Lifework

Manchester University Press

Lifework

On the autobiographical impulse in contemporary art, writing, and theory

Edited by

Moran Sheleg

Manchester University Press

Published by Manchester University Press
Oxford Road, Manchester, M13 9PL

www.manchesteruniversitypress.co.uk

British Library Cataloguing-in-Publication Data
A catalogue record for this book is available from the British Library

ISBN 978 1 5261 7247 1 hardback

First published 2024

Typeset
by Cheshire Typesetting Ltd, Cuddington, Cheshire

For those who have worked hard to make this book
and for those I share my life with

Contents

Figures

Contributors

Jo Applin is Walter H. Annenberg Professor in the History of Art at the Courtauld Institute of Art, London, where she is also Director of the Centre for American Art. She is the author of numerous articles, chapters and essays. Her books include *Lee Lozano: Not Working* (Yale University Press, 2018), *Eccentric Objects: Rethinking Sculpture in 1960s America* (Yale University Press, 2012), and *Yayoi Kusama: Infinity Mirror Room: – Phalli's Field* (Afterall Books, 2012). She is co-editor of *London Art Worlds: Mobile, Contingent, and Ephemeral Networks 1960–1980* (Pennsylvania University Press, 2018) and in 2016 she co-curated the exhibition *Flesh* at York Art Gallery, UK. Since 2014, Jo has been an Editor at *Oxford Art Journal*. She is currently writing a book about art and ageing.

Marquis Bey is Assistant Professor of African American Studies and English, and core faculty in Critical Theory and Gender and Sexuality Studies, at Northwestern University. Their work concerns questions of trans and nonbinary studies, Black feminist theory, and abolition. Their most recent books include *Black Trans Feminism* and *Cistem Failure: Essays on Blackness and Cisgender*, both published in 2022 with Duke University Press.

Lucy Bradnock is Reader in Modern and Contemporary Art History and Dean for Research at the Courtauld Institute of Art, London, and Editor of the journal *Art History*. Her books include *No More Masterpieces: Modern Art After Artaud* (Yale University Press, 2021), *Lawrence Alloway: Critic and Curator*, edited with Courtney J. Martin and Rebecca Peabody (Getty, 2015), and *Pacific Standard Time:*

Los Angeles Art, 1945–1980, edited with Rebecca Peabody, Andrew Perchuk, Glen Philips, and Rani Singh (Getty, 2011).

Alice Butler is an interdisciplinary writer and scholar based in the School of Arts and Humanities at the Royal College of Art who specialises in the intersections of recent and contemporary feminist and queer art, writing, and theoretical practices. She is currently finalising two books: a monograph on the sick pleasures and epistolary desires of Kathy Acker and Cookie Mueller's autofictional archives and an edited collection on gesture in interdisciplinary feminist practice. She is also at work on a new book that explores the minor intimacies of found materials in feminist art and writing practices.

Teresa Carmody 's books include *The Reconception of Marie* (Spuyten Duyvil, 2020), *Maison Femme: A Fiction* (Bon Aire Projects, 2015), and a forthcoming collection of autofictions, *A Healthy Interest in the Lives of Others* (2024). A co-founding director of Les Figues Press in Los Angeles, Carmody teaches creative writing at University of Nebraska Omaha.

Miguel de Baca is a senior program officer at the Getty Foundation in Los Angeles. Prior to that, he was Associate Professor of Modern and Contemporary Art History with tenure at Lake Forest College, where he was also the department chair. In 2017–2018, de Baca was the Terra Foundation Visiting Professor of American Art at the University of Oxford. He received his PhD from Harvard University and BA from Stanford. His publications include a 2015 monograph on the minimalist artist Anne Truitt, and an edited volume on identity and protest in American art (2015), among other essays and catalogue entries.

Rye Dag Holmboe is a psychoanalyst, art historian, and writer. He works in private practice and at the Camden Psychotherapy Unit, a mental health charity in London. Holmboe was an AHRC doctoral scholar at University College London and later held a Leverhulme Early Career Research Fellowship at the University of East Anglia. He has published widely in the fields of art history and psychoanalysis. His most recent books include *Nicol Allan: Collages* (Slimvolume, 2021) and *Sol LeWitt's Studio Drawings in the Vecchia Torre* (MIT Press, 2023). He is currently writing a monograph, *Howard Hodgkin's*

Interiors (MIT Press), which will be published in 2025 on occasion of an exhibition he is curating at Pallant House.

Margaret Iversen is Professor Emerita at the University of Essex. Her books include *Alois Riegl: Art History and Theory* (MIT Press, 1993), *Beyond Pleasure: Freud, Lacan, Barthes* (Penn State University Press, 2009), and *Photography, Trace, and Trauma* (University of Chicago Press, 2017). She edited, with Diarmuid Costello, a special issue on 'Photography after Conceptual Art' for *Art History* (2010) and another on 'Agency and Automatism: Photography and Art since the Sixties' for *Critical Inquiry* (2021). She also edited the Whitechapel Gallery/MIT Press 'Documents of Contemporary Art' volume on *Chance* (2010). *Writing Art History: Disciplinary Departures* (University of Chicago Press, 2010) was written in collaboration with Stephen Melville.

Susan Morris is an artist who also writes. Her work engages with periodicity and the involuntary mark, either through a form of diaristic writing or by diagrammatic works generated from data recorded by devices worn on the body and – more recently – from ambient light and sound recordings. Morris has won several grants and awards including, in 2010, a Wellcome Trust Grant to produce a series of Jacquard tapestries from data recording her sleep/wake patterns. In 2020, she was commissioned to make six large Jacquard tapestries for the library at St John's College, University of Oxford, based on sound recordings made in the college garden. This was completed in 2021, with accompanying artist's book published in 2022.

Alistair Rider teaches Art History at the University of St Andrews. His research focuses on late modern art, with a particular focus on abstraction and environmental themes. He is the author of *Carl Andre: Things in their Elements* (Phaidon Press, 2011) and *James Howell: Infinite Array* (Circa Press, 2021). Currently he is preparing a book on the temporalities of a wide range of artists' practices, called *Ongoing: Notes on Long Term Art Projects.*

Abi Shapiro is Curator at The Hepworth Wakefield with a specialist research interest in post-war sculpture and its critical histories. She has worked on curatorial projects such as *Kim Lim: Space, Rhythm & Light* (2023), *Hannah Starkey: In Real Life* (2022), *The Art of the Potter: Sculpture and Ceramics from 1930 to Today* (2023), *and Sheila Hicks: Off*

Grid (2022). She has previously worked as Research Curator, British Art 1945–1975 at Sheffield Museums, and taught at the University of York, City & Guilds of London Art School and McGill University. In 2017 she completed her PhD dissertation, *Ree Morton and Feminist Installation Art: 1968–1977*. In 2019 she published an essay in the exhibition catalogue *Ree Morton: The Plant That Heals May Also Poison* for the artist's retrospective at the ICA Philadelphia in 2018.

Moran Sheleg is a Leverhulme Early Career Fellow in the School of Art, Media and American Studies at the University of East Anglia. Before this she was a postdoctoral fellow at the Paul Mellon Centre and an Associate Lecturer at the Courtauld Institute of Art, London. Sheleg completed her PhD, which was funded by an AHRC/LAHP scholarship, at University College London in 2017. Her writing has appeared in several journals, edited volumes and exhibition catalogues. Her first monograph, *How to Make a Past: Ad Reinhardt versus Art History*, is forthcoming from MIT Press. She is currently completing a project on the work of Saul Steinberg.

Acknowledgements

Lifework began life before, but was indelibly marked by, the outbreak of COVID-19. A lengthy labour of love ensued that spanned actual childbirth, a global pandemic, and no end of national and international turmoil, all of which turned what would have been the daily graft of editing into a string of stolen moments of pleasure: reading, thinking, writing, re-reading, and finally, compiling this book. Along the way I was lucky enough to work with an esteemed group of colleagues whose voices fill its pages with a richness of ideas and variety of perspectives that resonate with each other in fascinating, often surprising, and illuminating ways. I am indebted to them all for their contributions.

I am extremely grateful to the editorial team at Manchester University Press, especially Emma Brennan, Katie Evans, and Alun Richards, who patiently and expertly guided this book from proposal through to publication.

My sincerest thanks to all the artists, photographers, museums, galleries, and estates who granted permission to reproduce their images, and especially to Moyra Davey for allowing me to feature her work – which incapsulates the dynamics between images and words, life and work, and private and public experience that animate every sentence of this book, while leaving their significance forever open to interpretation – both on the cover and throughout.

Moran Sheleg
London, 2023

Introduction: the life of work, the work of life

Moran Sheleg

An orange-gloved hand grips a pencil. Leaning on a boldly patterned bag placed on a lap, the other clutches a few sheets of paper, lifting them on a poised finger for stability amid the swaying of the subway carriage. *Orange Gloves* (2011), seen on the cover of this book, is one of a series of photographs taken by the Canadian artist Moyra Davey as she travelled on the New York metro. Like the busy commuters they portray, lost in their private thoughts, these images speak to the pressure of productivity felt by the artist – be they a writer, painter, photographer, whatever – whose work often happens in such moments of apparent mundanity. Yet the series to which they belong, *Subway Writers,* also hints at something beyond the seemingly introspective moments collected therein (by way of the mildly voyeuristic act of photographing strangers) and the lonely work of writing. As one scans the closely cropped photos, some of which are interspersed throughout this volume, one is struck by the activity surrounding these busy hands. Life goes on all around them and yet they remain steadfast in their task, scribbling on among the fleeting consequence of their shared setting on a commuter train. Puncturing a portion of the picture are several little squares of neon colour which transpire to be short strips of tape used to seal the folded image in preparation for, in this example's case, its transatlantic voyage and ultimate display at the Camden Arts Centre in London.[1] Bearing the marks of their own post-studio lives, these 'mailers', as Davey calls them, contain several temporalities, all alluding to the elapsed time in which the work of making art and the often very separate work of disseminating it happens. More than this, they chart a liminal zone in which the lines between life and work impinge, blur, and, at times, disappear altogether.

The first mention of 'lifework' as a single word (in English) that I know of appears halfway through Roland Barthes's hugely influential 1967 essay, 'The Death of the Author'.[2] The context within which this term appears in the essay is highly specific and deeply literary. The essay's own context, interestingly, was primarily art-historical, first appearing in the art magazine *Aspen*, in a double issue dedicated to the poet Stéphane Mallarmé and presented in a multimedia box that also featured writings by George Kubler and Susan Sontag, as well as recordings by artists and miniature models on paper of contemporary artworks by Sol LeWitt and Mel Bochner, among others.[3] Regardless of these layers of historical specificity, the title of Barthes's essay would quickly become what Jane Gallop has called a 'poststructuralist catchphrase' for the seeming excision of the writer and their life from any text, which would apparently from then on be seen as an object with a life of its own. Often coupled with Michel Foucault's 'What is an Author?' (1969), misgivings and misreadings would consequently abound despite, as Gallop states, Barthes's announcement of the author's 'friendly return' in 1971.[4] Further ripples of dissent would reverberate well into the 1980s, when, as Charles G. Salas has pointed out, the battle between the biographical and the 'transpersonal' or objective approach, particularly in art history, reached a climax.[5]

In Barthes's essay, Marcel Proust's novel *À la recherche du temps perdu (In Search of Lost Time)*, which took Proust almost fifteen years to complete and which he continued to obsessively revise until his death, is described as a form of 'lifework' in which the writer's life *as a writer* becomes the 'model' for their work. Through a twist of convention, Proust disproved the literary assumption that art should imitate life by effectively erasing the distinction between them, if under the guise of fiction. As Proust's enigmatic narrator muses, it is only at the end of the novel that the work of writing truly begins.[6] Self-reflexivity, borne out in this way, would become a hallmark of modernism, not only in literature and the visual arts but also in the field of semiotics – the study of signs and symbols, primarily lexical – to which Barthes dedicated the lion's share of his own life's work. Yet, the goal of his 1967 essay was to register the changing attitudes seen around the mid-twentieth century towards the idea of the 'self' as a distinct entity, or more specifically, as a fixed personhood with a secure political agency and, consequently, the products of that entity as a direct outcome of said agency. Driven by a discourse that sought to disrupt this foregone and problematic conclusion, the cultural critiques mounted by poststructuralism and postmodernism at that time seemed to herald the demise of the author and, ultimately, 'the birth of the reader'.[7] In essence, this amounted to a doing away with biographical readings of a person's work as the outcome of their life in place of an emphasis on the interpretation of a text (or artwork) free from the subjectivity of the hand that wrote (or made) it. However, in highlighting Proust's 'lifework', Barthes also pointed to its potential continuation in another form.

Barthes himself would become increasingly drawn to the diaristic mode in the years following 'The Death of the Author', as evidenced by his own consequent autobiographical writings (both public and private), from *Empire of the Sign* (1970) through to the 'mourning diary' he began after his mother's death in 1977 and kept until his own in March 1980 (which was posthumously published in 2009).[8] Dating his 'sudden about-face' to the writing of *The Pleasure of the Text* throughout 1973, Barthes recognised within this change of heart a more general and shared desire to '[put] a little bit of "psychological" affectivity back into intellectual production', in place of the detachedness dominating the 'theoretical superego' of the 1960s.[9]

As much as this earlier stance intended to pose key questions about the formation of subjectivity and, consequently, identity, its emphasis on the text as an object, according to Barthes, led away from the radical reinstatement of the subject supposedly at its heart. In a lecture given just two months before his death, Barthes denounced his famous essay, dismissing it as an exercise in structuralism gone too far that could not and did not stand the test of time.[10] Given as part of his conclusion to 'The Preparation of the Novel – From Life to the Work', an undergraduate course he was teaching at the Collège de France in Paris, Barthes suggested that the so-called 'return of the author' occurring by the outset of 1970s could be attributed to a wider renewal of interest in forms of life-writing, or 'biographical nebulae'. These included 'Diaries, Biographies, personalized Interviews, Memoires, etc.', reanimating not only literary theory but also artistic production and its analysis.

As is made clear throughout his lecture notes, Proust's novel still stood at the epicentre of this tidal shift for Barthes.[11] It is well known that while giving this final course Barthes was himself attempting to write a novel, tentatively entitled *Vita Nova,* that drew on his own extensive and experimental diary-writing as well as observations on the work of figures such as Proust, Gustave Flaubert, and André Gide. In his study of the French avant-garde return to this form, Sam Ferguson argues that Barthes's never-realised novel attempted a synthesis of the 'ideal' self, conveyed through descriptions of rich interior experience, and the 'incidental' self that emerges through the confessional, which lie on opposite ends of the diaristic spectrum.[12] While we can only speculate as to what his own may have contained, Barthes's conception of the diary-novel as a new form of writing capable of reinstating the author-subject also doubled as a symbolic *vita nova* (or new life) for the work of art.[13]

This renewed focus also mirrored the contemporary critical resurgence of the theories of Sigmund Freud, whose 1901 essay, *The Psychopathology of Everyday Life*, offered an early road map for navigating the inconsistencies of memory, of the kind Proust would so vividly convey in his novel. Freud would go on to develop this in texts such as *A Note upon the Mystic Writing Pad* (1924), invoking the eponymous toy as a metaphor for the way memories are inscribed onto the mind and never fully erased from it, no matter how remote or 'forgotten' they might seem. In her fascinating article on Freud's use of his own experiences as case studies throughout his career, Carolyn Laubender highlights how central self-narration is to psychoanalysis, in terms of both the analyst and the analysand.[14] While a sense of critical distance was somewhat restored to the field of subject formation via the work of Jacques Lacan, the increasing focus on individual experience emerging towards the end of the 1960s and into the 1970s would be further emphasised by others, such as Luce Irigaray, Julia Kristeva, and Juliet Mitchell, who were attempting to understand how difference affects processes of individuation.

Barthes's shift is thus significant not only in itself but also because it chimes with the wider critique of impersonality being mounted at that same moment by both feminist and postcolonial scholars. Seen through this lens, Barthes's proposals of the reinstatement of affectivity find a compelling parallel in the now-canonical feminist precept, 'the personal is political',[15] as well as a precedent in Frantz Fanon's fundamental explorations of 'double consciousness', as first posed by W. E. B. Du Bois (a contemporary of Freud). Fanon's use of psychoanalysis, in studies such as *Black Skin, White Masks* (1952) and *The Wretched of the Earth* (1961), homes in on the question of desire and its role in forming identities – both of oppressor and oppressed – under the power dynamics of colonialism as a sociopolitical and psychological regime.[16] Fanon, a psychiatrist as well as a psychologist, writer, and philosopher, interlaces his analysis with many accounts of his own experiences, all nestled among exegeses spanning from critical race theory to existentialism to phenomenology and beyond. For Fanon and others, violence appears as the driving force behind processes of oppression that colonialism, as much a psychological as a cultural phenomenon, fosters. For feminists, it was sexual difference that governed the power dynamics driving that same patriarchal structure. In 1974, Juliet Mitchell proposed that, rather than a challenge to feminism, psychoanalysis could offer a useful model for the analysis of what Jessica Benjamin later termed 'the problem of domination'.[17] Although controversial at the time, Mitchell's text has come to be seen as crucial to feminism's consequent investment in the disruptive potential of psychic life and its gendered (and otherwise differentiated) understandings. Similarly, Gilles Deleuze and Félix Guattari's 1972 study *Anti-Oedipus* suggested desire as a social force that shapes life in both revolutionary and reactionary ways.[18] While critiquing existing forms of psychoanalysis, it also contributed to a wider theoretical awareness and adaptation of many of its theses, some of which are discussed within the following chapters.

Even more pertinently, Barthes's shift in approach has come to be considered foundational to a genre of autobiography that emerged alongside both feminism and postcolonialism during the 1970s, which blends a diaristic style of writing with critical theory (as well as fiction) and has become known as 'autotheory'. Traced back to Barthes's 1975 'anti-autobiography', *Roland Barthes by Roland Barthes*,[19] 'autotheory' has recently been contextualised in terms of feminist art practice and employed in the field of critical race studies, as well as queer and transgender studies, as a form of praxis that brings the concept of the 'self' into direct dialogue with its lived experience in critically important, because socially and culturally revealing, ways.[20] Others have traced its origins back further to theoretical traditions beyond the purely literary.[21] So while the recent buzz around the term 'autotheory' might make it seem like an emerging art form, as well as a new way of writing or 'doing' theory specific to a contemporary moment, it actually stands as an interdisciplinary practice many decades (indeed, over a century) in the making.[22]

Although psychoanalysis, feminism, and postcolonialism were mounting important interventions in thinking around subjectivity and its political realities long before the 'return' signalled by Barthes, their convergence in the idea of 'lifework', as in the practice of 'autotheory', signals an ongoing tension. A tension between understandings of identity as, on the one hand, a scene of political struggle for liberation and, on the other, as a preoccupation imposed by late-stage capitalism. It is a struggle that fervently continues to this day in both theory and practice. The chapters gathered here consider the ways in which artists, writers, theorists, and historians have negotiated, and continue to negotiate, this perennial and ambivalent tie between life and work. Taken together, they raise broader questions about standing notions of what a life's work might constitute and, moreover, what it might (and might not) mean, as well as its implications. Although informed by different schools of thought, they all show how intrinsic the concepts of living and working are to each other, especially when they seem to collide or conflict, as has often been the case since the Industrial Revolution, and particularly after the 1960s and its ideological pursuit of self-actualisation (whether as protest or profit). A primary example of this tension are the strains felt by working mothers in a society that increasingly tells them they can have it all, and yet which, as Silvia Federici has most persistently and eloquently argued, functions on the exploitation of their domestic and unpaid, or 'reproductive', labour – not only child-rearing, but cooking, cleaning, and other necessary daily activities – which in many ways has only increased in the wake of the recent COVID-19 pandemic, even post-lockdown.[23]

Although the impetus for this book came about before the outbreak, the huge ramifications it had on this writer's own life, not least of all as a new mother, invested 'lifework' with a new set of meanings and associations, both within and beyond scholarship, that seemed increasingly urgent. Although 'work' in the old sense had to be delayed, it was not wholly replaced by 'life' – except in small, blissful, yet rare pockets of time – but more and different kinds of work. As any parent knows (and any child might imagine), having and raising children is the ultimate lifework. Yet, for the new mother especially it involves a succumbing of the self to the other, an agreement (either willingly made or imposed) to live, as Adrienne Rich put it, 'in the rhythms of other lives'.[24] Rich's *Of Woman Born*, a memoir-cum-critical-study of early motherhood and the division of labour punctuating life for so many women during the mid-twentieth century and beyond, would become a central feminist text that still resonates in its uncompromising honesty. At its core, however, is a reflection on how a mother might also (continue to) be a writer, a creative practitioner, and a critically important voice, amid the unrelenting demands on her time and efforts at home.

With everyday life forced to adhere to new norms during the pandemic, unprecedented pressures on the increasingly inseparable spheres of life and work arose across the demographic spectrum, with some lasting consequences. These have taken many forms, including: the loss of jobs and precarity of the employment market; the socioeconomic inequalities governing access to education, literacy, and work opportunities; the gender pay gap; the disenchantment with working realities and rejection of the slavish devotion to work subsequently dubbed 'The Great Resignation'; the work-from-home boom that has transformed life for many white-collar employees, converting living spaces into working spaces, or the indefinite suspension of work for huge numbers of blue-collar workers. While far from exhaustive, the themes guiding *Lifework*'s chapters attempt to address some enduring yet still urgent aspects governing this deep and far-reaching relationship. These include family and parenthood; the idea of the 'self', its formation, and regulation, through related notions such as self-expression, self-representation, self-surveillance, and self-improvement; mundane experience; illness and insomnia; memory; ageing; and what is gained and lost in the daily living of life, both internally and externally.

Labour as a determining factor of 'self', not just as a condition of survival but as a measure of social status and achievement, has of course found its extreme manifestation under neoliberalism.[25] Redefined through what Foucault famously called 'technologies of the self' – which are acts such as reading, writing, body augmentation, meditation, and so on – the formation of the subject under late capitalist society appears in the guise of seemingly liberatory rather than coercive means.[26] Several of the chapters collected herein address this apparent clash between the intellectual histories I have been outlining and the historical context in which they occurred and continue to take shape. My only regret is not having had more room to address how class figures here, and particularly in terms of the notion of 'lifework', which could be the topic of its own book. Much has been written about how the working class might be represented in the production and reception of contemporary art, following its apparent evisceration under neoliberal globalisation.[27] Yet, as Laura Marcus suggested some years ago, the power dynamics inherent to the writing – and by extension, one could add, the analysis – of autobiography, however radical in intent, still largely needs 'to shift for working-class autobiographies to be understood and "valued"'.[28] Several of the chapters included here do however broach, in their own divergent ways, the lingering problem of the subjective 'I' of the literary, artistic, and theoretical subject as a construct inherently prescribed as male, white, straight, and bourgeois. This also forces us to recognise that traditional modes of life-writing (be they textual, visual, or oral) are often far from egalitarian, given the economic and social restrictions on education and work mobility experienced by many in the developed world.

Indeed, following the technological and cultural revolutions experienced during the past decade alone, which have reshaped not only how we live and work but, just as crucially, how we share details of our everyday lives with others, the thought that a person could ever be divorced from the products of their labour (whether professional, creative, domestic, or habitual) seems unimaginable. It appears that under the sign of social media we have all become author-subjects, as well as voracious consumer-readers. Yet, of course, those same revolutions have led to the mass circulation and commodification of personal data and content creation that has resulted in what the artist and writer James Bridle recently called a 'new dark age' of technological connectivity and consequent personal alienation, not to mention corporate exploitation and political corruption.[29] The work of finding the lost author-subject amid this 'big data crisis', as it has been termed, has thus been taken up by artists and writers for whom autotheory, for want of a better term, has become a political imperative as well as a disruptive mode.[30] Bearing this in mind, the following chapters do not attempt to offer a conclusive definition of 'lifework' amid such an all-encompassing digital, and glaringly unstable and unsustainable, economy. Rather, they address ways in which artistic and critical labour has negotiated and made manifest certain points of pressure within the relationship between life and work under the pervasive cloud of a rapidly evolving technological and consumerist regime, with all its aesthetic, economic, social, gendered, and ethical consequences.

In the opening chapter, 'Diaristic diagrams', Margaret Iversen discusses a range of artists whose work opens up the dichotomy between the personal form of the diary and the impersonal structure of the diagram. Identifying two branches of this tendency, Iversen suggests that, when taken together, they prompt questions about the relationship between technologies of surveillance and techniques of self-examination posed by practices such as that of the London-based artist Susan Morris, who offers an account of her recent work in Chapter 2, 'Inarticulations'. In a first-person narrative, Morris discusses her use of self-monitoring devices and her habitual practice of collating a diary from the remnants of her daily life (such as receipts, emails, and text messages) into visual texts that – in the manner of an involuntary novel – together explore the limits of self-representation. Drawing on a distinctly modernist literary tradition from Virginia Woolf and James Joyce to recent writers like Maggie Nelson, Morris brings psychoanalytic and semiological theory to bear on her own work, itself both a comment on and contribution to an ongoing enquiry into what can and cannot be articulated about a life as it is lived, be it through writing, reading, making, or looking. In the next chapter, 'Valuing life', Alistair Rider further considers the temporal, subjective, and political vicissitudes thrown up by the idea of 'lifework' in contemporary artistic practice. Focusing on Adrian Heathfield's recent definition regarding the work of performance artist Tehching Hsieh, Rider argues that the 'life' which is referred to here is not straightforwardly that of the artist themselves, but a larger construct that relates to biopolitical definitions of human existence and the socioeconomic confines surrounding it, both moral and mortal.

This is one way in which, perhaps, examining autotheory's ascendancy – as well as that of the autobiographical impulse more widely – within contemporary art practice can lead to new insights into how artists have reckoned with the increasing dominance of the visual, or what Guy Debord in 1967 famously called 'the society of the spectacle', and to a greater degree the very imaging of the self, through an emphasis on the slipperiness and vagaries of language. Image–text relations here become charged by the exploration of subjectivity, which itself is revealed as a form of labour.

In many ways the growing interest in autotheory, as a mode of writing or making that incorporates autobiography into a critical response to the conditions and experiences of everyday life, reflects a wider historical recognition of the power structures inherent to late capitalism, whether in the home or workplace, and how art figures in relation to them. In her pioneering book, *The Problem with Work*, Kathi Weeks redresses the 'depoliticisation' of work as a symptom of capitalism's pervasive stranglehold on daily life. Despite a whole history of Marxist critique, the peculiar nature of contemporary labour as an insidious morality (and here Weeks highlights the term 'work ethic' as a potent example of the social value undergirding it) by which one comes to define an increasingly large proportion of one's life, even (and especially) if one is excluded from it, remains largely unexamined.[31] This is no less true in the humanities, which notoriously lack kudos on the job market compared to the social sciences, than in Weeks's concentrated field of political theory. Recent landmark studies in art history, however, have begun to redress this gap, particularly in relation to work by women and, importantly, what happens when one refuses to work.[32] Think of Jo Applin's book on Lee Lozano's radical and self-eviscerating decision to 'drop out' of the art world in 1970, which followed the artist's timely decision to 'boycott' other women the previous year.[33] The political potential of such gestures of refusal and self-repositioning are also explored by Kimberly Lamm in *Addressing the Other Woman*, through the relationship between image and word in the work of three American artists, Adrian Piper, Nancy Spero, and Mary Kelly, which she considers alongside (but independently from) that of three prominent feminist writers and theorists.[34] Regarding Kelly's important 1973 work, *Post-partum Document*, Lamm shows how writing functions as a site in which the maternal subject as a desiring being becomes legible through its inscription of an authorial 'I' that has long been defined by its passivity as the object of and vehicle for infantile subjectivity, particularly through Freudian psychoanalysis and the depersonalising language (and, at times, practice) of modern medicine.[35]

Significant too in this regard is the claim that autotheory is a practice inherently linked to feminist art and thinking, both about the conditions in which work takes place and the artwork or text as a site where such conditions can be pulled apart, examined, and reimagined. Arguing for autotheory's potency *as* feminist work, Lauren Fournier has provided a helpful overview of this tendency over the past fifty years.[36] But what about feminism itself as the work of life, that is, as a 'lifework', which both forms and exceeds the object or text? The remaining chapters in this book, although divided into four parts, imagine some of the multifarious forms that such a project might take.

Offering a close, contextual reading of Emily Dickinson's fragmentary 'envelope poems', Rye Holmboe highlights how these works stand as a reminder of the significance of the small, the quotidian, and the intimate – particularly when it comes to women's work. Dickinson's economical use of language in these tiny texts paradoxically conveys a set of wide-ranging and complex ideas, together playing with the logic of the envelope itself as a container for words, effectively turning them both psychically and metaphorically inside-out. Envelopes, as liminal boundaries between interior and exterior and as carriers of correspondence, also feature in Alice Butler's nuanced reading of the novelist Kathy Acker's work, her use of clothing as metaphor, and her 'kleptomaniac' tendency to reappropriate classic novels in her work, described as a form of 'close writing'. Aligning text with textile, Butler poses questions about the composition of subjectivity and suggests how its eroticism (and perversion) in Acker's work emerges as a vital feminist strategy. Where is the line, Butler asks, between the 'self' one makes, whether through self-fashioning, self-writing, or the act of living, and the 'self' others see, especially when one is ill, even dying? And how knowable by others, or by oneself, can this self ever fully be?

The idea of eroticism as a generative tool is further explored in Teresa Carmody's autotheoretical chapter, in which the author thinks through the desire generated by her research into the archives of fellow author Audre Lorde and the photographer Tee Corrine. Considering her own status as a queer woman whose strict Christian upbringing called for a prolonged period of self-redefinition, Carmody relives the experience of piecing together a personal history that is both rooted in and transcends the limits of individual memory to form a space in which multiple selves might coexist and speak to one another. This pilgrim's progress gone awry is mirrored in the colouring-in of an image, which reappears in various stages of completion throughout the chapter. This kind of polyvocal reckoning continues, in another direction, in Marquis Bey's self-reflective exploration of what the opposite, or rather the undoing, of autotheory as the writing of the monolithic 'self' might constitute. Looking to feminist, Black, and trans theory, Bey proceeds to consider a way of writing oneself into being that does not conform to standing conventions available for the definition of subjecthood, proposing the beginnings of a theory of the 'unself'.

The next set of chapters look to the historical moment and artistic landscape in which autotheory emerged, the 1970s, to ask broader questions about autobiography as a strategy of both making and interpreting art. Abi Shapiro examines how self-documentation and feminist analysis have at times worked to obscure the contradictions inherent to artistic projects involved in exploring the uneasy relationship between life and work, as well as image and text, such as that of the American artist Ree Morton. As a full-time mother to three children, Morton came to art-making relatively late, and her sudden death in 1977 meant that both her life and work were cut tragically short. Nevertheless, the abundance of written material Morton produced over her nine-year career points to the intimate ties between the details of her daily life, the hierarchies of contemporary artistic practice, and wider concerns of the time regarding the politics of women's lives, experiences, and representation. Considering how we might treat these writings as integral to – rather than as mere ciphers of – the artist's project, Shapiro makes the case for an approach that recognises 'lifework' as a self-critical form of artistic practice that goes far beyond the formal or the textual alone. Tracing a different tendency in art also produced during this time, Lucy Bradnock explores the conjunction between popular psychology and conceptual art being made predominantly in and around California. As Bradnock points out, a sense of identity crisis permeated these politically turbulent years in America and, as a result, a renewed focus on the individual emerged in both artistic practice and the wider cultural marketplace, with the former even at times mimicking the latter as well as driving it. Analysing the work of both men and women, Bradnock contextualises this trend in light of the parallels emerging between feminist discourse and the commercialised techniques of self-help flourishing at the time, suggesting that the artworks under discussion might expose how the liberatory project of self-actualisation, as imagined by the women's movement, coincided with the capitalist monetisation of it (particularly the conditioning and improvement of the self), as well as conceptual art's embroilment in this.

Melding some of the concerns raised in earlier sections, the final group of chapters further explores the themes of memory and motherhood, as well as female friendship and the crucial question of ageing, through the idea of a 'lifework' as something that is deeply rooted in but somehow exceeds the physical realities of routine life. Miguel de Baca examines Anne Truitt's early minimalist sculptures through the lens of loss and remembrance, proposing that they stage a form of 'lifework' as 'memory work'. Considering the coincidence and arbitrariness of Truitt's use of titles for her abstract sculptures, de Baca makes the case for an approach that accommodates the vicissitudes of what Proust famously called 'involuntary memory' within the processes of making and viewing art. Herself a keen reader of Proust, Truitt left the question of interpretation open, her work welcoming associations but evading meaning so that autobiography lingers without ever fully attaching itself to form. In contrast, the next chapter explores the late work of Louise Bourgeois, an artist who laced her art and writing with autobiographical details, often explicitly referencing aspects of the psychoanalytic therapy she underwent for many years. I consider how Bourgeois's fabric books produced between 2002 and 2007, in which literal fragments from the artist's past are stitched together to form abstract, non-narrative patterns, mirror the processes of writing and recollection through which certain bits and pieces of memory are lost and regained. Proust here returns, but in the guise of what is described as an 'anti-memoir' through which the silent maternal object of psychoanalysis is retrieved and remade. Taking the idea of 'lifework' to a terminal point, in the final chapter Jo Applin studies its valence when considered in relation to a person's lifespan, as understood through their work. Considering art as a measure of human time, Applin turns to gerontology to probe the fraught intersection of the 'lifework', feminism, and ageing, as the prospect of one's own ending comes ever closer into view.

There are many other artists and writers who could have been included in this book. A tome that took account of all the ramifications of a term such as 'lifework' would be impossibly long and most probably unreadable. Instead, it is hoped that this collection of chapters, by a range of established and emerging voices in different but increasingly overlapping fields, suggests certain critical directions for future thinking around the issues it raises, not least of all a renewed emphasis on lived experience, particularly that of women, governing much of the most interesting and important art and literature being made today within a context – that of North America and Europe – on the brink of self-destruction.

To return to the opening image, *Orange Gloves*, the conception of work posed by the luminous, velvet-covered hands of the unknown writer is not strictly the one we might associate with what most of us have devoted our adult lives to. Something about her activity seems resolutely, even indulgently, private, and the cropped view that disconnects her identity from her labour positions us as would-be peeping Toms to an opaque act of inscription. Yet, what exactly is it that we are spying? The page is turned away from us, forever concealing her thoughts (however salacious, imaginative, or banal) from view. Here work as process, the process of writing in a public place, is all that we see, while the product of that work remains a secret. Faced with this absence, thoughts inevitably turn to the work of the camera, our enabling intermediary, and the artist who wields it in place of a pen, pencil, brush, or chisel. The clicking finger (or thumb) poised to capture a moment, whose form is echoed in the other hands seen within the image, triggers a complex of touch whose only point of contact is within our own imagination. Barthes wrote that photographs carry within them the trace of death – and thus stand as the ultimate form of 'deathwork', perhaps.[37] Maybe by situating writing in an opposite register, one in which the work of a lifetime affirms the life inscribed within and through that work, it is possible to see why autobiography, and its other lives as autotheory, life-writing, or autofiction, not only survives but thrives when all else seems increasingly on the point of collapse. Is it not the very work of life, and the life registered through that work, that necessitates the 'lifework' in all its possible and potential forms?

Notes

1 The series was displayed as part of the exhibition *Moyra Davey: life without sheets of paper to be scribbled on is a masterpiece*, Camden Arts Centre, London, 11 April–29 June 2014.

2 Roland Barthes, 'The Death of the Author' [1967], in Stephen Heath (ed.), *Image-Music-Text* (London: Fontana, 1977), p. 144. The word 'lifework' (*Lebenswerk*) does appear in Walter Benjamin's 1929 essay, 'The Image of Proust', as translated by Harry Zorn, but without further definition. Reprinted in Hannah Arendt (ed.), *Illuminations: Essays and Reflections*, trans. Harry Zohn (New York: Schocken Books, 2007), p. 197. For more on the convergence of Benjamin's and Barthes's thoughts on the work of Proust, see Katja Haustein, *Regarding Lost Time: Photography, Identity, and Affect in Proust, Benjamin, and Barthes* (London: Routledge, 2012).

3 See *Aspen*, 5+6 (1967), The Minimalism Issue. For a detailed account of its genesis and contents, see Alexander Alberro, 'Inside the White Box: *Aspen* 5+6', *Artforum*, 40:1 (September 2001), 170–174.

4 Jane Gallop, *The Deaths of the Author: Reading and Writing in Time* (Durham, NC and London: Duke University Press, 2011), pp. 1–5.

5 Charles G. Salas, 'Introduction: The Essential Myth?', in Salas (ed.), *The Life and the Work: Art and Biography* (Los Angeles, CA: Getty Research Institute, 2007), p. 14. For a discussion of the 'transpersonal' or post-structural critique of authorship and the subject in art history, which touches upon Barthes and Foucault, among others, see Rosalind Krauss, 'Who Comes after the Subject?', in Salas (ed.), *The Life and the Work*, pp. 28–33.

6 As Barthes qualifies: 'Proust himself, despite the apparently psychological character of what are called his analyses, was visibly concerned with the task of inexorably blurring, by an extreme subtilization, the

relation between the writer and his characters: by making of the narrator not he who has seen and felt nor even he who is writing, but he who is going to write (the young man in the novel – – but, in fact, how old is he, and who is he? – – wants to write but cannot; the novel ends when writing at last becomes possible), Proust gave modern writing its epic.' Barthes, 'The Death of the Author', p. 144.

7 Barthes, 'The Death of the Author', p. 148.

8 Margaret Iversen further traces this trajectory in the introduction to 'The Diaristic Mode in Contemporary Art after Barthes', *Art History*, 44:4 (September 2021), 798–822.

9 Roland Barthes, 'Session of January 19, 1980', in *The Preparation of the Novel: Lecture Courses and Seminars at the Collège de France (1978–1979 and 1979–1980)*, trans. Kate Briggs (New York: Columbia University Press, 2011), p. 208.

10 Barthes, 'Session of January 19, 1980', p. 207.

11 Gallop concurs that, in his work of the early 1970s and most notably in *Sade, Fourier, Loyola* (1971), 'as it was at the end of *S/Z* [1970], Proust's autobiographical novel is here again, still the model'. Gallop, *Deaths of the Author*, p. 39.

12 See Sam Ferguson, 'The Return of the Diary in Roland Barthes's Vita Nova', in *Diaries Real and Fictional in Twentieth-Century French Writing* (Oxford: Oxford University Press, 2018), pp. 161–192.

13 Others have attributed Barthes's use of the term 'vita nuova' as a nod to both Dante and Michelet. See Kris Pint and Maria Gil Ulldemolins, 'Roland Barthes and the "Affective Truths" of Autotheory', *Mosaic: An Interdisciplinary Critical Journal*, 53:4 (December 2020), A Special Issue: Camera Lucida, 117–132.

14 See Laubender, 'Speak for Yourself: Psychoanalysis, Autotheory, and The Plural Self', *Arizona Quarterly: A Journal of American Literature, Culture, and Theory*, 76:1 (Spring 2020), 39–64.

15 As Teresa Carmody points out in Chapter 6 of this book, 'the personal is political' appeared as a subtitle given to Hanisch's text (originally 'Some Thoughts in Response to Dottie's Thoughts on Women's Liberation Movement') by Shulamith Firestone and Anne Koedt when they included it in their volume, *Notes from the Second Year: Women's Liberation. Major Writings of the Radical Feminists* (New York: Radical Feminism, 1970), marking it as a distinctly collective slogan.

16 See Fanon, *Black Skin, White Masks* [1952], trans. Charles L. Markmann (New York: Grove Press, 1967); and *The Wretched of the Earth* [1961], trans. Richard Philcox (New York: Grove Press, 1963).

17 See Mitchell, *Psychoanalysis and Feminism: A Radical Reassessment of Psychoanalysis* (London: Pantheon Books, 1974); and Jessica Benjamin, *The Bonds of Love: Psychoanalysis, Feminism and the Problem of Domination* (London: Pantheon Books, 1988).

18 See Deleuze and Guattari, *Anti-Oedipus: Capitalism and Schizophrenia* [1972] (Minneapolis: University of Minnesota Press, 1977).

19 Robyn Wiegman, 'Introduction: Autotheory Theory', *Arizona Quarterly: A Journal of American Literature, Culture and Theory*, 76:1 (2020), 1–14.

20 A useful collection of some recent thinking on autotheory's potential within these fields can be found in *ASAP/Journal*, 6:3 (September 2021), 'Autotheory'. Also see Lauren Fournier, *Autotheory as Feminist Practice in Art, Writing and Criticism* (Cambridge, MA: MIT Press, 2021).

21 As pointed out in Katherine Baxter and Cat Auburn, 'Introduction for Special Issue "Autotheory in Contemporary Visual Arts Practice"', *Arts*, 12:1 (2023), 11–12.

22 Alex Borstoff and Lauren Fournier, 'Introduction: Autotheroy ASAP! Academia, Decolonality, and "I"', *ASAP Journal*, 6:3 (September 2021), Autotheory, 489.

23 See Silvia Federici, *Wages Against Housework* (Bristol: Power of Women and Falling Wall Press, 1975).

24 Adrienne Rich, '"Anger and Tenderness" from *Of Woman Born: Motherhood as Experience and Institution* (1976)', in Moyra Davey (ed.), *Mother Reader: Essential Writings on Motherhood* (New York: Seven Stories Press, 2001), p. 91.

25 As Wendy Brown, a long-time scholar of neoliberalism, has argued: 'what changes with the rise of neoliberalism is a newfound construction of the subject and, increasingly, a newfound governance of the subject that renders it not simply as a creature of moral autonomy and self-crafting but as one that is relentlessly economically oriented in every aspect of life. This is a fundamental, radical shift.' Brown, cited in 'Invest Yourself! Wendy Brown in conversation with Isabelle Graw', *Texte zur Kunst*, 105 (December 2016), *The Individual*, 34–35.

26 See Foucault, *Technologies of the Self: A Seminar with Michel Foucault* (London: Routledge, 1988). Lois McNay charts Foucault's shift from a focus on the body to that of the self in his own intellectual trajectory, and the wider significance of poststructuralist thought for emancipatory politics, in *Foucault and Feminism: Power, Gender and the Self* (Cambridge and Malden, MA: Blackwell, 1992). She goes on to examine its relevance for the study of neoliberalism in 'Self as Enterprise: Dilemmas of Control and Resistance in Foucault's "The Birth of Biopolitics"', in *Theory, Culture and Society*, 26:6 (January 2009), 55–77.

27 See, for example, Jonathan Harris (ed.), *Globalisation and Contemporary Art* (Maldon, MA, Oxford and Chichester: Wiley-Blackwell, 2011); and Adele Chenowyth (ed.), *Museums and the Working Class* (London: Routledge, 2021). In his monograph, Anthony Grudin makes the case for how the egalitarian underpinnings of Pop Art – specifically, Andy Warhol's use of a lexicon of recognisable images and technologies aimed at a working-class audience, to which the artist himself initially

belonged – expose the precarity of such an artistic project under neoliberalism. See Anthony E. Grudin, *Andy Warhol's Working Class: Pop Art and Egalitarianism* (Chicago, IL: University of Chicago Press, 2017).

28 Laura Marcus, 'Border Crossings: Recent Feminist Auto/biographical Theory', in Selma Leydesdorff, Luisa Passerini, and Paul Thompson (eds), *Gender and Memory* (London: Routledge, 2017), p. 190.

29 James Bridle, *New Dark Age* (London: Verso, 2018).

30 See Carlos Castillo, *Big Data Crisis: Social Media in Disasters and Time-Critical Situations* (Cambridge: Cambridge University Press, 2016).

31 See Kathi Weeks, *The Problem with Work: Feminism, Marxism, Antiwork Politics and Postwork Imaginaries* (Durham, NC and London: Duke University Press, 2011).

32 A historical precedent can be found in the (anti)work of the Surrealists, as outlined by Abigail Susik in *Surrealist Sabotage and the War on Work* (Manchester: Manchester University Press, 2021).

33 Jo Applin, *Lee Lozano: Not Working* (New Haven, CT and London: Yale University Press, 2018).

34 These are: Angela Davis, Valerie Solanos, and Laura Mulvey. See Kimberly Lamm, *Addressing the Other Woman: Textual Correspondences in Feminist Art and Writing* (Manchester: Manchester University Press, 2017).

35 Lamm, *Addressing the Other Woman*, chapter 5.

36 See Fournier, *Autotheory as Feminist Practice.*

37 See Barthes, *Camera Lucida: Reflections on Photography*, trans. Richard Howard (New York: Farrar, Straus & Giroux, 1981).

Part I

Working lives

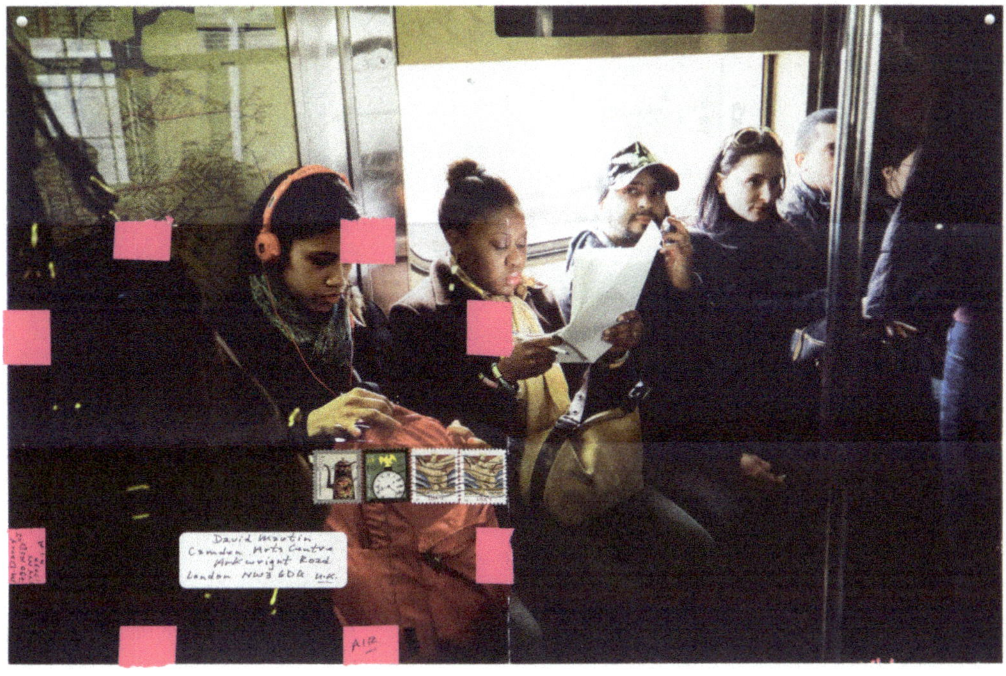

Moyra Davey, detail from *Subway Writers* series, 2011, C-print, tape, postage ink, 30 × 45 cm

1

Diaristic diagrams

Margaret Iversen

On the face of it, the diagram and the diary would appear to be antithetical forms. Diagrams graphically present information in a scientific, objective manner; they are abstract and impersonal. Diaries, on the contrary, are normally records of personal experience subjectively expressed. Yet most charts, diagrams, or graphs have a temporal axis and, to that extent, provide a sort of scaffold for works of art which aim to present information based on periodic observation or self-monitoring.[1] There are many examples of works of art that consist of photographs charting variations over time which are arranged for exhibition sequentially or in a grid format. Artists concerned about the rationalisation and standardisation of our experience of time and natural phenomena systematically record their observations. Others, more concerned with the contemporary conditions of daily life and labour, document their own activities. Examples of such diaristic diagrams are quite common in surveys of conceptual and post-conceptual art. Yet, rather than being treated as a specific genre, they are dispersed under several different rubrics as examples of the art of systems or series or as documents of performance.

In his influential article, 'Conceptual Art 1962–1969: From the Aesthetics of Administration to the Critique of Institutions' (1990), Benjamin Buchloh famously argued that conceptual artists were engaged in a project of negating the transcendental aspirations of traditional art by miming, 'with bureaucratic rigor', the positivist and instrumentalist logic of late capitalism.[2] Aiming to negate the high modernist cult of unmediated self-expression, they ended up affirming capitalism's rationalisation of work and bureaucratic procedures. Yet, it seems to me that conceptual and post-conceptual art is often aimed precisely at critiquing the effects that new technologies have on daily life, labour, and art practice. Such work explores the extent to which the technological conditions of modernity override what Jonathan Crary has called 'the periodic textures of human life'.[3] In order to convey their sense of a mutation in lived experience, these artists systematically record external impressions or subjective states and present the information gathered in graphs, charts, and grids. The graphic visualisation of information is a formal means of registering the rationalisation of time and work. Yet, as we shall see, the art in question also shows the diagram disrupted. The diaristic mode, I argue, puts pressure on the diagrammatic paradigm's formal structures. Diaristic diagrams perform a kind of critical mimesis of contemporary conditions while, at the same time, pointing to the inability of those formal means to adequately convey the affective and sensory dimensions of experience. The work demonstrates how clock time, artificial light, and work schedules conflict with cycles of the body and other natural rhythms. As the artist Susan Morris has observed, 'the body has an uneasy relation to the artificial systems of clock and calendrical time that structure our days'.[4] This chapter brings together a number of artists, from the 1960s to the present, whose work explores this and related tensions.

Growing interest in the diaristic diagram as a form is partly owing to the intensification, in recent decades, of our dependence on technology and our subjection to externally imposed time systems. In his book *24/7: Late Capitalism and the Ends of Sleep* (2013), Crary argues that the technologies of the Industrial Revolution and their associated work patterns have now been supplanted: the new Information Age runs on a homogenous time of sleeplessness. The title of the book, 24/7, refers to the daily twenty-four-hour availability of goods and services, but Crary expands its meaning to include the changed relation to time brought about by our adaptation to new information and communication technologies. The regime of 24/7 refers to 'the uninterrupted operating of markets, information networks, and other systems'. This continuous operation abolishes the distinction between night and day, work and rest, and ignores cycles and seasons – the rhythms and rituals of daily, monthly, and annual life. It also attempts to invade the 'useless' time of sleep which, as Crary notes, until recently could not be 'colonized by the massive engine of profitability'. Sleep is still to some extent embedded in cycles of activity and rest which are, for most of us, synchronised with solar light and darkness. Yet the pressure continually to work or consume necessitates 24/7 illumination of cities. This constant light exposure, Crary notes, destroys the shelter of darkness and the saving withdrawal of the self in sleep. He compares our situation to that of the 'sleep mode' of our devices, which is actually a state of perpetual readiness.[5]

Early anticipations of 24/7 society that accompanied the first mechanisation of labour are also discussed by Crary. Commenting on Joseph Wright of Derby's painting *Arkwright's Cotton Mills at Night* (1782), he draws attention to the strange conjunction of the rural landscape and a multi-storey factory building and, stranger still, the night sky with full moon and tiny gas lamps seen through the mill's windows. The painting announces, even at this early date, 'the rationalized deployment of an abstract relation between time and work, severed from the cyclical temporalities of lunar and solar movements'.[6] Workers, many of them children, were set to work in twelve-hour shifts, where they struggled to keep pace with the indefatigable machine. Such exploitative regimes common in contemporary society have been explored by the British artist Jeremy Deller. At the 2015 Venice Biennale's main exhibition, he drew attention to the rise of low-wage 'zero-hours' contracts as a new form of day labour in the service of digital economies. He displayed a banner emblazoned with the words, 'Hello, today you have day off', which is the grammatically incorrect text message received by workers in low-wage service industries who are not needed on that day. The textile banner of the sort paraded by trade unions ironically conveyed a message addressed to workers with no rights or union. Included in the same installation was a mannequin arm wearing a Motorola WT 4000, a tracking and messaging device that 'pickers' in large warehouses are obliged to wear to monitor and enforce time discipline. This is a real-time, digital version of Taylorist time-and-motion techniques aimed at maximising production.

The pressure of timekeeping on the worker is felt everywhere. The Belgian-born, Mexico-based artist Francis Alÿs is, like Deller, concerned with people living under precarious conditions of labour, although in a very different context. A work by him that is particularly relevant in this context is the video *Zócalo, Mexico City, May 22, 1999*, which was shot on a single day in May. The film, made in collaboration with Rafael Ortega, documents, from a high and distant point of view, a day in the life of the central square. From the raising of the flag at dawn to its lowering twelve hours later, people are seen waiting for casual employment, sheltering from the sun in the slowly shifting, narrow shadow of the giant, sundial-like flagpole. *Zócalo* graphically illustrates how time overshadows and dictates people's daily activity or inactivity.

The diagram is one of the many types of sign discussed by the American philosopher and semiotician Charles Sanders Peirce. He introduced a tripartite division of signs based on their differing means of signification: broadly, the icon depends on similarity, the symbol on convention, and the index on some physical proximity or existential connection. He understood the diagram as a sub-species of the icon because it sets up a relationship of similarity between logical or temporal relations of the phenomena and the spatial relations of the diagram.[7] Graphs or diagrams are a useful way of visualising information which varies with the passage of time – as exemplified by the ubiquitous line graphs of the rise and fall and rise of COVID-19 cases or stock-exchange prices. The diagram has a diaristic character if it regularly charts some aspect of the artist's daily experience. It focuses on a narrow bandwidth of experience and dispenses with the narrative form of a conventional diary. However, because of this restriction and its graphic display, it often produces new insights pertaining to the information charted. Personal diaries are to a certain extent periodic and repetitive, but they have a confessional intimacy that can only be hinted at in a diagram. Diaristic diagrams might be viewed as a hybrid of conceptual artists' preference for impersonal, anonymous presentation and a post-conceptual interest, particularly on the part of women artists, in taking lived experience and daily life as their subject matter.

In an essay that somewhat modifies the argument of 'Conceptual Art 1962–1969', Buchloh discussed the significance of artistic appropriations of the diagram. In 'Hesse's Endgame: Facing the Diagram' (2006), he argued that, after Duchamp, 'one of the principal dialectical oppositions in the medium of drawing has been the authentic corporeal trace and the externally established matrix'. On one side, drawing as desire – on the other, drawing 'as self-critical subjection to pre-existing formulae'.[8] Unlike prior models of drawing, the diagram would not trace desire, call forth corporality, or make a liberatory gesture; rather, it would register 'the disenchantment of the world and the total subjection of the body and its representation to legal and administrative control'.[9] As part of an extended analysis of Eva Hesse's work, Buchloh argued that the artist adopted the diagrammatic paradigm to signal her sense of alienation and constraint: she shows us a somatic record 'represented as totally constrained and submerged within the matrix of the purely machinic/technological registers'.[10] Although 'totally constrained', Hesse nonetheless inserted small marks of resistance in the form of traces of the body – 'residual and resistant forms of bodily authenticity and psychic autonomy'.[11] For Buchloh, Hesse adopted the diagrammatic mode in order to register her sense of the impossibility of any spontaneous, unmediated gesture under the coercive and instrumentalising regime of capitalism. Yet, at the same time, she subtly subverted that regime. For him, Hesse's drawings on graph paper both acknowledge the alienating structures of modern life and register a protest against them. This analysis provides a preliminary model for thinking about diaristic diagrams.[12]

The strategy outlined by Buchloh is well exemplified in Félix González-Torres's diagrammatic work *Untitled (Bloodworks)* (1989), although in this instance the graph has a temporal axis. The piece, which shows ascending and descending diagonal lines on two pencilled grids, is formally indebted to Hesse and also makes reference to Aleksander Rodchenko's *Line Drawing* of 1921, which consists of ruler-drawn diagonal line in crayon on a piece of graph paper. While Rodchenko's drawing carries connotations of a scientific outlook, González-Torres's is both diagrammatic and diaristic. Given the work's title and the fact that his partner, Ross Laycock, died of AIDS in 1991 after a long illness, the lines must allude to the daily count of the immune system's T-cells that measure the body's response to the AIDS virus.[13] The pair of images with their schematic lines might be thought, then, to represent hope and despair. Much of González-Torres's work aims to soften the diagrammatic paradigm's unyielding abstraction with traces of the body's vicissitudes over time.[14] Jörg Heiser's conception of 'romantic conceptualism' may be helpful in this context. This type of work, wrote Heiser, 'invests the Conceptual with what appears to be its antithesis'; it is about 'systematically treating the un-systematic'. He refers to Bas Jan Ader, who made a film of himself in floods of tears, *I'm too sad to tell you* (1971). His work, according to Heiser, is exemplary of the attempt to bridge the divide between intellectual systems and 'the spontaneous overflow of powerful feelings'.[15] I have organised a sample of relevant artists into two groups on the basis of the sources of the information they chart; the first, 'observational' group periodically records information gathered from external sources, while the second, 'self-monitoring' group is more concerned with tracking subjective states of circumstances that impinge upon the body.

Observational diaristic diagrams

A key figure in the brief history of diaristic diagrams is the leftist German artist KP Brehmer (1938–1997), who in the 1960s was affiliated with the Capitalist Realism group. His work takes the form of infographic diagrams, but also indicates what eludes that mode of representation. Brehmer appropriated economic and governmental bar charts, graphs, maps, and emblems in order to subvert them and, at the same time, purge his art of any aesthetic pretensions.[16] In this way, he reflected on the effects of the post-war rise of managerial and informational economies. As Helen Molesworth has observed, many conceptual artists 'made representations of work, such as diagrams, graphs, and flow charts'.[17] In Brehmer's work, however, sensation, affect, and aesthetics are nonetheless acknowledged. Some of his work, such as the series *Himmelfarben* (*Sky Colours*) (1969–76), includes a diaristic, temporal dimension. *Himmelfarben* is a seventeen-part series of watercolour paintings on graph paper, each part of which attempts to record the changing colour of the sky over a twenty-four-hour period. A note appended to an explanatory drawing states the following: 'The colour of the northern sky was observed each hour of the day, imitated and then transferred from the palette to the drawing. The colours corresponding to each hour of the day resulting [sic] in the colour scale of that day.'[18]

Himmelfarben is, I suggest, a critique of the coercive imposition of a rationalising and regulating regime governing every aspect of our lives. Ironically, its critique takes the form of apparently falling under that regime to the point of comic exaggeration. Yet the series, by attempting the impossible task of diagramming the elusive colours of the sky, gestures towards that which escapes representation.[19] Brehmer adopts a mock-scientific pose, no doubt aimed at subverting the German tradition of romantic landscape painting. His procedure involved 'clocking-in' each hour of the day to match and apply a patch of paint to a graph. Yet, against the background of this culturally imposed clock time, *Himmelfarben* alludes to planetary rhythms, the contingency and variability of weather conditions, and the ineffable colours of the sky. In addition, although Brehmer used commercial graph paper, he allowed his manually applied little patches of blues, greys, and blacks to spill over the lines of the grid and occasionally to pucker the paper and run down the page like tears. The artist's daily activity is severely restricted to a regular 'snapshot', but the day's work is expanded to 24 hours, effectively eroding the distinction between times for work and rest. The project must have severely disrupted his sleep.[20]

The American artist, Spencer Finch, also mimes and undermines the rationalisation of experience. *The River That Flows Both Ways* (2009) was a temporary public art project commissioned for the High Line in New York City (figure 1.1). In a manner similar to *Himmelfarben*, the work attempted to chart the changing colours of the Hudson River which flows parallel to the raised walkway, formerly an elevated railway line for freight trains. Finch decided to make use of an existing architectural feature on the site, a remnant of the old Nabisco factory featuring a wall of 700 mullioned panes of glass. From a tugboat drifting on the Hudson, he took 700 photographs of the water, one every minute, using a high-resolution digital camera. The period of sampling on 12 June 2008, from 9.15 am to 8.55 pm, amounted to 11 hours and 40 minutes. He pulled one pixel from each of the digital photographs, matched and printed the colours on film transparencies, sandwiched them between glass, and affixed them to the existing panes. The colours were arranged chronologically, from top left to bottom right, in the ready-made grid, so that the pale blues at the top give way to soft dusky purples and sea greens in the middle, and deep greys at the bottom when the sunlight reflected on the water had dimmed. The whole glass panel is, in its turn, subject to variable ambient light levels.

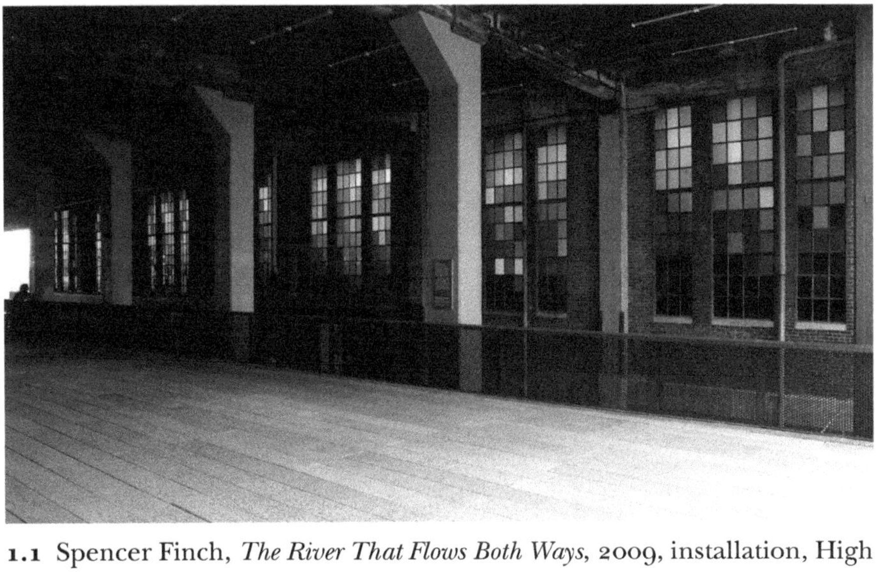

1.1 Spencer Finch, *The River That Flows Both Ways*, 2009, installation, High Line, New York

The River That Flows Both Ways has the luminous beauty of a stained-glass window. However, since it also closely resembles a pixelated blow-up of a digital image, it also draws attention to contemporary conditions of perception and representation. Finch acknowledges that it would be anachronistic to paint in the manner of Romanticism and Impressionism. Yet, at the same time, the work evokes the paintings of J. M. W. Turner and Claude Monet, both of whom, incidentally, made exacting studies of light and colour. Finch's observations are equally exacting, but, as Mark Godfrey nicely put it, he presents his findings filtered through 'layers of mediation'.[21] The artist's remarks on the history of attempts to categorise different types of cloud are illuminating in this context: he finds the attempts both 'appealing and also pathetic', since clouds are 'basically impossible to name [or] categorize'.[22] The title of the installation, *The River That Flows Both Ways*, refers to the native American name for the tidal river.

Finch's work, like Brehmer's, demonstrates the capacity of the grid to embrace the temporal dimension. This spatialisation of the passage of time makes it possible to view the work both as a temporal sequence and as an all-over pattern. The grid as a form is ubiquitous in the art of the twentieth century. As Rosalind Krauss pointed out, it has multiple connotations, including the assertion of an anti-mimetic impulse declaring the non-literary, purely visual, autonomous character of modern art. The grid can map the material, two-dimensional surface of the support or, in conceptual art, provide a neutral, pre-given matrix for entering information.[23] Yet, as we have seen, it can also represent time, as in a typical calendar grid.

The photographic practice of Austrian artist, Inge Dick, also involves tracking the shifting colours and light over a given period of time and engaging with layers of technological mediation. *Sommer Licht Weiss* (*Summer Light White*) (2013), for example, is a composite photograph made by extracting stripes of colour from a digital film of a white surface, recorded over the course of four days in June and July. Dick arranges the stripes chronologically, from top to bottom, in a single photograph, so that one can see, for instance, the bright pink tones of evening light before nightfall.[24] Such vivid colours are normally invisible because our eyes adapt to the different light levels. The camera, with fixed settings, does not. In Dick's work, the unnatural fixity of the camera's aperture enables the perception of something that would otherwise go unnoticed. This sort of affordance of technology was noted by Walter Benjamin in his discussion of the 'optical unconscious' and acts as a counter-argument to the idea that technology blunts perception.

Jill Baroff is an American artist whose ink-on-paper drawings are concerned with the periodicity of seasons and other natural phenomena. *A Month of Sundays (March)* (2015) explores the tension between measure and natural phenomena. Baroff explains that the drawing, which focuses on the lengthening days of spring, is 'composed of five lines drawn on a rectangular sheet of Japanese gampi paper separated by a distance determined by the length of the day for five Sundays in the month of March'.[25] Appropriately, the lines are drawn in a delicate shade of indigo. This rectangular sheet is then folded over to form a square. The fold introduces an element of chance aimed at subverting the data-based process in order better to reflect the 'individualised, sensorial experience of a given day'.[26] Folding the semi-transparent paper makes the lines on the left of the rectangle superimpose onto the others – in effect, folding time back on itself. This means that the drawing is no longer readable as a graph of objective measures of time, but rather suggests the inconsistency of lived experience. As Marcel Proust observed, 'the calendar of facts rarely corresponds to the calendar of feelings'.[27] For Baroff, strict measure, computer calculation, and diagrammatic display are inadequate means of capturing the variability of perception.

The work of all these artists is marked by a tension between the observation of natural phenomena and technical recording procedures. Their work makes periodic observations, systematically records, and diagrammatically presents some aspect of natural phenomena. They demonstrate the limits of the diagrammatic paradigm and make visible what would otherwise go unnoticed. Using technical recording equipment and graphic presentation, they show how subtle shifts in ambient colour, light, and shade strains the limits of representation.

Self-monitoring diaristic diagrams

The other loose grouping of artists I want to consider in this context is less concerned with observing natural phenomena. Instead, they record aspects of their own daily life and work experience. Although I refer to their practice as 'self'-monitoring, the self that emerges in their work is indicated only minimally, in outline. One early and influential exponent of a self-monitoring art practice was the Japanese-born artist On Kawara, whose work uncannily anticipated the digital revolution.

His series *I Am Still Alive*, inaugurated in 1969, consists of intermittent telegrams sent to friends and acquaintances from wherever the peripatetic artist was located. The message is always the same: 'I am still alive. On Kawara.' Yet the repetition of the declaration is hardly reassuring; the word 'still', in particular, seems to portend imminent death, as does the telegram – a means of communication usually reserved for urgent messages. The date, time, and place of filing and receipt were automatically recorded or stamped on the telegram. In this way, the artist's movements were tracked and recorded, leaving a low-tech data trail comparable to a smart phone or self-surveillance device. Other relevant examples include Kawara's series of postcards sent between 1968 and 1979 from far-flung hotels and rubber-stamped with the message 'I got up at . . .', stamped with a particular time. The cards provide minimal information about his location and sleep/wake patterns. As one critic noted: 'He spun art out of existential metadata – not the content of his life but its wreaths of attendant information – and his art ends up being about both how little and how much you can know from such stray facts, a half-century before the subject became a political hot-button issue in our epoch of data paranoia.'[28]

Kawara is best known for his series called *Today* or *Date Paintings*. Dating from 4 January 1966, until his death in 2014, there are eight thousand of them in all. Each canvas has the date on which it was painted inscribed in bold white paint against a dark ground; paintings unfinished by midnight were destroyed. Each painting is tied to the time and place of its making by writing the month in the language of the place where he was staying, and an accompanying page from a local newspaper of the same date. In effect, the place, time, and activity of painting were synchronised, but only briefly. Like a photograph, Kawara's *Date Paintings* are indexically tied to a time and place, but also immediately separated: the date now refers to a time long gone, not 'today'. While the dates are immediately readable, the canvases themselves, which are carefully painted in a range of subtle, hand-mixed shades of blues, greys, and reds, suggest something less accessible. Are they perhaps indicative of mood? Like all the work discussed here, they are curiously poised between strict impersonality and diaristic revelation. This ambiguity prompted Jeffrey Weiss to describe them as 'inherently paradoxical'.[29] Kawara's *Today* paintings are normally displayed in a single, eye-level chronological sequence, while his smaller works, such as the postcards, are arranged in a grid pattern.

Another early and influential example of an artist working in a diaristic and diagrammatic mode is Mary Kelly. Her groundbreaking

Post-Partum Document (1973–1979) channelled the trauma of the artist's own post-partum losses into an ambitious six-year project. Kelly's work was partly conceived as a response to conceptual artists who, she said, 'stopped dramatically short of synthesizing the subjective moment into their enquiry'.[30] It makes use of strategies of data collection, diagrams, and textual information alongside indexical traces.[31] As an artist with commitments to feminism and psychoanalysis, Kelly documented events as they unfolded in her own life, weaving a first-person-singular diary that narrated her lived experience as a mother together with medical, psychoanalytic, and sociological discourses aimed at analysing that experience and challenging the notion of an essential femininity. Graphs and charts from a variety of sources, such as a book on paediatrics and texts by Lacan, pepper the document, giving it an informational character. But Kelly also makes use of the mute and affecting language of the found object.[32] The work, consisting of 135 small units divided into six sections, is displayed in a chronological series in the gallery space, creating for the viewer an experience comparable to that of time-based media.

Another important example of the practice of periodic self-documentation is Eleanor Antin's *Carving: A Traditional Sculpture* (1972). Over the course of a month of dieting, she took daily photographs of her naked body posed so as to display four different views. In effect, she documented the 'carving' of her own flesh. The resulting 148 images, each recorded with an exact date, time, and weight, are arranged in a mural-sized grid reminiscent of Eadweard Muybridge's systematic photo-documentation of movement. It is a diary limited to a single aspect of self-observation that speaks of women's culturally engrained habit of self-surveillance and alienation from their own bodies.[33]

Self-monitoring is taken to an extreme by Taiwanese artist Tehching Hsieh. *One Year Performance 1980–1981*, for example, involved the artist punching a time clock installed in his studio every hour on the hour for a whole year. Hsieh made a time-lapse film of the performance which compressed his gruelling schedule into six minutes, during which time the artist's hair grew to shoulder length. He became increasingly tired and dishevelled as his vulnerable body failed to match the machinic rhythm to which he subjected himself.

The diaristic work of the Canadian artist based in New York, Moyra Davey, makes use of photography, video, and writing.[34] Several pieces are also diagrammatic diaries. *Bottle Grid* (1996–2000), for instance, consists of 54 gelatin-silver prints of empty whisky bottles taken over the course of 5 years. Davey explained the genesis of the piece:

> One day about twelve years ago, a blurred picture of an empty Johnnie Walker bottle turned up at the tail end of a contact sheet. It was a misfire, but I continued to take pictures of liquor bottles when they'd attained this state of depletion. Someone mentioned Morandi. I saw the totality of the images as a calendar, a marker of time denoted by a particular type of consumption.'[35]

Newspaper, Coffee (Receipts) II (2015–2016; figure 1.2), is a similar, although more complex, example. It consists of five analogue photographs of purchase receipts taken in the early 1990s. These were scanned and colourised by computer, folded, and sent through the post in 2016, and then arranged into a grid of twelve prints. The photographs show only one or two words from each receipt indicating the item purchased or shop visited. These are repeated, indicating a habitual behaviour pattern: newspaper, coffee, magazine, Blue Note, The Album. The work combines a great diversity of materials and techniques – found objects, obsolete dot-matrix type, analogue and digital photography, folded paper, sticky tape, postage stamps, and postmarks. Straddling two decades, the work seems like a fading trace of a former pattern of daily life.

The British artist Susan Morris has turned self-monitoring into an art form. She has made diagrammatic and diaristic drawings, prints, and Jacquard tapestries, as well as an unconventional diary, all of which involve some form of self-surveillance. She began the project in 2004, registering periodic 'symptoms' on commercial year planners, filling in certain squares of the grid and leaving others blank. Invoking Barthes, she referred to her process as 'notation degree zero'. The marks accumulate to form what she described as a 'nullifying cloud'.[36] This irregular pattern of gaps and squares may refer to days of 'being' or despondent 'non-being', as in the series in homage to Kawara called *I Am . . . (Still)*, or they might register spending patterns, or crying jags. It is unclear. The year-planner drawings are both intimate and impersonal, wet and dry.[37] Michael Newman discussed these works in the context of an essay on anti-portraiture, yet what he says about their ambiguously coded and opaque character applies to Morris's work generally and is worth quoting at length:

> The diagram's usual purpose of producing knowledge is reversed, and it becomes opaque in relation to the inferences that we are

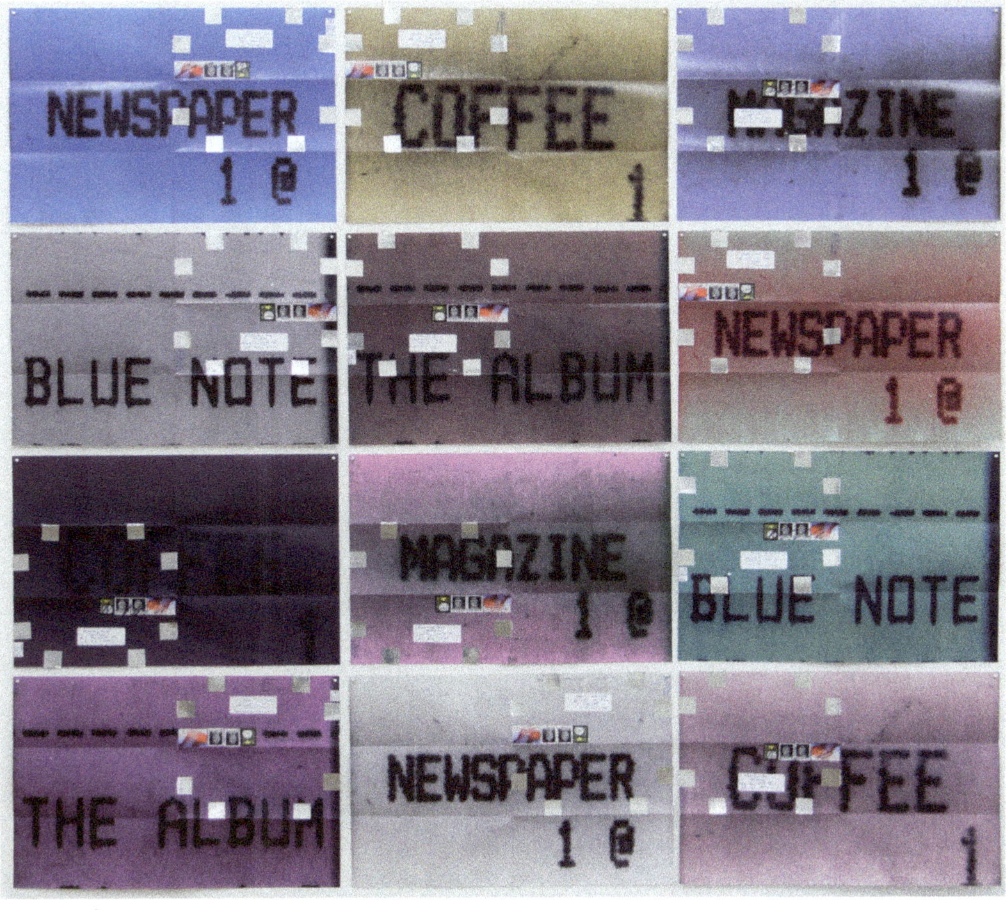

1.2 Moyra Davey, *Newspaper, Coffee (Receipts) II*, 2015–2016, 12 C-prints, copper, tape, postage, ink, 30.5 × 45.7 cm

forced to draw from its unreadable patterns. Abstraction is therefore given a double valence: on the one hand, it mimes the conversion of experience into data which renders exchangeable the singularity of the indexical (there at that moment the subject was in an unrepeatable situation which can be segmented into standardised units and tagged), while on the other hand it produced an experience which we could name 'aesthetic', marking the work as resistant to decoding. Morris's 'year planner' works are anti-portraits not only because (unlike the conventional portrait) they are non-representational, but also because as abstractions they exist in this double condition of standardisation and opacity.[38]

Newman refers to what I am rather clumsily calling 'self-monitoring diaristic diagrams' as 'data-portraits'.

In search of a less deliberate, more automatic, non-human, and 'truer' mark than the minimal handmade registrations of the year planner series, Morris began wearing an Actiwatch, a digital device usually used in a medical context to monitor periods of rest and activity. This was in 2005, long before the fashion for Fitbits and other self-tracking devices. At first, she made small infographic prints, *Actigraphs*, using the device's software. These ink-jet prints displayed her sleep/wake patterns as graphs using an array of coded, jewel-like colours. She then decided to use a Jacquard loom, partly because it was the first example of the mechanisation of human labour (which takes us back to Wright's cotton mills) and partly because it is a nineteenth-century invention whose original punch-card mechanism anticipated the modern computer. To make the tapestries, Morris fed the information from the Actiwatch into a complex algorithm that instructed the digital loom to display the data as a graph using colour-coded silk and linen threads. This process involved solving complex technical problems with the help of a master weaver, but she wanted the tapestries to shrug off all that labour so that they would appear effortlessly created, like 'the plumage of birds'.[39]

Some of Morris's tapestries are designed to capture the tension between artificial, socially imposed rhythms, and those tied to the Earth's rotation and orbit around the sun, as well as to the body's rhythms. *SunDial:NightWatch_Activity and Light 2010–2012 (Herringbone Weave)* (2017; figure 1.3), is a large tapestry that displays the Actiwatch's record of both activity and ambient light levels over a three-year period. It logged these two streams of data once every minute for 1,096 days. Simultaneously observational and self-monitoring, the tapestry combines both types of diaristic diagram. Vertical streams of variegated colour display activity levels, while the grey-scale streams are a record of concurrent ambient light levels (figure 1.4).[40] The sheer density of information and the use of a herringbone weave to distinguish the two data streams give the tapestry, when viewed at a distance, a beautiful, blurred, almost monochromatic quality, as its brilliant colours fade to grey. It looks like a landscape at dusk in the pouring rain, while also suggesting the involuntary fall of data. Digital bits are drowned in the seasonal waves of light and darkness. In 'Agnes Martin: The /Cloud/', Rosalind Krauss considered the difference between near and distant views. She suggested that Martin's work should be understood as setting up a dialectic between the objective tactile grid

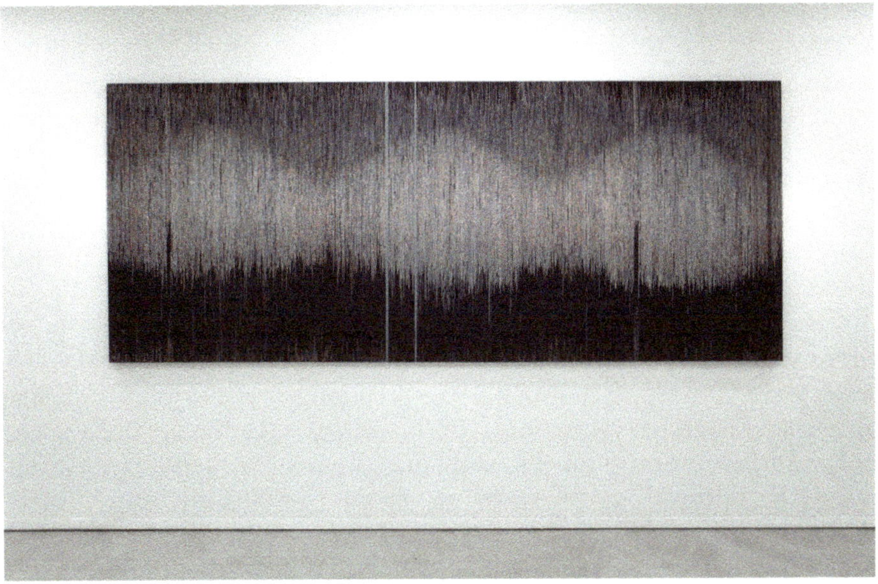

1.3 Susan Morris, *SunDial:NightWatch_Activity and Light 2010–2012 (Herringbone Weave)*, 2017, Jacquard tapestry: silk and cotton yarn, 130 × 312 cm

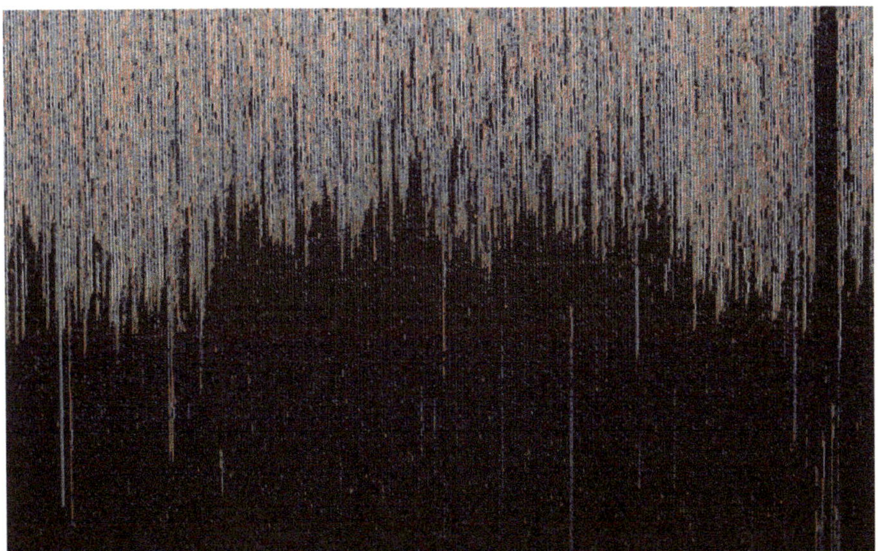

1.4 Susan Morris, detail from *SunDial:NightWatch_Activity and Light 2010–2012 (Herringbone Weave)*, 2017, Jacquard tapestry: silk and cotton yarn, 130 × 312 cm

(when seen up close) and the subjective cloudy, shimmering, optical veil (when seen further away). In other words, while Martin's grids figure vision's aspiration for clarity, they also picture an acknowledgement of its limits, its remainder.[41] As a description of the distant view of *SunDial:NightWatch_Activity and Light,* Krauss's phrase 'subjective cloudy, shimmering, optical veil' could hardly be bettered. It flickers between pictorial abstraction and dense information.

Although Morris's tapestries are primarily a record of her own activity and sleep patterns, they also make us aware of natural conditions and social circumstances – they display the periodicity of the seasons in the Northern hemisphere as well as our typical work schedules. The tapestry shows seasonal changes of sunlight intensity and longevity, passing through three summers where the light areas bulge and contract. It is noticeable that the profile showing morning is much flatter than the evening profile, indicating that Morris opened her curtains at the same clock-time, regardless of seasonal fluctuations. Evenings show up as speckled registrations of dim electric light that lasts late into the hours of natural darkness even up to midnight, at the top of the tapestry, and beyond, at the bottom. Low levels of activity during the night look like blue 'stars' against a black ground – an index of random restlessness.[42]

Long-term recordings draw attention to repetitive activities, the unconscious automatisms of everyday life, and to repeated natural rhythms like the rising and setting of the sun. Yet, as she notes, 'it remains clear that the subject being recorded is embedded in clock and calendrical time'. The tapestries show the effects of technological encroachment, the glitches in the system, and the body's resistance. They reveal, as Morris put it, 'the trace of a vaporous bodily unconscious that exists like a cast shadow alongside my everyday "self"'.[43]

For many artists since the 1960s, the diaristic diagram has acted as a means of formal restraint in treating autobiographical material. Some of these artists have also used a technical mediation alongside a diagrammatic format to register the increasing penetration of new technologies into every sphere of life, including the emergence of a 24/7 culture. While the diagram captures modernity's rationalisation of time and work, the diaristic content puts pressure on that paradigm. As we have seen, some diaristic diagrams capture the way that the infinite variations of the colours of the sky or sea, or the sun's reflected light, dissolve the strictures of the graph. Others show how the body, with its own behavioural unconscious and particular rhythms, habits, and moods, overflows the confinement of the grid.

Notes

This chapter develops ideas first published in the catalogue for an exhibition curated by Susan Morris. *A Day's Work* was held at Raum Schroth, Museum Wilhelm Morgner, Soest, Germany, from 26 January to 13 April 2019. My thinking and the choice of artists discussed owe a great deal to her original conception for the exhibition.

1 Pie charts and Venn diagrams are examples of infographics that lack a temporal dimension. For an overview of informational graphics see Edward Tufte, *Envisioning Information* (Cheshire, CT: Graphics Press, 1998).
2 Benjamin Buchloh, 'Conceptual Art 1962–1969: From the Aesthetics of Administration to the Critique of Institutions', *October*, 55 (1990), 119–124, 141, 143.
3 Jonathan Crary, *24/7: Late Capitalism and the Ends of Sleep* (London: Verso, 2013), pp. 9–11, 13.
4 Susan Morris, 'A Day's Work', in *A Day's Work* (Soest: Raum Schroth and Museum Wilhelm Morgner, 2019), p. 20. The catalogue includes an essay by me, 'Diagramming the Day', pp. 58–83.
5 Crary, *24/7*, pp. 9–11, 13.
6 Crary, *24/7*, p. 62.
7 Charles Sanders Peirce, 'Icon, Index, Symbol', in Charles Sanders Peirce, *Collected Papers. Vol. II: Elements of Logic* (Cambridge, MA: Harvard University Press, 1960), pp. 159ff; Charles Sanders Peirce, 'Logic as Semiotic: The Theory of Signs', in Justus Buchler (ed.), *The Philosophy of Peirce: Selected Writings* (New York: Harcourt, 1940), pp. 98–119. Although the diagram is mainly iconic, it has symbolic and, often, indexical aspects.
8 Benjamin H. D. Buchloh, 'Hesse's Endgame: Facing the Diagram', in Catherine de Zegher (ed.), *Eva Hesse Drawing* (New York and New Haven, CT: Drawing Center and Yale University Press, 2006), p. 117. For a different interpretation of the significance of the diagram see David Joselit, 'Dada's Diagrams', in Leah Dickerman (ed.), *The Dada Seminars* (Washington, DC: Center for Advanced Study in the Visual Arts, National Gallery of Art, 2005), pp. 222–239.
9 Buchloh, 'Hesse's Endgame', pp. 117–119.
10 This characterisation of Hesse's work appears in Benjamin Buchloh, 'Gabriel Orozco: Sculpture as Recollection', in *Gabriel Orozco* (London and Mexico City: Thames & Hudson and Museo Palacio de Belles Artes, 2006), p. 202.
11 Buchloh, 'Hesse's Endgame', p. 122.
12 For an interesting discussion of the diagram and a response to Buchloh, see essays by the American painter Amy Sillman. She found that adopting the diagram allowed her painting to combine spatial and temporal vectors, and provided a way to bridge the gap between thinking and making. 'Notes on the Diagram', *Paris Review* (12 November 2020),

theparisreview.org/blog/2020/11/12/notes-on-the-diagram/ (accessed 12 January 2021). See also her 'Alex Katz Chair in Painting Artist Talk', 3 December 2020, cooper.edu/events-and-exhibitions/events/amy-sillman-alex-katz-chair-painting-artist-talk (accessed 12 January 2021).

13 See Nancy Spector, *Felix González-Torres* (New York: Guggenheim Museum, 1995), p. 120.

14 I discussed this and other works by González-Torres in Iversen, 'Index, Diagram, Graphic Trace', *Tate Papers*, 18 (Autumn 2012), www.tate.org.uk/research/tate-papers/18/index-diagram-graphic-trace (accessed 12 January 2021). For an extended discussion of how Gabriel Orozco's work engages with these issues, see Iversen, 'Desire and the Diagrammatic', *Oxford Art Journal*, 39:1 (March 2016), 1–17.

15 Jörg Heiser, 'Emotional Rescue', *Frieze Magazine*, 71 (2002), 71–75.

16 See *Art into Society: Seven German Artists* (London: Institute of Contemporary Art, 1974), p. 62.

17 Helen Molesworth, 'Work Ethic', in *Work Ethic* (University Park, PA and Baltimore, MD: Penn State University Press and Baltimore Museum of Art, 2003), p. 27.

18 Brehmer's sky-colour charts bear comparison with Honoré-Bénédict de Saussure's invention, the 'cyanometer' (1789), a colour wheel of 52 different concentrations of Prussian blue from near-white to near-black which he used to gauge the varying blueness of the sky.

19 See also Doreen Mende (ed.), *KP Brehmer: A Test Extending Beyond the Action* (Seville: Centro Andaluz de Arte Contemporáneo, 2011), www.caac.es/descargas/libreto_brehmer_ing.pdf (accessed 15 July 2020).

20 *Himmelfarben* might be compared with the work of other conceptual artists who took an interest in tracking natural phenomena, such as the Dutch artist Jan Dibbets. See, for example, *The Shortest Day at the Van Abbemuseum, Eindhoven* (1970), or *Shadow Piece (The Shadows in my Studio as They Were at 27.07.69 from 8.40–4.10, Photographed Every Ten Minutes)* (1969).

21 Mark Godfrey, 'Measures and Pleasures', *Parkett*, 79 (June 2007), 19.

22 See the video interview with Finch made in conjunction with his exhibition at Turner Contemporary, 'The Skies Can't Keep Their Secret', May–September 2014, https://vimeopro.com/modusfilm/turner-contemporary/video/96259604 (accessed 12 February 2021).

23 Rosalind Krauss, 'Grids', *October*, 9 (Summer 1979), 51–64. Reprinted in Krauss, *The Originality of the Avant-Garde and other Modernist Myths* (Cambridge, MA: MIT Press, 1985), pp. 8–22.

24 See Gerda Ridler, 'The Colours of Summer', in *Inge Dick* (Munich: Galerie Renate Bender, 2014).

25 The same principle was used in one of John Cage's scores for *4′33″*, which had vertical lines at varying intervals dividing the otherwise blank horizontal pages and indicating the durations of the three movements. This version is called 'score in proportional notation'.

26 Email correspondence with the artist, 17 September 2018.

27 Marcel Proust, *In Search of Lost Time: Sodom and Gomorrah* (London: Everyman, 2001), p. 146. The quotation reads: 'It was only at that moment – more than a year after her burial, because of the anachronism which so often prevents the calendar of facts from corresponding to the calendar of feelings – that I became conscious that she was dead.'

28 Ben Davis, 'What On Kawara's Analog Wisdom at the Guggenheim Has to Offer a Digital World', *Artnet News*, 6 February 2015, https://news.artnet.com/art-world/what-on-kawaras-analog-wisdom-at-the-guggenheim-has-to-offer-a-digital-world-246126#:~:text=The%20greatness%20of%20Kawara's%20work,is%20painted%2C%20you%20are%20gone (accessed 4 January 2023).

29 Jeffrey Weiss, 'Bounded Infinity', in *On Kawara: Silence* (New York: Guggenheim Museum, 2017). One section of the Guggenheim show, *Self-Observation*, included the series *I Went* (1968–1997), *I Met* (1968–1979), and *I Got Up* (1968–1979).

30 Mary Kelly, 'Introduction: Remembering, Repeating, and Working Through', in *Imaging Desire* (Cambridge, MA: MIT Press 1996), p. xx.

31 Mary Kelly, *Post-Partum Document* (London: Routledge & Kegan Paul, 1983). I have written elsewhere about Kelly's work. See Iversen, 'Survey', in Iversen, Douglas Crimp, and Homi Bhabha, *Mary Kelly* (London, Phaidon Press, 1997), pp. 32–85.

32 On the 'informational look' in Kelly's and other artists' work see Eve Meltzer, *Systems We Have Loved: Conceptual Art, Affect, and the Antihumanist Turn* (Chicago, IL: Chicago University Press, 2013).

33 Buchloh discusses artists' interest in the chronophotography of Muybridge and Étienne-Jules Marey. Stressing its later use in Taylorist time-and-motion studies aimed at disciplining labour, he claims that avant-garde artists found in chronophotography a representational paradigm in which 'the actual conditions of somatic experience and subjecthood under advanced forms of capitalist production and control could be adequately recorded'. Buchloh, 'Hesse's Endgame', p. 121.

34 See Iversen, 'The Diaristic Mode: On Moyra Davey and Susan Morris', *Art History*, 44:4 (September 2021), 798–822.

35 Davey, 'Statement', murrayguy.com/projects/bottle-grid-1996-2000 (accessed 7 January 2020). See also Jess T. Dugan, 'Conversation with Moyra Davey', *Big Red and Shiny*, 79 (1 April 2008), https://bigredandshiny.org/4125/a-conversation-with-moyra-davey (accessed 7 January 2020). Reprinted in Davey, 'Empties', in Brian Sholis et al., *Moyra Davey*, with essays and interviews by Davey, Sholis, Ben Lerner, Élisabeth Lebovici, and Eric Rosenberg (Göttingen: Scotiabank/Steidl, 2019), p. 74.

36 'At the end of each year, each "completed" planner, with its squares either filled in or left empty, functions as a record of hidden or forgotten events that are either mundane or (to me) important and

meaningful; but with everything reduced to the same *degree zero* of mark making; to nothing but a kind of nullifying *cloud.*' Susan Morris, email to the author, 28 November 2020, emphasis added.

37 In her PhD dissertation, Morris cited the article referred to earlier by Jörg Heiser, 'Emotional Rescue'. See Susan Morris, 'On the Blank: Photography, Writing, Drawing' (PhD dissertation, University of the Arts, London, 2006), p. 75, https://ualresearchonline.arts.ac.uk/id/eprint/2309 (accessed 15 September 2021).

38 Michael Newman, 'Decapitations: The Portrait, the Anti-Portrait . . . and What Comes After?', in Fiona Johnstone and Kristie Imber (eds), *Anti-Portraiture: Challenging the Limits of the Portrait* (London: Bloomsbury, 2020), p. 54.

39 Morris's use of tapestry was also inspired by a discussion in W. G. Sebald's *The Rings of Saturn* (1995), in which the narrator praises seventeenth-century silk merchants' pattern books containing samples of woven textiles 'of an iridescent, quite indescribable beauty as if they had been produced by Nature itself, like the plumage of birds'. The silk pattern books seemed to him like 'leaves from the only true book, which none of our textual and pictorial works can even begin to rival'. The silk swatches give the impression of having fallen onto the page, having bypassed human intention or fabrication. Morris decided to make textiles of iridescent threads that emulate this kind of mark. W. G. Sebald, *The Rings of Saturn*, trans. Michael Hulse (London: Harvill Press, 1998), pp. 272, 286.

40 The tapestry is configured so that time travels upwards, beginning at 00:00 hours on 1 January 2010, at the bottom left-hand corner of the tapestry, and ending at 24:00 hours on 31 December 2012, at the top right. Each minute of the 1,096 days of the period was allocated two vertical threads, one for each of the two data streams of activity and light levels. Variation in activity levels is indicated by red, green, and blue threads, while light levels are shown in two shades of grey for artificial light, and white for solar light. Low data levels are black. Two sudden time-shifts mark travel to a different time zone. Periods of data loss are indicated by blank streams of solid green or grey.

41 Rosalind Krauss, 'Agnes Martin: The /Cloud/', in Barbara Haskell (ed.), *Agnes Martin* (New York: Whitney Museum of American Art, 1992). Reprinted in Krauss, *Bachelors* (Cambridge, MA: October/MIT Press, 1999), pp. 75–90.

42 This information is derived from the artist's book, *Sun Dial: Night Watch_Tapestry Dossier* (2015), and from conversations with Morris. See *Susan Morris: Self Moderation*, with essays by Briony Fer and Sadie Plant (Biel: CentrePasquArt, 2016). For more information, see Deirdre O'Dwyer (ed.), *Susan Morris, Sontag Montag*, with essays by Briony Fer, Margaret Iversen, and Ed Krčma (London: Five Years Gallery, 2009). For more resources, see www.susanmorris.com.

43 See Chapter 2 of this book.

2

Inarticulations

Susan Morris

The title of this chapter, 'Inarticulations' (a word not in any dictionary), is a play on the title of John Berger's last book *Confabulations*, which explores how language, like the body, houses the inarticulate alongside the articulate. Both writing and drawing, Berger argues, involve a search for the 'quivering almost wordless "thing"' waiting to be represented.[1]

I am a visual artist who has always worked with writing. By that I mean that I have written things, such as articles or essays, but also that my work engages with the formal attributes of writing. I am interested in making images that *look* like writing, and in a compositional logic that takes as its model things laid out on a page: the book, the letter, the diagram, and the musical score, for instance – all of which can be thought of as surfaces organised by design criteria privileging readability: flatness, the margin, and the grid. I also have an attraction to . . . *papery-ness.*

Figure 2.1 shows a very papery thing, made up of receipts tracking every transaction I made over the course of a year. Its title is *Expenditure*, which means both what I spend but also (crucially) *waste.* The accumulated receipts were not scanned – I felt this would have made them too pictorial – but transcribed, a gigantean task for which I used a professional typing service. The data was then organised chronologically. I used the same font throughout and a single colour: the violet of the dye used in carbonless copy paper, once widely used for invoices and receipts but now almost obsolete. The information was printed at a scale of roughly 1:1 to that of the original receipts (which, in reality, varied in font size), resulting in a work that covered a large wall in its entirety, like wallpaper.[2]

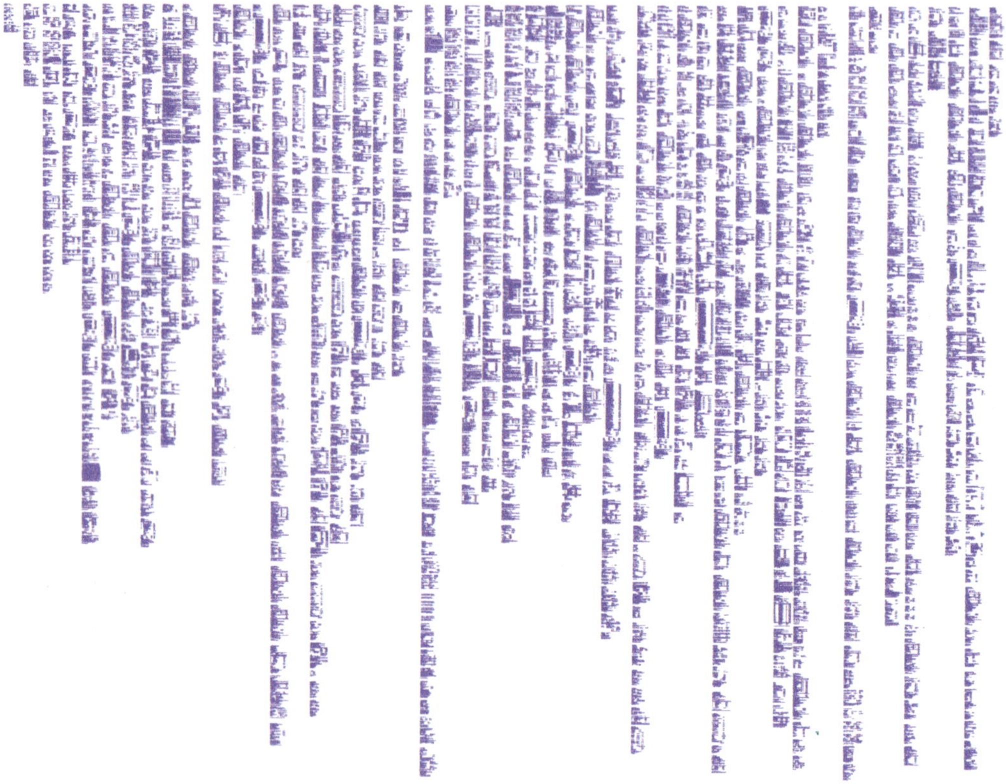

2.1 Susan Morris, *Expenditure*, 2016, inkjet on paper, 400 × 637 cm

The columns of figures go down in vertical streams. But something else is going on, operating horizontally, that cuts across this downward movement and interferes with it, like an undertow:

You were served today by Paul. How did we do? Like us on Facebook! Check out our back-to-school offers, all through September. Valentine's Day for two, only £14.99. From the Co-Op – Now!

This horizontal activity, a machinic 'chatter' that registers seasonal changes, the coming and going of shop and café workers with names that appear and disappear, and so on, points to another of my interests, writing that exhibits the properties of the mark – in particular, the indexical mark. Something registers in these extra pieces of *peripheral* information that is both part of the flow of money and outside it too.

Another papery thing I have made takes the form of a diary. This, like many of my more conventional artworks, is the result of a long-term recording project. It consists of a series of day-to-day (often hour-by-hour) notations recorded over the course of an entire year (2011), interwoven with material sampled from the real (or exterior) world, such as photographs, drawings, and diagrams, but also uncited quotations, snatches of overheard conversation, dialogue drifting in from the radio and scanned newspapers, 'found' writing and images that are embedded in the text like a bus ticket in a cubist collage. The receipts are in there too.

The diary project was made in relation both to ideas around automaticity in art, as exemplified by the writing or drawing

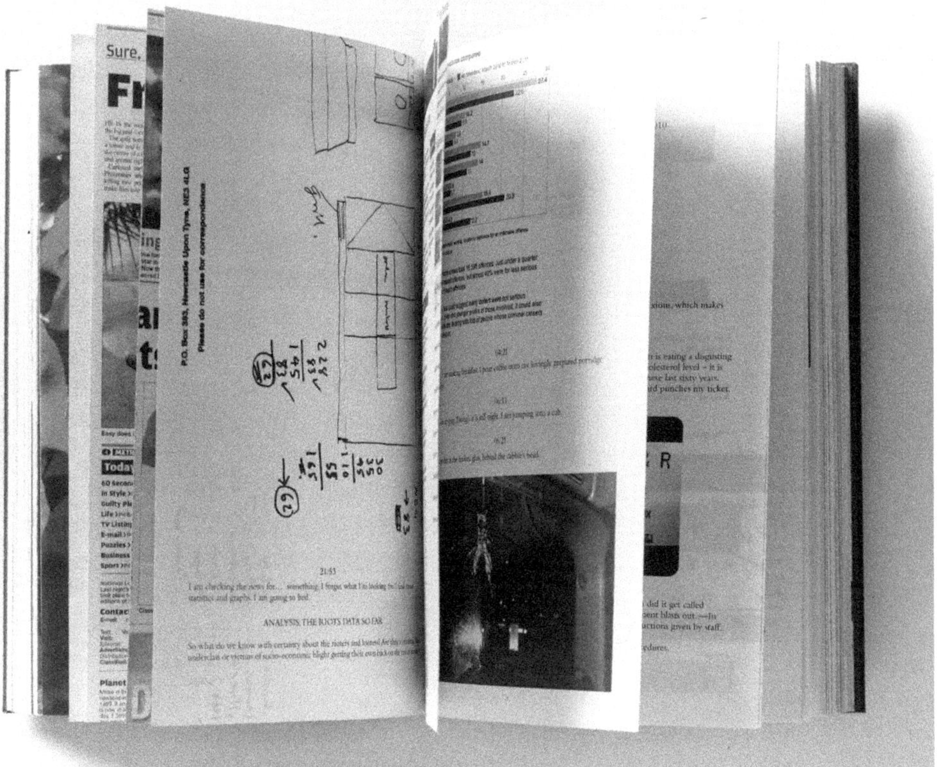

2.2 Susan Morris, detail from *de Umbris Idæarum [on the Shadow Cast by our Thoughts]*, 2021, 12 × softback books, each 21.5 × 13 cm, with shelf. Printed paper and wood, 23.5 × 37.2 × 13.5 cm

initiated by the Surrealists in the 1920s, and to the *encounter* – the 'sudden violent shock' that, for Virginia Woolf, signalled 'some real thing behind appearances'.[3] James Joyce thought this phenomenon through in relation to the epiphany – the sudden manifestation of the 'whatness' of an object or a gesture. For Proust, it took the form of an involuntary remembrance closer to forgetting; to a kind of ecstatic oblivion, when self-realisation coincides with self-obliteration, an encounter with something *outside* of self; outside of language's shared communicatory system.[4]

It is significant that these writers were all working in the wake of photography, the invention of which, as the linguist Ann Banfield has argued, produced a new kind of sentence structure – one that leaves the 'I' of the first person *out*. Woolf, for example, often appears to be recording the external world from the viewpoint first revealed to us by the photograph – i.e., of no one at all. The instruments of 'modern science', Banfield writes, allowed 'the viewing subject to see, to witness, places where he is not, indeed, where no subject is present . . . He therefore directly observes . . . the appearance of things in his absence' and, by inference, his *own* absence, as revealed by these recording devices.[5] Banfield draws our attention to the question repeated throughout Woolf's novel *The Waves* (1931): *how to describe a world without a self?* Each time this question is asked it is followed by the statement 'There are no words.' Or – as one of the novel's characters, Bernard, falteringly realises – there are only the little, broken, breathless words that 'lovers use'.[6]

Triggered by the encounter with the photograph, this kind of writing, in which words fail, may take the form of a *lover's discourse*, which – as Roland Barthes suggests – reduces us to subjects capable of little more than 'outbursts of language'.[7] In his later works, beginning with *Roland Barthes by Roland Barthes*, through to his final work on photography, Barthes developed a writing style that became ever more fragmentary and notational: broken words, broken sentences, or sentences that break off. Texts split into paragraphs that retain the character of the fragment, written in little bursts, like snapshots. In a posthumously published lecture, Barthes describes the process of his note-taking in similar terms to those one might use for taking a photograph. His aim is to get his own 'personal and internal scoops' – 'to "swipe" directly from life' – and he often uses the same words to describe the immediacy or 'suddenness' essential to both notetaking and photography: the moment is one of '*satori*'; of '*kairos*'.[8] As Barthes suggests, writing itself 'is precisely *there where you are not*' – language, like the photograph, excludes a vital part of the subject (the part that is *not* subject).[9] So in order to come close to what is located, literally, in a no man's land, you need 'a howl or cry', an 'utterance' – something that is neither fully inside nor fully outside meaning, or that is on the edge of meaning: *littoral*.[10]

Much of my recent visual practice has drawn upon the theme of selfhood's intermittent or flickering character. Using medico-scientific devices I have made works, such as screen prints, large ink-jet prints, and Jacquard tapestries, out of data recorded directly from the body. These trace a vaporous bodily unconscious that exists, like a cast shadow, alongside my everyday 'self'. What is important for me here is that the traces produced by these digital recording devices might also be classified as indexical marks, or signs.

An indexical sign is classified as such because it has a direct, physical link to the thing that caused it. 'Shadows', as Rosalind Krauss reminds us, are 'the indexical sign of the objects' that cast them.[11] Likewise, every photograph records the physical imprint of its object. Digital technology is often blamed for breaking this direct link between an object and its analogue. But digital technology is interesting to me precisely because it allows me to make recordings of things that *do not* have a specific location: *orphan* shadows, thrown by an invisible object, rather like the 'smoke without fire' that Walter Benjamin recognises in a photograph, when 'a space informed by human consciousness gives way to a space informed by the unconscious'.[12]

In other words, digital technology makes it possible to record something that is connected to a cause, but in a much more remote, complex, and mysterious way. For instance, if my heart is beating excessively fast at a certain moment and is recorded as doing so in the data converted into one of my tapestries, there is often no way of knowing exactly *why* it is behaving like that. It is a sign with a referent that remains enigmatic, elusive. But we encounter these sorts of signs every day, as the character Marcel in Proust's *la Recherche* knew only too well. Something announces itself, 'like the rush of blood to the face of a person who is unsettled, or like a sudden silence' – the evidence of something impossible to decipher.[13] 'Strong emotion must leave its trace', as Woolf writes in *Moments of Being*. Her idea is that one day 'some device will be invented by which we can tap' or record them.[14]

Digital technology allows me to produce images (such as my tapestries) that trace something enigmatic but related to the body; a body in the grip of a rhythm dictated by its own, unruly desire. But my thought is that the things that fall into the image – automatically, involuntarily – might also fall across a sentence, might also *mark* a sentence, like a shadow. Denis Hollier has described the early, autobiographical writings of the Surrealists as attempts to find, in literary space, 'the equivalent of what a shadow is in pictorial space'.[15] In their attempts to embed the index into their writing, these writers wanted to ensure, as Hollier argues, that the resulting text contained an element of 'incommunicability': a *break* in communication.[16]

This idea – that writing could also index (point to) something *outside* language – interests me. The problem was: how could 'I' write it? How could the use of the first person generate what Hollier describes as an 'autobiographical *precipitate* of the index'?[17] This question resolved itself once I started working in the diaristic mode, where entries written one day and forgotten the next bring about a paradoxical conjunction between the 'I' of the first person and the *absence* of self implied by automaticity. So it was that on 1 January 2011, and for the rest of that year, I submitted myself to what Michael Levenson has described as the 'tyranny' of the diary form, entrusting myself – as Barthes said of his own diary keeping – to *the banality that is in me.*[18]

The most intense moments I have experienced have often been when I am writing, when I find myself 'hardly aware of [anything], but the sensation . . . the feeling of ecstasy . . . of rapture' that overtakes me, forcing me to stop, in the street, on the train, and scribble frantically in my notebook.[19] For this reason, when I decided to keep a diary, I thought that the resulting text would be full of compelling insights and poetic observations. Not so. Indeed, while some of the motivation for this project came out of an interest in Virginia Woolf's delight in 'rubbish reading', I admit some perplexity at the realisation that I have met this with my own *rubbish writing.*[20]

Yet perhaps there is value in all this detritus? Freud suggested that the best place to look for the truth of the subject was by sifting through the rubbish of their discourse. He found this in his patient's dreams – noting too that these dreams could never be fully reassembled; that they always had the fragmentary, 'nonsensical' characteristic of a rebus. Similarly, Walter Benjamin's *Arcades Project*, which also juxtaposes unrelated (textual) fragments in a process 'intimately related to that of montage',[21] has been described as a way of writing about an entire civilisation 'using its rubbish as materials'.[22]

The value of rubbish writing has also been discussed at length in Lacan's commentary on James Joyce, whose books, Lacan suggests, are a form of *lituraterre* – a neologism that (in French) brings mud, dirt, and the earth into literature.[23] It is also based on a play on the words 'letter' and 'litter'. A letter is usually intended for a reader. Litter, on the other hand, is more likely to end up on a rubbish heap. *Litura* in Latin means 'erasure' or 'blotch'. A manuscript is *liturarius* when full of such things. My diary, which I kept doggedly for the year, aspired to this state, gathering everything into it. Like the magnetised toy canine that the artist Francis Alÿs dragged through the streets of Mexico City in his 1991 performance piece, *The Collector*, things stuck to me. But more than that too: stuff from the 'world' actually *interfered* with 'me'. In fact, as Hollier has pointed out, autobiography tends to suffer interference from the immediate. 'What is a private diary', he asks, when technologies of media and communication have insinuated their way 'into the innermost recesses of privacy?' The truth is that the writing of the private diary (the journal) is often *prompted* by the reading of what we could call the public diary (the [in French] *journal*).[24]

The title for my 'diary project' – which for years (channelling Joyce) I also referred to as 'Work in Progress' – is *de Umbris Idæarum [on the Shadow Cast by our Thoughts]*.[25] The piece consists of twelve books, housed in a purpose-built shelf, one for each month of the recorded year. Clearly, there is a lot of material from the real world, stamped, as it inevitably is, with real time and dates. The *journal* is in the journal, alongside cinema tickets, letters, and 'litter' (such as flyers), and so on, not to mention thousands of itemised receipts, emails, and text messages, all interspersed with the 'text' – the writing itself – which, rather than reflecting the interiority of a constructed self, also appears to be sampled from the world 'outside'. This is because the words I use often seem to echo the machinic clatter of the world I am inhabiting, as if the things I 'say' are simply gleaned or plucked from my immediate environment. Unconsciously or not, I mimic what I read, the conversations I share, what I hear.

The 'I' of the diarist is migratory, fluid, unfixed. As opposed to the memoir, which is typically written from a fixed standpoint, the diary continually changes its perspective and thereby undoes the

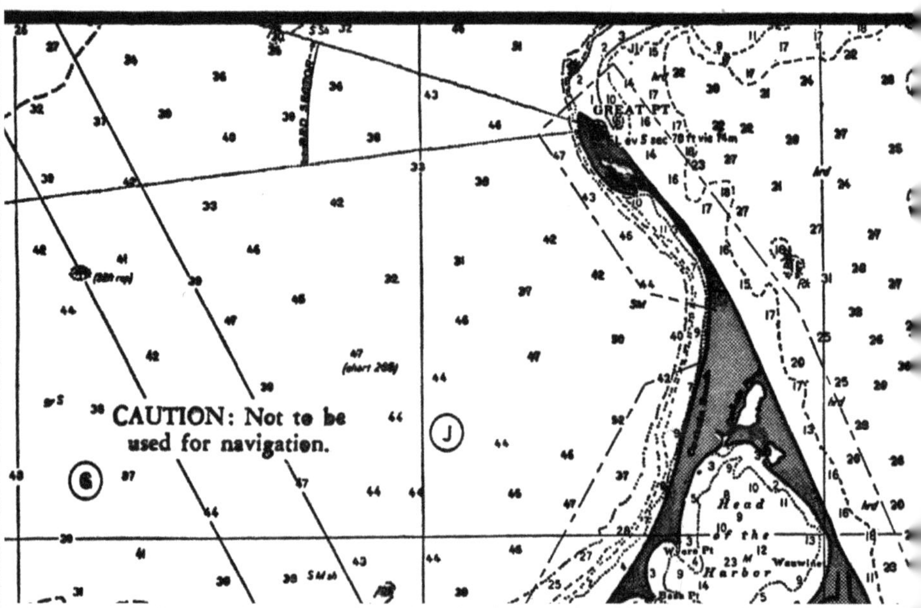
GREAT PT
CAUTION: Not to be used for navigation.
Head of the Harbor

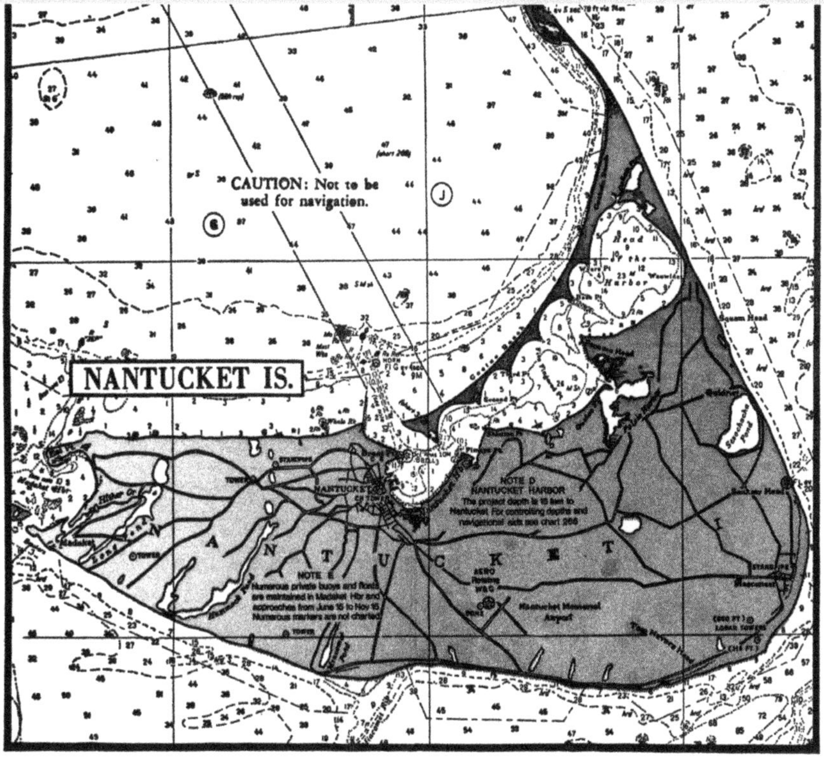

11:00

I am awake.

I am thinking. Last night. Was I drunken and foolish? I am thirsty. I am hot. A feeling of despair! I remember surfacing, briefly, in the night.
But can I be bothered to get water?

11:45

I get up. I am feeling relieved. I have finished the work that took up so much of my time last year - all year, in fact. I can't imagine doing it again and hope that my new project is more playful, less duty bound. Above all - it should be FACTUAL.

My intention? To keep a journal.

I am thinking about Roland Barthes, who loved to read biographies for their accounts of mundane things, such as the fluctuations of weather and other "petty details of daily life: schedules, habits, meals, lodging, clothing." Factual details, unlike someone's "insipid moral musing" retain their immediacy and relevance to our lives. Or so Moyra Davey says, in her book *The Problem of Reading*.

On the kitchen table, the napkin from last night's supper.

NOT TO BE USED FOR NAVIGATION

Put the biography down, she recommends, and look out the window. Try your hand at recording the scene, "stimulating… in its unselfconsciousness, its irrelevance, its perpetual movement."

Woolf had a passion for the letters, diaries, and travel journals of ordinary men and women of bygone days. In "Street Haunting," her 1930 *flaneuse*'s account of a twilight walk through the streets of London for the purpose of buying a pencil, she recounts stepping into a secondhand bookshop, the home of all the "wild" and undomesticated books, and pulling off of an upper shelf a faded little volume, a wool-merchant's chronicle of a business trip through Wales, written and self-published a hundred years prior. In an almost Proustian evocation of the serendipitous, sensory retrieval of memory—the idea that something buried and forgotten may be summoned to life once again through chance encounter—she describes how the chronicler "let flow… [into his account] the very scent of hollyhocks and the hay together with such a portrait of himself as gives him forever a seat in the warm corner of the mind's inglenook." These "relics of human life" constitute the "rubbish reading" to which Woolf is so devoted: "it may be one letter—but what a vision it gives! It may be a few sentences—but what vistas they suggest!" It is the "matter-of-factness," the unpremeditated quality of these writings that is key to Wolf's delectation of them. Like the Surrealists who seized on the evocative, hallucinatory power of the found-object, Woolf prized her chance literary finds and wrote of the paroxysms of pleasure they elicited with an intensity and craving of a gourmet.

(Roland Barthes, in his book *The Pleasure of the Text*, expresses

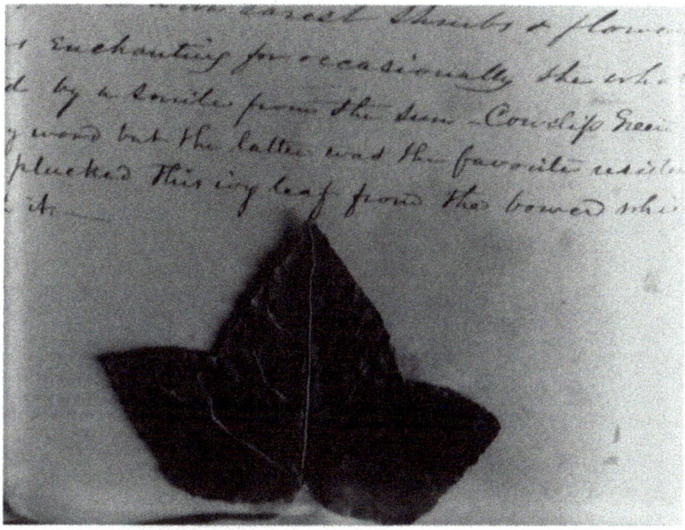
… sweetest shrubs & flowers
… enchanting for occasionally she …
… by a ramble from the dear Cowslip Green
… wood but the latter was the favorite resort
plucked this ivy leaf from the bower whi…
… it.

14:05

I am eating lentils that sink in my belly like a stone.

15:35

Parched. I am staring at a blank page. Nothing to say!

Parchment.

I type 'parched' into Google. A set of options fall down the screen.

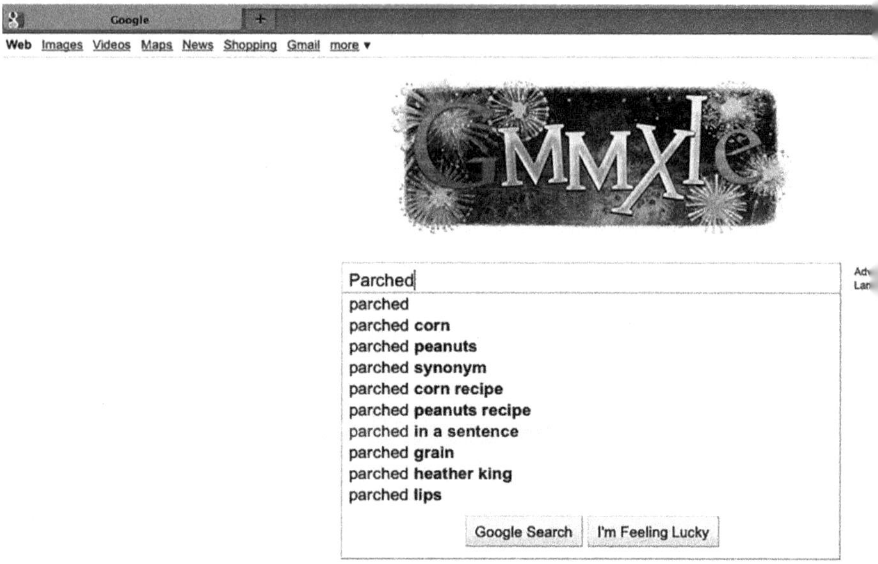

16:17

An email. From Sissu. It is a page from John Cage's *Mushroom Book*. A recipe and a song.

Sissu writes nothing in the email but the subject heading says

for susan
for a sound year ahead

MUSHROOM BOOK

I

Bake *Polyporus frondosus* (buttered,
seasoned, covered)
until tender. Chop.
Steep wild rice 5 x 20'
in boiling water (last water salted).
iGoogle | Search settings | Sign in
Combine.

Voices singing Joyce's Ten Thunderclaps
transformed
electronically to fill actual
thunder envelopes; strings playing star
maps transformed likewise to fill
actual raindrop envelopes (rain
falling on materials representing history of
technology).
(McLuhan.) Last rain not falling
(wind instruments), i.e. present moment.
Music becomes nature (Johns).

Man/Earth: a problem to be
solved.

highway system (Ivan Illich): a false utility.

no water unless necessary.

Hunting for *hygrophoroides*, found
abortivus instead.
Returning to get more *abortivus*, found
ostreatus in fair condition. South to
see the birds, spotted *mellea.*
Hunting is starting from
zero, not looking for.

19:30

We are going to the movies. Catfish.

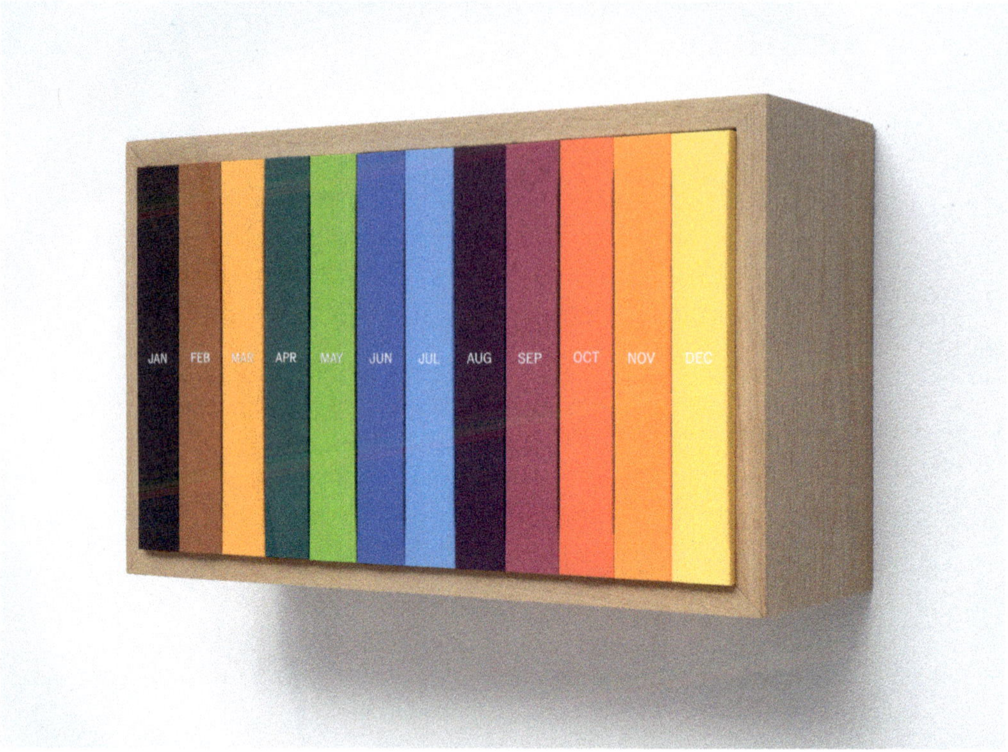

2.3 Susan Morris, *de Umbris Idœarum [on the Shadow Cast by our Thoughts]*, 2021, 12 × softback books, each 21.5 × 13 cm, with shelf. Printed paper and wood, 23.5 × 37.2 × 13.5 cm

work of each preceding entry. There is always a slight sense of unease when you read what you wrote 'last night'. As Stephen Dedalus observes, in Joyce's *A Portrait of the Artist as a Young Man*, 'I was someone else then.'[26] So the diary's retrospective view is daily rendered obsolete as life outstrips it; each entry brings a new retrospect, inviting a restless process of self-correction, self-revision, and, arguably, a kind of self-erasure.[27] A text accumulates, littered with blotches, blanks, and erasures, or, as Lacan put it, with *failure, impediment, split* – the ways in which unconscious activity makes its presence felt. In the gaps, lapses, and silences across the page there is *being* which is *not* the 'I', or is an 'I' that has something about it that is both unspeakable – 'meaninglessness surrounds it' – and unlocatable.[28] Indeed, as the year of my diary-keeping progressed, a question about the *tense* of the text emerged – perhaps as a by-product of the repeated attempt to record 'presence'. No sooner is each entry written than it is in the past. The reader therefore encounters the diary in a kind of future anterior, the tense that Barthes claims is the property of the photograph: both 'this *will* be' and 'this *has* been'. 'In front of the photograph of my mother as a child,' Barthes writes, 'I shudder like Winnicott's psychotic patient *over a catastrophe which has already occurred.*' If 'every photo is this catastrophe', are there also instances of written sentences that operate in a similar way?[29]

Nothing catastrophic happened to me personally in the year I kept the diary. However, there were many, *many*, actual catastrophes, such as the Fukushima nuclear disaster in Japan and the right-wing terrorist attacks in Norway, and many fictional disasters, particularly in films released that year. These seemed to mirror each other in a rather unsettling way, with parallel themes running through both.[30] The diary recorded this peculiar coincidence of real and fictional disasters – floods, earthquakes, random shootings, the deaths of our heroes, and the betrayal of the people by our leaders – all of which culminated in a feeling of dread: an *anticipation* of catastrophe. A kind of post-apocalyptic atmosphere permeates the text; not so much melancholia as fear – a *shuddering.*

On top of this, as the diary went on, I started to feel more and more detached, like a non-human recording machine. Gradually I found that I was adopting quite a psychotic relation to the world, by which I mean one that does not understand language as a series of substitutable signifiers but instead takes every word at face value – so that the graffiti on the walls, the patterns of birds in flight, the shape of the clouds, and even the whispering of the trees, for example, were all encountered as messages addressed *to me alone.* This approach was not without the occasional, unexpectedly humorous effect – during the month of September, for example, almost every time I left my analyst's house, an apple fell on my head. Given, however, that the majority of all the narratives that surround us are received through the same apparatus (phone/computer screen), the difference between fiction or fantasy and (so-called) reality can get confused. Very early on in the diary – at 12.15 on 27 January, to be precise – I write that when you record it 'just as it happens, as it unfolds, life starts to seem little more than a massive hallucination'.

'The recent past always presents itself as though annihilated by catastrophes', writes Benjamin, quoting Adorno, in *The Arcades Project* which, because of its fragmentary form, was one of the many

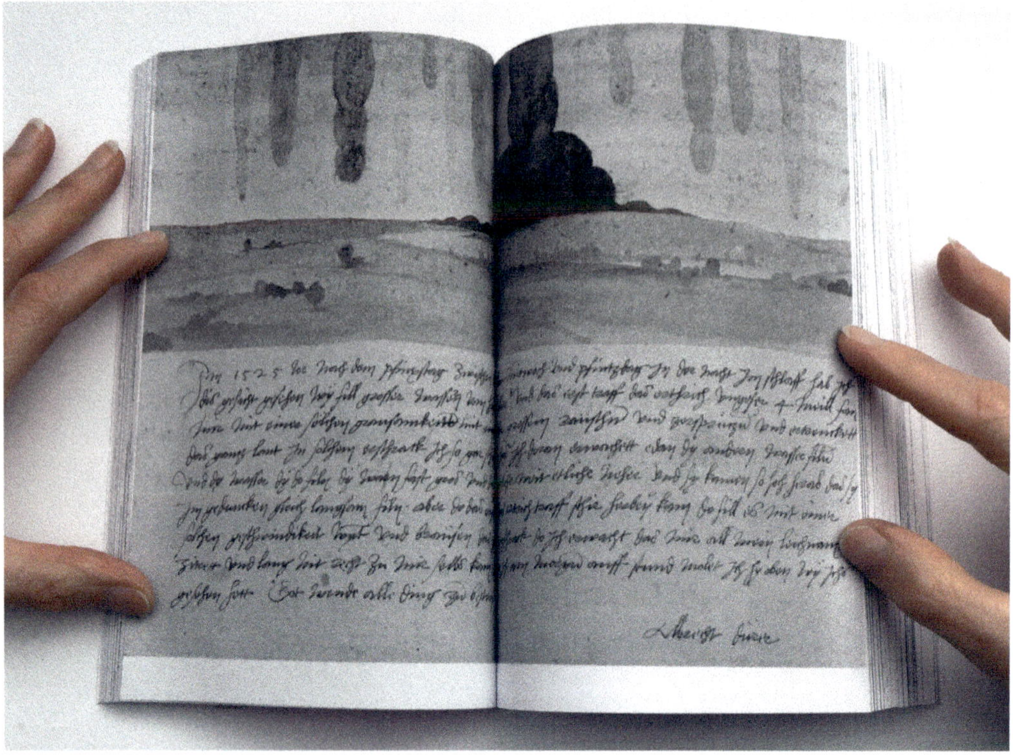

2.4 Susan Morris, detail from *de Umbris Idœarum [on the Shadow Cast by our Thoughts]*, 2021, 12 × softback books, each 21.5 × 13 cm, with bespoke shelf. Printed paper and wood, 23.5 × 37.2 × 13.5 cm

models for the diary.[31] Another was the combination of image and text in Albrecht Dürer's *Dream Vision* (1525), a watercolour painting accompanied by writing that recounts a nightmare, a deluge that 'drowns the whole land'. This image ended up in the diary, of course, but media reports of real events, such as the floods in Australia and Thailand, echoed this image, as if it were some sort of *template of dread.*

Page after page records imagery that describes the world as if after an apocalypse, although this was not planned nor anticipated. I deliberately made sure that no people appeared in any of my photographs (which I also tried to take as if by a disembodied recording device, like a drone.) The only images of people are from printed sources such as newspapers, so a feeling of emptiness permeates the book. I was particularly attracted to sites of dereliction, where old notices and spray-painted texts appear like coded messages on walls and pavements. I am there, in the diary, but maybe I am not – maybe it is just a machine talking to itself, its messages circulating by themselves, like a malfunctioning Amazon 'Alexa', or a radio stuck between channels.

There is also a sense throughout the text of things being in limbo. Stuff happens but nothing is resolved – there is no ending; certainly no denouement. There is the unresolved nature of my relationship with my partner, but also of my work. My studio practice seems to be in some sort of hiatus. Although, in my memory, I seemed to have always been in the studio – and certainly work gets made and is being exhibited (I talk about the various stresses of that) – still it appears as if I was not there. Those parts of my life went unrecorded. Instead, I seem always to be in the street, in the in-between spaces, on my way somewhere or on my way back. Yet this may just be the nature of the diary's 'ongoingness', with the attempt to capture everything leaving, paradoxically perhaps, vast chunks of unrecorded time.

I referred above to the fact that everything, all information, comes to us through the same devices. That is basically how I made the piece. I gathered the material by using the Evernote app, usually through my phone, but as all my devices were synced together I just added stuff using whatever was immediately to hand (iPad, laptop, or phone) typing in, or more often dictating (while on the move), the diary entries, as well as scanning material, taking photographs, or recording audio material from the radio or television. When it came to laying it out, the only rule I had was that the *time* of each diary entry would run like a column down the centre of each page. Everything else had to fall into place around that. So, all the material, no matter how diverse, is organised chronologically and it is all held or contained in the same digital storage system.

There is no reference in his book on photography, *Camera Lucida,* to the source of the idea that Barthes evokes when discussing tense. In his *Mourning Diary,* however, where he refers to it in three separate entries, the editor directs the reader to psychoanalyst D. W. Winnicott's paper 'Fear of Breakdown' (1963). Fear of breakdown, fear that 'the unit self' will collapse, fall to pieces, is, Winnicott suggests, fairly universal – it is on his list of 'primitive agonies'. But the main idea in Winnicott's paper is the suggestion that fear of a breakdown is always the fear of something that has *already been experienced.*[32] The subject scans the future for an experience that is in the past.

'Falling to pieces, falling for ever', shudders the writer Maggie Nelson, who has also been reading Winnicott, and whose 'Fear of Breakdown' she quotes throughout her 2015 book *The Argonauts*. In the book, Nelson is searching for a holding environment – which could simply be the right word (name) or phrase – that allows a fluid, transitory identity to thrive. But she is aware at every turn (falling in love, becoming a mother, finding a mother) how fragile, and how vulnerable to collapse, identity always is.

Nelson's work repeatedly conjures up Barthes's injunction to give voice to this thing that 'is "unreal" i.e. intractable': a stubborn, perverse, ungovernable thing that we must, so to speak, tune into.[33] Her writing, she states, comes out of a need 'to pay homage to the transitive, the flight'.[34] Nelson seems to concur too with Barthes's idea that a discourse might be considered purely as *structure*; as holding place for the 'multiple traces' of the 'I' to be staged. Here the 'utterance' might be considered as something nebulous, drifting . . .

'A frequent image', writes Barthes in his autobiographical book *Roland Barthes by Roland Barthes*, 'is that of the ship *Argo*, each piece of which the Argonauts gradually replaced, so that they ended up with an entirely new ship, without having to alter its name or its form.'[35] Hence, for Barthes, the *Argo* stands for a structural identity that allows the material that constitutes it to be continually replaced. It can do this, he suggests, by a process of two 'modest actions': substitution and nomination. So, is the *Argo* itself 'an object with no other cause [i.e., referent] than its name'?[36] Nelson picks up on this when she suggests the *self* as Argo. And she names this self 'snowball' – destined to melt, to crumble, or disappear.

Nelson assembles her text (her 'self') by gathering together many different voices so that both text and self stay open, constantly *becoming*. She takes this technique from Barthes, confessing in an interview that she 'totally stole' his mode of marginal attributions, in order to build something out of fragments, a collage that has inscribed within it a becoming in which one never becomes, whose rule is a 'certain turning' – like a clock, perhaps.[37] This is a ventriloquising reminiscent of the great works of mourning assembled by W. G. Sebald. Writing from a place of exile, Sebald also allowed his work to be permeated by multiple voices – to create a mobile, mutable 'I' alongside images of things collapsing. 'Like ashes the low cliffs crumble,' he writes, reciting A. C. Swinburne's poem *By the North Sea* (1880), 'and the banks drop down into dust.'[38] Here Sebald embeds Swinburne's text into his own, so that one line is 'spoken' by two voices.

Ventriloquism produces a disembodied voice, then, or one that comes from the wrong part of the body or from someone else's body, which is put to subversive use, like an undercurrent that moves against the tide. A writer who is ventriloquising channels or picks up, as if her body were a radio receiver, the voices of the dead and buried, as well as those of the restless undead.

Fear of death is one of a number of applications Winnicott makes for his theory, alongside fear of emptiness, the feeling of non-existence.[39] Fear of dying, or of being already dead, may actually be a pretty widespread cultural anxiety, related to language's peculiar operation – we are both inside and outside it. In her posthumously published 'Sketch of the Past', Virginia Woolf writes movingly of how at some moments and without reason something happens and the shield that protects us suddenly cracks, at which point 'in floods reality'.[40] 'Again I had that hopeless sadness,' she writes, 'that collapse I have described before; as if I were passive under some sledge-hammer blow; exposed to a whole avalanche of meaning that had heaped itself up and discharged itself upon me, unprotected, with nothing to ward it off.'[41]

For Winnicott, it is this feeling of falling, 'falling for ever' – as the repetition of an event in the past – that is dreaded yet obsessively sought.[42] This situation is not confined to the analyst's couch. An obsessive search in the future to understand something that has happened in the past could easily describe the structure of many science-fiction films; one might think of the *Terminator* series, but also of Chris Marker's 1962 film *La Jetée*: 'the story of a man, marked by an image from his childhood'. Sent back into the past by time-travelling scientists, he comes to realise that what he has witnessed as a child was his own death as an adult.

La Jetée is a disjointed, fragmentary collage-film consisting almost entirely of stills so that, even as it moves forward in linear time, it is cut through with stroboscopic flashes of blindness, where the darkness is aligned with intuition or knowledge. The poet Claudia Rankine, in *Don't Let Me Be Lonely* (2004), uses a similarly disjointed form, with fragmentary notations that explore themes of toxic poisoning, sleeplessness, medicated depression, and fear of death, cut through with blank pages – *white* spaces this time.

Throughout Rankine's poem, again and again, the question is asked and rearticulated: when does death – when *did* death – actually occur? Are we now in fact always already dead? When did the event – the toxins, the poison, the cancer, the terrorists – enter our body and end our lives, send us over to the disunited realm of the dead, the breathless? For instance, 'say the eyes are resting when the phone rings and what this friend wants to tell you is that in five years she will be dead . . . The lump was misdiagnosed a year earlier. Can we say that she might have lived had her doctor not screwed up? If yes – when does her death actually occur?'[43]

What underpins Rankine's questions about death, as well as her desire to locate the precise moment that the death occurred, revolves around the question of race, the exclusion of a whole people from the 'we' that speaks in America. This exclusion has unsettling repercussions. 'In college,' she writes, 'when I studied Hegel, I was struck by his explanation of the use of death by the state. Hegel argued that death is used as a threat to keep citizens in line. The minute you stop fearing death you are no longer controlled by governments and councils . . . The relationships embedded between the "I" and the "we" unhinge and lose all sense of responsibility. That "you", functioning as Other, now exists beyond our notions of civil and social space.'[44]

Later (in a passage about the first person that really resonated for me), Rankine describes a conversation she has had with her editor that goes badly:

> I understand that what she wants is an explanation of the mysterious connections that exist between an author and her text. If I am present in a subject position what responsibility do I have to the content, to the truth value, of the words themselves? Is 'I' even me or am 'I' a gearshift to get from one sentence to the next? Should I say we? Is the voice not various if I take responsibility for it? What does my subject mean to me?[45]

Rankine's video series *Situations,* which she makes with her partner the artist John Lucas, presents another example of the ventriloquising I discussed earlier. These voices from or *of* the dead – projected through Rankine's body from beloved poets who 'whisper in her ear', or from external sources such as the television – echo throughout her poems. *I thought I was dead. You thought you were dead? / Is she dead? Is he dead? Yes, they're dead.* The presence of these restless spirits is hinted at throughout the printed pages of the book by photographs of a television set. A few have messages on them. 'YOUR LIFE IS WAITING', the manufacturers of antidepressants tell us, commanding us to *stop being dead* – but most are of televisions stuck between channels, screens filled with white noise or 'snow'. Yet out of these fragments, the collected quotations, newspaper reportage, and flashes of imagery from the media, out of this *gleaning*, Rankine builds a voice that 'quivers', in the terms defined by Berger for poetry or drawing – as expression of a kind of *dis*integration; a not belonging.

There is also a death – a fading away or collapsing; a *being corpse* – that occurs in Joyce, or at least to the character Stephen in *A Portrait of the Artist as a Young Man.* Faced with a situation that causes him extreme anxiety, Stephen slips or fades away, like a shadow. He casts off his body (his body as self) as easily, he says, 'as a fruit is divested of its soft ripe peel'.[46] He feels himself falling and lets himself go. *Portrait* is an expression of extreme anxiety in language, which resolves itself (at least for the writer, Joyce) by moving from 'straight' writing to something very different indeed. As Lacan argued, Joyce saves himself from the psychosis that threatens to engulf the character in his book by his own writing – through which he (literally) makes a name for himself – for *his* 'self' (Argo). Joyce's particular, structural mode of writing holds him together, stops him falling to pieces. And around the 'voice', heard particularly in *Finnegans Wake,* an identity crystallises – as precipitate; as snowball.[47]

Interestingly, *Portrait* ends with fragments of a diary. It is worth noting too that Joyce, whose writing Lacan uses as an example of the *lituraterre* mentioned above, was the ultimate ventriloquist, with *Portrait* containing approximately ten quotations in every dozen pages. Later this ventriloquism interrupts, disrupts, the words themselves, to create neologisms that, when read aloud, allow Irish to be spoken through English. 'How different are the words *home, Christ, ale, master,* on [the Englishman's] lips and on mine!', Joyce's character Stephen protests. '*My soul frets in the shadow of his language.*'[48]

Lacan's concept of *lituraterre* suggests litter, letters, and their erasure (a pun that is more obvious in French, since one can always hear *rature* – erasure or crossing out – in the very signifier). It hints, too, at the limit or border of a territory, be it the sea, a hole, or language, literature, itself. Here rubbish writing takes on a new validity and function – rubbish escapes from or falls out of the neat chain of symbolic signifiers that produce meaning. A *lituraterre* – the literature of the littoral – as a discourse made up of rubbish which erases itself as it is being written may be what we need as subjects, both to hold ourselves together and to allow us to fall apart, to fall to pieces or stay fluid, to flow, but also to speak outside the master discourse in order to disrupt it.

The separation of our shit from other areas of our living space is, apparently, what makes humans different from animals. Both Lacan and Nelson mention this. For Nelson, it makes her 'feel at home in her species'. There is 'no civilisation without the sewer', asserts Lacan.[49] But what happens if a whole people are identified as the shit from which we want to separate? And what if you are part of that group that has been designated as trash?

Rankine and Nelson speak from that position, as does Joyce. For Lacan, it is the *only* place from which to speak; the only place to move from totality to fragments; to make holes in writing, and thereby create self-identifications that resist simple categories of either/or. Nelson draws on Barthes's idea of the Neutral for this, 'being that which, in the face of dogmatism, the menacing pressure to take sides, offers novel responses: to flee, to escape, to demur, to shift or refuse terms, disengage, to turn away'.[50]

True discourse is discursive. It runs; like mercury, it spills. This liquid metal as a metaphor for discourse is attractive, but Mercury the deity is very appropriate too, as he is the god of poetry, of discourse and exchange, but also of travellers (Mercury is the guide of souls to the underworld), of boundaries (i.e., the littoral), of luck, and of thieves.

Joyce was a thief. Lacan shows how – by using wordplay, condensation, neologism, displacement, pun, riddle, allusion, ideogram, misspelling, combination of incongruous words and phrases, words from different languages, absence of punctuation, stress on the sounds of words, the fading self – Joyce created hallucinatory and chaotic texts, situated on the edge of meaning.[51] Throughout his course on the novel, Barthes repeatedly returns to the suggestion that 'moments of Truth' should be scattered randomly throughout a text. In this way any narrative would be interrupted with 'the sudden *bursting forth* of the uninterpretable, '"scattered" within its fabric'; something, or *nothing* – rubbish perhaps – that 'possesses an evidential force'; a wordless, nameless 'presence'.[52]

In my own work, I have been trying to think about a particular kind of mark-making, one that could be classified as indexical, and looking at ways in which this mark can be embedded or manifested in writing; to put pressure on language, expose its limit or edge. This means that there are things in some of the material that I collected that I could not really see. For example, looking back through the pages now, I am amazed to discover two newspaper articles that warn in great detail of the threat of a global pandemic. I had included them because I liked the diagrams that accompanied the articles. I did not for one moment think that there would actually *be* a pandemic, the impact of which is still unknown because similarly impossible to see. However, I think it is safe to say that a catastrophe *has* occurred, although perhaps not *the* catastrophe, which might be related to the increasingly evident effects of climate change or to something else altogether, something that's already here but to which we are also completely blind.

This year I started another diary. Ten years separate the first from the current recording project, which has the working title of *s/Wake*, intended to evoke both a wake – Finnegan's? – but also, the *aftermath*. The long gap in time between one work and the other, in what may become a series, reflects an already established methodology in my practice. For instance, I have two other bodies of work made out of text either 'found' or generated in accordance with a set of rules, a process I repeat every five years.[53]

This diary, the 2021 diary, records a very real event after it has happened – or it is being made in the aftermath of that event (although of course every recording is of the aftermath of something). It takes the same basic form as the 2011 diary, with all material organised around a central 'spine' of time entries. I have made the decision not to include photographs or images of any kind this year, but the basic rules still apply: as much as is consciously possible, I exclude my own, subjective, point of view. I continue to incorporate 'any old rubbish' as it comes my way, which is added to the ever-expanding text without judgement. This means the same operation of blindness and erasure is at play as before, so that new entries often cancel out previous ones. I cannot actually remember what went into the diary yesterday, last week, and certainly not a few weeks ago, and that is how I want it to be. There will be no revision of the completed text. This is so I do not miss the things I cannot currently see.

Tomorrow will be the last day of May 2021, so I am already five months into this project. This morning, 30 May, I had my second vaccination. My hopes are high, despite reports in the news that indicate potential problems with virus variants. But for the first three months of this year, in England, we were in severe lockdown. I have almost forgotten what it was that we were not allowed to do, but I know we were not allowed to do much, and anyway the cinemas, galleries, cafés, restaurants, and all 'non-essential' shops were closed and the weather was awful.

Those winter months were grim and dark; repetitive, without texture. The writing – what I recorded from the media, from the books I was reading, from the copious amounts of television I was watching, and of the conversations between friends and family (which, if in real life, had to be conducted outside, on the empty streets or on our daily walks, but which most often took place by text, WhatsApp, or over Zoom) – reflects both the tedium but also our efforts to entertain ourselves. Always present in the background is an undercurrent of fear, like white noise. Almost everything we do, and everything we say – in the media or in our conversations – occurs in the shadow of the Coronavirus.

I sometimes think that this activity is closer to a kind of 'death-work'. I am always recording and writing, I have no time to live! But what interests me, and keeps me at it, is the knowledge that I do not know what I am actually writing as I am writing it. Life – that 'real

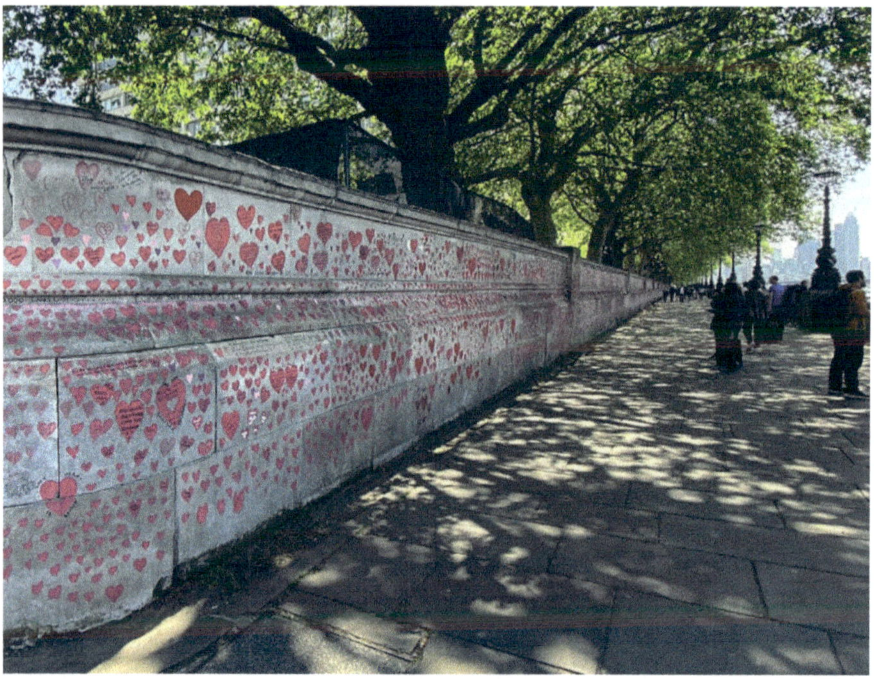

2.5 The National Covid Memorial Wall, 2021

thing behind appearances' – keeps breaking in. In addition, the fragmentary form of the text and the ever-accumulating amount of unrecorded time *between* each diary entry draw the reader's attention to another kind of white noise, or undercurrent, within the text. Something is being written in the gaps and silences, the interruptions, fractures, and splits, which shows that 'evidence' may not be what or where we think it is. In this way, the material I leave out of the diary – unconsciously or not – creates a space in language for things that cannot be put into words.[54]

Susan Morris,
London, May 2021

Notes

1 John Berger, *Confabulations* (London: Penguin Books, 2016), p. 4.

2 Of course, the scale at which this piece is reproduced in this book renders this information invisible. However, there is another horizontal/vertical movement operating here on the page, between the reproduced image and the words used to describe it. For installation shots of the work, plus details, see: http://susanmorris.com/self-moderation-installation-shots (accessed 2 November 2022).

3 Virginia Woolf, 'Sketch of the Past', in *Moments of Being* (London: Pimlico, 2002), pp. 84–85.

4 Here something – 'a disturbance (to civilisation)' – erupts, which Roland Barthes, following Proust, knew well. Roland Barthes, *Camera Lucida* (London: Vintage, 2000), p. 12.

5 Ann Banfield, 'Describing the Unobserved: Events Grouped Around an Empty Centre', in Colin McCabe, Nigel Fabb, Derek Attridge, and Alan Durant (eds), *The Linguistics of Writing: Arguments between Language and Literature* (Manchester: Manchester University Press, 1987), p. 265.

6 Virginia Woolf, *The Waves* (London: Penguin Books, 1992), pp. 221–227. See also: 'I begin to long for some little language such as lovers use, broken words, *inarticulate* words, like the shuffling of feet on the pavement.' *The Waves*, p. 183, emphasis added.

7 Roland Barthes, *A Lover's Discourse* (London: Vintage, 2002), p. 3.

8 Roland Barthes, 'Daily Practice of Notation', in *The Preparation of the Novel: Lecture Courses and Seminars at the Collège de France (1978–1979 and 1979–1980)*, trans. Kate Briggs (New York: Columbia University Press, 2011), p. 90.

9 Barthes, *A Lover's Discourse*, p. 100, emphasis added.

10 In his later work, Barthes repeatedly returns to the idea of the photographic 'Encounter' – met with a cry at 'the end of all language', 'a *satori* in which words fail'. Barthes, *Camera Lucida*, p. 109. For 'a howl,

a cry', see also Bernard in *The Waves*, p. 227. For 'an utterance', see Barthes, *A Lover's Discourse*, p. 3.

11 Rosalind Krauss, 'Notes on the Index', in *The Originality of the Avant-Garde and Other Modernist Myths* (Cambridge, MA: MIT Press, 1986), p. 198. In this essay Krauss also explores the 'collapsed shifter' – "I"'.

12 Walter Benjamin, 'A Small History of Photography', in *One Way Street* (London: Verso, 1997), p. 243.

13 Marcel Proust, *In Search of Lost Time, Volume 5: The Prisoner*, trans. Carol Clark (London: Allen Lane, 2002), p. 77. Proust also expresses a desire to record these 'precious compounds' and does so in terms that evoke early photographic methodology – for example, when he wishes to 'process' them by 'electrolysis'.

14 Virginia Woolf, *Moments of Being* (London: Pimlico, 2002), p. 81.

15 Denis Hollier, 'Surrealist Precipitates' ('Précipités surréalistes'), *October*, 69 (Summer 1994), 124.

16 Hollier, 'Surrealist Precipitates', 113.

17 Denis Hollier, 'Surrealist Precipitates', 130, emphasis added.

18 Michael Levenson, 'Stephen's Diary', in Mark A. Wollaeger (ed.), *James Joyce's A Portrait of the Artist as a Young Man: A Casebook* (Oxford and New York: Oxford University Press, 2003), p. 186; Roland Barthes, *Mourning Diary* (New York: Hill & Wang, 2010), p. 17, emphasis added.

19 Woolf, *Moments of Being*, p. 81.

20 The second spread from the opening pages of *de Umbris Idæarum* consists of a photograph from Moyra Davey's book *The Problem of Reading*, embellished with my post-it notes. This is one of many found texts and images in the diary that, assembled in the order that I encountered them, set off various associative chains. In this case, I was attracted to Davey's description of Woolf's 'rubbish reading'; her 'passion for the letters, diaries, and travel journals of ordinary men and women of bygone days', with these considered as 'relics of human life'. Moyra Davey, *The Problem of Reading* (Los Angeles, CA: Documents Books, 2003), pp. 22–23. See also Virginia Woolf, 'How Should One Read a Book?', in *Virginia Woolf: Essays on the Self* (London: Notting Hill Editions, 2014), p. 71.

21 J. M. Coetzee, 'The Man Who Went Shopping for Truth', *Guardian*, 20 January 2001: www.theguardian.com/books/2001/jan/20/history.society (accessed 2 November 2022).

22 Walter Benjamin, *The Arcades Project* (Cambridge, MA: Belknap Press of Harvard University Press, 1999), [N1,10], p. 458.

23 Jacques Lacan, *Lituraterre:* seminar of 12 May 1971. First published in the review *Litterature (Larousse)*, 3 (1971), republished in *Ornicar*, 41 (April–June 1987), 5–13.

24 Denis Hollier, 'Timeliness and Timelessness', in *Yale French Studies*, 93 (1998), The Place of Maurice Blanchot, 106. See also 'Contingent

Selves: Simone de Beauvoir's Use of the "Journal Intime"', in Rachel Langford and Russell West (eds), *Marginal Voices, Marginal Forms: Diaries in European Literature and History* (Amsterdam and Atlanta, GA: Editions Rodopi, 1999), pp. 136–146.

25 This title originates from a passage in *The Rings of Saturn* by W. G. Sebald, a key text for me, influencing both my writing but also the making of my tapestries. W. G. Sebald, *The Rings of Saturn* (London, Harvill Press, 1998), p. 272. See also Margaret Iversen, 'The Diaristic Mode in Contemporary Art after Barthes', *Art History*, 77:4 (September 2021), 798–822.

26 James Joyce, *A Portrait of the Artist as a Young Man* [1916] (London: Penguin, 2000), p. 261. See also p. 274 for the character Stephen Dedalus's encounter with what he had written 'the night before'.

27 Michael Levensen, 'Stephen's Diary', in Mark A. Wollaeger (ed.), *James Joyce's A Portrait of the Artist as a Young Man: A Casebook* (Oxford and New York: Oxford University Press, 2003), p. 190.

28 Rosalind Krauss, 'Notes on the Index', p. 77. For indexicality and 'meaninglessness' see also Susan Morris, 'On the Blank: Photography, Writing, Drawing' (PhD dissertation, University of the Arts London, 2006), https://ualresearchonline.arts.ac.uk/id/eprint/2309/ (accessed 2 November 2022).

29 Barthes, *Camera Lucida*, p. 96, emphasis added.

30 Examples of the films I am talking about include Lars von Trier's *Melancholia*, Jeff Nichols's *Take Shelter*, and *Another Earth*, directed by Mike Cahill.

31 Benjamin, *Arcades Project*, [K4,3], p. 397. For more on the Dürer work, see: https://theparisreview.tumblr.com/post/58075304454/albrecht-durer-dream-vision-1525-a (accessed 2 November 2022). Note that Benjamin also states that 'the art of citing without quotation marks' is essential to this work. Benjamin, *Arcades Project*, p. 458.

32 D. W. Winnicott, 'Fear of Breakdown', in Clare Winnicott, Ray Shepherd, and Madeleine Davis (eds), *Psychoanalytic Explorations* (London: Karnac Books, 2010), p. 87, emphasis added.

33 Barthes, *A Lover's Discourse*, p. 3.

34 Maggie Nelson, *The Argonauts* (London: Melville House, 2016), p. 66. This book is also, obviously, a lover's discourse.

35 Roland Barthes, *Roland Barthes by Roland Barthes* (London: Papermac, 1995), p. 46.

36 Barthes, *Roland Barthes by Roland Barthes*, p. 46.

37 Maggie Nelson, *Argonauts*, p. 66.

38 W. G. Sebald, *Rings of Saturn*, p. 160.

39 Winnicott, 'Fear of Breakdown', p. 92, 95.

40 Woolf, 'Sketch of the Past', p. 145.

41 Woolf, 'Sketch of the Past', p. 90.

42 Winnicott, 'Fear of Breakdown', p. 89.
43 Claudia Rankine, *Don't Let Me Be Lonely* (London: Penguin, 2017), p. 8.
44 Rankine, *Don't Let Me Be Lonely*, p. 84.
45 Rankine, *Don't Let Me Be Lonely*, p. 54.
46 Joyce, *Portrait of the Artist as a Young Man*, p. 87, 161, emphasis added.
47 Stephen's repeated psychic collapses are discussed in detail in 'A Young Man Without an Ego' by Geneviève Morel, in Parveen Adams (ed.), *Art: Sublimation or Symptom* (London: Karnac Books, 2003), p. 138.
48 Joyce, *Portrait of the Artist as a Young Man*, p. 205.
49 See Santanu Biswas, 'A Literary Introduction to "Lituraterre"', in Biswas (ed.), *The Literary Lacan* (Calcutta: Seagull Books, 2012), p. 178.
50 Nelson, *Argonauts*, p. 139.
51 See Biswas, 'A Literary Introduction to "Lituraterre"', p. 185.
52 Adam Thirlwell, 'My Novel, My Novel', *New Republic*, 8 December 2010, https://newrepublic.com/article/79745/novel-roland-barthes-realism (accessed 2 November 2022), emphasis added.
53 These have been written about by Sadie Plant; see 'Compelled to Count', in Susan Morris et al., *Susan Morris, Self Moderation* (Vienna: Verlag für moderne Kunst, 2016), http://susanmorris.com/self-moderation-catalogue-essays/#essay2 (accessed 2 November 2022).
54 The National Covid Memorial Wall is a public mural painted by volunteers to commemorate victims of the COVID-19 pandemic in the UK. Organised by the campaign group Covid-19 Bereaved Families for Justice, it has no legal status.

3

Valuing life

Alistair Rider

If the narrative of the artist's life and works is 'one of the oldest models in the Western literature of the visual arts', as Gabriele Guercio writes in his history of the artist's monograph, then it should not come as a surprise that, sooner or later, critics would conjoin these two terms and the neologism 'lifework' would enter art discourse.[1] Might this not imply, then, that the word is merely a novel, alternative way of expressing the familiar idea that any work of art is genetically linked to its maker, and is thus the sedimented testimony of a unique, historical life? Writers and critics do occasionally use the term to imply nothing more nor less than this. In a review of a retrospective exhibition of the work of Hannah Wilke, for instance, the curator Johanna Burton refers to the artist's documentation of her final illness as 'the end of Wilke's lifework'.[2] Similarly, in one of his articles, the film-maker Hollis Frampton alludes to the absence of meaningful stylistic development 'within the lifework' of the photographer Paul Strand.[3] In both these examples, the word 'lifework' could be straightforwardly replaced with 'oeuvre', although perhaps to contemporary ears the former word conveys more powerfully the sense that, collectively, artists' works form a dynamic whole, and that this totality bears witness to the singularity of the maker's life. From this perspective, any artwork can be regarded as an excerpt from a lifework, although *only* once it is understood that creative individuals are conveyors of unique meanings, the significance of which is inscribed in their creations.[4]

This is just one way in which writers have applied the term. In other scenarios the word is used in ways that imply that lifeworks are instead a generically distinct category of art. Just over a year after his essay on Strand, Frampton singles out Eadweard Muybridge's eleven-volume photographic series, *Animal Locomotion*, as his 'lifework'. It qualifies as such, he infers, not on stylistic grounds, but because of its magnitude – its ambitious, excessive proportions – and because it preoccupied him for close to two decades.[5] Likewise, Thomas McEvilley's volume, *The Shape of Ancient Thought* (published in 2001), is described in the art critic's obituary as a 'nearly eight-hundred-page lifework'.[6] In these instances, 'lifework' is being used as an anglicised synonym for a *magnum opus*, or a *chef-d'oeuvre*. So, from this point of view, Jay DeFeo's *The Rose* (a painting she painstakingly created between 1958 and 1966), Simon Rodia's *Watts Towers* (which he laboured over for thirty-three years, from 1921 to 1954), or Zofya Rydet's *Sociological Record* (her photographic project to document the interior of every household in Poland, commenced in 1978 and pursued continuously until her death in 1997) would all qualify as lifeworks. Understood in this sense – as a synonym for 'a life's work' – the term lifework is not just descriptive but evaluative. It is a way of classifying a specific creative output as of superior cultural value relative to all the artist's other works, vindicating the significant expenditure of energy and time it entailed. And, as anyone familiar with French nineteenth-century art discourse will know, artists who self-consciously and ambitiously commit to delivering a *magnum opus* are gambling with their reputation, because creators of failed *chefs-d'oeuvre* are accorded little sympathy. If the finished product is deemed inconsequential (as was the verdict on Frenhofer's murky canvas in Honoré de Balzac's well-known story, *Le Chef-d'œuvre inconnu*), or fails to materialise, then the lonely hours and years that were poured into its realisation are written off as a misdirected and squandered usage of time.[7]

I can also think of a third path by which the term lifework enters the lexicon of modern art, in ways that are subtly distinct from the above two senses. In these instances, lifeworks tend to be exclusively associated with a specific class of modern artists, who are firmly committed to an all-embracing notion of creativity that is not necessarily associated with any particular *métier* or area of expertise. Such artists are generalists. They refuse to distinguish between day-to-day living and their art activities, so that it becomes impossible to tell for certain where their art ends and ordinary life begins. Artist and work chiastically merge: their creative zeal amplifies the sense of vivacity of their life, and their unique life is perceived as essential to the significance of their art. 'A painter must paint a single masterpiece, constantly,' affirms Yves Klein, for example, in France in 1957, 'and thus become a sort of atomic battery, a sort of constantly radiating generator that impregnates the atmosphere with his pictorial presence fixed in space after its passage.'[8] Guercio, who has written perceptively about this leitmotif in modernist art, traces its roots to Gustave Courbet, specifically to his canvas *L'Atelier du peintre* from 1855, his monumental celebration of the entanglements of his work and his creativity, his life, and his cultural milieu.[9] Guercio also credits Pablo Picasso as a significant early twentieth-century exponent, although Marcel Duchamp, along with the Fluxus movement of the 1960s, clearly also embraces facets of this tendency.[10] For such artists, the attractiveness of referring to their creations as 'lifeworks' is its genericity. It applies equally to any art form and may refer to the making process as much as it does to the end results. No doubt this is why, for instance, the Hungarian artist György Galántai named his retrospective at the Ernst Múzeum in Budapest in 1993 'Lifeworks'. The accompanying catalogue is organised in a way that impresses on the reader the fluidity of his creative workflow. Meanwhile, on the back cover, the artist adds an endorsement in the form of a citation attributed to none other than Duchamp: 'My art, you could say, is simply that I am alive.'[11]

In each of these three applications, and despite their differences in sense, the life that is at stake in the lifework is always understood to be a property of a named, creative individual. However, Adrian Heathfield, a writer on contemporary performance and other live arts, has recently advanced a definition of a lifework as a means of distinguishing a specific class of contemporary work, one in which the sense of life it discloses is more quotidian, and inclines more to biological persistence than it does to ennobling notions of ingenuity or inventiveness. It is a provocative analysis, and so I shall devote this chapter to unpacking its premises. As with all classifications, the criteria it accentuates orient the account towards particular ends and, in ways I hope to elaborate, this makes the term more suitable for illuminating certain works rather than others.

Heathfield first invoked the term 'lifework' in collaboration with Tehching Hsieh, a Taiwanese-born artist who created six landmark durational performance pieces in the United States between 1978 and 1999. In 2009, they co-produced a major volume on these works with MIT Press, which featured the word in the title.[12] Here, lifeworks are presented as an apt name for Hsieh's extended performances, because once they were under way, they absorbed every facet of his existence for significant periods of time. The first, for instance, named *One Year Performance 1978–1979*, involved the artist sealing himself in solitary confinement in a cell for twelve months, and relying on a friend to provide him with food, fresh clothing, and to remove his waste. Four carefully documented, year-long performances followed, each involving similar strictly enforced self-impositions. After these, Hsieh enacted a single thirteen-year plan, in which he vowed to make art yet not show it publicly, thus withdrawing entirely from the art world.[13] These 'serial durational aesthetic experiments', Heathfield writes, plunge 'art into the barely legible, in the intertwined realities and tumultuous forces of (a) life'.[14]

Although the definition of a lifework advanced here is obviously tailored to Hsieh's practice, Heathfield intimates that analogous art tendencies can be recognised in the work of other contemporaries, and, furthermore, extend further afield than performance. In particular, he singles out the Japanese-born artist On Kawara and the Polish painter Roman Opałka, both of whom explore the idea of 'a life sentence traced within the limits of art'.[15] In particular, it is Opałka's life-long recursive practice, which involved painting the number continuum on identically sized canvases, and which he pursued from 1965 until his death in 2011, that Heathfield identifies as the most pertinent to Hsieh's. Heathfield presents Opałka as an artist who persisted with a rigorous painterly programme that indexically depicted the flow of his life in real time. The project thus encompassed his entire corporeal being, in a way that Hsieh would pursue even more unrelentingly.[16]

In his account of Hsieh, Heathfield intimates that the sense of life that is presented within the works themselves is not wholly specific to Hsieh's biography, even though he still considers the six lifeworks to be constitutive of a single oeuvre, and constitutive of a coherent, meaningful 'life trajectory'.[17] Yet immediately after he states that all of 'Hsieh's artwork presents itself as (a) life.'[18] So why set the indefinite article in parentheses? And, if this 'life' is not exclusively individuating a named subject, then what is it? The simplest answer is that it is merely the abstract, indefinite state of being alive: it is life's metabolic dimension.

In a subsequent essay from 2014, this time on the Slovenian collective Janez Janša, Heathfield pushes his definition further in this direction:

> A lifework might be defined as art that involves the subjection of a life to a projected, sustained, and all-consuming creative practice,

> where the body of the artist and their lived experience becomes a formative content inseparable from the artwork. Lifeworks often involve extended durations in order to mark and incorporate lived change, processes of accrual, aging, personal and material transformation: they trace the singularity of a *bios* in movement.[19]

The processes listed in this second sentence are wide-ranging: it is unclear, for instance, how much of an actual difference Heathfield means to imply between transformations that are 'material' or those that are 'personal'. On balance, though, the factors he mentions tend towards those elements of life that, in isolation, would be the least meaningful for a biographer who was attempting to portray the distinctiveness of a named individual. In themselves, the physical manifestations of growth, maturation, and senescence reveal little about the deliberate, conscious exercise of a person's agency. They are merely the impersonal, biological laws that apply to all living things, even if they always manifest themselves in singular and distinct ways. Accordingly, I read this definition as suggesting that artists who embark on such durational projects expose a certain absence of control over these facets of their lives, yielding a glimpse of themselves as 'anybodies' rather than 'somebodies', disencumbered of prestige and distinction as they are swept along in life.[20]

Heathfield is surely correct in his observation that the most distinctive aspects of lifeworks so defined is their relationship to temporality. All art – spatial or time-based – obviously entails a quantum of time, either to complete, or to be performed, or to be apprehended by the recipient; certain works also have particularly long gestations. But lifeworks are distinguished because the span of time set aside for their undertaking is fundamental to their intent, and to their import. Lifeworks are those in which the time of the artist(s) or participant(s) is deliberately used up. And because the time expended is so clearly sensed as actually having been experienced, lived through, sustained, or even endured by those involved, it is hard not to compare the way that time has been spent with how we, as viewers, consider our own lives. Relative to us, lifeworks often register as an exorbitant, excessive, or purposeless expenditure of time. In a world in which life generally seems pressured, with so many competing expectations placed on 'our' time, part of the allure of lifeworks surely derives from the exhibition of a drawn-out, concentrated devotion to a self-selected activity, whatever this happens to be.[21]

With this in mind, I want to turn to a work by the London-based artist David Connearn called *Mappa Mundi: Drawing to the Extent of the Body* (figure 3.1). Created in 1984, it could be described as process-based, partly inspired by constructivist-inspired line exercises the artist had encountered at Camberwell School of Art in the 1970s under the tutelage of Norman Dilworth. The drawing consists of an abstract shape – a circle – that was built up from the repeated inscription of

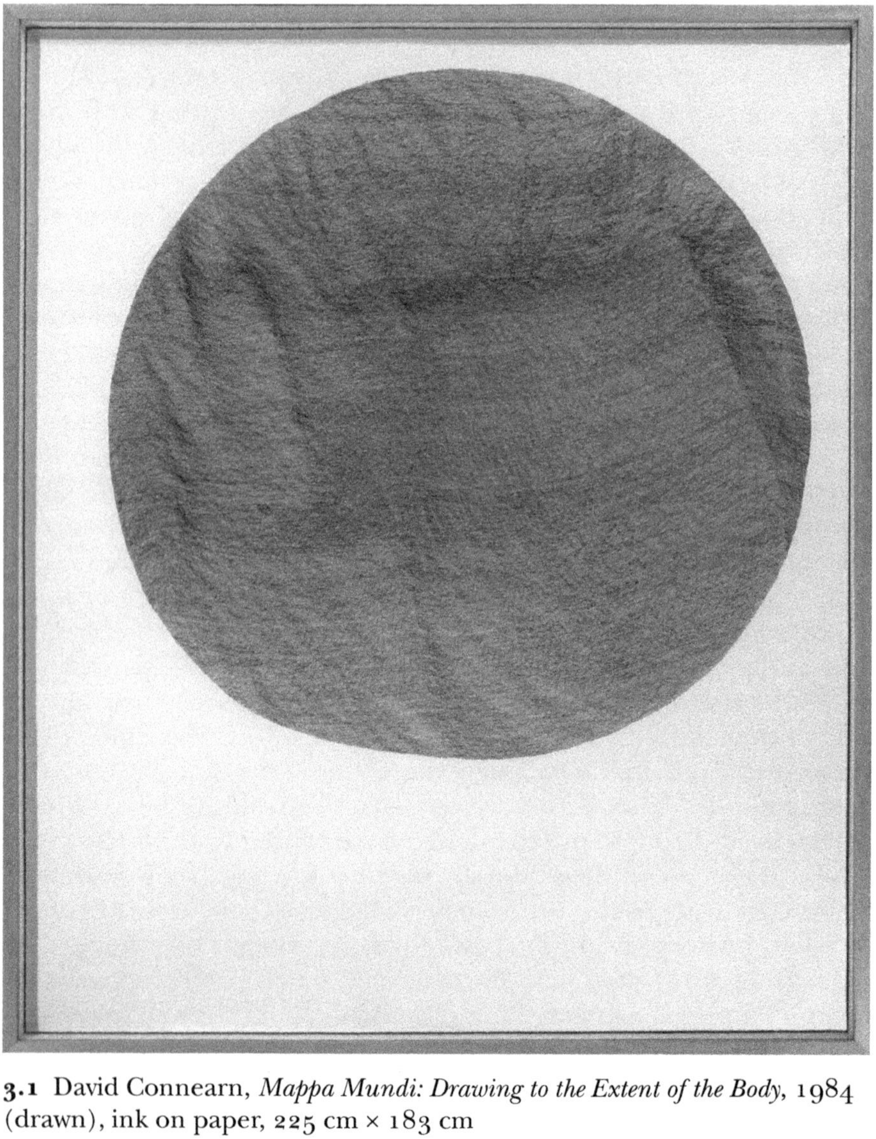

3.1 David Connearn, *Mappa Mundi: Drawing to the Extent of the Body*, 1984 (drawn), ink on paper, 225 cm × 183 cm

hand-drawn vertical lines over the course of many weeks. Of course, in the scheme of things, a few weeks is barely any time at all. But everything is relative, and we can regard this drawing as a lifework on the grounds that the duration entailed in its making is instrumental to its import. To produce this large-scale work, Connearn rigidly stood at one fixed point, secured his easel so that the sheet stretched above him and almost to the floor, and then, working with his dominant hand, and without stretching or bending his torso, covered as much of the paper as he could reach with hundreds of thin, horizontal ink lines.[22] He was careful to ensure that each line followed the path of the one preceding it, retaining a minute, even distance across its length. Yet faint hand tremors mean that the lines do not remain taut, and invariably diverge from their desired trajectory, especially at those points when he found himself assuming awkward, off-balanced postures. The completed work incorporates wild undulations, particularly in the lower half, as small instances of errancy higher up are incrementally magnified as he consciously reacted, dutifully shifting his fingers and wrist to compensate for them in the lines below. The marks themselves are not expressive, although they are expressions of the coordination of hand and mind in movement, operating in an assiduous fashion over a prolonged period. The completed work thus invites viewers to contemplate the patient, focused activity that was invested in its making. A recognition that this is a work that was intentionally slow and time-consuming to create seems therefore fundamental to its identity.

This is not a drawing that registers lived change in as extreme a fashion as we witness in the lifeworks of Opałka or Hsieh. That said, if *Mappa Mundi* is the transposition of a focused thought, translated through the body over time into a tangible accretion, then it is also the trace (in Heathfield's words) of 'the singularity of a *bios* in movement'.[23] The wave patterns within the circle are not preconceived or even contrived: they arise merely as an emergent effect of Connearn's micro-adjustments as he focused on duplicating the course of the line that lay directly above. Thus, we see in this work the motivating intent that sets the drawing in motion, incrementally distorted by the proprioceptive responses of the reactive body, which acts as an echo-chamber, even as it aspires to concentrate exclusively on the hand holding the pen, progressing forward over the surface of the paper. For these reasons, *Mappa Mundi* is arguably an exemplary exploratory chart of a self – an embodied consciousness – as it arises through a durational practice.

Invoking a notion of selfhood deserves some qualification, because Connearn's drawing is not an investigation of anything as substantiated as a distinct personal identity. The 'self', of course, is a composite and abstracted notion, formed from the various culturally and historically specific languages that we employ to describe our inner lives. There is also considerable variation among psychologists, psychotherapists, philosophers, and cultural analysts regarding how much status they attribute to it. At one end of the spectrum, the self is used as a term merely to refer to a pre-reflective cognisance of bodily processes (of the kind exhibited by newborns). Then there is the experiential self to which phenomenologists refer in their accounts of bodily self-awareness, and it is this sense of selfhood that seems pertinent to Connearn's practice. Meanwhile, at the other end of the scale, selfhood is understood to be an extended and wide-ranging phenomenon, involving personal memory and a disposition to employ narrative structures in the attainment of integrative self-definition.[24] With few exceptions this is the sense of self to which those academics and writers whose research addresses the genres of autobiography, life-writing, and self-portraiture largely subscribe. In these cultural fields, the self is widely understood to be associated with emotional depth, an authentic inner life, consistency of character, not to mention a sense of agency and moral accountability. However – and this is the point I need to stress – if we follow Heathfield's definition, then these premises cannot be carried over straightforwardly into the realm of lifeworks. It is often claimed that autobiographies or self-portraits are valid expressions of a distinct, authorial 'I', who is living a life that is uniquely theirs, yet such assertions do not seem applicable to these works.

There are two grounds for saying this. First, there are many sustained, durational works which involve lived experience, and yet self-expression, or the articulation of an ego, is simply not a motivating factor. Hsieh's lifeworks are a good example, and I can think of others, such as, for instance, Peter Dreher's long-term series, *Every Day is a Good Day* (figure 3.2).[25] In 1972, the West German figurative painter created a small still life of an empty water glass on a white table, set against a blank ground, in his studio in St Märgen, high up in the mountains of the Black Forest.[26] Two years later, he had the idea of depicting the same motif around a handful of times. But then he realised that there was no need for him to cease, and he continued to depict the same glass, positioned in the same way and viewed from an identical point, until around 2012, when, it seems, old age prevented him from continuing.[27] Sometimes, he painted the glass by day, and the natural light from a nearby window is shown glinting on the object in innumerably different ways, so that no two canvases are ever exactly the same. At other times, he depicted the glass by night, illuminated by a spotlight, the position of which he barely touched during the thirty-eight years that he spent sitting before this scene. But while there is no variation in the light conditions in the night-time versions, as the decades pass, the works do vary stylistically. In the earliest versions, he accentuates the rounded lineaments of the glass, while in the later canvases it is the translucency of the material that he emphasises. In the second half of the 1970s, the ground incrementally darkens, and then in the early 1980s, it begins to lighten again. And so on. Once a large number of his canvases are displayed sequentially, gradual modifications of this kind are perceptible, yet, as with the variations in Connearn's lines, they do not appear to be the outcome of conscious deliberation.

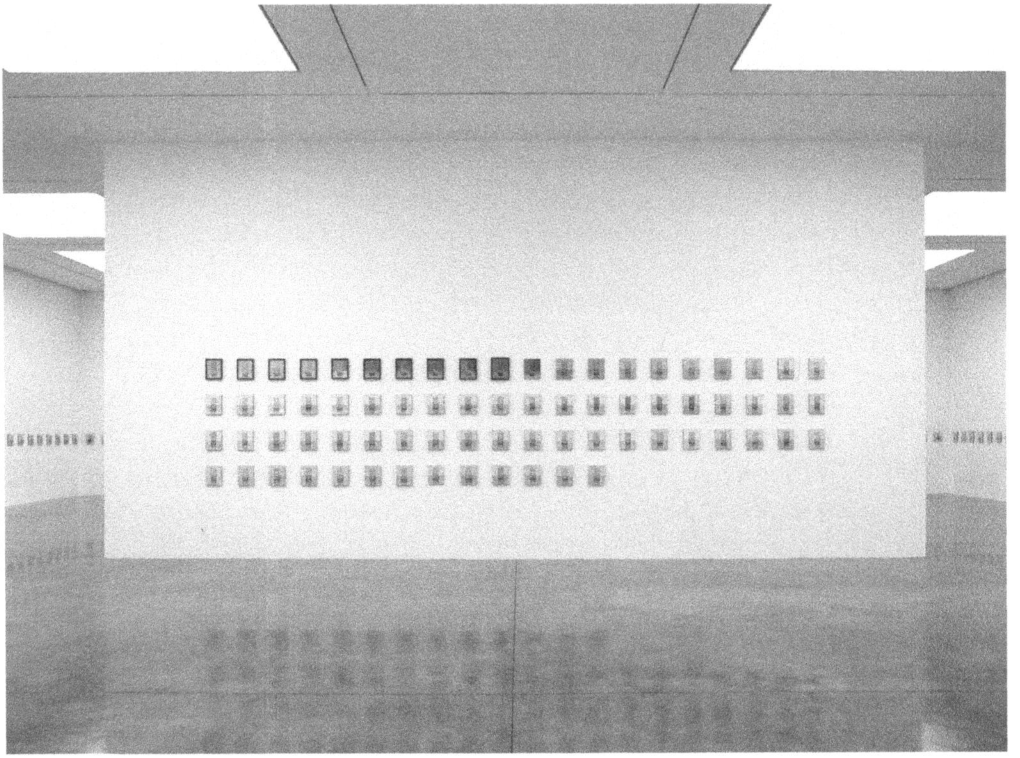

3.2 Peter Dreher, *Every Day is a Good Day*, since 1974, installation photograph

They arose from the painter's perceptual and painterly facilities and habits, and therefore to attribute any larger expressive signification to them feels inappropriate.[28] My point, in short, is that if we want to locate in Dreher's series a sense of self, an agency, then we cannot say that it is necessarily expressive, or that it is of a reflective, synthesising nature. Instead, the paintings reveal only the workings of an experiential self, attentive to the present moment, absorbed in the task at hand.

Of course, some artists have embarked on substantial, durational works with the express motive of attaining a non-artistic, personal goal, such as self-improvement, or even religious enlightenment. Take the American performance artist Linda Mary Montano, for instance, who participated with Hsieh in the making of his *Art/Life One Year Performance 1983–1984*. In the early 1980s, Montano had become an advocate for what she termed 'living art': 'Living art divides time in actual time and ART. . . . The artist may choose as much of this time as they think they need to transform and change themselves. When it is intended that a specific time together will be designated as time for LIVING ART then that time will become ART and not time.'[29] From 1984 until 1991, Montano completed *7 Years of Living Art*, which was immediately followed by *Another 7 Years of Living Art*. For Montano, this fourteen-year experiment became a highly ritualised, ascetic way of life. It is also a work that incorporates autobiographical, self-reflective commentary in the form of annual diaristic reports on her physical, mental, spiritual, and artistic advancement.[30] But because Montano's 'living art' practices focus so explicitly on personal transformation and its articulation, I wonder whether there are better reference points for exploring her art than that which Heathfield's lifeworks definition provides.[31]

Then again – and this is the second reason – there are other durational works that do appear to involve a clear element of self-affirmation or self-realisation, yet, despite this, also incorporate an additional facet that appears to have nothing to do with selfhood and seems beholden to an entirely different logic. A case in point is Adrian Piper's work, *What Will Become of Me*, commenced in 1985 and which remains ongoing (figure 3.3). It consists of a shelf of glass jars, flanked on either side by two framed and printed texts. The one on the left is written in the first person and is confessional in tone. It details how 1985 was an acutely challenging year for the artist. Her father had died of cancer, and her marriage was collapsing. Then she discovered that her colleagues at the university

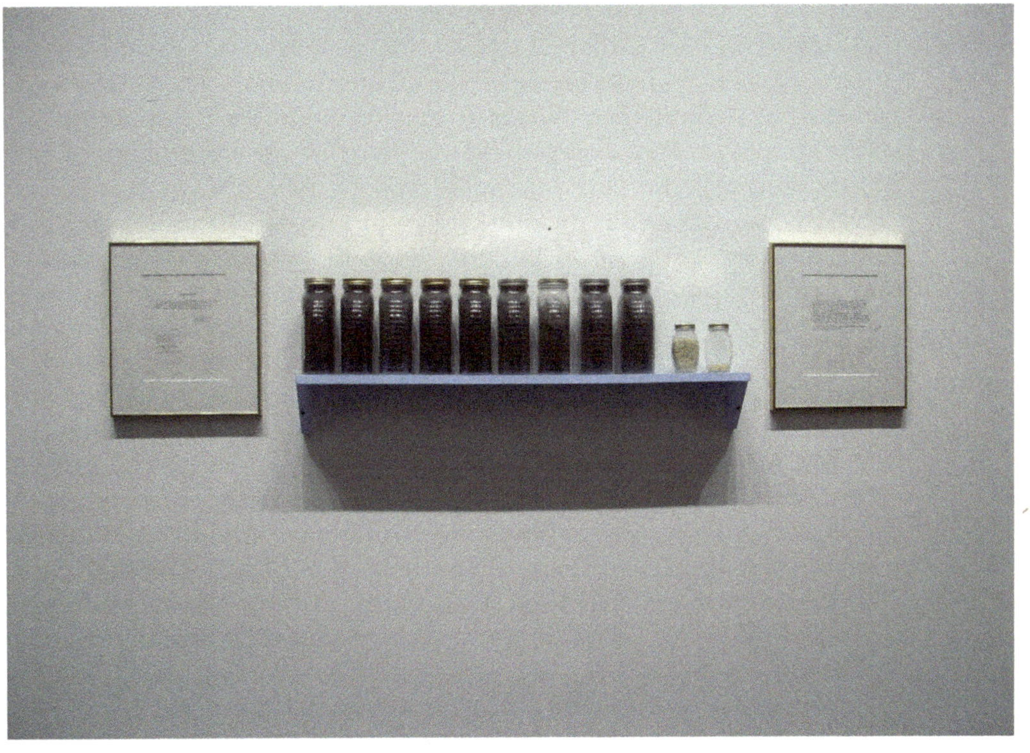

3.3 Adrian Piper, *What Will Become of Me*, since 1985, honey jars, hair, fingernails, skin, shelf and two framed texts, dimensions variable

where she worked were conspiring against her to ensure she did not obtain tenure. Personally, and professionally, this felt like an end point. And yet the text closes on a note of resolve: 'I felt sure that if I could just hold myself together for long enough to escape from Ann Arbor, I'd be alright.'[32] Meanwhile, the text on the right assumes the form of a legal contract and is signed by a notary. It is written in a voice that is as impersonal as the first was intimate, while also doubling up as an explanatory caption for the accompanying shelf. It clarifies that these are empty honey jars, filled with samples of the artist's hair, nails, and skin, which have been collected since 1985, and to which she will continue to add until her death. It then states that the final addition will be a jar containing her cremated ashes, and the text concludes with an expression of her wish to bequeath this work to the Museum of Modern Art in New York.

What Will Become of Me therefore inscribes Piper in three registers. First there is the intimate voice of an 'I' who speaks of personal experience. Then there is an appeal to her legal identity as author. This enshrines the personal voice as hers, plus the resulting work as her moral property. This component is also promissory, insofar as it binds the author-artist to a prescribed future course. Finally, in the third component, discards of the materiality of her embodied self, her life, are exhibited in the form of a relic-like display of otherwise meaningless exuviations. In isolation, this element divulges little of her character, or her distinctive qualities as an individual. But, accompanied by the two texts, the jars and their contents testify that she did survive this personal crisis – at least physically – and, for this reason, they feel freighted with additional significance.

At the University of Michigan, Piper not only furthered her art career, but was also a professor in the Department of Philosophy. During the 1970s she had completed degrees in the subject, first in New York, before completing a doctoral thesis in 1981 at Harvard, with a spell at the University of Heidelberg in between. She focused on metaethics, and her PhD dissertation mounts a strong defence of rationality as axiomatic for self-understanding.[33] In 1985, she published a revised extract in *Philosophical Studies*, which argues for a conception of selfhood premised on Kant's moral law.[34] This paper makes it crystal clear that Piper values highly the pursuit of a rationally meaningful life. As she argues in her conclusion, only by self-analysis of past experiences and behaviour can an individual attain a healthy, integrated, and unified sense of self. For her, selfhood is an attribute of a person that must be cultivated, and which is susceptible to forces of disintegration if it is not grounded in comprehension.[35]

Details of Piper's perspectives on ethics, which she has advanced in her academic writings, do inflect an interpretation of *What Will Become of Me*. It shifts the focus to all those attributes of Piper's character that are not presented by the shelf of jars. The excess hair, nails, and dried skin fragments indexically refer to physical growth, yet this growth becomes metaphorical, not merely literal, implying 'development' in a broader sense. Indeed, we might conjecture that Piper's ritual process of adding samples to the jars every few years affords her an opportunity to reflect on the course of her life: its unity, her past and future plans, not to mention the incremental augmentation of self-knowledge that longevity and experience bring. The jars' contents are therefore perhaps best seen as emblematic of the personally extraneous. They are, arguably, doubly discarded: initially, as bodily waste, and then again when they are symbolically deposited in the glass containers, so as to be conserved for perpetuity in the aspic of art. These, perhaps, are the dimensions of life that can be deemed as of the least significance to Piper. What matters is the ongoing pursuit of a consciousness, which cannot be represented.

However, there is a dimension to Piper's work that I have not yet mentioned, even though it is difficult to overlook. And this is the evidence of Piper's physical ageing, evident in the incremental greying of the hair fragments, which is especially noticeable in the jars furthest to the right. In the previous reading, it is a principle of growth that is accentuated, and the account is premised on the assumption that there is an overriding identity, an essence, an ego, an agency, that transcends any changes in Piper's personal and physical circumstances. If, however, we approach *What Will Become of Me* from the purview of Heathfield's definition of a lifework, then we need to engage more directly with the process of physical change that is incorporated within the work.

There is much to be said about cultural responses to ageing, which vary substantially according to one's gender.[36] But here I want to reflect more broadly about what we mean by ageing per se. Its workings and wide-ranging effects tend to be suppressed, or at least downplayed, in accounts of life that focus on the unique ways they are lived. It is one of those transformational processes that the philosopher François Jullien describes as 'silent', on the grounds that it is so undifferentiated and gradual that it largely goes unnoticed: 'just as "everything" ages within us,' he writes, 'we do not see ourselves becoming old'.[37] Ageing, he explains, affects all aspects of a subject simultaneously, and, even if we can review its effects on various aspects of our physiognomy, the steady transition in operation still feels elusive. Nor is it a phenomenon that can be considered as a detachable supplement or attribute of individuality. It is utterly integral to our identity, even if it is also selfhood's inherent vice, incrementally working as a disintegrative force over time. Perhaps most unsettlingly of all, Jullien observes that ageing is a goalless process, tending towards no specific result. Unlike, for instance, self-development, it tolerates no thoughts of ideal end states, such as mastery, expertise, wisdom, or enlightenment; indeed, it has nothing whatsoever to do with endings and beginnings: it is 'always already underway'.[38]

It is noticeable how Piper plans for her death to be represented in *What Will Become of Me*. Her instructions for the inclusion of her ashes within the work imply a continuity between the contents of the jars during and after life, as if her final remains are no more and no less life's by-product than nail or hair trimmings. Death is envisaged not as an abrupt event, but as a sequential stage in a process that is already in train, as if dying is already soundlessly at work in life. To approach Piper's lifework from the point of view of transformations is thus to understand life and death as an interconnected fluidity. And perhaps there is a case to be made that *What Will Become of Me* is as much, or even more, about this than it is a work of self-representation, in which personhood is conceived as a synthesised unity, continuous until curtailed by death.

The question that remains to be asked is what there is to gain from addressing durational works in these terms. What rationale is there for devoting so much attention to this less individuated dimension of life? Is it anything more than the cultivation of a sensibility for traces of embodiment and corporeality? Or a sensitivity to instances in which a felt, empathetic connection arises between a viewer and a more generalised feeling for life as an undifferentiating force? Think, for instance, of the justification Roman Opałka provides for his conscious efforts to maintain formal and stylistic consistency from one year to the next: it was necessary, he explains, so that less controllable rhythms, such as those pertaining to his inner mental state or varying levels of wakefulness or exhaustion might register on the surfaces of his canvases.[39] 'I was content', he writes, 'to transcribe a biological situation which is universal: at every moment of our lives, our body is transformed. . . . When I add a unit to the number I have just painted, I obey this same law of evolution. I create an evolving and therefore different work, which nonetheless presents itself in a state of perpetual becoming.'[40] ('Je me suis contenté, par cette opération, de transposer picturalement une situation biologique qui est celle de tous: à chaque instant de notre vie, notre organisme se transforme. . . . Lorsque j'ajoute une unité au nombre que je viens de peindre, j'obéis à cette même loi d'évolution.') Opałka's explanation of his work conforms perfectly with the terms of Heathfield's lifework definition: what else is the artist describing other than the tracing of 'the singularity of a *bios* in movement'? To many ears, however, this may well sound like a retreat from historical explanation in favour of all-too-familiar vital truths. Indeed, is this not merely a reflection of the increasingly ubiquitous trend in the twentieth and twenty-first centuries to define life in terms drawn primarily from biology and from medical practice?[41]

To respond to these reservations, some level of intellectual contextualisation of Heathfield's interpretation of lifeworks is necessary. Because, although never stated explicitly, his predisposition to pay greater attention to life's anonymous, biological dimension is one that is also shared by many contemporary theorists, particularly those inspired by the writings of Gilles Deleuze. Late in his career, Deleuze advanced a philosophical definition of life as an impersonal, immanent force that exists in a permanently suspended state, such that it remains unattributable to any one individual.[42] In an important gloss on Deleuze's position, Giorgio Agamben asks if there is anything more to this than an account of bare, nutritive life, one that is very distant from the realms of consciousness, personhood, or memory. But his verdict is that Deleuze's position is considerably more subtle.[43] Agamben argues that biological life is primarily a theoretical categorisation which is essential for any hierarchisation of life forms or lives. Lives that are valued or privileged are always seen as superior to 'mere' metabolic processes, and, without this grounding definition, it becomes impossible to establish discriminatory classificatory systems for determining the values of specific lives. For Agamben, though, Deleuze's account of life as an immanent force undoes all such rankings and groupings, and instead imposes a radical principle of 'indetermination', one in which 'the vegetative and the animal, the inside and the outside and even the organic and the inorganic, in passing through one another, cannot be told apart'.[44]

These discourses, philosophical though they are in nature, are not intended to be read in isolation from more pressing, contemporary sociological issues. Both Deleuze and Agamben are writing in full awareness that the ways in which life is conceptualised have a direct bearing on how populations are managed in the modern state. In short, they are responding to the conditions that Michel Foucault defined as 'biopolitics', which was the term that he had coined in the late 1970s to describe the mechanisms of governance in post-sovereign societies.[45] Foucault's perspective on these issues had been shaped by his former teacher, Georges Canguilhem, who, in his landmark study, *The Normal and the Pathological*, had defined life as a reactive activity, never indifferent to the conditions in which it arises.[46] And because living beings have an innate tendency to exploit their environment for their own advantages, life can be defined as a process of constant adaptation.[47] Foucault's contribution was to apply this insight to modern history, through an analysis of how the apparatuses of institutional power co-opt this dynamic so as to regulate a population. This is achieved through instigating environmental modifications or intervening in the living conditions of a social group, in ways that impose artificial external norms on the lives of subjects. Foucault understood these various biopolitical techniques as indicative of how power operates in modernity, not as a repressive, violent force, but as a positive and enabling programme. It operates through manipulation, by imitating the dynamic of life itself, so that what subjects experience as the fulfilment of their personal potential is, in actuality, a socially fashioned norm.

Whereas Foucault was careful never to define life in positive terms, Deleuze's antipathy to the operations of biopolitical managerialism, as outlined by Foucault, led him to consider life as a force that was inherently hostile to all externally imposed regulatory strictures. As Maria Muhle has written in a helpful analysis, Deleuze approached life as an 'ontological support for a resisting force', which he regarded as separate from the operations of power, as if there were 'a power of life' that 'exceeds the power *over* life'.[48] This premise has motivated many subsequent intellectuals, including Agamben, who have looked to life to locate an essential, vital force, which is innately indifferent to the operations of power.[49] Consider, for instance, Josephine Berry's book, *Art and (Bare) Life*, which concludes with the verdict that, in the face of late capitalist biopower, art's sole capacity for future resistance involves reanimating the avant-garde ambition of transforming itself into a praxis of life, although *only* if life is conceived 'without fixed horizon or identity'.[50]

An awareness of this agenda helps in explaining Heathfield's rationale for defining lifeworks in the way he does. His discussion of Hsieh's art is also attentive to the inherent biopolitical dimension in some of his works, particularly *One Year Performance 1980–1981*.[51] For this piece, Hsieh had installed a worker's time clock in his studio, and, foregoing proper sleep, assigned himself the task of punching timecards, on the hour, every hour, twenty-four times a day, for twelve months. It was a work in which Hsieh exposed himself – manically, excessively – to the machine's managerial logic, which biometrically records human productivity in regularised quanta of labour time. Having punched the clock, Hsieh immediately photographed himself, taking a single frame on a 16mm camera, meaning that, at the year's end, he had created a stop-motion animation of his year-long performance that runs to just over six minutes.

Throughout this film, Hsieh maintains a consistent frontal posture, exposing the transformative, physical toll that the undertaking has wrought on his countenance in accelerated time.

The animation also results in a disturbing, uncanny jerkiness, which Heathfield evocatively describes. He points out that the depicted figure 'is neither fully present, nor self-coincident; it is not owned by its subject, and it exists in a radical state of discontinuity and fray'.[52] Caught in this state of alterity, he refers to Hsieh's animated image as 'coursing with a vital energy; . . . rapidly trembling and mutating in the grip of a relentless, machinic condensation of time'.[53] What is significant about this 'vital energy', and which Heathfield recognises, is its affective, infectious force. Hsieh's agitated form clearly registers with viewers as expressive, although, at an emotional level, it remains disturbingly opaque and enigmatic. In the terms of Eric L. Santner, we might describe Hsieh's comportment as 'creaturely', a concept the literary theorist reserves for defining a dimension of human existence that arises at moments when there is a fundamental breakdown in the realm of meaning. Santner specifically attributes these instances to points of somatic distress, when lives have been abandoned to acute levels of arbitrary authority.[54] He refers to this failure in symbolisation as triggering an 'excess of pressure', which he provocatively defines as 'a kind of life in excess of our biological life and of our life in the space of meaning'.[55] I interpret this as implying that when life is subjected to extreme external restrictions, something of it, or in it, precipitates an effect in the field of signification that remains enigmatic, fugitive, and incapable of being assimilated.

I want to underline that such efforts to address life's impersonal dimensions are principally motivated by an attentiveness to the operations of the insidious, managerial techniques that are seen to define so many dimensions of contemporary existence. Once life is understood as not exclusively an individuated and individuating property of the artist-creator, then it becomes possible to approach lifeworks as mimetic of broader, biopolitical realities. They can be conceived, moreover, not merely as dystopian illustrations of actual living conditions, but as demonstrations that, however entrenched biopolitical regulation appears, some facet of life nonetheless eludes capture.

Indeed, these are the terms in which Susan Morris, a fellow contributor to this volume, describes her art practice. Between 2005 and 2010 Morris wore a biometric sensor which measured her changing levels of physical activity in relation to the amount of ambient light in her environment. Over the ensuing years, she represented this data as colour-coded graphs that were woven on a Jacquard loom into tapestries, in recognition of the significant historical role this apparatus played in the mechanisation of modern labour practices. Yet Morris's objective in this body of work, titled *SunDial:NightWatch,* was not merely to emblematise the tortuous work conditions that automated technologies institute or to analogise her own life experience with those of nineteenth-century weavers. It was to uncover the extent to which bodies are inherently resistant and unruly in the face of socialisation processes.[56] In her words, her works reveal traces of 'a body in the grip of a rhythm dictated by its own unruly desires'.[57] Lifeworks, confirms Heathfield, 'are oriented towards an insistent regeneration of fugitive affects that *for some time* evade the existent forms of capture by capital and its social and cultural agencies'.[58]

Approaching works as evidencing vital signs of life's inherent autonomy – conceived as an impersonal, essential value – makes most sense when the artworks in question tacitly allude to instrumental power and its resistance, themes which are made manifest when artists adopt programmes or practices that are envisioned in response to actual forms of social subjectification. But Heathfield's lifework definition might be less apposite when used to describe works that appeal to viewers as political subjects with some degree of collective responsibility for society's overall direction. Such works are responding to an inequality, as when, for instance, in 2017 Connearn created a suite of drawings that was motivated by the plight of undocumented migrants who were attempting to seek asylum in the UK. At the time, they were constrained in a camp outside Calais in northern France, and, among them were an estimated five hundred minors, who, under European Union and UK law, had a potential legal right to enter the country, yet were being impeded from applying by the then British government. Connearn, a British citizen, felt an ethical obligation to respond through his art to the plight of these children. In one group of works, he drew five hundred horizontal lines across square sheets of paper – one line symbolising each child. In his studio, he then began a slow, recursive, meditative process of overwriting each line in differing shades, thus obscuring its identity and emblematising the government's disregard for the children's rights (figure 3.4). Through such allusive, graphic acts of erasure, Connearn aspired to enact a sustained gesture of empathy with lives lived in extreme states of precarity.[59]

To discuss Connearn's more recent works in terms of the defiant, autarchic conceptions of life that inspire biopolitical interpretations of art would be misleading, because it would distract from the fact that these drawings are informed by a human rights-based, politicised understanding of life. This is an altogether different proposal. These are drawings that are motivated by the consequences of a xenophobic politics on those who are at most risk from institutions who refuse to observe the rule of law. It is not an art inspired by a premise of vitality as a resisting force. So, if there is a lesson to be drawn here, it is that although life is a

3.4 David Connearn, *Refuge 4 (Amnesis)*, 2017, white and coloured acrylic inks on 300 gsm Fabriano Artistico paper, 97 × 97 cm

familiar-enough word, how it is defined varies considerably, and no more so than when it comes to 'lifeworks'.

Notes

1 Gabriele Guercio, *Art as Existence: The Artist's Monograph and Its Project* (Cambridge, MA: MIT Press, 2006), p. 1.
2 Johanna Burton, 'Hannah Wilke, Ronald Feldman Fine Arts', *Artforum*, 46:4 (December 2007), 353. Burton uses this term in the context of a description of Wilke's series *Intra-Venus* (1991–1992). Her point is that it is a body of work that enables viewers to see the artist's self-portraits of her younger self in a profoundly different light.
3 Hollis Frampton, 'Meditations around Paul Strand', *Artforum*, 10:6 (February 1972), 52–57.
4 See Guercio, *Art as Existence*, chapter 3.
5 Frampton, 'Eadweard Muybridge: Fragments of a Tesseract', *Artforum*, 11:7 (March 1973), 43–52.
6 David Frankel, 'Thomas McEvilley', *Artforum*, 51:10 (Summer 2013), 56.
7 On the fable of failure in French nineteenth-century art, see Paul Barolsky, *A Brief History of the Artist from God to Picasso* (University Park: Pennsylvania State University Press, 2010), chapter 8.
8 Yves Klein, 'Some excerpts from my journal of 1957', in *Overcoming the Problematics of Art: The Writings of Yves Klein*, trans. Klaus Ottmannn (Putnam, CT: Spring Publications, 2007), p. 14.
9 Gabriele Guercio, 'The Form of the Indistinct: Picasso and the Rise of "Generic Creativity"', *Res*, 63:4 (Spring–Autumn 2013), 147.
10 Guercio, 'The Form of the Indistinct', 143–144.
11 *Galántai: Lifeworks* (Budapest: Artpool and Enciklopédia Kiadó, 1996). In the introductory essay, Géza Perneczky underlines that Galántai preferred not to distinguish between his living and working environment: 'I had seen George's work many a time, but for the most part in their home . . .. [V]isitors would inadvertently take them for improvised chairs. What else could serve as the key to these objects' aesthetic correlations if not the original mentality manifest in the composite word "life works"?' See Perneczky, 'The Sculptor's Progress from Word-Collages through Allegories to the Fluxus Concert', p. 8.
12 Adrian Heathfield and Tehching Hsieh, *Out of Now: The Lifeworks of Tehching Hsieh* (Cambridge, MA: MIT Press, 2009).
13 It was an act that has echoes of Lee Lozano's inexplicable yet choreographed disengagement from all art practices in the late 1960s. See Jo Applin, *Lee Lozano: Not Working* (New Haven, CT: Yale University Press, 2018), pp. 129–151. For a more general reflection on contemporary

artists who have withdrawn from the art world, see Martin Herbert, *Tell Them I Said No* (Berlin: Sternberg, 2016).

14 Heathfield, 'Impress of Time', in *Out of Now*, p. 16.

15 Heathfield, 'Impress of Time', p. 18.

16 Heathfield, 'Impress of Time', p. 18.

17 Heathfield, 'Impress of Time', p. 56.

18 Heathfield, 'Impress of Time', p. 57.

19 Heathfield, 'Life Re-encased', in *Janez Janša: Life II [in Progress]* (Ljublana: Maska, the International Centre of Graphic Arts and Live Art Development Agency, 2014), p. 13. In this essay, Heathfield lists Opałka and Hsieh as precedents. His essay addresses *Life II [In Progress]*, a complex performance piece and accompanying photo-documentation, involving a group of participants who produce the work periodically over multiple years.

20 These terms are inspired from John Rajchman. See his introduction to Gilles Deleuze, *Pure Immanence: Essays on a Life*, trans. Anna Boyman (New York: Zone Books, 2001), pp. 13–14.

21 For a provocative and wide-ranging psychosocial reflection on how lived time is experienced currently, see Lisa Baraitser, *Enduring Time* (London: Bloomsbury Academic, 2017). Boris Groys also discusses the temporality of art projects in his essay, 'The Loneliness of the Project', in *Going Public* (Berlin: Sternberg Press, 2010), pp. 70–83.

22 David Connearn, conversation with the author, December 2018.

23 Heathfield, 'Impress of Time', p. 57.

24 For two important accounts of a bodily and experiential sense of self, see Evan Thomson, *Mind in Life: Biology, Phenomenology, and the Sciences of Mind* (Cambridge, MA: Harvard University Press, 2007); and Galen Strawson, 'The Self', *Journal of Consciousness Studies*, 4:5–6 (1997), 405–428. Two classic accounts of bodily self-consciousness include Maurice Merleau-Ponty, *Phenomenology of Perception*, trans. C. Smith (London: Routledge 2002); and Francisco J. Varela, Evan Thompson, and Eleanor Rosch, *The Embodied Mind: Cognitive Science and Human Experience*, revised edition (Cambridge, MA: MIT Press, 2016). For examples of theories of extended selfhood, see Marya Schechtman, *Staying Alive: Personal Identity, Practical Concerns, and the Unity of a Life* (Oxford: Oxford University Press, 2014); and Paul Ricoeur, *Oneself as Another*, trans. Kathleen Blamey (Chicago, IL: University of Chicago Press, 1992). This mapping of conceptions of selfhood is indebted to Shaun Gallagher's introduction, 'A Diversity of Selves', in Gallagher (ed.), *The Oxford Handbook of the Self* (Oxford: Oxford University Press, 2011).

25 Heathfield discusses the absence of self-expression in Hsieh's work in 'Impress of Time', p. 26.

26 For an illustration of the initial canvas, see Peter Dreher, *Tag Um Tag is Guter Tag* (Düsseldorf: Galerie Hans Mayer, 1990), p. 5.

27 See Peter Dreher, 'Conversation Notes, February 2012', in *Peter Dreher: Hommage an die Malerei* (Frieburg: Museum für Neue Kunst im Augustinermuseum, 2012), p. 148. Although I have been unable to verify definitively that the series concluded in 2012, I have uncovered no evidence of canvases created after this date.

28 For a provocative study that questions the relation between painterly style and subjective temperament, see James D. Herbert, *Brushstroke and Emergence: Courbet, Impressionism, Picasso* (Chicago, IL: University of Chicago Press, 2015). Whitney Davis also explores the implications of makers' lack of awareness of their stylistic behaviour in chapter 4 of his *A General Theory of Visual Culture* (Princeton, NJ: Princeton University Press, 2011).

29 Linda M. Montano, *Art in Everyday Life* (Los Angeles, CA: Astro Artz, 1981); reprinted in Jennie Klein (ed.), *Letters from Linda M. Montano* (London: Routledge, 2005), p. 151.

30 See *Linda Mary Montano, 14 Years of Living Art* (Brattleboro, VT: CX Silver Gallery, 2017).

31 The same might equally be said for works such as Mary Kelly's *Post-Partum Document,* her six-year analysis of the mother–child relationship, which she completed between 1973 and 1979.

32 On the institutional challenges Piper faced within academia, see Vanessa E. Jones, 'The Fallen Academic Star of Adrian Piper', *Journal of Blacks in Higher Education,* 36 (Summer 2002), 120–123.

33 Adrian M. S. Piper, 'A New Model of Rationality' (PhD dissertation, Harvard University, 1981).

34 Adrian M. S. Piper, 'Two Conceptions of the Self', *Philosophical Studies,* 42:2 (September 1985), 173–197.

35 Piper, 'Two Conceptions of the Self', 194.

36 For two publications that address cultural gerontology, see Mike Featherstone and Andrew Wernick (eds), *Images of Aging: Cultural Representations of Later Life* (London: Routledge, 1995), and Roberta Maierhofer and Ulla Kriebernegg, *The Ages of Life: Living and Aging in Conflict?* (Bielefeld: Transcript, 2014).

37 François Jullien, *The Silent Transformations,* trans Krzysztof Fijalkowski and Michael Richardson (London: Seagull, 2011), p. 98.

38 Jullien, *The Silent Transformations,* pp. 55–59.

39 Roman Opałka, 'Meeting through Separation', in *OPALKA XIX* (São Paulo: Biennale Internationale de São Paulo, 1987), unpaginated.

40 Roman Opałka, *OPALKA 1965 / 1 –* (Paris: Flammarion, 1992), p. 27.

41 On this wider tendency, see Nikolas Rose, 'The Value of Life: Somatic Ethics and the Spirit of Biocapital', *Daedalus,* 137:1 (Winter 2008), 40. See also chapter 5 of his book, *The Politics of Life Itself: Biomedicine, Power, and Subjectivity in the Twenty-First Century* (Princeton, NJ: Princeton University Press, 2007).

42 See in particular Gilles Deleuze's essay, 'Immanence: A Life', in *Pure Immanence: Essays on a Life*, trans. Anne Boyman (New York: Zone Books, 2005), pp. 25–33.
43 Giorgio Agamben, 'Absolute Immanence', in *Potentialities: Collected Essays in Philosophy*, trans. Daniel Heller-Roazen (Stanford, CA: Stanford University Press, 1999), pp. 231–238.
44 Agamben, 'Absolute Immanence', p. 233.
45 See Michel Foucault, *Security, Territory, Population: Lectures at the Collège de France, 1977–78*, trans. G. Burchell (London: Palgrave Macmillan, 2007); and *The Birth of Biopolitics: Lectures at the Collège de France, 1978–79*, trans. G. Burchell (London: Palgrave Macmillan, 2008).
46 See Georges Canguilhem, *The Normal and the Pathological*, trans. Caroline R. Fawcett and Robert S. Cohen (New York: Zone Books, 1991), pp. 128–130.
47 Canguilhem, *Normal and the Pathological*, pp. 143–144.
48 Maria Muhle, 'A Genealogy of Biopolitics: The Notion of Life in Canguilhem and Foucault', in Vanessa Lemm and Miguel Vatter (eds), *The Government of Life: Foucault, Biopolitics and Neoliberalism* (New York: Fordham University Press, 2014), p. 94, 96. For a clear articulation of Deleuze's position, see his book, *Foucault* [1986], trans. Seán Hand (London: Continuum, 1999), p. 77.
49 Agamben's emphasis on what he terms a 'form of life' (an idea he appropriates from Ludwig Wittgenstein) is specifically advanced as a means of conceiving of life as inseparable from the way it is lived, in accordance with its own norms. Agamben is explicit that 'forms of life' stand 'always and above all power'. See 'Form-of-Life' [1993], in *Means Without End: Notes on Politics*, trans. Vincenzo Binetti and Cesare Casarino (Minneapolis: University of Minnesota Press, 2000), p. 4.
50 Josephine Berry, *Art and (Bare) Life* (Berlin: Sternberg Press, 2018), pp. 321–322.
51 For Heathfield's account of this work see 'Impress of Time', pp. 30–36.
52 Heathfield, 'Impress of Time', p. 36.
53 Heathfield, 'Impress of Time', p. 32.
54 See Eric L. Santner, *On Creaturely Life: Rilke, Benjamin, Sebald* (Chicago, IL: University of Chicago Press, 2006), chapter 1.
55 Santner, *On Creaturely Life*, p. 34.
56 For Morris's account of *SunDial:NightWatch*, see http://susanmorris.com/sun-dial-about/ (accessed 10 April 2021).
57 Susan Morris, 'Drawing in the Dark', *Tate Papers*, 18 (Autumn 2012), 31.
58 Heathfield, 'Life Re-encased', p. 14, emphasis added.
59 Connearn's drawings were exhibited at Patrick Heide Contemporary Art, London, in February 2018.

Part II

Enveloping me

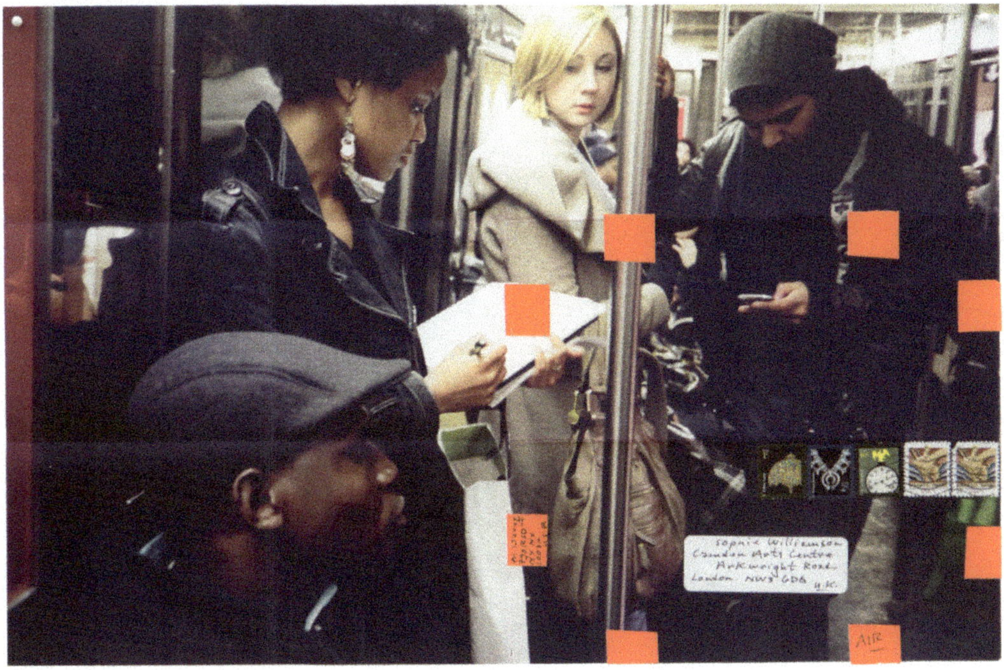

Moyra Davey, detail from *Subway Writers* series, 2011, C-print, tape, postage ink, 30 × 45 cm

4

Folds

Rye Dag Holmboe

One of the most striking things about Emily Dickinson's envelope poems is the way in which the shape of the support helps to decide the shape of the text. To make the poem shown in figure 4.1, dated 1873, an envelope was carefully unfolded, and a scalpel used to incise a rectangle where a stamp must have been, a little bit of paper left dangling from a corner. The paper surface was turned to a 45-degree angle on a wooden lap desk and only then did Dickinson begin to write, allowing the interventions to determine where each line started, as well as the spaces between words. The envelope's shape even impacted on the integrity of words, as in the line, 'And yet we know / that gentle clock / Meant nought / but / going home.' When it reaches the incision, the word 'meant' is cut in two: 'me-ant'. A small violence is inflicted on meaning, invisible when the poem is reproduced in print. Likewise, 'Esoteric time', with which the poem ends, is also time out of joint: 'tim / e'.

It would be interesting to know how much Dickinson improvised, if she knew what she was going to write before putting pencil to paper. Did a crease, fold, or cut change the content of the poem as she wrote? Was the line 'going home' written next to the incision to suggest that home was, for Dickinson, something akin to an absence, a void, a cut? Or did the poem take shape in her mind and, according to the characteristics of the support, only then be written down? I would hazard that she used the envelopes as constraints, which, paradoxically perhaps, gave her the freedom to improvise. This helps to account for why, when a word gets close to an edge or corner, letters are sometimes twisted out of shape, bunched up, or forced down a line. The problem Dickinson faced was not only how to end but how to continue.

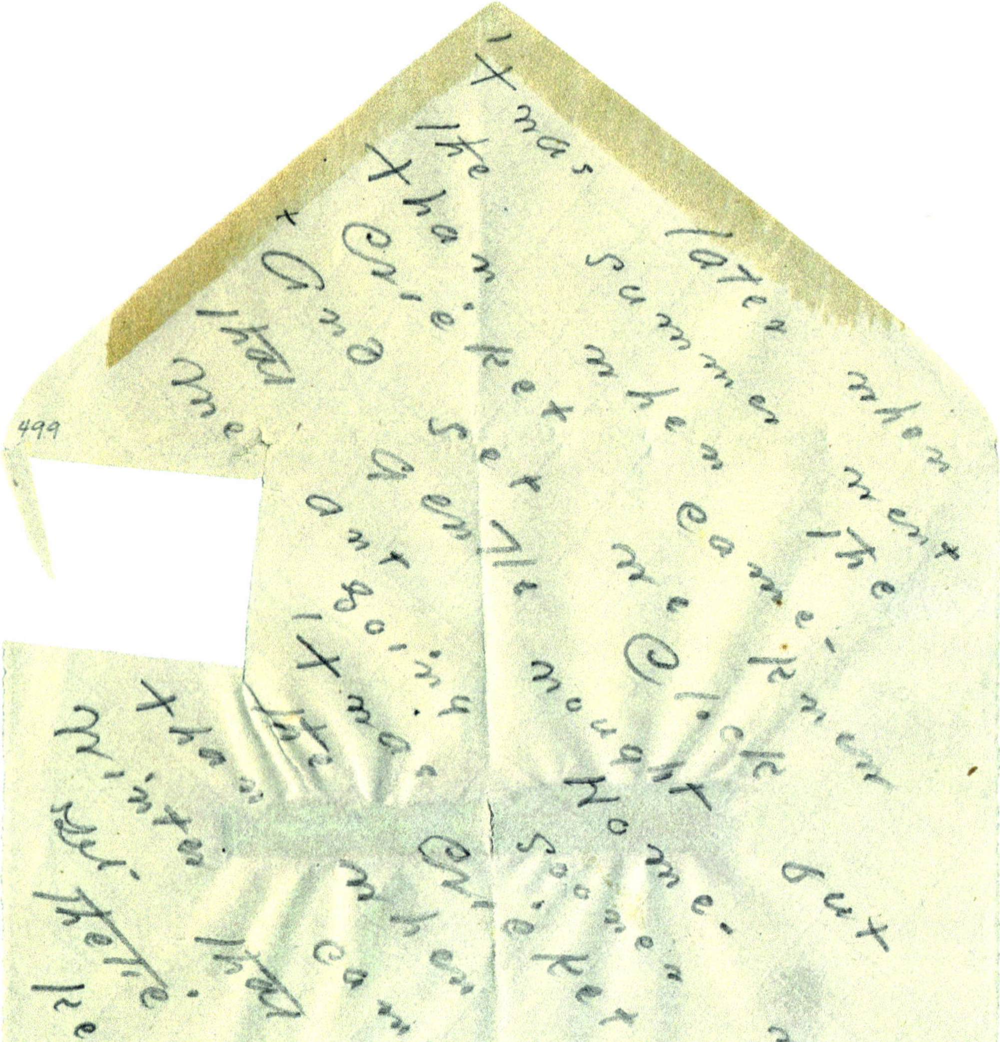

4.1 Emily Dickinson, from GORGEOUS NOTHINGS

The folds used to make an envelope typically take the form of a rhombus, a short-arm cross, or a kite. In Dickinson's poems these structures were sliced or steamed apart, gently pulled out of shape, flattened, and cut. While the support she chose to write on can make the poems look throwaway, unspoken for, like flotsam and jetsam, as if she had just picked up any old scrap of paper and decided to write on it ('scrap' is a word often used to describe these poems), the artist Jen Bervin was right when she observed just how deliberate and meticulous the preparatory process was: 'What looks simple, simply is not.'[1] The surface of Dickinson's lap desk, now at Amherst College Library in Massachusetts, 'is positively riddled with myriad fine cuts'.[2] Envelopes were treated like specimens in a natural history museum, dissected and decomposed, then carefully stored in a drawer.

The envelope poems are at once deeply personal and anonymous. To read them is to be invited into an intimate paper world usually reserved for the recipient of a love letter. I have only ever seen them in facsimile, but it is easy to imagine how delicate they would feel in the hand, how the smaller fragments would ask to be held in the palm, as might a bird, or a butterfly. This intimacy is belied by a sense of distance or detachment, a common experience when reading Dickinson. It is unclear for whom they were written – a prolific writer, she published only ten poems in her lifetime, all anonymously – and while Dickinson uses words to become her own observer, she does so in an elliptical, almost encrypted way.

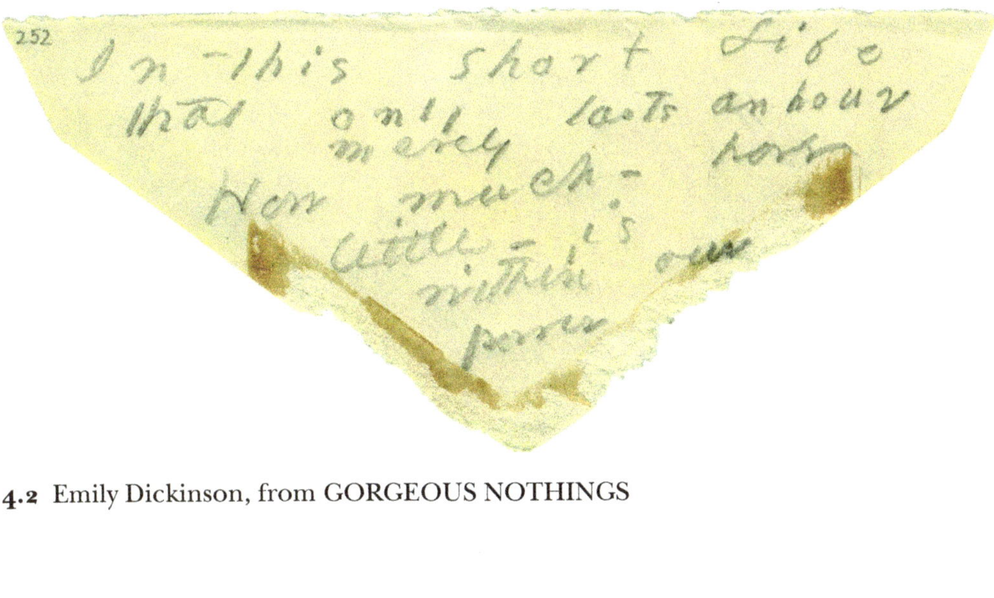

4.2 Emily Dickinson, from GORGEOUS NOTHINGS

Even when you get this close you never really feel like you know her. That the poems were written on the surface of envelopes adds to this effect: meaning would usually be concealed within an envelope and not without, which suggests that a surface reading, where your eye just follows the shape of the letter, could be as appropriate as a search for deeper meaning.

As the envelope poems suggest, Dickinson wrote many letters: at least 1,150. Only one half of the correspondence survives, because Lavinia Dickinson, following her sister's wishes, burnt the other half after her death in 1886. Few copies of Dickinson's own epistles exist, and the ones that do were victims of 'scissored deletions', as one of her biographers put it.[3] Details were literally cut out by Lavinia to protect her sister's privacy. Most obscure are the three 'Master letters', which were addressed to the Master, who Dickinson never names. These letters are unusual for adopting a tone both passionate and pleading. Nobody knows who the Master was, or indeed if the Master ever existed. Was the Master a lover, an omnipotent object, like God or the Devil, an alter ego? We will never know. What matters, though, is that for Dickinson the process of writing needed an addressee – in phantasy or in reality – with which to commune. Though she worked alone, within the confines of her bedroom, often at night, the epistolary form facilitated that process, in both her internal and external worlds. We never write to no one; a letter always has an addressee, even if they are imaginary.

In the digital era, it would be easy to lend the envelopes a nostalgic character they were unlikely to possess. The historian James Ward has described how it was only after 1840, with the invention of machines able to tesselate, cut, fold, and press sheets of paper, that envelopes were commonly used when sending letters.[4] Until then the page was simply folded in half. When Dickinson was working on her poems, machine-made envelopes were current; the stationery was modern, not nostalgic. Her decision to write on envelopes was due to her 'New England thrift', as Bervin noted, and to her pragmatism.[5] We know that the envelopes she used were produced by machines because of details such as the bands of gum mechanically applied on the sealing flap, which replaced the wax seals used in the first half of the nineteenth century, when envelopes were still handmade. Others were embossed by a machine, and, as in the first example above, you can sometimes make out the presence of a grid in the sheet, which shows that the format of the page was predetermined, printed to be turned into a standard-sized envelope.

Dickinson's handwriting is both constrained and enabled by the grid, entering into a tension with it. Strokes, swashes, finials, Cs curling into the open counter, all remind us that handwriting is first a form of pattern-making, which is only later pressed into the service of meaning. One contemporary described her writing, beautifully, as 'the fossil-tracks of birds'.[6]

Paper, and therefore letter-writing, moreover, were not as cheap as one might think. As she was born in 1830, as a teenager it would have cost Dickinson twenty cents, or roughly six dollars in today's money, to send a letter that travelled more than 150 miles by rail.[7] In the 1840s, American citizens turned to cheaper private carriers, which almost put the Post Office out of business. Congress responded by subsidising the postal service, which in 1845 slashed letter postage to ten cents, depending on the distance travelled. This decision was practical but also ideological, aimed at integrating the United States through the establishment of post routes that connected western and southern territories, the Missouri River to the Pacific Ocean. The railway network used to deliver post and other goods was responsible for the standardisation of time across America.[8] Until 1883, time was measured according to the movements of the sun, maintained by a public clock; powerful rail companies put paid to these natural cycles and their local expressions in the name of accuracy and efficiency. Standard time, then known as 'Railroad and Telegraph Time', was resisted by meteorologists, who thought it inaccurate and artificial. Time was indeed out of joint.

In 1863, postal prices were standardised at three cents per half-ounce. The same year also marked the first time that letters were delivered to the home; unless they were carried on horseback, a mode of transport still cheaper and faster than stagecoaches or trains, Dickinson would have needed to walk to the local post office to send or receive letters.

The time such journeys took were factored into the letters Dickinson wrote. Knowing that you need to wait changes what you write. This is true of all forms of communication, where, as a rule, the less time a message takes to reach its recipient the more compressed it is. Time shapes space. Dickinson was keenly aware of this. What struck her most about the telegraph, a technology invented in 1837 and implemented over the course of the mid-nineteenth century, was its ability to transcend time and space, to make information almost instantly available, so making messages shorter. '"I see Thee" Each responded straight / Through Telegraphic Signs', goes

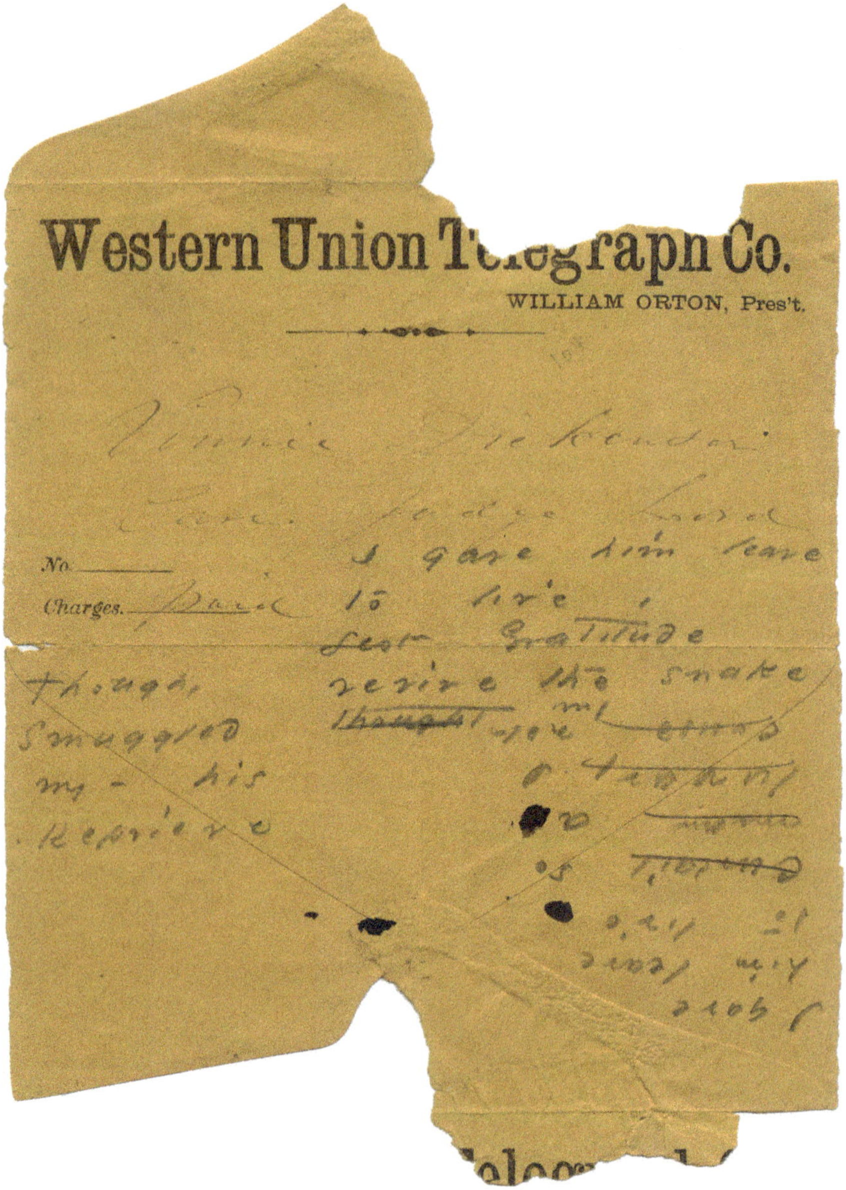

4.3 Emily Dickinson, from GORGEOUS NOTHINGS

one poem. 'The Ropes – above our Head' are always 'Continual – with the News', goes another.[9] One envelope poem was drafted on yellow telegraph paper (figure 4.3), which bears the heading: 'Western Union Telegraph Co.'.

Like the railways used to deliver post, telegraphs were seen to symbolise the union of the country. Dickinson wrote the earliest envelope poem in 1864, at the height of the Civil War, which corresponded with her most productive period as a poet. Amherst, a town in Massachusetts where Dickinson lived, lost many men conscripted to fight for the Union. The myth that Dickinson was not implicated or aware of the goings-on in the world around her has long been put to rest.

The Civil War impacted letter-writing in a particular way. In the mid-1860s, blockades were enforced by Unionists and their European allies, designed to cut off the confederate South from trade and resources. This led to rising costs and a scarcity of writing materials, envelopes in particular; the machines needed to make them only operated in the industrialised North. Women were compelled to handmake envelopes using other materials, such as wallpaper, maps, marine charts, song sheets, invoices, or train and ship schedules. Philatelists know these envelopes as 'adversity covers' because of the difficult conditions under which they were made (for examples, see figures 4.4 and 4.5).

In 1885, one Miss Anna Simpson of Pendleton, South Carolina, described how she made these envelopes during the war and the materials with which she wrote:

> A favorite night's employment was found in making envelopes. No bits of white paper suitable for writing with pen and ink could be wasted on envelopes. Thus it happened that wall paper and sheets with pictures on one side, taken from 'United States Explorations,' served to make envelopes, neat enough. These we stuck together with gum from peach trees. Ink was made from oak balls and green persimmons, with rusty nails, instead of copperas, to deepen the color. The noisy goose supplied our pens.[10]

Such resourcefulness was widespread. Patricia Kauffman, a leading authority on Confederacy letters, has recounted how, towards the end of the war, the adhesive quality of gum on stamps deteriorated. The problem was solved by using needle and thread to fasten the stamps to covers. Adversity covers were also washed and reused. 'Charlotte says be sure to wash this envelope & send it back', reads one such letter. 'We have a mania for economy just now as you perceive.' Kauffman compares these practices to the famous scene in *Gone With the Wind* where Scarlett O'Hara makes a dress out of a green velvet curtain.[11]

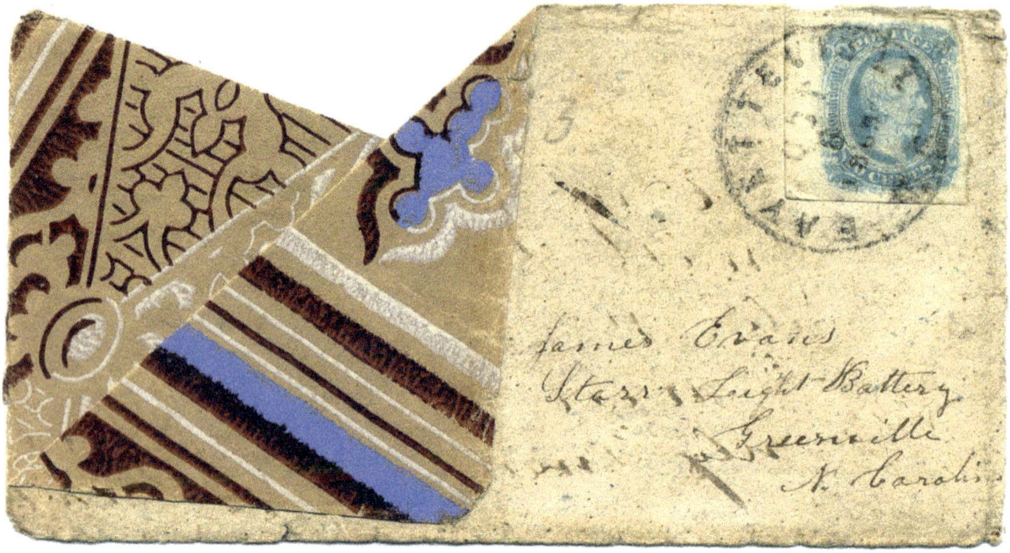

4.4 'Adversity cover'

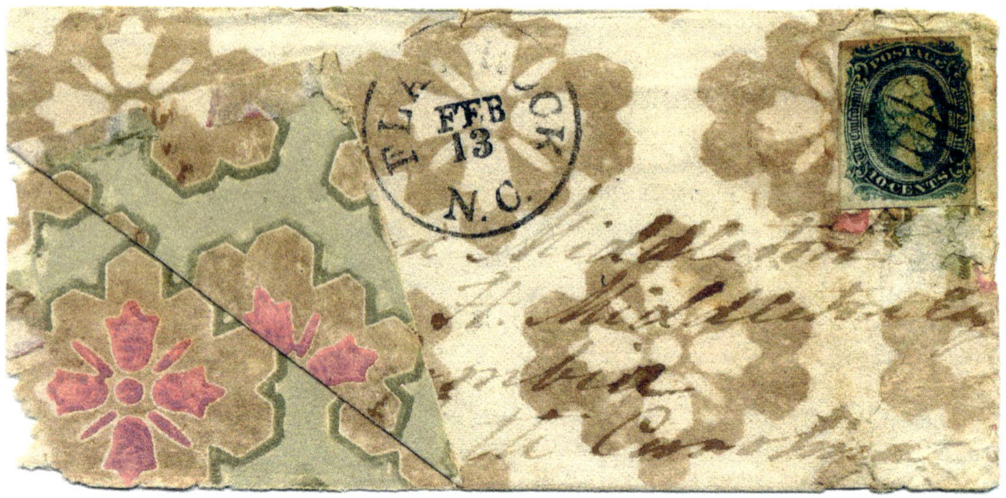

4.5 'Adversity cover'

The adversity covers were born out of hardship, if not abjection. Yet, like Dickinson's envelope poems, they reveal an aesthetic sensibility. Mostly the wallpaper was reversed so that the blank side could be used for writing on, but there are rarer examples in which the wallpaper design is on the outside of the envelope, where its decorative aspect is more pronounced. The pleasure and surprise at finding a coloured pattern on the surface of an envelope or in its pocket is easy to imagine. This may explain why to my eyes, at least, the adversity covers always look like love letters (envelopes made with care have a particular resonance, at once emotional, psychic, and bodily). There is in fact one example made of floral wallpaper, owned by Kauffman, which did contain a love letter, together with a small, pressed fern leaf that plays, unconsciously perhaps, on the relationship between folds and foliations.

'As there are / Apartments in our / own Minds that – / we never enter / without Apology – / we should respect / the seals / of others', wrote Dickinson in one envelope poem, in the last decade of her life (figure 4.6). There are, no doubt, many such apartments whose doors will be forever closed to us, and that is as it should be. When Dickinson died, her death certificate listed her occupation as 'at home'.[12] It may be more than a matter of chance that, in the mid-nineteenth century, while the bourgeois domestic interior became a private refuge from the outside world, the mass-produced envelope should have gradually privatised the letter.

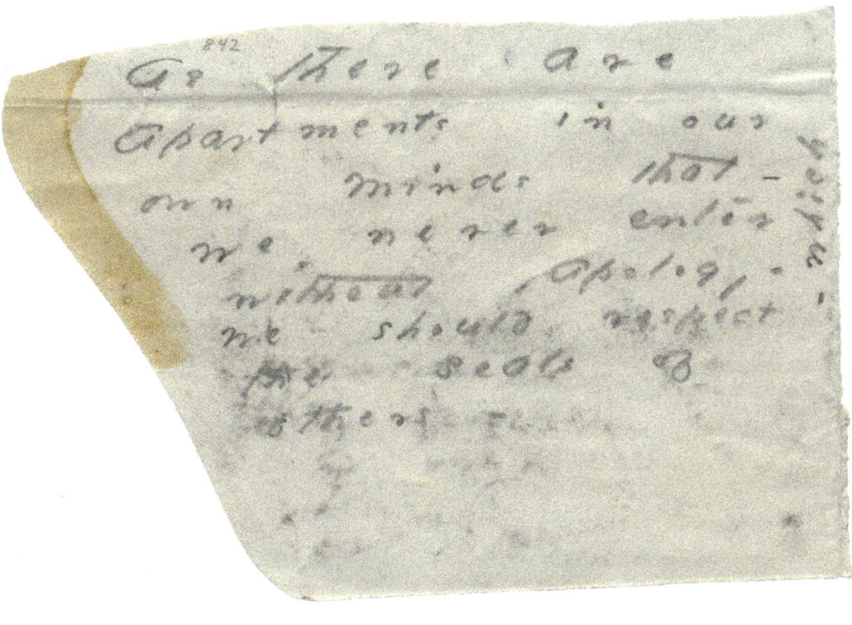
842
As there are
Apartments in our
own Minds that –
we never enter
without Apology –
we should respect
the seals of

4.6 Emily Dickinson, from GORGEOUS NOTHINGS

Dickinson's envelope poems play upon and invert these tropes, turning them inside out and outside in. As do the adversity covers. Wallpaper covered the walls of apartments in the privacy of the home, providing them with an internal envelope. A room was also an interior whose own exterior could be cut, pinched, creased, and folded into an envelope. 'The Inner – paints the Outer – / The Brush without the Hand', to borrow Dickinson's words from another set of poems. Though she was writing under different constraints, the adversity covers help us to see that the epistolary form Dickinson adopted was itself a fold – a fold in history, a fold within a fold, so to speak.

It takes a certain kind of sensibility to make such things, to feel free to repurpose materials as the means to communicate with others. A modernist paradigm is found in the figure of the ragpicker, who has long been connected to the modern poet (Baudelaire in particular).[13] Finding value in detritus, the historical leftover, what gets cast out or abjected – this all matters, and not only to poets. Artists can be ragpickers, too, showing the same wish to salvage, the same mania for economy. After all, the envelope poems are visual things concerned with shape and pattern as much as they are textual things. Processes of unfolding and cutting were as important to the composition of the poems as writing, and the experience of reading them hinges on how the support is held in the hand, whether you decide to turn a poem over, or around – they can be read in many ways.

Yet, like their Southern counterparts, Dickinson's envelope poems offer a different paradigm with which to think the modern, quite unlike the ragpicker. Pattern-making is as important as form, continuity as discontinuity. What counts is not only the fragment in its relation to an imagined whole or totality – melancholically held to be lost – but rather the fold, a figure of topology which, like the crease that secures it, opens up distinctions between the private and the public, the interior life and the exterior one, the sensible and the intelligible.

Notes

This text was written on the occasion of *The Gorgeous Nothings*, an exhibition curated by the artist Susan Morris at Bartha Contemporary, London, in 2022. It was originally published in the accompanying pamphlet.

1 Jane Bervin, 'Studies in Scale', in Marta Werner and Jen Bervin (eds), *Emily Dickinson: The Gorgeous Nothings* (New York: Christine Burgin/New Directions, 2013), p. 8.
2 Bervin, 'Studies in Scale', p. 9.
3 Alfred Habegger, *My Wars Are Laid Away in Books* (London: Penguin, 2002), p. 436. See also Hillary Kelly, 'Master Narrative: Who Did Emily Dickinson Write Her Love Letters To?', *Los Angeles Review of Books*, 22 July 2012, https://lareviewofbooks.org/article/master-narrative-who-did-emily-dickinson-write-her-love-letters-to/ (accessed 24 May 2023).
4 James Ward, *Adventures in Stationery: A Journey Through Your Pencil Case* (London: Profile Books, 2014).
5 Bervin, 'Studies in Scale', p. 11.
6 Thomas Wentworth Higginson, cited in *Emily Dickinson: The Gorgeous Nothings*, p. 12.
7 See Winifred Gallagher, 'A Brief History of the United States Postal Service', *Smithsonian Magazine*, October 2020, www.smithsonianmag.com/smithsonian-institution/brief-history-united-states-postal-service-180975627 (accessed 24 May 2023). See also Boyce Upholt, 'The Tumultuous History of the U.S. Postal Service – And its Constant Fight for Survival', *National Geographic*, May 2020, www.nationalgeographic.com/history/article/tumultuous-history-united-states-postal-service-constant-fight-survival (accessed 24 May 2023).
8 See Alexis McCrossen, *Marking Modern Times: A History of Clocks, Watches, and Other Time Keepers in American Life* (Chicago, IL and London: University of Chicago Press, 2013), chapter 4.
9 Dickinson cited in Jerusha Hull McCormack, 'Domesticating Delphi: Emily Dickinson and the Electro-Magnetic Telegraph', *American Quarterly*, 55:4 (December 2023), 574.
10 Patricia A. Kauffman, 'Resilience in Hard Times: Adversity Covers', in *Stamp Collectors Quarterly*, 12, unpaginated.
11 Kauffman, 'Resilience in Hard Times', unpaginated.
12 Martha Ackmann, *These Fevered Days: Ten Pivotal Moments in the Making of Emily Dickinson* (New York: W. W. Norton, 2020), p. xiii.
13 The most well-known example is Walter Benjamin's essays on Charles Baudelaire. See Walter Benjamin and Michael W. Jennings (ed.), *The Writer of Modern Life: Essays on Charles Baudelaire*, trans. Howard Eiland (Cambridge, MA and London: Belknap Press of Harvard University Press, 2006).

5

The perversity of her envelopes, or, Kathy Acker's sick clothes and kleptomaniac close writing: a reply to sender

Alice Butler

The snake is an invitation: I see and touch sickness and pleasure

Four hooped earrings sway from her left earlobe. Horned amulets are pinned through her right. Both of her eyebrows are pierced, cutting two twinkles of light across the surface of her rouged skin, underneath delicate brown hairs. Her shaved head is growing back tufted in a sandy shade of blonde, which pops brightly against her rosebud lip and loose-fitting trouser suit of black velvet sheen and gold clasp details. A glimpse of Versace at the waist. It is a soft and oversized jacket that slips from her shoulder, as she shifts her hip and twirls, arms splayed outwards, making the jacket flare and flutter like wings, murmuring in motion. Simultaneously direct, playful, and vulnerable, it is a pose that leaves the garment and her body undone, rather than fastened or covered. Her exposed chest and stomach (navel decorated with a purple jewel piercing) are revealed in this flip from back to front. Slithering down her small frame – first around her neck, and then her clavicles (risking suffocation) – is the head and body of a gem-stoned snake, splashed with ruby-red crystals for eyes. The snake's arrowed head points towards her absent breasts, scarred by the trace of a knife.

Or the enfleshed line of writing.

This is a portrait that depicts – in many ways recognisably – the American writer Kathy Acker (1947–1997). After arriving in London from her native New York in early 1984, she stayed for five years, fled back to her home town, then returned again (via a stint in San Francisco and world-crossing book tours) in time for this

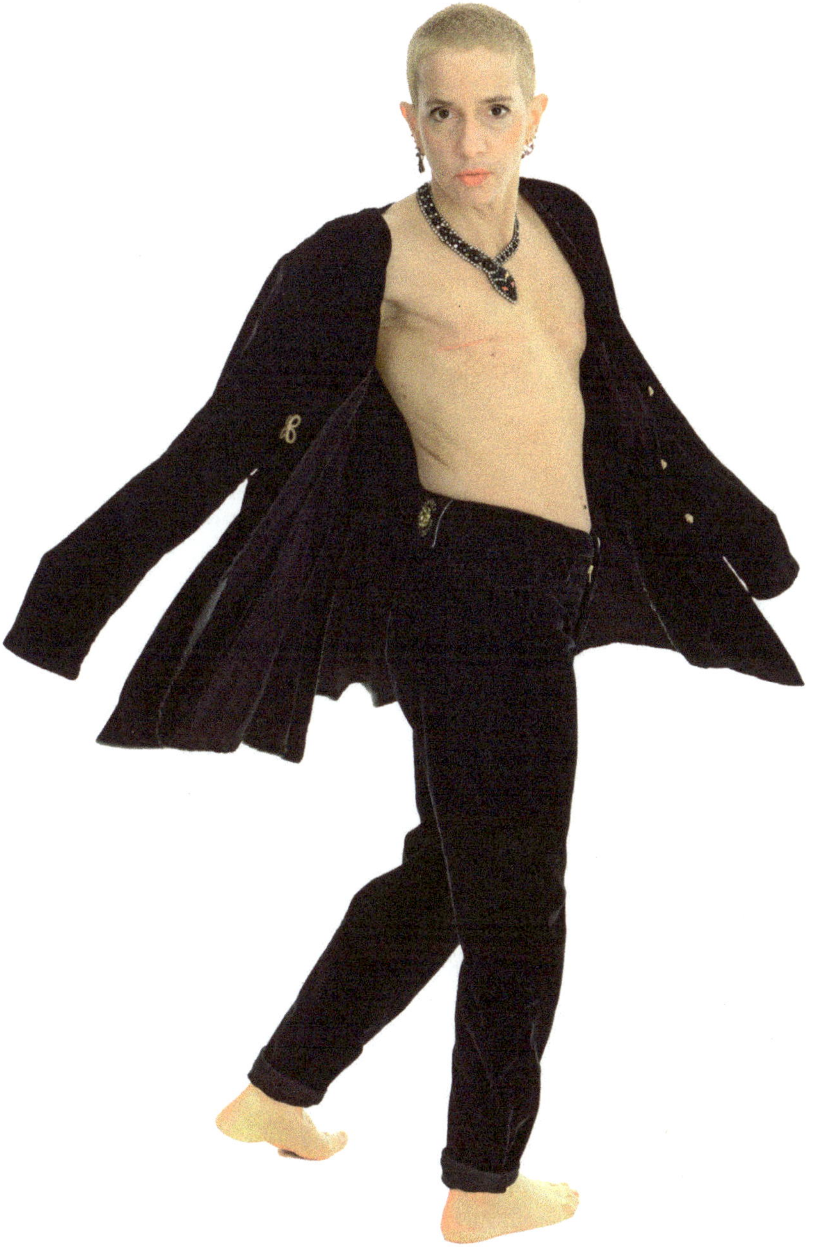

5.1 Del LaGrace Volcano, *TWIRL, Kathy Acker, London*, 1997, digital C-print, 55.8 × 48.2 cm. Reproduced by permission of the artist

picture, which re-produces the sartorial spectacle for which she had become known: a self-imaging, punk collage of piercings, peroxide buzz-cut, worked physique, embellished epidermis, and deconstructed designer clothes. Her literary work was defiantly cross-genre, and evolved a transdisciplinary relationship to postmodernist visual and performance art practices, as she developed so-called 'intentions' to facilitate her writing:[1] be it automated, diary notations exploring sexual and sensual experiences at home and work (her first self-published work, *Politics* (1972)); first-person rewritings of copied texts (in serial novels contained in mail-art chapbooks, such as *The Childlike Life of the Black Tarantula by the Black Tarantula* (1973)); epistolary interventions crossing with plagiarised passages (in *Great Expectations* (1982) and *Don Quixote (which was a dream)* (1986)), as well as other forms of translating, copying, drawing, and dialoguing.

Such methods created a fractured formal landscape for her feminist investigations of sex and gender, and the social and patriarchal constructions of language, in capitalist society. While characters' identities move freely across gendered, sexual, historical, and geographical norms in her archive of writings (which as well as comprising novels informed by art and experimental poetry, also included a screenplay, a libretto, and essays about, or rather *with*, art and culture), the stereotype of the young girl made sick by class and gender oppressions is the subject through which she often speaks with subversive political energy and perverse desire. *Don Quixote*, for example, begins in the abortion clinic; its protagonist is lovesick: 'When she was finally crazy because she was about to have an abortion, she conceived of the most insane idea that a woman can think of. Which is to love. How can a woman love?'[2]

Interwoven within her sick-girl corpus, Kathy was – and I use her first name to embody and address, *intimately*, the ways her life and fiction meshed – also the author of her own sartorial scenography, which was visualised in texts, photographs, performances, and her own lived experience: close to its operatic end, involving pain and pleasure, as she listened to a recording of *La traviata* on her sickbed (as one of her artist friends once told me) at an alternative treatment centre in Tijuana, Mexico, before her death on 30 November 1997 from a cancer that had spread and spread. As I will pattern together in this chapter via piecemeal parts, and borrowed words and bodies that move across time, I consider the 'sick' aspects of her clothing archive as items that articulate deviations *away from* ('perversions', I call them) regulatory norms relating to gender, sexuality, healthcare, and the literary artwork itself. I hereby depart from Sara Ahmed's reading of perversion as a spatial, sexual, and social term that describes the 'willful determination to counter or go against orthodoxy, but also to what is wayward and thus "*turned away* from what is right, good, and proper"'.[3] Kathy's sartorial perversions, I argue, function as extensions of her perverse writing practice, whereby perversion is channelled in *forms* that deviate from disciplinary norms, and *scenes* that deviate from social and sexual conventions. Not only did her dressing, and her dresses, nourish the making of the work – or *heal* the body (like a bandage dressing to an open wound) – but they also became a significant medium for her compartmentalised creative practice: the sick garment as a piece to be handled, then threaded through, interwoven within, the perverse patterns of her writing.

As she told an ex-lover, the artist, writer, and editor Jonathan Miles, in a letter dated 1983: 'I have to make *all* my living' – which includes the sewing,[4] the shopping, the dressing – 'as interesting to myself as my writing'.[5] '*As* interesting': that is, equal *to* the blurred, embodied, performative lines of clothing and writing. For when writing can be understood as performance, as Kathy had shown in the Eleanor Antin-inspired identity game-play of *The Childlike Life*, or the epistolary re-enactment of Laure and Georges Bataille's relationship in the later *My Mother: Demonology* (1994) ('I act through the novels', she told Sylvère Lotringer in 1991),[6] then perhaps performance (insofar as it involves the doing of 'clothing' and the object itself) can be 'read' as a kind of writing, too.[7] I pick up the loose threads that dangle from the question marks of another epistolary performer, Dodie Bellamy: 'The clothes are superfluous to Kathy's writing, her real legacy – or are they? Could there have been a Kathy Acker without the clothes?'[8]

And I also embroider my own: could the sickness of her clothing practice be a way into thinking about, and *with*, the feminist politics of her living and writing of sexual, social, and creative *perversion*? I am particularly indebted to the capacious critical writing of Eve Kosofsky Sedgwick – the links between textiles, sickness, and perversion made in her work: from the essays that became part of the 1993 collection *Tendencies*, to the essays, talks, and textiles which she was working on in the later years of her life before her death from breast cancer in 2009 – in probing the possibilities of this question. In doing so, I fold these projects closer together, from the earlier essays' interest in the crossings of queerness as existing 'across genders, across sexualities, across "perversions"',[9] to the later pieces' rootedness in reparation, affect, and the non-dualisms of textile art and Buddhist practices.[10]

In the 1999 talk 'Come As You Are', Sedgwick recognises overlapping threads between earlier and later studies, namely around 'nondualistic approaches to ideas and genres [– working, for example, at the boundaries between poetry and prose, between activism and scholarship]'.[11] And it was within her activism and scholarship that a visceral and political entanglement with queer death and disease was explored, first in the confluent AIDS and cancer contexts that shadowed her writing of *Tendencies*, where she described queer identification as existing across the 'ontological crack between the living and the dead';[12] and then again in the reparative and non-dualistic approaches to mortality that became woven throughout her later work. The close spaces between living and dying was a persistent occupation for Sedgwick, and this commitment to non-dualism stretched into all aspects of her life and work (the crossed threads between them), as she pulled apart binary thinking towards writing, genre, and discipline, erotic life, and gender, sexual, racial, and bodily identity, recognising in the essay 'Queer and Now' (and mining weaving for a queer metaphor of perversion) that the 'loose ends . . . can't be made to line up neatly together'.[13] Departing from Sedgwick's threaded writings, I interweave the non-dual and the queer in this chapter to rethink the 'sicknesses' of Kathy's transdisciplinary texts and textiles as erotic spaces of feminist perversion, which produce rearticulations of sexual desire and gendered embodiment.

In *TWIRL*, the velvet-vivid photograph of her by the artist Del LaGrace Volcano, Kathy's clothes help tell her sick story of embodiment. The photograph was part of a series of Acker portraits by Volcano, which included the profiles that accompanied Kathy's 1997 autobiographical essay for the *Guardian*, 'The Gift of Disease': a lacerating description of the personal and political circumstances of her breast-cancer diagnosis, double mastectomy, and rejection of Western medicine. To borrow the words of the contemporary artist Johanna Hedva, she is a 'sick woman', suffering a gendered disease (which has "come to her", but is not part of her), resistant to the forces of the 'Western medical-insurance industrial complex' that thinks it understands her.[14] Hedva's 2016 essay 'Sick Woman Theory', which theorises the sick woman as a subject of many 'guises' representing all of the 'the un-cared for, the secondary, the oppressed, the non-, the un-, the less-than', has helped me to read the image of Kathy's open ready-to-fly jacket hanging loose over her mastectomised, muscular frame, *differently*, more *perversely*: it has helped me to unravel its sick textures and sick textualities (for text and textile both share the same etymology in the verb 'to weave'); the ways her clothing intersects with her words as a creative form of political energy and reparative survival.

I now read the wearing of the jacket as an anti-capitalist, anti-patriarchal gesture of care for one's own body and the bodies of other sick women *like* her. 'You don't need to be fixed, my queens – it's the world that needs fixing', writes Hedva, whose portrait accompanying the essay features the artist in a shocking red kaftan, lips, nails, and hair painted black, surrounded by a blanket of medications while reclining on their bed. Kathy's breastless body covered in diamonds communicates a similar message (and so does the image of Sedgwick dressed in tight Lycra black crop top and shorts, her oversized 'divine' frame exceeding the elasticated edges, not long after being diagnosed with breast cancer) – the subversive, sartorial agency of the vulnerable, which is interwoven into the writing and back again.[15] What resources or pleasures, then, might clothes provide the sick woman writer? How might clothing (so often a feminised object, designed and manufactured to cover the body in erotic servitude to the male gaze, or bracketed within the terms of domestic labour) help to subvert or repair the feminising impositions of breast cancer as a gendered disease?[16]

'I am going to tell this story as I know it', begins Kathy in 'The Gift of Disease'. It is a piece of exacting attention ('I want to describe as exactly as possible what it is like to experience conventional cancer medicine') and at times jarringly clinical and 'un-sentimental'.[17] 'I have never been sentimental', adds Kathy: 'Perhaps just to say that it happened. In April of last year, I was diagnosed as having breast cancer. I had had a history of breast lumps but, until this time, none of them had been malignant. A biopsy revealed that the mass involved was no less than five centimetres in diameter.'[18] But in spite of the text's empirical gloss, this is a sick story that is viscerally *hers*, a work of embodied knowledge that traverses 'the ladder between the case and the universe', as Lauren Berlant writes of Anne Boyer's 'meditation on modern illness' (breast cancer), *The Undying* (2019).[19] The reparative energy of sentiment and the paranoid exposure of ideology are stitched into the same textual fabric[20] – shifting scales – from the corporate scene of 'big business' and the spiralling lists of treatment costs in the medical-industrial complex, to the intimate life narrative of Kathy's (more affordable) breast-removal surgery, her veins 'plugged' with liquid, her head and eyes covered in a green cap, her jewellery and the skin around it plastered with tape.[21] 'I was being reduced to something I couldn't recognise', remembers Kathy – which gives way, after receiving the news from her surgeon that the cancer had spread, to a 'realisation':

> I realised that if I remained in the hands of conventional medicine, I would soon be dead, rather than diseased, meat. For conventional medicine was reducing me quickly to a body that was only material, to a body without hope, and so, without will, to a puppet, who, separated from her imagination and vision, would do whatever she was told. . . . I knew I wanted to live. To live was to stay alive and to not be reduced to materiality.[22]

Spreading the lustrous wings of her velvet jacket – uncovering her operated-upon body with the embodied and artistic agency of a twirl – Kathy denies the medical marker of 'meat'. She rejects the capitalist and patriarchal regulatory norms that seek to exploit her body, and the bodies of other sick women suffering from 'cancer, Aids and immune diseases in general'[23] who remain uninsured, uncared for in this 'unbearable' reality.[24] Kathy's sick clothes and sick writing – stitched and restitched together as a work of parts (like a dress) – tell a different, more wayward, story. The perverted, as Ahmed gestures towards, is that which '"turns astray" or moves off the straight line',[25] which Kathy embodies, turning away from the biopolitical matrix of power, its control of medicine, gender, and sexuality: the 'straight line' denoting 'that which moves *without any deviation* towards the "point" of heterosexual union' and reproductive sexual acts.[26] As Kathy describes the effects of her wilful deviation: 'Belief in conventional medicine is so deeply engrained in our society that to walk away from conventional medicine is to walk away from normal society.'[27] She performs it, too, in her pose, the erotic velvet of cut-breasted exposure, which also signals a disappearance of the maternal breast, delaying the (essentialist) 'point' of 'heterosexual union'.[28]

Rather than passing judgement on the decisions Kathy made regarding her treatment (namely her rejection of chemotherapy and subsequent embrace of alternative therapies such as macrobiotic diets and psychic healings that pledged an indebtedness to non-Western traditions), I desire to unpick the complex entanglement of binary dualisms interlaced within her texts and textiles. Indeed, despite a chorus of voices (friends, colleagues, publishers, fellow writers) expressing affective responses and remembrances ranging from anger and dismay to the ruling of a death wish, the most probable situation is that Kathy refused chemotherapy due to an intricate network of economic, affective, and medical reasons, which Boyer attends to in *The Undying*, even entering an approximation of Kathy's disease statistics into a prognosis database, which she had used to help her make decisions about her own cancer treatment. 'There wasn't a cure then', muses Boyer, 'There isn't one now. In making a principled judgment to live according to her own values, Acker did the best anyone could do.'[29] And those values to and for living emerge in 'The Gift of Disease' (text and textile: I attend to it as a work of parts: interlaced, following Sedgwick, one 'beside' the other: like the spatial, textural, interweaving of warp and weft),[30] with the realisation of a non-dualist corporeal imagination and subjectivity in chronic sick time ('I live as I believe, that belief is equal to the body').[31]

Recognising that reality is not necessarily '*what's true,* but . . . *what's realised,* what is or has become real', and that 'reality in this sense, as it happens, may be entirely orthogonal to the question of truth',[32] Sedgwick was thinking with similar ideas in the essays and talks that both intersected with, and directly commented upon, her textile practice, which flourished (as Kathy's sick clothes also intimate) during and beside her own embodied experience of the 'bardo of dying', in which there may be 'years of good health or ill health, of pain or its relative absence, of lassitude or energy', or more likely an unpredictable mixture of all of these, 'on a worsening trajectory'.[33] In Sedgwick's work on realisation; on the nondualism of realisation separate from truth (not to mention a 'spacious antagonism to several of the linear logics that enforce dualistic thinking' in general);[34] on the difference between knowing and realising (one's mortality, for example): she enveloped herself in Buddhist thought. And in so doing, Sedgwick approached it as a practice rather than an epistemology, which resurfaced again in her textile work and the 'exciting intimacy with nonbeing' she realised in cutting up kimonos and making appliqués, collages, and woven pieces from them.[35] Sometimes, she even printed overlaid medically scanned images of her bone tissue onto the fabrics themselves, in a sick woman's gesture of care, reparation, and creativity.

Hence, while Sedgwick may have downplayed the artistic, intellectual, or queer significance of her textiles and the conceptual linkages between her visual and writing practices, her critical work was dominated by (as I have also thrillingly succumbed to) 'textile vocabularies' of queerness[36] – the 'open *mesh* of possibilities, gaps, overlaps, dissonances and resonances, lapses and excesses of meaning when the constituent elements of anyone's gender, or anyone's sexuality aren't made (or *can't* be made) to signify monolithically', which defines the capaciousness of queer identity in *Tendencies* that materialises queerness-as-texture.[37] And the textiles themselves also signify an unravelling of binary oppositions. Iconographically for example, the indigo-dyed, cyanotype textiles that incorporate images of late Tang- and Sung-dynasty Chinese bronze sculptures of Guan Yin, the Bodhisattva of compassion, are 'queer little gods', to borrow Jason Edwards's phrase, which 'embody and represent the kaleidoscopic slippage between male and female, passive and active, Occidental and Oriental'.[38] Materially, also, Sedgwick's compositions were often frayed at the edges, formed of rags or cut pieces, which invoked a language of unfinished loose ends or borders, even vulnerabilities. Her textiles hereby conceptualised the shifting ground of queerness, sickness, and the bardo of dying in the objects' material composition. And in even more phenomenological terms, Sedgwick's turn to textile art was also a turn to multisensory modes of perception, crossing between seeing and touching and affect. Exploring these 'middle ranges of agency' (as she describes 'the field in which most of consciousness, perception, and relationality really happen'), *through* textiles, and *beside* writing, at a time when she learned the cancer for which she had been treated several years earlier had become chronic and incurable, brings into focus an intense re-engagement with the self as unfinished, split, medial, edgewise, and enduringly in process.[39] Wrapped up in the criss-crossings of textile yarns is the promise of non-dualistic, middling relations, a space of chronic *means* (rather than ends), a touching of pleasure with pain, where the binary oppositions of life and death, form and emptiness, mind and body, can thrive in reparative terms.

I pull again on Kathy's own loose ends; I caress the shedding skin of her velveted epidermis. Her semi-clothed body beats at a Sedgwickian non-dualistic boundary: between the living and the dying, the healthy and the sick, the animate and the inanimate, a piece of girl and a piece of boy. The picture's performative blurring of masculine and feminine gestures is an extension of Volcano's representation of sexual subcultures and gender-variant bodies, collected in the 1991 book *Love Bites: Photographs.* After Volcano first fleetingly met Kathy outside a cinema in East London, and then again in San Francisco, where Kathy read a draft of the artist's writing in progress ('Memoirs of a Pussy Licking Sodomite') at Red Dora's Bearded Lady's Café, they became close friends towards the end of Kathy's life, as they lived only a short bus ride from each other in north London.[40] Volcano's work has since engaged more intensely with intersex representation and activism (the artist was born 'with an intersex variation', but it was with the 1995 work, *Self Portrait with Beard,* that Volcano turned towards 'uncovering the ambiguity in my gender that had always been there').[41] Gender-deviating lines similarly emerge in the artist's 1997 portrait of Kathy, through the shifting, polymorphous, corporeal presence of a sick body traversing life and death and moving through a textured network of possible identifications.

Sedgwick identified as queer along similarly interwoven lines in the essay 'White Glasses', in which she describes the flourishing affinity she feels with her friend, Michael Lynch, due to a shared experience of illness. For in spite first feeling (fearing?) upon receiving her diagnosis that, 'Shit, now I guess I really must be a woman', Sedgwick explores the identificatory *distance* from 'mysteries of essential femaleness' that actually emerged, as she too found herself, in the course of the text's development, 'to be ill and writing'.[42] Becoming even closer to Michael – learning again from him, in an echo of AIDS activist energies, 'how to be sick – how to occupy most truthfully and powerfully, and at the same time constantly to question and deconstruct, the sick role'[43] – the intimate, gender-crossing refractions between them is embodied in a fashion accessory: two matching pairs of white glasses. And uncovered in the crossings between feminine and masculine that are couched in Kathy's clothed and accessorised but un-breasted and un-shoed body, or in the wrinkled crush of her rolled-up trouser bottoms raising the prospect of a body and identity who is also crushed (broken up into multiple particles), or in the prickling pleasures of velvet suggesting a self-directed autoeroticism that is neither homo- nor hetero- as it delays reproductive couplings, is a queer, embodied, erotic intervention into the dualisms of sickness, sexuality, and gender, as performed in her visual and haptic text/ile practice.[44]

The portrait's clinical white background could be seen to suggest the punishing space of the hospital that Kathy describes in 'The Gift of Disease', where halls give way to more halls in a panopticonic effect, and then to a room which is 'huge and colder than the hall', containing 'something that was partly a table and partly a bed', with 'machines that looked like Dr Seuss animals' connected to it.[45] She is 'told to climb on it and lie' on her back. Then, 'thick straps were placed around' her arms and legs, and 'buckled tightly'.[46] It is rendered as a Foucauldian scene of biopolitical medical control that recalls other misogynistic and homophobic medical discourses of the past, which Paul B. Preciado attends to in *Testo Junkie: Sex, Drugs, and Biopolitics in the Pharmacopornographic Era* (departing from Foucault) as disciplinary machinations of 'sexopolitics' wherein 'the discourse on masculinity and femininity, as well as techniques of normalizing sexual identity, have turned into governmental agents of the control and standardization of life'.[47] Patient-ghosts pathologised (such as the androgyne, the onanist, the hysteric – the sick woman being a subject of many guises – plural 'identities . . . that must be studied, recorded, hounded, hunted, punished, cured')[48] return in the shadows of Kathy's sartorial image to gaze back and gesture with traces of desiring agency.

This stance echoes the more direct challenges made by Sedgwick against such forces in earlier essays, such as 'Jane Austen and the Masturbating Girl',[49] and also in her dialogic cancer memoir that folds poetry, essay, and case notes together, *A Dialogue on Love*. In this book she tells her therapist how she would 'spend hours and hours a day as a child in my bedroom masturbating', but that the intensity of this 'autoerotic life' has disappeared with the diagnosis, her 'quasi-medical' fantasies only now 'warmed' by the masochistic effects of the waiting room (as the intervention of Kathy's erotic gesture into an expanded hospital surround also suggests).[50] While the temperature of Sedgwick's fantasies is at a more comfortable rather than 'horrifying' level of heat here,[51] relational linkages between the sick and the erotic are nonetheless carved out in these scenes, when Sedgwick's perverse fantasies are pleasured by the exposing effects of the hospital intercom calling her name.[52] This hints at the room (or 'the fullness', as Sedgwick describes elsewhere) the sick woman can make for gestural glimpses of erotic relief and perverse pleasure, in resistance to the punishing surrounds (within and beyond the body) of sickness itself.[53]

I touch again Kathy's textured essay. The phrase, 'My search for a way to defeat cancer now became a search for [a] life and death that were meaningful',[54] echoes Audre Lorde in its non-dualistic philosophising ('There must be some way to integrate death into living, neither ignoring it nor giving in to it')[55] and also Sedgwick, with her understanding of the extended bardo of dying as 'electric with spiritual possibility'.[56] For these sick woman writers, it is the turning of 'fury' at one's own 'limitations into some more creative energy',[57] a finding of 'strength',[58] or fullness in work and writing which sustains them in sick pleasure and protest and which is viscerally materialised in Kathy's handwritten drafts of novels, plays, and essays in her notebooks (including 'The Gift of Disease', originally entitled 'On My Healing' – as she scrawled on its front cover: 'that is the end of my experience of western medicine. I walked away').[59] Could that 'energy' as it exists across all work, all practice, also be woven throughout all aspects of their life: the lived embodiment of their texts and textiles? By rubbing text and textile together (between my thumb and forefinger), I am gesturing towards the possibility that clothing – *like* writing and *as* writing – opens out the 'power of the erotic', as Lorde terms it: a deeply sensory, emotionally charged 'lifeforce', which mixes doing and feeling with thinking, and desiring, and in so doing, provides 'energy to pursue genuine change. . . . in the face of a racist, patriarchal, and anti-erotic society'.[60] However, while Lorde sees the erotic as a 'nurturer of all our deepest knowledge',[61] somehow *subservient to* the writing and thinking, in Kathy's version, living and writing flourish on the same non-hierarchical plane of activity. In this space, clothing becomes an erotic and poetic *practice* that is powerful, in the sense that it is also critical (as complex as its textured composition), nurturing as it does an embodied and perverse reimagining of the sick woman's body.

The surface of her clothing comes into close, erotic contact with her skin. It is electrified, like hairs standing on end, alive and *lively* 'vibrant matter', to borrow Jane Bennett's term describing non-human forces and tendencies which can 'aid or destroy, enrich or disable, ennoble or degrade us'.[62] Vitally material, the velvet shelters her cut flesh, dashed with scars where there once were stitches (threads, *things*). In learning and listening to her body anew, as she describes in 'The Gift of Disease', Kathy discovers its connected pieces, an assemblage of 'connected bodies, as soul, as energetic, as emotional, and as physical', which remembers 'all that happened to and within the body', including, perhaps, its surgical stitches and the (inanimate) clothing that rubs it closely.[63] This is a reparative process for Kathy: a remaking of her body, with hope and wilfulness (this is the 'perverse potential of will', writes Ahmed),[64] erotic imagination and *creative* vision – the overlapped threads of a feminist practice which animates the politics of non-dualistic perversions through clothing and writing.

Once again, the snake necklace grabs my eye, my *throat*, as I remember that the same animal motif illustrates the front cover of Boyer's book. 'To see a snake', Boyer writes, 'is also to think of the way a snake slithers out of its skin, the way it has to rub its skin against something hard so that the skin begins to loosen and also the way the snake must generate sufficient new skin so that the old might be left behind'.[65]

The snake, I now realise, is an invitation to dream what other stories are possible as I endure in restitching (accompanied by a reparative desire akin to Kathy's own bodily remakings) a new skin for Kathy's clothes. But while Kathy's approach to healing grasps for a 'self which is always whole',[66] this essay's skin-shedding-regeneration shows its scars, the fragmentary pieces, departing more closely from Sedgwick's conceptualisation of reparation in *A Dialogue on Love* as a fitting of the pieces back together that do not always cohere to a past self.[67] My restitchings also flourish in close relation to her subsequent understanding of reparative reading as a queer critical practice rooted in affect and love, which, drawing on Melanie Klein, seeks pleasure, rather than forestalls pain (or exposes it as a paranoid reader), repairing and reassembling the 'murderous part-objects into something *like* a whole' that could never be fully healed or complete.[68] This reimagined whole provides sustenance and nourishment to vulnerable 'selves and communities' as a method to overcome all kinds of discrimination, oppression, and stigma,[69] with Sedgwick's writing in particular holding a visceral relationship to the energies of AIDS activism (which also cannot be separated from her queer experiences and absorbed identifications of life-limiting chronic disease).[70] Sarah Schulman writes in the 2012 book-length essay *The Gentrification of the Mind* that 'AIDS and gentrification have stripped away the context' of Kathy's memory, a violence that also manifested in the erasure, as well as fetishisation, or pathologisation, of her clothed body in published writings 'on' or 'about' her that emerged during her lifetime and after her death.[71]

And yet, rather than committing to a diagnostic pathway of paranoid exposure, I continue to make excess room for erotic speculation, cross-temporal corporeal intimacy, and *writer-to-writer love,* to articulate both sickness and pleasure.[72] This reparative methodology, which writes close to clothed skin, crosses bodies and time in a similar way to Sedgwick's 'Memorial for Craig Owens', which declares their relation a 'fairly strange – *not* to say rare – form of love, the love of part-objects and snatches of print, glimpses and touches of a largely unfamiliar body', following his death from AIDS-related illness in 1990. No less 'real' than romantic love, it is 'love at a distance, or even just reading and writing', a space in which the physical and affective 'touch' of the essay brings the living into closer contact with the dead in a queer gesture of love.[73] Jane Gallop has described Sedgwick's address as justifiably 'indecent', recognising how, in the context of AIDS, 'Queer theory in the early nineties was energized – and politically justified – by the embrace of precisely such indecencies.'[74] I am writing in a different time, a different place, *to* and *with* a different sick body – who once also nearly braved a public announcement of grief in the form of a love letter (to her close friend, the photographer Robert Mapplethorpe, following his death from AIDS-related illness)[75] – but the risk with which she opened and performed the fraying boundaries of her desire and disease deserves a similarly illicit response. To write close to clothed skin – *with love* – is to pick and rub and speculate how far the sick energies of her clothing stretched.

When Kathy first arrived in London in early 1984, it did not take long for the British press to want her, *eat* her – with her cartoon costumes and outlandish display that collaged lace, leather, leopard print, and Lycra (more easily funded after she received a large lump-sum inheritance upon her grandmother's death, gifting her the freedoms of financial privilege).[76] She wears a stretchy black jumpsuit, its front cut away to reveal her then round breasts, in a portrait taken by Mapplethorpe in 1983. The picture likely stems from a shoot at his West 23rd Street studio that was documented in an episode of *The South Bank Show* dedicated to her life and work. Pausing from her pose, she tells the interviewer that the relationship to the camera (which I take to mean clothing too) is not so far removed from 'the same sort of play I do in my writing with identity . . . because an image is rigidity, and I'm always interested in seeing an image being able to fluctuate to another identity. Or an identity fluctuate to another identity. And this is one way I do it.'[77] She performs such fluctuations in *Great Expectations* when she stitches together the plagiarised opening from Dickens's famous *Bildungsroman* alongside the real-time, autobiographical placement of her mother's suicide and grandmother's death, producing a shifting, schizophrenic, and intertextual "I".[78] When *The South Bank Show* episode was screened on British television sets a year later, she was no longer living in the Lower East Side loft it documents, but hopping between friends' houses in London, basking in the warmth of a rapidly increasing media profile. Indeed, while she still published with more intellectual journals such as New York's *Wedge*, alongside the novel-experiments,[79] she could now be found in music and fashion magazines, like *NME* and *Blitz*, where she wrote in 1985 that: 'In New York there's a kind of . . . community agreement about who's out and who's in . . . But here it's very different, you can be trendy at one point, and then you're not.' 'THIS IS HYPE CITY!' she warns, 'HOW YOU DRESS IS HOW YOU ARE!'[80]

Made visible by the hype city, Kathy was also *hystericised* by it, like the photographed subjects of Jean-Martin Charcot's 'living museum of pathology' living centuries apart from her.[81] She too suffered from the fetishising, pathologising effects of the representational image that Peggy Phelan challenges in *Unmarked: The Politics of Performance*. 'This fetishization of the image', writes Phelan, 'is the risk of representational visibility for women. It secures the gap between the real and the representational and marks her as Other.'[82] Kathy alluded to the violence of this image *marking* while speaking to Sylvère Lotringer in 1991: 'In England it was absolutely horrible . . . the media image is so much of this kind of sexual image. I'm very well-known there and I get tons of work, but to say that they like what I do, no, I wouldn't say that. They fetishize what I do.'[83] And this fetishisation also occurred in obituaries after her death. In *The New York Times*, a tone of ridicule teetering on misogyny inflected the frame of mourning, with notable space given to her punk image: 'Ms. Acker cut a well-known figure in the East Village scene of the '80s, favouring leather clothes, spiky hair styles, red lipstick and stiletto heels.'[84] Schulman writes that this is 'how the diminishment process works', transforming her into an 'object of mockery'.[85] Even Gary Indiana, a close friend of Kathy's and a former collaborator, claimed in a *London Review of Books* essay that 'she had the cachet of a fetish object and did her best to look like one', suggesting that she was complicit in her own victimisation-*as*-fetish.[86] But focusing as it does on appearance, rather than authorship, Indiana's reading of the role she played in her own self-fashioning does not quite tease out the ways she was always subject *and* object in her performance of clothes *and* clothing (noun and verb: like *practice*).

She wove her *sartorial image like text.*

What, then, if I were to think of the subject/object crossings interlaced within the meaning of 'Kathy' in similar ways to the ancient poet 'Sappho': as a visual *and* verbal 'set of texts', as Page duBois writes in *Sappho is Burning*, 'gathered in her name'?[87] Sappho's fragmentary corpus, which Kathy later imitated in her initial comings to writing,[88] makes impossible the task of ever knowing her completely: her words, her body, her translations, have been scattered and crushed (often fetishised) across time and history. And within these first-person fragments, boundaries are consistently blurred between subject and object, love and hate, pleasure and pain, straight and queer, disrupting, in an ancient echo of Kathy, 'various paradigms of Western civilization'.[89] Thinking with this body-in-pieces, duBois invites a relationship to the past and its fragments that does not 'focus on the restoration of lost wholes, or even on the tragic impossibility of the reconstitution', but rather to 'read what we have', to dream and desire and speculate these fragments reparatively anew.[90]

Michael Ann Holly calls this (in dialogue with the object-relations theory of Melanie Klein, which Sedgwick's own affective and queer vision of the reparative also speaks from) the melancholic impulse of art-historical writing. 'We cannot let the life of these lonely works of art [*or sartorial image-texts*] entirely disappear', writes Holly, before adding: 'If this is pathological, so be it; if it is symptomatic of melancholy rather than mourning, it is nevertheless the only romantic, reparative act in which caretakers can engage . . .'[91] 'Simultaneously enlivening and paralysing',[92] the melancholic writer is held by the still-bleeding, open wound of art history, its paradoxical (and often painful) presence and absence, with the process of writing itself becoming 'that act of touching that cannot let go'.[93]

Possessed, decades after her death, I cannot let her stray garments go. I read and write *to* them, and *with* them: closely, affectively, passionately, even *perversely* (absorbing an assemblage of reparative reading strategies hinted at by Sedgwick, namely her references to 'imaginative close reading' and the '"over"-attachment to fragmentary, marginal, waste, or leftover products').[94] And I do this for *Kathy*, the sick woman: it is for her I take this *risk.*[95] I tease at the powers of her erotic, the perverse threads of her sick clothes: the ways they became entangled with her writing as sartorial texts. (A set of texts gathered in her name.)

I match perversion with perversion.
I risk the prick of a needle.
I speculatively repair an erotic afterlife that dwells (non-dualistically) in pleasure as well as sickness.

Confession: I am a melancholic writer, as I get closer to the clothes of the dead

For years now I have been touching and tracing the words in her worn worlds. I have obsessed over her clothes, in life, through writing, and in my dreams. Is this fandom? Or melancholy? Or love? Or could it be all of these perversions at once? 'I can't be normal because I can't stop loving', the words of Don Quixote in Kathy's *Don Quixote* fill my mouth.[96] I have scoured charity shops for leather trousers, lace bodysuits, and velvet trouser-suits, to fantasise our intimate merging, so I can steal in some way closer to the perverse vitalities of her clothing archive, from life to writing and back again.

First, it was the photographs that absorbed my (autoerotic) attentions: the 154 prints of trousers (neon pink and yellow 1991 Versace jeans luridly printed with the Pop Art faces of Marilyn Monroe and Betty Boop); skirts (flared and pleated, schoolgirl minis); dresses (tight bodycon sheaths hugging close to the absent figure or stretchy and mangled full-length gowns); jackets (leather bikers frilled in pink shag fur or blazers with a cut-out torso); two-pieces (top-to-toe sailor smock and bottoms), and shawls (trimmed in tails of fox fur), which were photographed by the artist Kaucyila Brooke soon after Kathy's death and exhibited as a series at the Berlin Biennale in 2004.[97] The series displays a carousel of carnival clothes hanging off metal hangers against a plain white background, suspended, stretched, or contorted by the artist using invisible thread, injecting life and form and energy into them. Slipping between vision and touch, I felt *enveloped* by these documents (which depict only a fragmented selection of the writer's clothing archive, cared for by the executor of her Estate, Matias Viegener). As an object, the photograph articulates a piercing relationship to past lives, and garments do too, with moth-eaten holes, ink stains, and bleached surfaces inscribing temporal passages in materiality itself.[98] I rubbed the images with my eyes, gazed at them through texture, to trace Kathy's lost body-in-pieces, its authorial energies, in Brooke's spectral reanimation of her disembodied things.

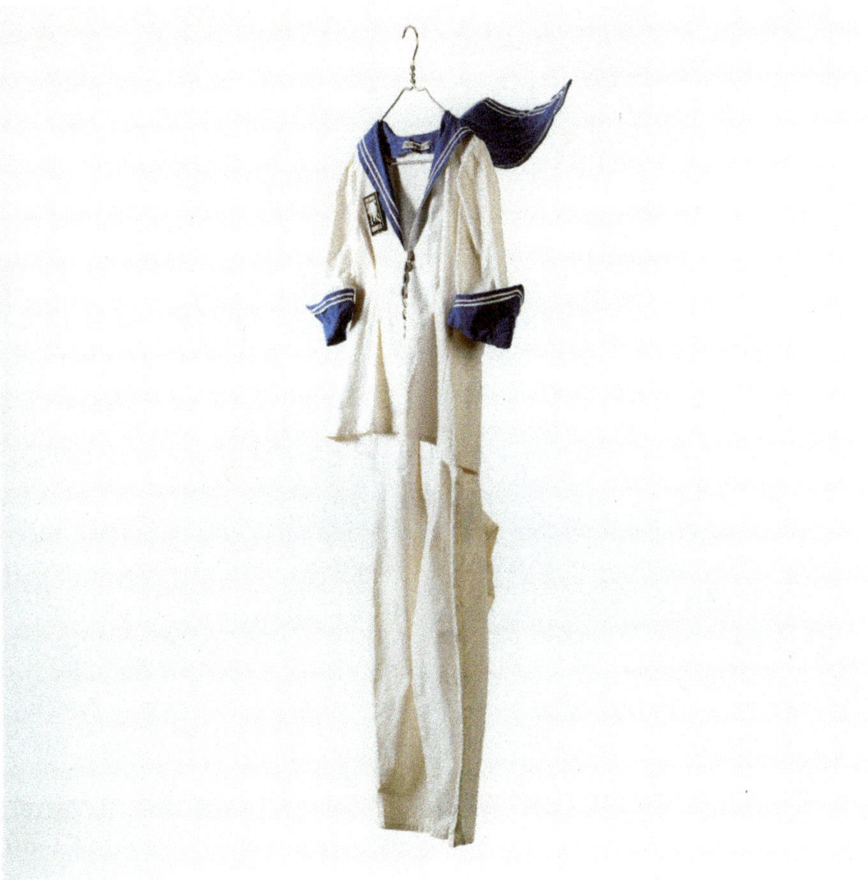

5.2 Kaucyila Brooke, *Untitled 118*, from *Kathy Acker's Clothes, 1998–2004*, colour photograph, 38.1 × 38.1 cm. Reproduced by permission of the artist

The simultaneous presence and absence of her clothed body – in portraits taken by Michel Delsol within an empty penthouse suite of Manhattan's Gramercy Park Hotel and reproduced on the metallic-tinted Grove Press book covers in the 1980s – manipulated this ambivalence further. These beloved part-object paperbacks, 'weird holographic projections' of her name and public persona, lie strewn across my desk, infiltrated with felt-tipped lines and pencilled annotations (messages of correspondence) across the years of my loving her.[99] Silver spine upon silver spine; her creased papers pile up (showing age like a dress) in this intimate, domestic archive gathering pieces of love.

She wears a zipped bodice that hugs her closely at the waist for the front cover of *Great Expectations*, sandwiched by a black lace bra and flared striped skirt. Her hair is shaved neatly, and then gelled at the roots (freshly dyed dirty peroxide). A gigantic diamond earring weighs down one heavily pierced ear. The other lobe is out of shot as she turns her head to the side, eyes averting the photographer's gaze: a pose she replicates, but this time with back turned, for the close-up cover image used for *Don Quixote*. In this cropped picture, her rose-tattooed skin enveloping her body appears to have been cleaved apart with the allusion of torn paper. I catch a glimpse of the author's greyed-out silhouette in severed fragments not wholes, which echoes the strategies developed by Kathy in the novel itself, as stolen texts become intermeshed with autobiographical contexts, producing slippages and disorientations for the reader. Leslie Dick calls this mode of self-presentation, which was expressed in live performances as well as the photographic, a 'threat and a promise' wherein the body was rendered an 'obstacle . . . mediating between the reader and the text'.[100]

In *Don Quixote*, for example, the 'knight-to-be' protagonist of *Don Quixote* is also a 'very sick girl', poised to have an abortion, as Kathy also experienced in 1985.[101] While in hospital, she began reading Cervantes's original text, copying out sections because she 'couldn't think'.[102] It is a process of endurance that opens up a space of feminist rewriting (surprisingly reparative), as the crazy, sick, infected, bedbound, heartbroken, wounded, nymphomaniac, irrational Don Quixote – who aborted her baby as a perverse refusal of 'normalcy, which is the capitulation to social control' – transforms feminised 'sickness into a knightly tool'.[103] Sickness, in this novel, manifests as a wilful turning away from the norm, as a feminist purging and *perverting*: 'swerving rather than straightening, deviating from the right [or expected] course', as Sara Ahmed describes the queer potential of perversion. Ahmed's analysis draws on Sedgwick's etymological analysis of 'queer' as being related to the turning, twisting, transversing, *perverting* associations of the Indo-European word 'twerk', which also echoes the etymological root of 'sick' in 'weak' and its underlying meaning as 'twisted, bent'.[104] The sick emerges as a perverse force, bending things out of place, remaking the world with twisting textures.

Gary Indiana has written that 'Attacking capitalism while dressed in Valentino can look like absurdist theatre', and that Kathy's 'extravagant self-presentation often worked against her'.[105] Of course, it seems fairly apparent, given the extent of the boxes marked 'Acker's

Clothes' (in Kathy's own rounded script) and stored in Viegener's Los Angeles home, that Kathy was a shopaholic: a finding that can produce a destabilising effect.[106] For to go from anti-capitalist writing to the devouring of clothes to the blurred, seemingly contradictory lines of consumption and art-collecting in my getting to know 'her' can feel like falling through a series of 'trapdoors', as Bellamy has also described of Kathy's paradoxical politics and praxis: 'as soon as you think *I'm getting this* the floor drops beneath your feet'.[107] In an interview with Rosemary Bailey in 1984, Kathy gave some reasoning to her purchases: 'Street fashion is where the art is for poor people. I can't afford to buy a painting so if I get some money I go buy a dress.'[108] And in the process, the (hardly 'street fashion') designer garments piled up (thanks to her inheritance): Comme des Garçons, Jean-Paul Gaultier, Betsey Johnson, and Vivienne Westwood.

Rather than attempt to unpick these paradoxes, I am thinking with the *excess* in those stacks, the boxes that she carried and the boxes that remain. Could her addiction to clothing, I gesture, also make her another iteration of *a very sick girl* – a girl made sick by capitalism and its feminising effects – suffering from the pathological impulse to collect and buy, maybe even to thieve?[109] Critics have provided their own case histories, echoing the nineteenth-century gendering of women's object veneration as disorder or disease.[110] But following Emily Apter's feminist rereading of sexual fetishism – which seeks to destabilise the line between feminine pathology (as sickness) and male perversion (as agency), and instead revise such practices that depend on the touching, collecting, and thieving of corporeal objects and sartorial things as 'the semiosis of a subversively erotic practice, thoroughly "perverse" in its own terms'[111] – I am speculating an alternative afterlife. I encounter desire, imagination, wilfulness, and waywardness in her sick clothes. She is a perverse clothing fetishist (I am turning Freud's use of this term inside out, echoing Apter):[112] tantalised by velvet, and with a serpent round her neck. Writhing, desiring, *re-birthing*.

When I saw her Westwood pirate jacket hanging on a domestic wooden hanger at an exhibition of her writings, objects, and artworks,[113] I danced around its polymorphous shape, tried to enter her (however dangerous or deviant this felt; my loving her this way). As Roland Barthes writes in *A Lover's Discourse:*

> I must resemble whom I love . . . I want to be the other, I want the other to be me, as if we were united, enclosed within the same sack

> of skin, the garment being the smooth envelope of that coalescent substance out of which my amorous Image-repertoire is made.[114]

I tried to meet her within that ghostly envelope, which was far from smooth: its vertical lines of white stitching upon admiral-navy cloth interrupted by tucks and gatherings at the chest and shoulders. 'I always wanted to be a sailor,' said Kathy, 'to wander' in 'wonder'.[115] These words pulsed in and around those stitches, reminding me of the ways she waywardly wandered in her writings through texts and worlds, sexualities and genders. I peered around the garment's jagged corners, like a 'pirate' happening upon 'buried treasure. The dreamer, the dreaming, the dream.'[116] I inched closer to her disembodied rags. My eyes darted along the sinuous lines of the wrinkles at her elbows ('wrinkles that in the technical jargon of sewing are called memory').[117] Then, crossing between the senses in this middle ground of agency, I reached my hand out – to this archived piece of her body – in a spontaneous gesture of touching desire. I fantasised us seizing one another down the dark tunnels of the jacket's interior: a greeting and a farewell combined.[118] Before I physically left the jacket (suspended in space; swinging through time), I attempted to catch the flavour of her smell, the ancient vapours of sweat stuck to the item's browned insides overlaid with a yellow-on-red Westwood label. Gigantic, she becomes waste: a 'second grave for the loved being',[119] which comes alive differently again (that is melancholy) in my writing her here.

I climb inside the perversity of her envelopes.

Picking perversion from the grave, and the visceral textures of her kleptomaniac close writing

Kathy wears slippery leather – that most fetishistic of fabrics – in an author portrait taken by Kate Simon in 1987.[120] As a long-sleeved dress, it falls at her bent knees. She balances on the back of a wooden chair, wearing worn pixie boots. A plastic Casio watch around her right wrist, a brass cuff around her left, a dropped earring, and another snake necklace taking form as a rope of unbejewelled metal are the other sartorial details of the picture. It was commissioned and circulated to coincide with the publication of her novel *Don Quixote*, which makes her pose – a riff on Rodin's bronze sculpture that is symptomatic of interiority, enlightenment, and intellectual genius, *The Thinker* – more complex in its playfulness, as the second part of the book begins: 'BEING DEAD, DON QUIXOTE COULD NO LONGER SPEAK. BEING BORN INTO AND PART OF A MALE WORLD, SHE HAD NO SPEECH OF HER OWN. ALL SHE COULD DO WAS READ MALE TEXTS WHICH WEREN'T HERS.'[121] In the process, they become hers/Don Quixote's (the boundaries blur) in a perverse act of possession.[122] Don Quixote's quest for love is also a quest for writing, which happens through reading ('to write is to read', the author essayed elsewhere)[123] – through copying and *stealing*. The novel was Kathy's attempt, she often said, to do a 'Sherrie Levine painting' in prose, in a nod to the artist's photographed reproductions of Walker Evans portraits.[124]

I turn again to the leather portrait; see alchemy in Kathy's necklace-rubbing gesture: the possession, then transformation, of canonical male texts that do not officially, or legally, belong to her/ Don Quixote. 'My world isn't about ownership', she once said.[125] An inanimate thing, it has animated my imagination.[126]

It is the hand that unleashes such magic. She rubs and rubs and rubs the physical object/text that she venerates in autoerotic pleasure (in a perverse encounter *with* the fetish, not *as* the fetish, reframing the critics' case-noting of her). The clothing fetishists that populate Gaétan Gatian de Clérambault's 1910 psychiatric case histories of female kleptomaniac patients were judged by their doctor as being 'passive in their [*masturbatory*] contact with silk' – the stolen object of their desires.[127] By contrast, when referring to male perverts' onanism, de Clérambault described it as an act of imagination and creativity: 'throughout masturbation with the fetish they project splendid scenes'.[128] Kathy's clothing fetishism, I argue, offers a way out of this gender bias: it projects its own splendid scenes, which hint at the creative agencies and desires of her sick absorption of clothes, as well as the role kleptomania itself plays in her writing practice. At the time of its medicalisation in the nineteenth-century, kleptomania was understood, writes the artist Sharon Kivland, as a 'modern and feminine disease, a new neurosis of perverse desire, a sexual disorder at the heart of capitalism'.[129] Revealing how far its codes and conditions pressed into Kathy's present, this echoes Preciado's categorisation of the disease (alongside breast cancer) as one of the many 'semiotechnical codes of white heterosexual femininity belonging to the postwar pharmacopornographic political ecology'.[130] Kivland also draws our attention to the ways hysteria (kleptomania's pathologised kin) was thought to come about by an addiction to novels, to 'improper reading', which veers

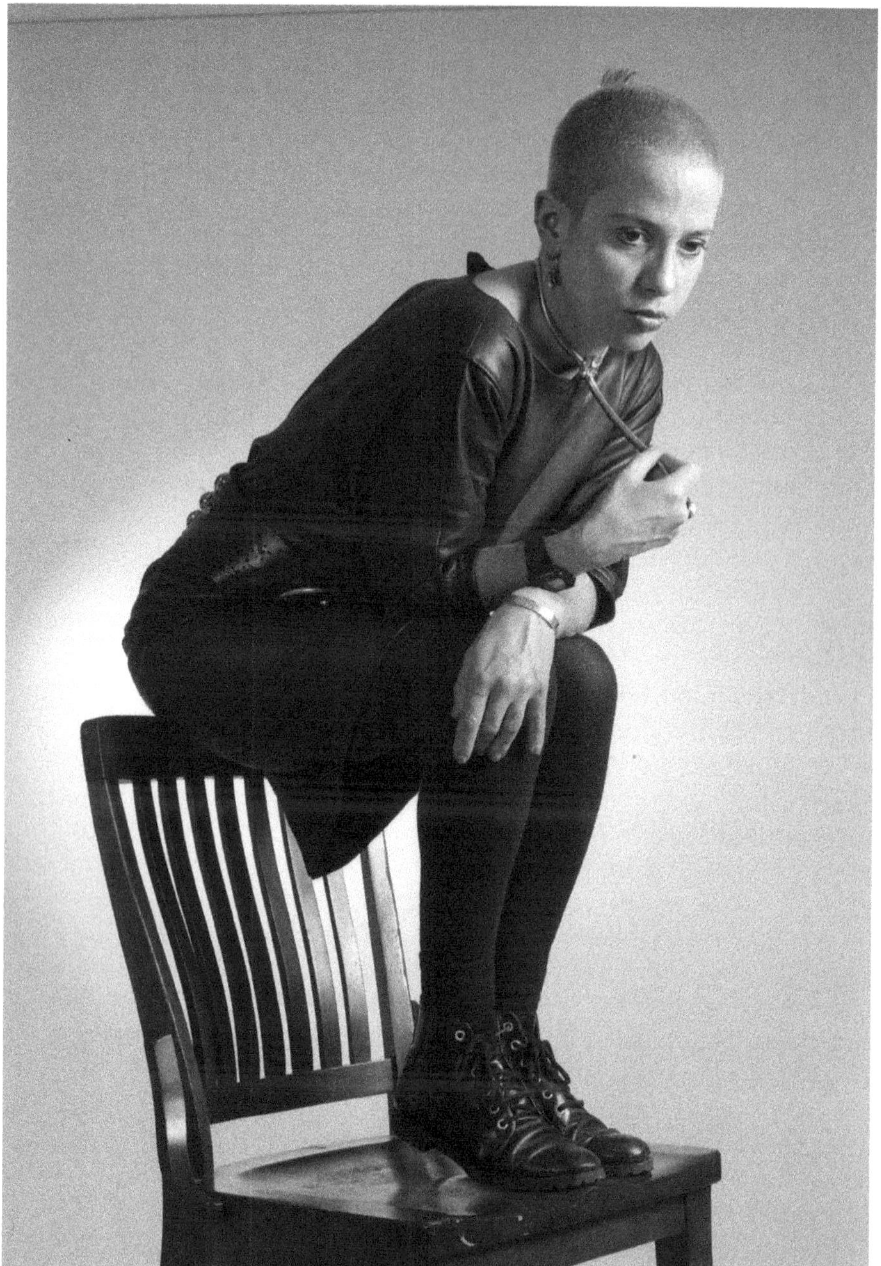

5.3 Kate Simon, *Kathy Acker, NYC, 1987*, 1987, silver gelatin print, 20.3 × 25.4 cm. Photo © Kate Simon. Reproduced by permission of the artist

on autoerotic.[131] Kathy was shamed (even forced to publicly apologise) for such practices,[132] for her 'indecent' unravelling of literary property, of texts that on paper were not her 'own'. Manifesting in what I term her *kleptomaniac close writing*,[133] this is an anti-capitalist, anti-patriarchal gesture (as she writes in the 1989 essay, 'Nobody *really* owns anything. Dead men don't fuck'),[134] which also connects with the perverse as a wandering from the law.

Kathy described her radical approach of stealing, collaging, and rewriting texts as being rooted in the 'tactics of guerrilla warfare' and as 'the only possible chance for change, for mobility, for political, economic, and moral flow' in the postmodern age of late capitalism.[135] It was a deconstructive assault on the structures, strictures, and singularities of originality and identity – how each self, as well as each text, is a composite of overlapping threads. Such tactics have been more commonly read as representative of a paranoid reading of existing texts through suspicious acts of plagiarism.[136]

I, however, have picked perversion from her sartorial grave, its kleptomaniac textures and reparative desires. She is a kleptomaniac in clothing and writing (and clothing *as* writing). To newly consider her erotic work through this term is to signal the specificities of a practice of theft that is intimately entangled with the perverse pleasures of her own sexual (and sick) lives, as the materials of stolen text and intimate life matter meet viscerally at the cut-up, close edges of her writing. She steals with the perverse desire of a literary kleptomaniac, to pervert and transform the stolen text. This kleptomaniac close writing, therefore, also highlights the ways writing this way – cutting, copying, *weaving*: using haptic techniques like textiles – is full of autoerotic, bodily sensations. The critics' case histories dismissed her for raising 'literary masturbation to an anti-art form', to quote from a review of her 1996 novel *Pussy King of the Pirates*.[137] But for Kathy, the bodily erotics of masturbating and writing were closely related, as when she breaks into a series of notational inscriptions formed while 'moving through orgasm or orgasms' in her analysis of bodily languages in the essay 'Seeing Gender'.[138] It is a perverse writing of pleasure that deviates from the aim of heterosexual, genital acts, echoing the queer thrills sought by the kleptomaniacs who had come before her. To emphasise the kleptomaniac qualities of her practice is thus also to place her work in a cross-historical legacy of sick women with perverse, political agency.

Their perverse desire is often haptic, as they pilfer silk, or swatches of poems, or even love letters (one of the sentimental fetish objects recognised by Apter as being preserved by women in 'lugubrious' nineteenth-century practices of keepsake preservation and manic collecting).[139] Snippets of poetry or letters are purloined by Kathy's hand in *Don Quixote*. In the second piece of the novel's second section that is interwoven with stolen revisions, Kathy interrupts a Latin poem by Catullus with epistolary insertions, embroidering perverse desire into the text and shocking it into transmission. She forms a correspondence with Catullus's poem that is sexual, even masochistic, as she pierces the other's text, places her body in between its clauses. To cite: 'fulsere quondam candidi tibi soles, / cum it hurts me to remember I / did act up today, a way of / saying "I'm not perfect," / forgive my phone call'.[140] The effect is a raw ripping open of desire and text – a splintering of the original – which brings it into a *closer* autoerotic relation with the visceral textures of her own sexual life (her fractured words recall intimate correspondences with another, later named more directly as 'Peter', when she places in parentheses within the Latin: '(My awful telephone call. This is my apology, Peter. Do you accept?)').[141]

The autobiographical matter becomes for Kathy another stolen text, with the spectre of 'Peter' a likely mutation of Peter Wollen, the British filmmaker and critical theorist, who Kathy engaged in an epistolary and real-life love affair in 1983, before she twisted and re-enacted those letters in novelistic performance. In the preceding part, Kathy's autoerotic attentions produce a frantic exchange between the stolen object (transcriptions of Andrei Bely's 1913 novel *Petersburg*) and the direct specificity of her own desires as expressed in self-stealing, purloined letters.[142] Bely's text is placed into close contact with her own abject writing: epistles that begin directly 'Dear Peter' and contain within them perverse declarations of lovesickness ('If I see you, I'll want you. If I don't see you, I'll die') and masochistic outpourings ('I can't stand living without you. I hate this day after day constant waiting-for-you: you're not here: all my hours spent in longing for what's not here').[143] She performs the lovesick condition *to excess,* subverting and perverting psychiatric histories of lovesickness that categorise it as a feminine neurosis triggered by diseased convulsions in the womb (this echoes the sexist diagnoses attached to kleptomaniacs and hysterics of the past). Kathy's lovesick letter-writing comprises repetitions and distractions that suggest disorderly autoerotic attentions, where she writes 'to Peter' but always in relation to herself, between 'You' and 'I', constructing a rhythm that appears to build to the crescendo of climax where pleasure merges with pain. 'You are my madness', she writes, 'Come in me, my madness.'[144]

Sickness and sexual fantasy intertwine in Kathy's 'autoerotic life' in letters; hers is a perverse coming that is conjured by the *absence* of a body.[145] She deviates from the promise of union to waywardly wander in the pleasures of writing. The letter is a promise when other forms of communication fail, as she repeats verbatim in another lovesick message: 'I can't say over the telephone what I want to say to you: "Please touch your cock because I can't touch your cock now and I have to touch your cock."'[146] The telephone fails, but the direct address and intimacy of the letter facilitates a sexual finding and perverse fantasy. Kathy's kleptomaniac close writing involves two acts of stealing: from the patriarchal domain of literature and from the visceral textures of her written life. It is by weaving the two together, I propose, that the paranoid violence of her deconstructive desire to read and copy 'male texts which weren't hers' slips away to make room for a reparative revisioning of female desire – where the 'sick' impulses of the pathologised are re-owned and reshaped by Kathy in autoerotic, epistolary excess. The purloined letter containing visceral *traces* of her own life transforms the literature it closely rubs up against, revealing the abject, difficult, complex, and contradictory angles of female perversion. For a writer who claimed to have no imagination in the urge to destroy language, a surprising act of care emerges for the sick woman in all her many guises.

RSVP: I tear the envelope open

She pilfered, and then stuffed, perverse letters of desire and care within the *envelope* of her kleptomaniac close writing. It is an enclosure where text and body touch. It is a wrap for her stolen words. It is a covert embrace, like the words stitched into the clothing that covered her. Like the object of the envelope – be it a container for writing, or a garment, or even the body itself – kleptomania itself is rooted, etymologically speaking, in secrecy and concealment. It is linked to the Greek *kleptein,* meaning 'to steal, act secretly', which comes from the Proto-Indian European **klep-* that denotes the verb 'to steal'. This is both an extension of its root **kel-*, meaning 'to cover, conceal', and similar to the Latin *clepere,* meaning to 'listen secretly to'.[147] In this, my return-to-sender envelope-as-essay (which has caressed my skin, like cloth), I have speculated a similar space of erotic proximity, to move dangerously closer to (like a kleptomaniac dancing through the shadows) Kathy's set of texts gathered in her name. From sick clothes to sartorial texts to close writing, I have been enveloped by her objects in a melancholic haunting that gives way to an afterlife.

But rather than seal the envelope, I open it (traversing the always belated 'cut between past and present').[148] I open it as a gesture of care, for her, the sick woman weaving and writing perversion. I have touched her, and she has touched me, and we have touched the open mesh: of life, death, desire, and writing.

RSVP

Notes

1 Kathy Acker cited in Sylvére Lotringer, 'Devoured by Myths: An Interview with Sylvére Lotringer', in Kathy Acker, *Hannibal Lecter, My Father* (New York: Semiotext(e) Native Agents Series, 1991), p. 3. Here Acker describes how her interest in 'intention' and 'methodologies' came from her alignment with the poet David Antin and conceptual art.

2 Kathy Acker, *Don Quixote, which was a dream* (New York: Grove Press, 1986), p. 9.

3 Sara Ahmed, *Queer Phenomenology: Orientations, Objects, Others* (Durham, NC and London: Duke University Press, 2006), p. 78.

4 Chris Kraus, *After Kathy Acker: A Biography* (London: Allen Lane, 2017), p. 45. Kraus refers to the ways a young Acker often 'baked bread, designed and sewed her own clothes' in the slow summer months in San Diego after she finished her degree in May 1968. I speculate that her skills as a seamstress never left her.

5 Kathy Acker cited in Kraus, *After Kathy Acker*, p. 214, emphasis added.

6 Acker, cited in Lotringer, 'Devoured by Myths', p. 20. Acker also acknowledges a performance art context for her early writing and mail-art distribution in Ellen G. Friedman, 'A Conversation with Kathy Acker', *Review of Contemporary Fiction*, 9:3 (Fall 1989), www.dalkeyarchive.com/a-conversation-with-kathy-acker-by-ellen-g-friedman (accessed 21 April 2021).

7 In my understanding of Acker's writing 'as' performance, I am indebted to the work of Della Pollock in the essay 'Performing Writing', in Peggy Phelan and Jill Lane (eds), *The Ends of Performance* (New York and London: New York University Press, 1998), pp. 73–103.

8 Dodie Bellamy, 'Digging through Kathy Acker's Stuff', in *When the Sick Rule the World* (South Pasadena, CA: Semiotext(e) Active Agents Series, 2015), p. 140. Bellamy notes the influence of Acker's work on her epistolary novel-in-fragments, *The Letters of Mina Harker* ('Inspired

by Kathy, in it I stole from anything and everything that crossed my path' [p. 128]), which also emerged in an early letter-essay by Bellamy to Acker; see 'Delinquent', in *Pink Steam* (San Francisco: Suspect Thoughts Press, 2004), pp. 134–141.

9 Eve Kosofsky Sedgwick, 'Foreword: T Times', in *Tendencies* (Durham, NC and London: Duke University Press, 1993), p. xii.

10 See Eve Kosofsky Sedgwick, *Touching Feeling: Affect, Pedagogy, Performativity* (Durham, NC and London: Duke University Press, 2003) and Jonathan Goldberg (ed.), *The Weather in Proust* (Durham, NC and London: Duke University Press, 2011).

11 Eve Kosofsky Sedgwick, 'Come As You Are', in Jonathan Goldberg, *Come As You Are: After Eve Kosofsky Sedgwick* (Goleta, CA: dead letter office, BABEL Working Group, an imprint of punctum books, 2021), p. 111.

12 Eve Kosofsky Sedgwick, 'White Glasses', in *Tendencies*, p. 257.

13 Eve Kosofsky Sedgwick, 'Queer and Now', in *Tendencies*, p. 13. For a further discussion of Sedgwick's theories and practices in the context of the 'woven', see Katy Hawkins, 'Woven Spaces: Eve Kosofsky Sedgwick's *Dialogue on Love*', *Women & Performance: a journal of feminist theory*, 16:2 (2006), 251–267.

14 Johanna Hedva, 'Sick Woman Theory', *Mask Magazine*, 24 (January 2016), www.maskmagazine.com/not-again/struggle/sick-woman-theory (accessed 22 April 2021).

15 For Sedgwick's reading of 'divinity' as a state of defiance and abjection shared by overweight women and gay men, see Michael Moon and Eve Kosofsky Sedgwick, 'Divinity: A Dossier A Performance Piece A Little-Understood Emotion', *Discourse*, 13:1 (Fall–Winter 1990–1991), 12–39.

16 In the essay 'The Gift of Disease', Acker refers to statistics determining that 'one out of every seven women' are being diagnosed with breast cancer in the Bay Area, and there has been no media outcry; while Audre Lorde, writing earlier in 1979, asserts that 'we cannot afford to look the other way, nor to consider the incidence of breast cancer as a private or personal problem. It is no secret that breast cancer is on the rise among women in America'. Lorde also analyses the intersectional impacts of this rise, highlighting deteriorating mortality rates 'if you are poor, or Black, or in any other way part of the underside of this society'. See Acker, 'The Gift of Disease', *Guardian*, 18 January 1997; and Lorde, *The Cancer Journals* (London: Penguin Classics, 2020), p. 54.

17 Acker, 'Gift of Disease'.

18 Acker, 'Gift of Disease'.

19 Lauren Berlant, 'The Undying', *4Columns*, 9 June 2019, www.4columns.org/berlant-lauren/the-undying (accessed 22 April 2021).

20 My understanding of reparative sentiment and paranoid exposure comes from Sedgwick's theorisation of reparative and paranoid reading strategies, in which reparative stances are defined by affective motives to love, to repair, to 'assemble and confer plenitude', while paranoid stances are defined by the suspicious urge to expose and anticipate hidden violences. See 'Paranoid Reading and Reparative Reading, or, You're So Paranoid, You Probably Think This Essay Is About You', in *Touching Feeling*, pp. 123–151.
21 Acker, 'Gift of Disease'.
22 Acker, 'Gift of Disease'.
23 Acker, 'Gift of Disease'.
24 Hedva, 'Sick Woman Theory'.
25 Ahmed, *Queer Phenomenology*, p. 78.
26 Ahmed, *Queer Phenomenology*, p. 78.
27 Acker, 'Gift of Disease'.
28 Ahmed, *Queer Phenomenology*, p. 78.
29 Anne Boyer, *The Undying: A Meditation on Modern Illness* (London: Allen Lane, 2019), chapter 3.
30 For Sedgwick's discussion of 'beside' as a non-dualistic critical practice of 'spatial positionality', see 'Introduction', in *Touching Feeling*, pp. 8–9. Sedgwick's proposition of beside – insofar as it allows a 'number of elements' to 'lie alongside one another, though not an infinity of them' – connects with the book's broader discussions of haptic perception and texture, implied by the textile artist Judith Scott's sculptural bundle of yarns that provides the book its frontispiece.
31 Acker, 'Gift of Disease'.
32 Sedgwick, 'Reality and Realization', in *Weather in Proust*, p. 208.
33 Sedgwick, 'Reality and Realization', p. 214.
34 Sedgwick, 'Introduction', p. 8.
35 Sedgwick, 'Making Things, Practicing Emptiness', in *Weather in Proust*, pp. 70–71.
36 Jason Edwards, 'For Beauty is a Series of Hypotheses? Sedgwick as a Fiber Artist', in Lauren Berlant (ed.), *Reading Sedgwick* (Durham, NC and London: Duke University Press, 2019), p. 74.
37 Sedgwick, 'Queer and Now', p. 8.
38 Edwards, 'For Beauty is a Series of Hypotheses?', pp. 76–77.
39 Sedgwick, 'Making Things, Practicing Emptiness', p. 79.
40 Email correspondence with Del LaGrace Volcano, April 2023.
41 Del LaGrace Volcano cited in Edward Siddons, 'Del LaGrace Volcano's best photograph: my blue mascara masculinity', *Guardian*, 15 August 2019, www.theguardian.com/artanddesign/2019/aug/15/del-lagrace-volcano-best-photograph-between-genders (accessed 22 April 2021).
42 Sedgwick, 'White Glasses', p. 263, p. 256.

43 Sedgwick, 'White Glasses', p. 261.
44 My understanding of the (once pathologised) autoerotic as queer is informed by Sedgwick's essay, 'Jane Austen and the Masturbating Girl', in *Tendencies*, pp. 109–129.
45 Acker, 'Gift of Disease'.
46 Acker, 'Gift of Disease'.
47 Paul B. Preciado, *Testo Junkie: Sex, Drugs, and Biopolitics in the Pharmacopornographic Era* (New York: Feminist Press at the City University of New York, 2013), p. 69.
48 Preciado, *Testo Junkie*, p. 75.
49 In 'Jane Austen and the Masturbating Girl', Sedgwick writes: 'The identity of the masturbator was only one of the sexual identities subsumed, erased, or overridden in this triumph of the heterosexist homo/hetero calculus. But I want to argue here that the status of the masturbator among these many identities was uniquely formative', p. 117.
50 Sedgwick, *A Dialogue on Love* (Boston, MA: Beacon Press, 1999), pp. 45–48.
51 Sedgwick, *A Dialogue on Love*, p. 47.
52 Sedgwick, *A Dialogue on Love*, p. 48.
53 Sedgwick, 'Introduction', p. 24. The book's frontispiece picture of disabled textiles artist Judith Scott conveys, for Sedgwick, 'an affective and aesthetic fullness that can attach even to experiences of cognitive frustration'. It is this complex 'fullness' that Sedgwick writes *into* and *with*.
54 Acker, 'Gift of Disease'.
55 Lorde, *Cancer Journals*, p. 5.
56 Sedgwick, 'Come As You Are', p. 110.
57 Lorde, *Cancer Journals*, p. 8.
58 Acker, 'Gift of Disease'.
59 Acker's 'The Gift of Disease' ring-bound notebooks and typescripts are contained in Box 20, Folder 4 of the Kathy Acker Papers, David M. Rubenstein Rare Book & Manuscript Library, Duke University. An early version of the essay in annotated typescript form is titled, 'On My Healing'.
60 Audre Lorde, 'Uses of the Erotic: The Erotic as Power', in *Your Silence Will Not Protect You* (London: Silver Press, 2017), p. 30, p. 25, p. 30.
61 Lorde, 'Uses of the Erotic', p. 26.
62 Jane Bennett, *Lively Matter: A Political Ecology of Things* (Durham, NC and London: Duke University Press, 2010), p. ix.
63 Acker, 'Gift of Disease'.
64 Sara Ahmed, *Willful Subjects* (Durham, NC and London: Duke University Press, 2014), p. 12.
65 Boyer, *Undying*, chapter 9.

66 Acker, 'Gift of Disease'.
67 Sedgwick, *A Dialogue on Love*, p. 7.
68 Sedgwick, 'Paranoid Reading and Reparative Reading', p. 128, p. 137, p. 128, emphasis added.
69 Sedgwick, 'Paranoid Reading and Reparative Reading', pp. 150–151. Since the essay begins with Sedgwick reflecting on a conversation with a friend and AIDS activist scholar, Cindy Patton, about the origins of the virus, the vulnerable self or community as a 'sick', vulnerable self or community is implied at the essay's close.
70 As well as the essay's opening remembered conversation, Sedgwick also refers to 'the brutal foreshortening of so many queer life spans' through AIDS, and her own specific experiences of 'living with advanced breast cancer', which have 'deroutinized' '"normal" generational narrative[s]'. Sedgwick, 'Paranoid Reading and Reparative Reading', pp. 148–149.
71 Sarah Schulman, *The Gentrification of the Mind: Witness to a Lost Imagination* (Berkeley and Los Angeles, CA and London: University of California Press, 2012), pp. 7–73.
72 For an expanded discussion of sickness and pleasure, see Alice Butler and Gemma Blackshaw, 'Sick Women Correspondents: Practices of Care in Cross-historical Love Letter Writing', *MAI: Feminism and Visual Culture*, 10 (Spring 2023), https://maifeminism.com/sick-women-correspondents-practices-of-care-in-cross-historical-love-letter-writing/ (accessed 2 May 2023).
73 Sedgwick, 'Memorial for Craig Owens', in *Tendencies*, p. 104.
74 Jane Gallop, 'The Queer Temporality of Writing', in *The Deaths of the Author: Reading and Writing in Time* (Durham, NC and London: Duke University Press, 2011), p. 88.
75 Acker, 'Epitaph: Kathy Acker on Robert Mapplethorpe', *The Face*, 2:8 (May 1989), 36.
76 See Kraus, *After Kathy Acker*, p. 181.
77 Acker speaking on *The South Bank Show*, directed by Alan Benson, screened on 1 April 1984 on ITV.
78 See Acker, *Great Expectations* (New York: Grove Weidenfeld, 1983), p. 5.
79 The second edition of *Great Expectations* came out with New York's avant-garde Grove Press in late 1983, before *Blood and Guts in High School* in the spring of 1984, both of which were then published by London's Pan/Picador in a triple volume with *My Death, My Life by Pier Paulo Pasolini*, the book's UK launch dovetailing with Acker's London move.
80 Kathy Acker cited in Mark Issue, 'Blood and Guts in Hype City', *Blitz*, 34 (September 1985), 22.
81 Didi-Huberman, 'The figurative incarnation of the sentence (notes on the "autographic" skin)', cited in Carol Mavor, 'Odor Di Femina:

Though You May Not See Her, You Can Certainly Smell Her', *Cultural Studies*, 12:1 (1998), 56.

82 Peggy Phelan, *Unmarked: The Politics of Performance* (London: Routledge, 1993), p. 6.

83 Acker cited in Sylvère Lotringer, 'Devoured by Myths', p. 20.

84 Rick Lyman, 'Kathy Acker, Novelist and Performance Artist, 53', *The New York Times*, 3 December 1997, www.nytimes.com/1997/12/03/arts/kathy-acker-novelist-and-performance-artist-53.html (accessed 22 April 2021).

85 Schulman, *Gentrification of the Mind*, p. 54, p. 76.

86 Gary Indiana, 'Ackerville', *London Review of Books*, 14 December 2006, www.lrb.co.uk/the-paper/v28/n24/gary-indiana/ackerville (accessed 22 April 2021).

87 Page duBois, *Sappho is Burning* (Chicago, IL: University of Chicago Press, 1995), p. 3.

88 McKenzie Wark's review of the *Kathy Acker: Get Rid of Meaning* exhibition at Badischer Kunstverein in Karlsruhe, Germany (5 October–2 December 2018) supports this. After hearing Acker's biographer, Jason McBride, give a reading of his in-progress work at the exhibition's symposium, Wark proffers that the young Acker was 'writing Sappho imitations', along with 'taking cinema courses, shoplifting books, but was not all that political'. See McKenzie Wark, 'Kathy Acker: *Get Rid of Meaning*', review of *Kathy Acker: Get Rid of Meaning*, *The Brooklyn Rail*, 5 February 2019, https://brooklynrail.org/2019/02/artseen/Kathy-Acker-Get-Rid-of-Meaning (accessed 13 March 2019). For more on the rehabilitation of Sappho in Acker's novels, see Katherine Wasdin, 'The undead past in Kathy Acker's *Blood and Guts in High School*', *Classical Receptions Journal*, 9:2 (2017), 268–286.

89 duBois, *Sappho is Burning*, p. 25.

90 duBois, *Sappho is Burning*, p. 64.

91 Michael Ann Holly, *The Melancholy Art* (Princeton, NH and Oxford: Princeton University Press, 2013), p. 21, emphasis added.

92 Michael Ann Holly, *Melancholy Art*, p. 6.

93 Michael Ann Holly, *Melancholy Art*, p. 23.

94 Sedgwick, 'Paranoid Reading and Reparative Reading', p. 145, p. 150. Here I am also departing from Meridith Kruse's analysis of Sedgwick's 'perverse close reading' in 'Sedgwick's Perverse Close Reading and the Question of an Erotic Ethics', in *Reading Sedgwick*, pp. 132–140.

95 'Risk' is often involved in reparative methods, suggests Sedgwick, who describes, in dialogue with Melanie Klein, the shift towards 'a sustained *seeking of pleasure* (through the reparative strategies of the depressive position)' as a 'distinct, often risky positional shift' away

from the 'self-defeating strategies for *forestalling pain* offered by the paranoid/schizoid position'. Then, later in the essay, she reinforces how the reparative position 'undertakes a different range of affects, ambitions, and risks'. See 'Paranoid Reading and Reparative Reading', p. 137, 150.

96 Acker, *Don Quixote*, p. 33.

97 See Kaucyila Brooke, 'Kathy Acker's Clothes', *Art Journal*, 72:2 (2013), 104–105.

98 For more on this relationship, see Carol Mavor, 'Collecting Loss: Photographs, Dresses, "Paperies"', *Counterpoints*, 220 (2004), 15–38.

99 Sedgwick, 'Memorial for Craig Owens', p. 104.

100 Leslie Dick, 'Seventeen Paragraphs on Kathy Acker', in *Lust for Life: On the Writings of Kathy Acker* (London: Verso, 2006), p. 112.

101 Acker, *Don Quixote*, p. 16.

102 Kathy Acker cited in Ellen G. Friedman, 'A Conversation with Kathy Acker'.

103 Acker, *Don Quixote*, pp. 17–18.

104 Ahmed, *Willful Subjects*, p. 11. 'sick (adj.)', *Online Etymology Dictionary*, www.etymonline.com/word/sick#etymonline_v_23485 (accessed 20 October 2022).

105 Indiana, 'Ackerville'.

106 Bellamy, 'Digging through Kathy Acker's Stuff', p. 131, p. 140.

107 Bellamy, 'Digging through Kathy Acker's Stuff', p. 130.

108 Rosemary Bailey, 'The Pornographic Imagination of Kathy Acker', *The Face*, 45 (January 1984), 23.

109 Sharon Kivland, 'EN TOUTE INTIMITÉ', performance-lecture, Freud Museum London, London, 31 May 2019.

110 In such practices as represented by Guy de Maupassant's novelistic fiction (an example of fin-de-siècle modernist writing that 'fused the medical *observation* with the literary chronicle of behavioral aberration'), Emily Apter uncovers 'the outline of a sentimental sickness . . . akin to the great feminine pathologies of the nineteenth century: hysteria, hypochondria, somnambulism, and frigidity'. See *Feminizing the Fetish: Psychoanalysis and Narrative Obsession in Turn-of-the-Century France* (Ithaca, NY and London: Cornell University Press, 1991), p. xi, pp. 100–101.

111 Apter, *Feminizing the Fetish*, p. 106.

112 While Freud patronisingly and universally declared at the Vienna Psychoanalytic Society in 1909 that 'all women . . . are clothes fetishists', Apter delves deeper into the term, in the effort to ground 'a feminist ontology of femininity in the constructions, both erotic and social, of a certain kind of *Verkleidungstrieb* ("will to dress," "sartorial drive") or clothing fetishism (65–66)'. See 'Unmasking the

Masquerade: Fetishism and Femininity from the Goncourt Brothers to Joan Riviere', in *Feminizing the Fetish*, pp. 65–98.

113 *I, I, I, I, I, I, I, Kathy Acker*, Institute of Contemporary Arts, London, 1 May–4 August 2019, was the first UK exhibition dedicated to Acker's work and influence that brought together her documents, recordings, videos, manuscripts, and objects, in dialogue with other artists and writers past and present.

114 Roland Barthes, *A Lover's Discourse: Fragments*, trans. Richard Howard (London: Jonathan Cape, 1979), pp. 127–128.

115 Acker cited in Lotringer, 'Devoured by Myths', p. 23.

116 Kathy Acker, 'Seeing Gender', in *Bodies of Work: Essays* (London: Serpent's Tail, 2006), p. 166.

117 Peter Stallybrass, 'Worn Worlds: Clothing, Mourning and the Life of Things', in Dan Ben-Amos and Liliane Weissberg (eds), *Cultural Memory and the Construction of Identity*, (Detroit, MI: Wayne State University Press, 1999), p. 28.

118 My thinking on the paradoxical presence and absence of Acker in my memorial-writing is informed by Jacques Derrida's short piece, titled 'Adieu', which was delivered at Emmanuel Levinas's funeral in 1995. Derrida writes: 'The greeting of the *à-Dieu* does not signal the end'. See Jacques Derrida, *Adieu to Emmanuel Levinas*, trans Pascale-Anne Brault and Michael Naas (Stanford, CA: Stanford University Press, 1999), p. 13.

119 Roland Barthes, *Camera Lucida: Reflections on Photography*, trans. Richard Howard (New York: Farrar, Straus & Giroux, 1981), p. 64.

120 This photograph was found within the Ira Silverberg Papers, MSS. 110, Box 41, Folder 28, Fales Library and Special Collections, New York University Libraries.

121 Acker, *Don Quixote*, p. 39.

122 Acker cited in Friedman, 'A Conversation with Kathy Acker'. Acker tells Friedman that 'there's a certain amount of ironic distance between me and Don Quixote, a distance that varies'.

123 Acker, 'Reading the Lack of the Body: The Writing of the Marquis de Sade', in *Bodies of Work*, p. 66.

124 Acker in Friedman, 'A Conversation with Kathy Acker'.

125 Acker cited in Lotringer, 'Devoured by Myths', p. 23.

126 This effect is similar to Barthes's writing of the punctum as the partial detail of the photograph that generates an affective response and expansive interpretation. For Barthes also, these details are often sartorial, as his intimate discussion of the 'slender ribbon of braided gold' in a James Van der Zee photograph elucidates. This object cuts Barthes's emotions and memories, reminding him of a relative who once wore a similar item, and who died alone, with no-one to pass on the necklace to, but a 'family box of old jewelry'. *Camera Lucida*, p. 53.

127 Gaétan Gatian de Clérambault cited in Leslie Cahmi, 'Stealing Femininity: Department Store Kleptomania as Sexual Disorder', *differences: A Journal of Feminist Critical Studies*, 5:1 (1993), 41, emphasis added.

128 de Clérambault, cited in Apter, *Feminizing the Fetish*, p. 107.

129 Kivland, 'EN TOUTE INTIMITÉ'.

130 Preciado, *Testo Junkie*, pp. 120–121.

131 Kivland, 'EN TOUTE INTIMITÉ'.

132 This reached an apex with what has been called 'The Harold Robbins Affair'. It was a damaging incident – creatively and personally exposing – that resulted in Acker being forced to write a public apology to the bestselling practitioner of soft erotica, Harold Robbins, for plagiarising several pages of his 1974 novel, *The Pirate*, in her 1975 work *The Adult Life of Toulouse Lautrec by Henri Toulouse Lautrec*. When Fred Jordon, Acker's US editor at Grove Press, found out about the furore, he called Robbins himself, who stressed in response that Acker had his full permission to appropriate from his work, and that to accuse her of plagiarism was shockingly 'ill-informed'. See Kraus, *After Kathy Acker*, pp. 232–235.

133 This builds on previous work around Acker's 'close writing' of autobiographical performance. See Alice Butler, 'Fan Letters of Love', in Catherine Grant and Kate Random Love (eds), *Fandom as Methodology: A Sourcebook for Artists and Writers* (London: Goldsmiths University Press, 2019), pp. 149–164.

134 Acker, 'A Few Notes on Two of My Books', in *Bodies of Work*, p. 10.

135 Acker, 'Postmodernism', in *Bodies of Work*, p. 4.

136 'Plagiarism' is also the title of the first chapter of Acker's *Great Expectations*, which weaves Marcel Proust, Pauline Reage, Pierre Guyotat, Ben Johnson, Propertius, and Dickens together, in an embodied insurrection of the 'original'. Yet, Acker did not always like the term being applied to her work, as she explained, 'To be guilty of plagiarism, according to the law, is to represent somebody else's material as your material. I haven't done that. I have always been very clear that I use other people's material. . . . I've always talked about it as a literary theory and as a literary method.' See Lotringer, 'Devoured by Myths', pp. 12–13.

137 David Kelly, 'Books in Brief: FICTION', *The New York Times*, 3 March 1996, www.nytimes.com/1996/03/03/books/books-in-brief-fiction-085260.html (accessed 26 April 2021).

138 Acker, 'Seeing Gender', p. 167.

139 Apter, *Feminizing the Fetish*, p. 99.

140 Acker, *Don Quixote*, p. 47.

141 Acker, *Don Quixote*, p. 48.

142 Focusing on letters-as-literatures, rather than the more intimate aspect of letters, Rod Phillips has also adapted Edgar Allan Poe's

phrase 'the purloined letter' to consider Acker's borrowing from Nathaniel Hawthorne's 1850 novel *The Scarlet Letter* in *Blood and Guts in High School* (1984) as an act of revisionist, feminist writing. See Rod Phillips, 'Purloined Letters: *The Scarlet Letter* in Kathy Acker's *Blood and Guts in High School*', *Critique: Studies in Contemporary Fiction*, 35:3 (Spring 1994), 173–180.

143 Acker, *Don Quixote*, p. 43.

144 Acker, *Don Quixote*, p. 44.

145 Sedgwick, *A Dialogue on Love*, p. 47.

146 Acker, *Don Quixote*, p. 47.

147 'kleptomania (n.)', *etymologyonline.com*, www.etymonline.com/word/kleptomania (accessed 20 October 2022).

148 Holly, *Melancholy Art*, p. 116.

Part III

Autotheory as medium and message

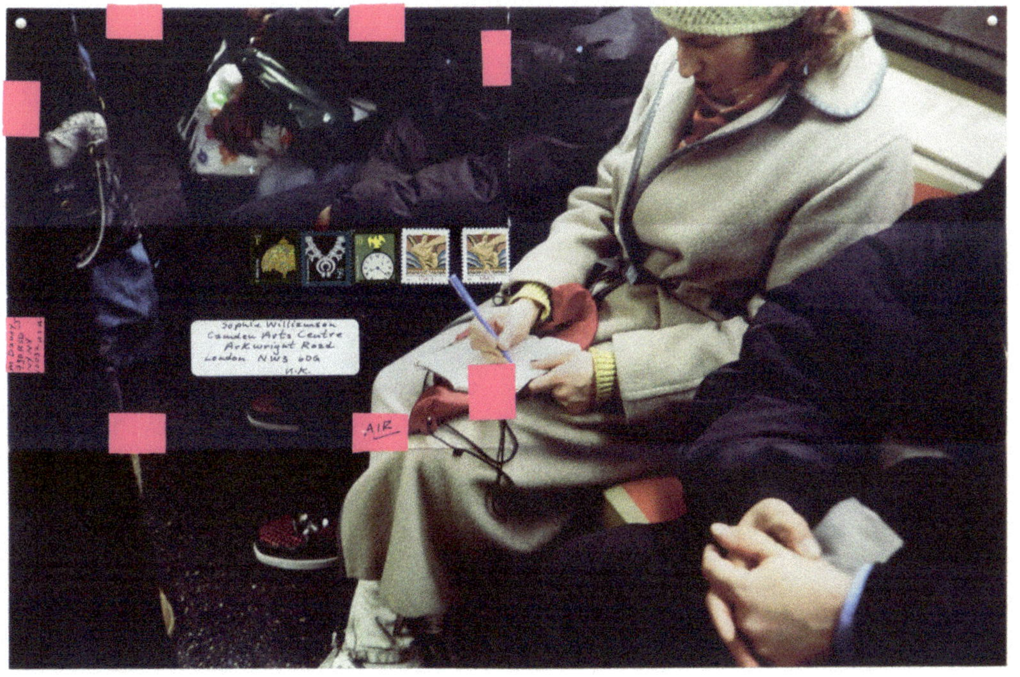

Moyra Davey, detail from *Subway Writers* series, 2011, C-print, tape, postage ink, 30 × 45 cm

6

At the altar of her divine: on Audre Lorde and Tee Corrine

Teresa Carmody

> It is a place to concentrate spiritual power and experience.
> It is a thing I craft with my hands and heart and head . . .
> Requa Tolbert, artist, psychiatric nurse[1]

> Do altar in a shoe box?
> Previous reader, marginalia written in red ink[2]

The gathering began even earlier, before you were born.

On top: two framed photographs.

First, Audre Lorde, smiling in large-framed eyeglasses. Outside, the cityscape behind her, Eastern city, sunrise, air, and breath. Thought and intellectual curiosity. Fresh start. 'The body is an instrument, like a wind instrument', says adrienne maree brown in conversation with her sister, Autumn, on their podcast, *How to Survive the End of the World.*[3] This episode is about sustaining love.

Second, Tee A. Corinne, peering above a 35mm camera she holds at chin level. Scene: interior, a wall in the West, all water, shifting forms like feelings do. 'Divination', says Selah Saterstrom, 'is a place where we risk more poignant relationships with uncertainty, which is in and of itself a revolutionary strategy.'[4] The word *revolution* first referred to celestial bodies; *revolve* roots through *revolver*, 'to change, change direction, bend around'.[5]

Inside: two preserved roses, light blue, Northern colour, earth blossom, materials and materiality, cannot see a rose without remembering your name. Between these: a photograph of you, trucker's cap over short bleached-blonde hair, skinny tie, aviator glasses. Boyish. The first time you met your neighbour friend, J, she would not play with you because she read you as *boy*. You think of this when you realise you are not.

Inside: seven-day candle with seven colours, seven saints in syncretic relation with seven African powers. Southern fire, transformation, light of wand flame away that which does not align. You purchased this candle several years ago, noting your discomfort – residual religious trauma mixed with questions of appropriation, colonisation, authority, how you might be continuing and/or transforming harm. Yet something inside said *yes* and when you gathered this material, the rainbow candle wanted to be lit.

You realise you are not
heterosexual despite decades of social grooming.

You paste magenta, cyan, black line drawings of cunts on the inside of a shoebox turned altar. You weave image over image over mirror from a sex-education workshop offered at a weekend retreat for HIV/AIDS workers in Thailand. You remember the lesbian teaching the workshop and how you had, by that point in life, had sex with more than one woman, but were still wrestling with your queer.

I am looking at *The Cunt Coloring Book*, a 1975 work by the American lesbian artist and writer Tee A. Corinne. Initiated in 1973 as a teaching tool for sex-education groups, Corinne's vulvas are visually compelling – black line drawings that linger between abstraction and representation. The book's first image includes arrows pointing from part of the image to anatomical term: clitoral shaft, clitoral hood, clitoral head, plus *caña del clitoris, prépuce clitoridien, Glans* (= *Eichel*) *des Kitzlers*. *The Cunt Coloring Book* is a multilingual switch. Keywords: relational aesthetics, participatory art, erotic education as play.

In 1963, Corinne was an art student at Pratt Institute, having moved there from Florida. This was before the internet, before 1968 challenges to US obscenity laws that, in many states, classified even information about birth control as 'obscene' and thus illegal. Corinne was learning about nude paintings by artists such as Michelangelo but could not view these paintings because it was not allowed.

So maybe, like Corinne, you decide at home that evening to draw a picture of your own vagina, legs spread before a mirror, seeing this part of yourself, strange yet familiar, an intimate unknown. Perhaps, like Corinne, you tear up that drawing before anyone (a husband,[6] or cis-het male lover) knows. Fast-forward to 1973 and the US Supreme Court ruling that women have the right to privacy and liberty and legal authority over their bodies, including the right

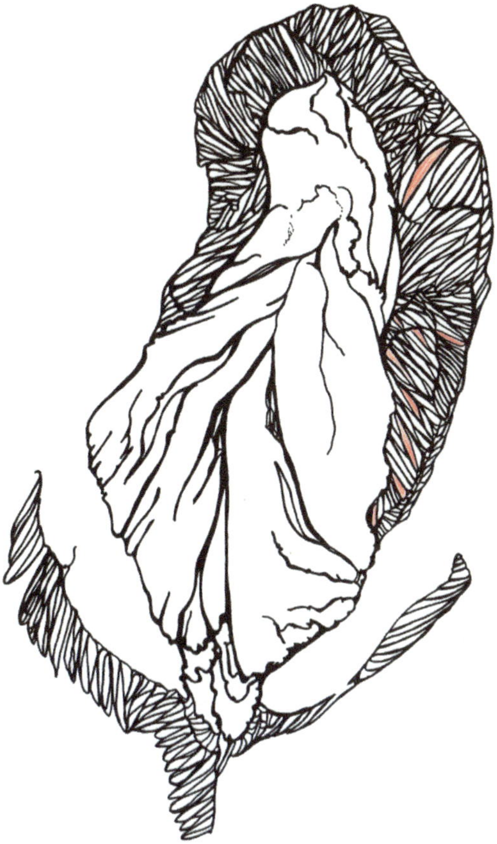

6.1 From Tee Corinne's *The Cunt Coloring Book* (1975), colouring by the author, Teresa Carmody, in stages. Stage 1

to abortion, and in a wave of excitement and necessity, you ask your friends to pose as you make pictures of their cunts. You have, by this point, left your husband or male lover, and are doing things with women that were previously unimaginable: sex, yes, but also talking, letting your imagination grow. 'The drawings in this book are of real women's cunts', writes Martha Shelley in *The Cunt Coloring Book's* short introduction. Why colouring? Corinne explains in an equally succinct foreword: 'Coloring is a way for the child in each of us to revision and reclaim this portion of our bodies from which we have been estranged.'

I speculate on Corinne's encounters with her friends and lovers – one woman opening her legs to her friend's artistic eye. There was not a model yet for this experience. Or for many of the knowledge-generating encounters of second-wave feminists. In her

Introduction to Corinne's 1982 *Yantras of Womanlove*, Margaret Sloan-Hunter describes the first time she had sex with a woman – not the sex, but the discussion beforehand, how they both sincerely believed the sex would not be as good because there was no penis or 'male aggressor to initiate'. That was 1970. By the time Sloan wrote this piece in 1979, she sees the irony, that women know *even better* how to give each other orgasms. The problem, wrote Sloan-Hunter, was not only 'basic ignorance' of sexuality, but the lack of 'images in our own minds of what we could possibly do with each other in bed'. She ends this piece with a note about the power of seeing her own naked body in *Yantras of Womanlove*. How she smiled. How 'she no longer feels uncomfortable with the light on when she is making love'.[7]

( )

Realising you are not heterosexual shifts your relationship to your sexuality. To your body. Both *become* yours as you become someone new: queer, lesbianic outlaw, unmarriageable because it is the noughties and gay marriage is not legal.

This claim to your own body and sexuality, to your own pleasure – that is what you have been taught to fear, were told you were not capable of handling. 'Take care of my Teresa', your dad once said to the boyfriend who would not kiss you on your mouth or read your writing. Your father, who wouldn't teach you about cars because you weren't a boy (you took a basic automotive class from a feminist car-dyke instead), who scoffed at your college education because you didn't know how many pounds were in a ton (2,000; you looked it up later). Our economic and social structures run on the libidinal energy of humans, which patriarchal religions and ideologies have divided into class-, race- and gender-based systems of authority, while suppressing human sexuality, quarantining sex from source, the energy which animates all life. This idea comes from Austrian psychoanalyst and social psychologist Wilhelm Reich, who wrote in the 1930s about the correlation between sexual suppression and human exploitation, noting that such suppression began with the end of matriarchies and goddess cults that enjoined the spiritual and sexual, and with the 'establishment of an authoritarian patriarchy'. Reich describes how authoritarian structures – the family, the church, the military – distort what is natural and good within the child towards an impotent yet fervent feeling of religiosity and nationalism, fuelled by an unconscious brimming with repressed energies, which subsequently emerge as 'cruel, sadistic, lascivious, rapacious, and envious impulses'. Reich distinguishes these distorted energies from what he calls our *biologic core*; to Reich, humans are 'an essentially honest, industrious, cooperative, loving, and if motivated, rationally hating animal'.[8] To Reich, teaching children to fear their capacity for pleasure teaches them self-fear; and this, ultimately, infantilises humans while 're-creating the life-negating ideologies' which give rise to authoritarianism and dictators.

I trace a thread from Reich's *biologic core* to Audre Lorde's notion of the erotic. 'We have been raised to fear the *yes* within ourselves, our deepest cravings', writes Lorde in her 1978 essay, 'The Uses of the Erotic: The Erotic as Power'. For Lorde, the erotic is a deeply held internal resource within each of us, a feeling of deep inner connection, a physically embodied awareness of our life-force and capability, of our intuitive inner-knowing and capacity for joy. For life. The erotic is spiritual and sexual and sensual – it 'heightens and sensitizes and strengthens all experience'. To embrace the erotic as a resource within we begin 'to live from within outward', writes Lorde; we become 'responsible to ourselves in the deepest sense'.[9]

You realise you are not heterosexual and give yourself a *yes*. The first of many, sounds a slow moan.

( )

I have written about friends and ex-friends since I first began writing, with or without their consent, but always consciously grounded within my perspective – me, or the character based on me, narrating from that limited perspective. It took years to recognise this obsession: writing about my friends. How when you are queer, the friendships may run hotter, have a different charge, become a primary relationship of found and chosen family, often more reliable, more nurturing than your family of origin, especially parents, especially my mother, who cannot, will not, accept herself, and thus me, as whole. She still believes, after twenty years, that I am not gay, 'deceived', she calls me, so I learn to accept the way she cannot mother me. The way I must learn to mother myself.

And a friend becomes a mother. A writer becomes an artistic or spiritual ancestor. A friend who is a writer becomes a living ancestor. A book by a writer already dead becomes a consciousness capable of holding multiple truths.

Like Audre Lorde's *Zami: A New Spelling of My Name*. First published in 1982, Lorde describes *Zami* as 'a biomythography' – life + myth + writing the story of coming into her own creative, political, and sexual awareness. Community, especially queer or gay-girl community, is integral to her narrative. 'Zami', writes Lorde, is 'a Carriacou name for women who work together as friends and lovers.'[10] Her story is their story is her story: singular and plural. These are women who have filled and broken Lorde's heart, including her mother, and Lorde describes them and her younger selves with clarity and compassion, even as they sometimes hurt themselves and each other. After the traumatic end of her first long-term live-in lesbian love affair – with Muriel – Lorde hears 'the sky fill with a new spelling of [her] own name'.[11] A rupture opens a pathway. Through and changed anew.

As Zami, Lorde becomes a chorus from beginning to end. 'To whom do I owe the power behind my voice?' I read this as a beautifully queer inversion of the first sentence of *David Copperfield*,[12] which is often attributed as the first autobiographical novel in Anglophone literature. Both books begin with a question, but while Dickens's narrator worries about whether or not he will be herocentric, Lorde's question recognises the interconnection and interdependence from which every human comes. *To whom*, asks Lorde, and her unitalicised next paragraph answers with a description of her father as 'distant lightning' compared to the more immediate '[i]mages of women flaming like torches . . ., stand[ing] like dykes between me and the chaos'.[13] Lorde credits these women, 'kind and cruel', as leading her home.

May this be an offering to the flamey dykes who lit and light and will the way.

You realise you are not heterosexual and remember how the first person you spoke to on your first day of college was the 'school dyke'. It was the early 1990s and the college was small enough for one person to have this reputation, though you did not know about her or the school. But you wanted a cigarette. Needed one, you decided, though you had given up three weeks before in a fit of religious fervour. Across the courtyard, you spot B. Short dark hair, blue jeans. Smoking. She had a throaty voice and a curious expression. You liked talking with her and were thrilled when she showed up a few weeks later, this time because she was dating R who lived down the hall. R was a first-year, like you, and according to your roommate, R did not know she was a lesbian until she fell for B. How does someone know

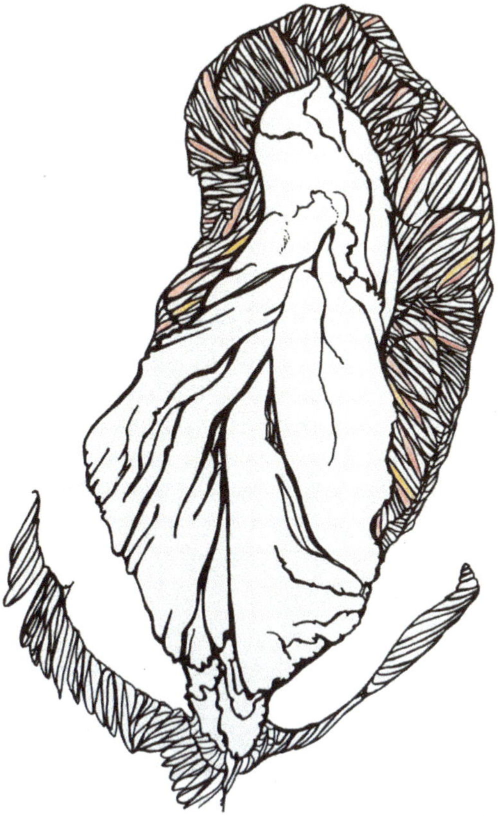

6.2 From Tee Corinne's *The Cunt Coloring Book*, 1975, colouring by the author, Teresa Carmody, in stages. Stage 2

or not know? You tried not to stare as they held hands and kissed, lips full and soft; you felt a charge in your body you did not trust. Was this what bigotry felt like? You were learning about homophobia and sexism and the algorithms they produced in social behaviour, though you did not have that language either. As a young child, you had learned the word 'homosexual' from Christian radio, and that being 'gay' meant doomed to hell. You felt defensive about not being gay, and when you later realise that you are not heterosexual, you see this defensiveness differently, the looking and not-looking, the felt charge within your body signalling desire and fear of that desire. Even later, a therapist tells you that, neurologically, excitement and fear feel nearly the same in the body.

Within a few years, most of your friends will be gay or bisexual, including your boyfriend and the married Christian woman you met at the church you attended for a few months after you moved out West, still too scared to not try, at least, to believe in your mother's mean god. The married Christian woman confessed that while she loved her husband, she married to 'leave the lifestyle'. This was the one friend you made at church. Even later, you revel in the attraction of affinities, that even as you resisted your own intuitions, you surrounded yourself with lesbians, transmen, fags, dykes, plus artists, writers, thespians, and queens. Queerness and fluidity. Gender in the head.

( )

Four years before the publication of *Zami*, Lorde delivered her paper, 'The Uses of the Erotic: The Erotic as Power' at the Fourth Berkshire Conference on the History of Women.[14] Moving past what she calls the exploitative idea that flattens the erotic into mere 'sensation', meaning the 'pornographic', Lorde describes the erotic as a 'resource', a well of information 'firmly rooted in the power of our unexpressed or unrecognized feeling'. She intones words like *deepest* and *nonrational knowledge, spiritual* and *revelation*; the erotic, she writes, 'is a measure between the beginnings of our sense of self and the chaos of our strongest feelings'.

A measure: is Lorde speaking temporally? Like moments of intensity – when I am angry or aroused and quit knowing myself as myself, caught in a surge of emotion. Though as the intensity dissipates, I return to myself, and hopefully to a sense of curiosity about what activated such a strong response. With age and a regular meditation practice, this experience has changed, so I can be increasingly present even during these moments, and the measure of time between not knowing and knowing lessens as I recognise and accept my feelings as they are and direct my emotional energy with intention and skill. A portal to greater self-connection.

A measure: is Lorde speaking musically? About rhythmic patterns, like dancing or singing or painting or having sex, and how the experience of self becomes no more or less than all that surrounds, molecules moving from one form into another like that example I remember from a lecture on meditation: at what point does a bite of apple stop being an apple and become part of the one who eats?

Even after your realisation, you sometimes worried you had been tricked into being gay. Tricked because pastors had warned that others would make 'sin' seem pleasurable and good, that the best deceptions were always coated in truth. Tricked because you wanted to be friends with the queers, who seemed so cool, like your first girlfriend's group of friends, a bunch of artists and writers and

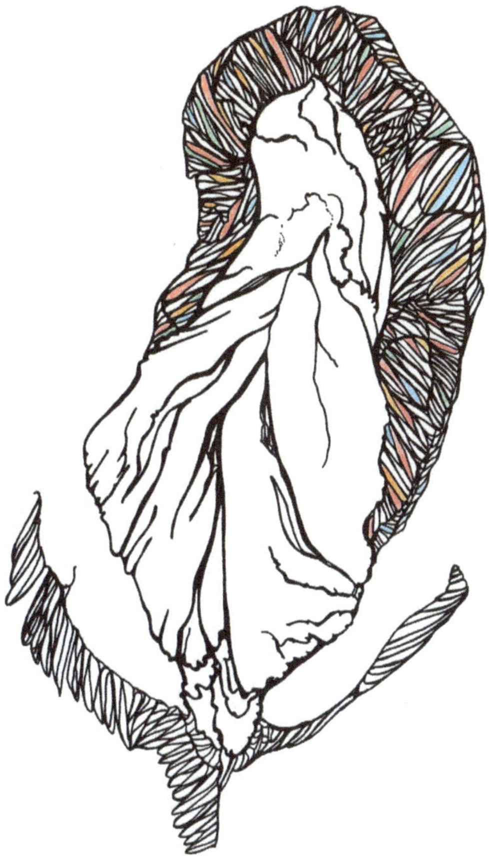

6.3 From Tee Corinne's *The Cunt Coloring Book*, 1975, colouring by the author, Teresa Carmody, in stages. Stage 3

musicians – were you just trying to fit in? Tricked as you withstood all the usual accusations: that coming out was you acting out, making it *all* about you, lying and being dramatic, determined to hurt your mother or destroy the family, falling under the influence of friends or the spirit of homosexuality who was stronger, your sister said, on the West Coast where you lived. And because you had been Church-manipulated for many years, had learned that rebellion was like the sin of witchcraft and the only thing worse than being gay was being a witch, never mind a gay witch, you could not image yourself as rebellious until you were in your mid-twenties, you forget your exact age though remember where you were (in the kitchen of that small rental you shared with the boyfriend who would not read your writing), the time of day (midday, lunch, you were eating a sandwich), and it made you want to laugh and vomit, this realisation that leaving your childhood home could be called *rebellious,* because to you, it was pain and brain fog to be there, and you did what you did (left, left, left) in order to live.

You realise you must write this essay by making an altar. *Must* is an intense word and it is not the first altar you have made. When you began studying divination – when was that? Did it begin with entering S's apartment in downtown Denver, with tarot cards and a bouquet of flowers (for there must always be an offering – look, another *must*), something given for something gained? Or did your divinatory study begin with purchasing that tarot deck at BodhTree in West Hollywood, one weekend morning after sex but before marriage, so early in your relationship with your now ex-spouse that the children – her children, but they are also your children, not legally but spiritually – say they have always known you to be a card reader? They knew this you before you could perceive her. Before you could enter more deeply into the felt space of divination, not as a parlour game or newspaper horoscope, but as a way of encountering the mysterious and unfathomable. A way of listening to your deep nonrational knowledge, of speaking back to the querent something they know but could not yet speak.

( )

Instead of asking friends, I consult two chosen mothers: Audre Lorde and Tee A. Corinne, foremothers or dyke-moms.[15] In the summer of 2019, I consulted Lorde's papers at Spelman College in Atlanta. For a week, I leafed through journals, photographs, and draft manuscripts, a typed, edited version of 'The Uses of the Erotic'. I took pictures, noting sentences she later deleted, sentiments sharped in published versions. I did not know what I was looking for but knew that Lorde's essay on the erotic rang differently after I began studying divination, which is to say, after I began healing from spiritual trauma and turned towards another way of listening. I knew that 'The Transformation of Silence into Language and Action', a paper Lorde first delivered on the 'Lesbians and Literature Panel' (yes, there was only one) during the 1977 MLA Conference, had been one of my touchstone texts as a young writer. 'You're never really a whole person if you remain silent', wrote Lorde, quoting her daughter,[16] which validated my *need* to speak this terrified silence lest I murder myself – of this I was certain – from the inside out.

I experience the archive itself as a kind of sensorium; the artist's felt presence lingers within the papers and objects she has left behind. The collection holds her point of view: what she saw, letters received and kept (as opposed to those she wrote and sent), her journals and saved syllabi and poetry flyers. Notes scribbled in margins or in the front of a notebook (Please Return–Reward), dreams (the artist's, her child's), handwritten on lined notepaper. A list of stones and their protective qualities: 'chalcedony: against lunacy, promotes strength, clarity'. In Lorde's archive, I absorbed feelings of excellence and nurturance, a palpable quality of presence and Lorde's thoughtful determination to love and trust herself and her work regardless. 'As a Black lesbian mother in an interracial marriage,' Lorde noted in a 1982 talk honouring Malcolm X, 'there was usually some part of me guaranteed to offend everybody's comfortable prejudices of who I should be.'[17] Lorde insisted on defining herself and refusing 'other people's fantasies for [her]'. This extended to roles at poetry readings. After finishing her set, Lorde would often turn to the audience and ask: 'Why are you here? . . . What do you feel?'

By the time I visited Tee Corinne's papers in the summer of 2022, the world had visibly shifted. The lingering global COVID-19 pandemic meant I wore an N-95 mask, as did the other researchers sitting in the Special Collections and University Archives at the University of Oregon, Eugene. Two years of virtual meetings and a desire to support transfolx led many, myself included, to reconsider and write our pronouns (she/they) alongside our login name and Zoom rooms unbinarised before our eyes. Uprisings during the summer of 2020 protesting police violence and the state-sanctioned murder of Black people, including George Floyd, led organisations, including academic departments, to write and adopt anti-racist statements, which prompted a predictable right-(white)wing backlash. While I was in Oregon, public universities in Florida, where I live, were deleting these statements from department websites in order not to flag themselves to the Governor, whose 'Stop Woke' Act threatened funding loss for teaching students about racism. Earlier, in June, the Dobbs *v.* Jackson decision in the US Supreme Court overruled Roe *v.* Wade, taking away the constitutional right to privacy, liberty, and bodily autonomy for women and child-bearing people.

Why are you here? To connect with others.[18]

What do you feel? Grief and curiosity. Gratefulness, yet fleeting comparisons that lead to judgement (of self, of others). Compassion, then awe for feminist foremothers, when there is a mass enough movement, it cannot be stopped, grief again, how many different

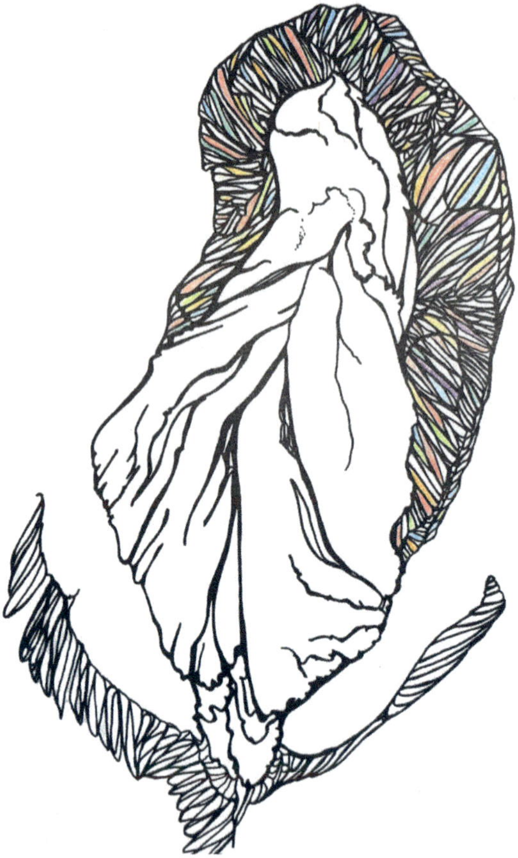

6.4 From Tee Corinne's *The Cunt Coloring Book*, 1975, colouring by the author, Teresa Carmody, in stages. Stage 4

species lost today, plus energy moving from the tip of my head through to my pelvis, arousal, yes, turned on.

Because I am interested in Corinne's spirituality, I request a box holding 'destiny cards' – a deck Corinne made using, as she often did, accessible materials on hand: photographs, a printer, an X-Acto knife, a photocopier. Each card includes collaged images from Corinne's life – family, friends, herself at different ages. Sometimes, a bit of text. In gold, Corinne signed each card's front, while their backs hold a black-and-white illustration of vines, leaves, and flowers, against a grid as regular as wires in an old window screen.

I decide to ask Corinne about this essay. I settle into my chair, ground, and begin working the cards. *Dear Tee* – I peek at the librarian, who is watching but does not intervene. *What would you like to come through?* The first card pops inverse; two images of women in a workplace.[19] At the bottom, eight women, all seemingly white, pose around a desk or table with some kind of paper in the middle. Perhaps they are working on *The Blatant Image*, a feminist lesbian magazine Corinne started with Ruth Mountaingrove and other women in 1981, the reason Corinne moved to Southern Oregon. 'We asked,' wrote Corinne, '"How has the women's movement changed the way we see? What kinds of photos are being produced and published now that haven't been seen before?"'[20] This card is bifurcated, and the other image includes two women, also seemingly white, holding a large paper. I sit with the card long enough for the picture to come into focus: these women, who by their fashion and hairstyles lived in the early to mid-twentieth century, were also publishing some kind of art or political magazine.

Why are you here? There is an unease in how we are working together and an invitation to come into communal alignment around a purpose or project. This is art. Being together in the reading, not singular, a way to perceive and honour difference. And: there is hurt and disagreement; you must attend to each other's feelings. Create space for listening. For learning how to give and receive care. Self-connection lubricates your connections with others, your capacity for intimacy and difference. So many systems (white supremacy, patriarchy, body terrorism)[21] work to keep us numb and disconnected, which is why a path towards dissolution easily gains momentum. How do we engage and shift this? How do we turn towards the wholeness of who we are?

What do you feel? The card of unease is flanked by two other groups: ancestors and feminist activists. The first card images Corinne's bio-family: three females; one male. They are in Florida, Corinne's birthplace, surrounded by palm trees. A woman (Corinne?) holds a camera; another wears a veiled hat and a dress with a Victorian-era collar. The third woman coordinates a striped polo shirt and midi skirt while leaning against a palm trunk, smiling at the viewer. Meanwhile, the man is a disembodied head floating inside the gap of a tree. He looks frightened. The women are resourced, full bodies, there is water in the middle, your self-belief is your strength and your protection, the women sing a song:

'One two three, can't pick your mommy. Four five ten, oh yes I am. Eight six nine, don't need to fix her. Seven times fine, time is a lie.'[22]

The other card holds six images of women: gathering, performing, publicly reading, dancing, smiling, standing with their non-human animal companion. Corinne is among them, a centre image in shadow, camera in hand. On this card, she wrote in fine black ink: 'Destiny is more than just a card you play.' Destiny is a coming together. A way to hold yourself in community. Destiny looks simultaneously in multiple directions, and for this we need each other. We cannot, writes Lorde, give in to a fear of feeling or of bringing all of ourselves to our creative, political, spiritual work. To Lorde, such giving in 'is a luxury only the unintentional can afford, and the unintentional are those who do not wish to guide their own destinies'.[23] 'Lesbian strength', writes Joan Nestle in the 1979 foreword to lesbian photographer JEB's book *Eye to Eye*, 'is a strength based not on the conquering of a weaker adversary, but on the refusal to be less than who we are. It is a strength nourished by our rejection of one world and the joyous, glorious and difficult dedication to the creation of another.'[24]

Why are you weeping? Because you will break my heart and I will choke yours and you will weave my heart back together and I will sing yours.

For both Lorde and Corinne, being out and visible as lesbians was fundamental to living and creating. Lorde wrote that for her there was 'no difference between writing a good poem and moving into sunlight against the body of a woman I love'.[25] Corinne turned towards the book – photos, stories, poems – as a private exhibition space after repeated censorship from public exhibitions, noting that 'writing erotica is a radical and extremely political act'.[26]

The Cunt Coloring Book is arguably Corinne's most well-known work, still in print and available in alternative independent bookstores around the country. It is a simple and elegant concept: a series of line-drawn labias, designed to be coloured and that demonstrate the variety and beauty of this marvellous organ. Sized like a standard colouring book, 8.5 × 11 inches, it has one image per page. While some include a connected groin or leg, most of these vulvas float in negative space, like sea creatures or pressed flowers. In some, a few lesbian fingers are present, tips pulling her inner lips apart. Other times, the vulva is nearly surrounded – à la Lady de Guadalupe – with heavy strokes for hair. Leafing through the pages can feel overwhelming, at least to me – these images simultaneously similar and dissimilar, of a body part so consistently absent from public discourse and view. Contrast the visibility of the labia with the penis; consider this sentence on Planned Parenthood's educational website: 'While vaginas are just one part of the vulva, many people say "vagina" when they really mean the vulva. But the vulva has a lot more going on than just the vagina.'[27] *Destiny is more than just a card you play.*

In Corinne's colouring book, the vulva cannot be pinned into a platonic form, for there are too many shifting differences between them; like a lover, the reader must search each page for the clitoris, and without her lover's moaned affirmation, she may not know if she has found the spot. If a platonic form is about the *essence* of a thing, an idealised form, the 'chairness' of a chair, tell me what is the 'vulva-ness' of a vulva? A combination of pleasure, pee, and blood, oh portal into the world? Corinne's images appear too different to be the same, even as their similarity stands. They are like faces, but without easily located features that ground me as viewer. The clitoris does not resemble the nose.

Lorde often began talks by grounding her audience within her own positionality: Black lesbian feminist warrior poet. 'I am

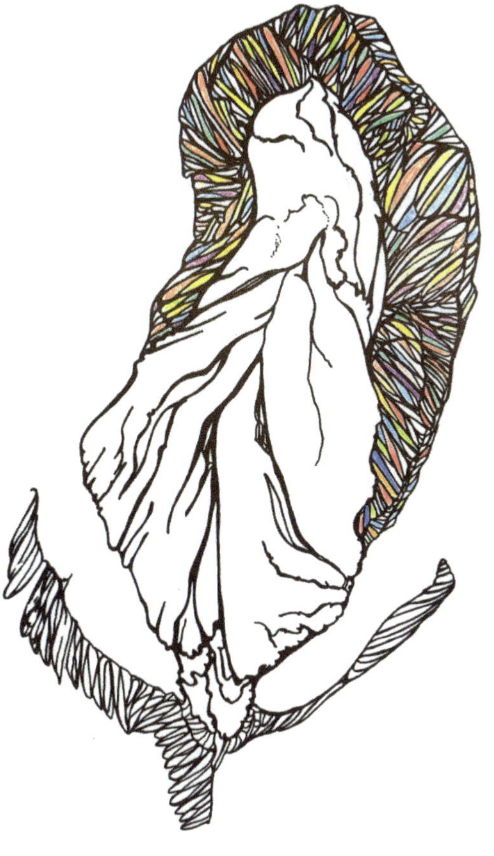

6.5 From Tee Corinne's *The Cunt Coloring Book*, 1975, colouring by the author, Teresa Carmody, in stages. Stage 5

profoundly thankful that I have a son,' she wrote to organisers of a Lesbian/Feminist conference she did not attend, 'since he helps to keep me honest'. The conference disallowed entry to boys over the age of ten. Lorde and her then partner Frances Clayton penned the letter together, warning about an 'oversimplified approach to the nature and solutions of any oppression, as well as the danger inherent in an incomplete vision'.[28] Keenly aware of her own intersectionality,[29] Lorde's list of self-identifiers was not shorthand essentialising but paratactic awareness of her own compounded multiplicity. A series of internal yeses. No wonder Lorde is such a major force, whose work continues to shape so many fields of inquiry: poetry, gender and women studies, critical phenomenology, Black studies, American studies, disability studies, pedagogies, and queer lit, to name a few. Some of her lines have become as ubiquitous as the second-wave feminist slogan 'the personal is political'. About that slogan: in 1969, Carol Hanisch wrote what she called a memo responding to another staff member, Dottie Zellner, 'who contended that consciousness-raising was just therapy', and questioned whether or not this work was truly 'political'.[30] Hanisch's memo, published the following year in *Notes from the Second Year: Women's Liberation*, was subsequently titled 'The Personal is Political' by editors Shulie Firestone and Anne Koedt, with input by Kathie Sarachild. In other words, the title which became a slogan emerged collectively, like the systemic knowledge the groups were creating by positing and honestly answering questions – such as, 'What happens in your relationship if your man makes more money than you? Less than you?' – then tracing the patterned power dynamics apparent in their overlapping experiences and beliefs. Intellectually perceiving these patterns is a first knowing, a beginning; *You realise you are not heterosexual but do not know how to live a body free.*[31]

'Abstractions', wrote Lorde, 'do not alter feeling. Images do. Images work best when they are concrete and particular.'[32] She wrote this in a notebook list of ideas she wanted to convey to women attending a poetry workshop. Ten years earlier, at the Second Sex Conference in New York, she spoke against the lack of Black feminist and lesbian representation. 'To read this program is to assume that lesbian and Black women have nothing to say about existentialism, the erotic, women's culture and silence, developing feminist theory, or heterosexuality and power.'[33] Lorde had understood that she would be responding to papers about the 'the role of difference within the lives of american [sic] women'; at the conference, she discovered she *was* the difference, that hers was the only panel with input from Black feminists and lesbians.

As Lorde wrote over and again, in order to live more fully, with more integrity and care for all humans, we must press into our differences. Explore them, instead of fearing them. 'It is not our differences which separate women, but our reluctance to recognise those differences and to deal effectively with the distortions which have resulted from the ignoring and misnaming of those difference.'[34] How do we know when it is a distortion or something else? When I saw B and R kiss in college and felt strange in my body – uncomfortable and embarrassed, afraid to look and wanting to look – how did I know if it was internalised homophobia or desire or both and then some? As Lorde notes, each person is built from 'blueprints of expectation and response, old structures of oppression' that become internalised, sometimes so deeply that we might not realise they are there. These blueprints manifest in patterns of 'guilt, hatred, recrimination, lamentation, and suspicion'. She offers what has rightfully become a Lordean proverb – 'For the master's tools will never dismantle the master's house' – about the need to tend to our insides as we enact outside change, because our personal healing and political futures are fundamentally connected to our ability and willingness to dismantle supremacist structures. This exceeds the question of enacting change from *within* an institution or system because that institution is also *inside you*. You *are* the house. Your guilt, fear, lament, and envy are flush with information about beliefs built into you. Note: these beliefs are not you. But until you acknowledge them, they will replicate, inside and out. Remember the Hermetic adage: *As within, so without.*

Self-connection is a feeling job, for the beliefs were stored with feeling and must be felt in their release. This alone scares many back into numbness; or rather, it scared me. At different points I have been so ashamed of particular feelings or experiences that it seemed safer (and more familiar) to self-criticise than to acknowledge the damaging events and attendant beliefs about my self-worth. But if I cannot look at the terror and loathing inside me, the part some part of me would like to estrange or annihilate, how can I hold another human close?[35]

Self-connection is a collaborative project, for the toxic voices and distorted histories each human has internalised need to be alchemically countered with other ways of knowing and perceiving, including experiences and stories from those who have been marginalised, denied humanity, suppressed.[36] We learned one way of perceiving; we can learn another. Like I have learned to call a friend when I am in a shame spiral, because sometimes I need another's validation and nurturance. Again, as Lorde reminds us: 'the need and desire to nurture each other is not pathological but redemptive, and it is within that knowledge that our real power is rediscovered'.[37] We need, and we need each other.

And perhaps it is obvious, but self-connection is also a solo job, for only you can bring your hurt and fearful yous to the altar of your holiest divine; only you can come into integrity with your deepest knowing, encounter what Lorde calls your 'erotic guides'. I am still getting to know mine, but every time I turn towards myself with compassion and gratefulness, I feel these parts of myself more fully alive. For the erotic leads towards self-trust and power. Not over others but within yourself. 'In touch with the erotic,' writes Lorde, 'I become less willing to accept powerlessness, or those other supplied states of being which are not native to me, such as resignation, despair, self-effacement, depression, self-denial.'[38]

Driving home from a sunset picnic with friends. I flip through Florida radio stations, pause on a sermon, the pastor's voice rising and falling in familiar cadences. He is talking about the sanctity of Christian marriage.[39] *Marriage,* he says, *is about vows, not feelings, and this vow is a contract made with God and your spouse. To break the vow is to live in selfishness. To live in selfishness is to live in misery, to be forever wrong.* More than his words, I hear the fear beneath them. How he minimises feeling as untrustworthy, turned that mistrust into contempt. He does not like it, either, when couples write their own vows. *The traditional vows,* he says, *have lasted for over 400 years.* He wants language fixed and stable. *Like God is,* he might say. But a fixed god is a dead god, for all that lives shifts and changes: plants and animals, mindsets, and neural pathways.[40] Even rock is formed through the slow exertion of steady change and documents, like job descriptions, are reimagined and revised by the body who inhabits the position.

In the car, the pastor's fear is infectious. I feel a wave of self-mistrust, a compulsive yearning for the certainty of another's worldview. Seven years passed between my first girl-kiss and me fully coming out of the closet; another ten to realise the hell-panic no longer lingered in my energetic field. I had given up the intellectual idea of hell long before, but my nervous system had not received the memo. And sometimes, it still activates. In the car, I feel a clutch of wrongness spread through my body, I have made one too many bad decisions, become banished, forever estranged. No wonder your marriage ended in divorce. But wait, I interrupt my accuser; I wanted that marriage to end. When I realised she could not, would not be there when I most needed (hello, mother; hello, lover); when I realised I used her problems and ambitions to avoid sitting with myself. In the car, the panic is an energy body of sensation; I can notice it and let it go. Relax into the deeper feeling always already present. Your divinity, my throne.

( )

Divination is ritualised method for meeting the divine. In art practices, divination genuflects to chance-based, procedural methods and to relational aesthetics, whereby the diviner, or artist, becomes a facilitator and the art or cards or altar space opens a site for exchange. 'An altar', writes Kay Turner, 'makes visible that which is invisible and brings near that which is far away; it makes the potential for communication and exchange between different but necessarily connected worlds, the human and the divine.'[41]

I take a photo of my own vulva. I am in my school office on a Saturday afternoon. I have closed the blinds. Am wearing a skirt. Had not planned this photo session when I came to campus, but as I begin making photocopy art from the *The Cunt Coloring Book*, I decide to include my own, to juxtapose one vulva over another. Mine and hers. At the site of this altar, this essay, written and simultaneously assembled in a shoebox prepared with paint and cloth, glue and photos, flowers and thread, lines from letters written by Lorde (for her handwriting as much as thoughts), and coloured images of Corinne's drawings (yes to her hands, too). Home altars such as these, writes Kay Turner, embrace the 'aesthetics of relationship' between the personal and the cosmic. As art, the form is also the content: the materials that comprise the altar *are that* which is offered to Lorde and to Corinne, to my feminist ancestors, holy Sappho, spirit goddexx, grand-funky-she-gods. Every object placed on an altar is there for a reason that exceeds reason. In Turner's book, Rose Wognum Frances notes: 'Once you put an object in relation to another, it tells a story, it makes a different reality . . . This is the beginning of all art, to take this thing and put it in relation to that thing.'[42] This is the beginning of an altar: to alter patterns and energies, to open the self to change.

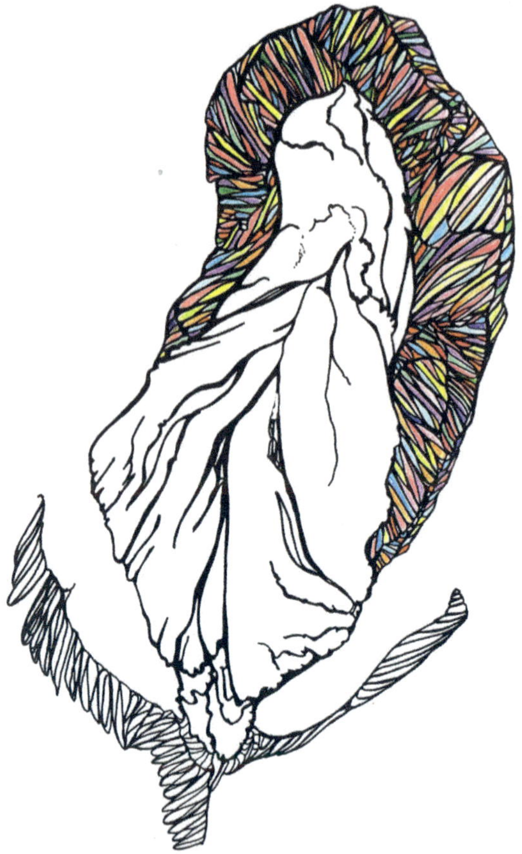

6.6 From Tee Corinne's *The Cunt Coloring Book*, 1975, colouring by the author, Teresa Carmody, in stages. Stage 6

Instead of asking my friends for their stories, I read them mine, an earlier version of this chapter with stories of sexual encounters. I will leave those specifics on a back deck under a smoggy Los Angeles night sky. *You need more sex in your stories,* said a former male writing teacher to one of my students. That same male writer thought each story should have an epiphany, a quick spurt of realisation. I know how to spurt, but why would I want that every time? When I can also learn a slow, long moan, the 'considered phrase, "It feels right to me."'[43] There are so many ways of knowing. A yes to sex, with who and when I want to, is about learning to read my body. A long-term relationship. She did not know how to read me, said R, so she broke it off with her lover. Where is the body in this text? During divination, S says you are always reading three creatures: the querent, the cards, the reader. To whom do I owe the power of my voice?

If an altar is a site for altering the relationships between various objects and energies, then writing, too, becomes a kind of altar, a site infused with intention and desire. Writing opens space for something else to come through. Ordinary objects – we call them words – take on extraordinary significance. Cardboard, paint, fabric, glue. Sequins, patterns, pink and ultra-sheen. Doilies and mirrors, clay and silver gelatin. The altar casts a shadow on the wall behind it. A shadow in the shape of a church. Your holy darkness. Queer divine.

Notes

1 Kay Turner, *Beautiful Necessity: The Art and Meaning of Women's Altars* (London: Thames & Hudson, 1999), p. 29.

2 Turner, *Beautiful Necessity*, p. 47.

3 Autumn Brown and adrienne maree brown, 'Sustaining Love', 20 October 2022, *How to Survive the End of the World*, audio podcast, ed. Zac Rosen, endoftheworldshow.org (accessed 25 October 2022). The sisters were sharing their 'Flumes of Awe': adrienne spoke about taking voice lessons, while Autumn shared wisdom from Angela Davis about how in the 1960s and 1970s their activism was about *producing knowledge*.

4 In 2022, Saterstrom recorded monthly homilies that meditate on the Chariot card, which were held online for members of her website, fourqueens.org. This quote comes from the session, 'The Chariot, Burying the Halleluiah', 1 March 2022. For more on divinatory poetics, see Saterstrom, *Ideal Suggestions: Essays on Divinatory Poetics* (Buffalo, NY: Essay Press, 2017).

5 'revolution (n.)' and 'revolve (v.)', *Online Etymology Dictionary*, etymonline.com/search?q=revolution (accessed 25 October 2022).

6 Corinne was married at the time and tore up this picture, even as she became quite interested in nude or erotic art. Before the marriage ended, she was trying to get her husband to pose nude for her. He refused. In her introduction to *Dreams of the Woman Who Loved Sex*, Corinne gives a much more nuanced description of her early sexual education during this time, from *The Story of O*, to 'how to' books, to *My Secret Garden* by Nancy Friday. See Corinne, *Dreams of the Woman Who Loved Sex* (Austin, TX: Banned Books, 1987), Tee A. Corinne Papers, Coll. 263, Special Collections and University Archives, University of Oregon, Eugene, Oregon, https://archiveswest.orbiscascade.org/ark:/80444/xv98508 (accessed 20 November 2022).

7 Margaret Sloan-Hunter, 1987, 1995, Box 25, Folder 4, Tee A. Corinne papers, Coll. 263, University of Oregon Libraries, Special Collections and University Archives. 'Introduction', in Corrine, *Yantras of Womanlove* (Tallahassee, FL: Naiad Press, 1982) pp. 11–14.

8 Wilhelm Reich, *The Mass Psychology of Fascism* [1933], trans. Vincent R. Carfango (New York: Farrar, Straus & Giroux, 1980), p. xi.
9 Audre Lorde, 'Uses of the Erotic: The Erotic as Power', in *Sister Outsider* (Freedom, CA: Crossing Press, 1984), p. 58.
10 Lorde, *Zami A New Spelling of My Name: A Biomythography* (Berkeley, CA: Crossing Press, 1982), p. 255.
11 Lorde, *Zami*, p. 239.
12 'Whether I shall turn out to be the hero of my own life, or whether that station will be held by anybody else, these pages must show.' Charles Dickens, *David Copperfield* [1850] (Mineola, NY: Dover Publications, 2004), p. 3.
13 Lorde, *Zami*, p. 3.
14 She gave this paper again at the First National Feminist Perspective on Pornography Conference in San Francisco. It is a pleasure to hear the women laugh: Pacifica Radio Archives, KPFK, 'Eroticism and pornography/Audre Lorde', produced by Helene Rosenbluth, broadcast on 4 March 1979, https://archive.org/details/pacifica_radio_archives-KZ0884 (accessed 20 November 2022).
15 Question: how does shifting the appellation shift the social relationship?
16 Lorde, 'The Transformation of Silence into Language and Action', in *Sister Outsider*, p. 42.
17 Lorde, 'Learning from the 60s', in *Sister Outsider*, p. 137.
18 My trip out West included visits with so many family members and friends: Anna Joy and Caty, Connie, Matias, Zach, Pam and Sara, Alyssa, Prageeta and Mike, Janice, a poetry reading where I saw Stacy and heard about Joanna Russ holding a fiction workshop while lying on a mattress in her office.
19 A note in Lorde's archive, typed on her letterhead with a Staten Island address: 'I think I did not go far enough in talking about the erotic force in work. I believe that women touch this connection more easily because of our capacity for labour rather than the actual experience of giving birth. But our bodies know what it is ultimately to labour and to produce, and the intense pleasure of this hardest of work so aptly named labour. / That can be a measurement of how intensely satisfying a job well-done can be.' Writing, 'The Uses of the Erotic', July 2019. Audre Lorde Papers, Box 16, Folder 2.1.052, Spelman College Archives, Atlanta, Georgia.
20 Tee Corinne, 'The Blatant Image: Making a Magazine', paper delivered at the Women in Photography: Expanding Connections conference, June 1989, Bryn Mawr College. Tee A. Corinne Papers, Box 38, Folder 24, Coll. 263, Special Collections and University Archives, University of Oregon.
21 See Sonya Renee Taylor, *Your Body is Not an Apology* (Oakland, CA: Berrett-Koehler, 2018).

22 Back in Florida, I met up with M for a spirit tour of Cassadaga Spiritualist Camp. We were outside, holding an EMF meter, when Micaiah asked, 'Is time a lie?' The machine lit up in affirmation.

23 Lorde, 'Uses of the Erotic', p. 54.

24 JEB (Joan E. Biren), *Eye to Eye: Portraits of Lesbians* (New York: New York Anthology Editions, 2020), p. 7. Originally published in 1979 by Glad Hag Books. Also see this conversation between JEB and Alexis Pauline Gumbs, who is writing a biography of Audre Lorde: www.youtube.com/watch?v=lw_aUQm_WUk (accessed 20 November 2022).

25 Lorde, 'Uses of the Erotic', p. 58.

26 Tee Corinne, *Dreams of The Woman Who Loved Sex*, p. vii.

27 www.plannedparenthood.org/learn/health-and-wellness/sexual-and-reproductive-anatomy/what-are-parts-female-sexual-anatomy (accessed 19 November 2022).

28 Lorde, 'Man Child: A Black Lesbian Feminist's Response', in *Sister Outsider*, p. 77. Also Audre Lorde Papers, Box 15, Folder 1.2.359, Spelman College Archives.

29 Kimberlé Crenshaw, 'Demarginalized the Intersection of Race and Sex: A Black Feminist Critique of Antidiscrimination Doctrine, Feminist Theory and Antiracist Politics', *University of Chicago Legal Forum*, 1:8 (1989), 139–167.

30 The original title was 'Some Thoughts in Response to Dottie's Thoughts on a Women's Liberation Movement'. Carol Hanisch, 'The Personal Is Political: The Women's Liberation Movement classic with a new explanatory introduction by Carol Hanisch' ([1969] 2009), www.carolhanisch.org/CHwritings/PIP.html (accessed 20 November 2022).

31 This is also why autotheory *is* a feminist practice demonstrating the personal as political, an idea offered by Lauren Fournier and Arianne Zwartjes. Autotheory extends the practice of consciousness-raising to art. In autotheory, the reader/artist traces questions and patterns found within both a body of knowledge (philosophical or texts) and their own body-person, to generate new knowledge.

32 Audre Lorde Papers, Section 2.5, Journals, Box 5, 35, 1989–1990, Spelman College Archives.

33 Lorde, 'The Master's Tools Will Never Dismantle the Master's House', in *Sister Outsider*, p. 110.

34 Lorde, 'Age, Race, Class, and Sex: Women Redefining Difference', in *Sister Outsider*, p. 122.

35 I am thinking about this passage from Lorde's paper, 'The Master's Tools Will Never Dismantle the Master's House': 'Racism and homophobia are real conditions of all our lives in this place and time. *I urge each one of us here to reach down into that deep place of knowledge inside herself and touch that terror and loathing of any difference that*

lives there. See whose face it wears. Then the personal as the political can begin to illuminate all our choices.' 'The Personal is Political Panel', Second Sex Conference, New York, 29 September 1979, emphasis added.

36 Let your intuition choose your guides, knowing this is a lifelong process.

37 Also from 'The Master's Tools Will Never Dismantle the Master's House', comments given at 'The Personal is Political Panel', Second Sex Conference, New York, 29 September 1979.

38 Lorde, 'Uses of the Erotic', p. 58.

39 I first heard this emphasis on Christian marriage at my Evangelical Christian cousin's wedding, after a landmark ruling in Obergefell *v.* Hodges that guaranteed marriage equality for LGBTQ+ couples. Since state-sanctioned marriage had become more inclusive, some Christian pastors felt the need to emphasise the bigotry of their views. I am using the word 'bigotry' here in both its contemporary and etymological understandings, for the word 'bigot' may root through the Germanic oath *bi God*, and thus a definition from the 1590s is 'sanctimonious person, religious hypocrite'.

40 'God is change'; this is the central tenet of Earthseed, the religion in Octavia Butler's *Parable of the Sower* (1993) and the *Parable of the Talents* (1998). Butler attributes this philosophy or religious tenet to her Black teen protagonist, Lauren Oya Olamina. Writer, pleasure activist, and visionary adrienne maree brown draws on Butler's Earthseed to write *Emergent Strategy: Shaping Change, Changing Worlds* (Oakland, CA: AK Press, 2017).

41 Turner, *Beautiful Necessity*, p. 23.

42 Rose Wognum Frances, cited in Turner, *Beautiful Necessity*, p. 96.

43 Lorde, 'Uses of the Erotic', p. 56.

7

Autotheorising the unself

Marquis Bey

An account must be given. Not an account of who I am, as it will quickly become clear why this is not quite the aim here. The given account is one of where this meditation stems from. That non-originary origin is an intellectual one, a sociopolitical one, an ethical one. This account begins with an idea. Or a series of ideas concatenating in astounding ways. One idea: sometimes, and perhaps most times, it is believed that this thing we call the self is simply a name for that fundamental, unmediated I-ness; a transparent descriptor of merely that which I am, which takes the personal pronoun 'I'. But those other times, that are not the sometimes or most times when this is believed, posit the self as something quite differently textured. We might suggest here that the 'self' inflects in fact not a transparent mirrored reflection of 'I', nor the simple naming of the coalescence of that which is contained in my supposed body; instead, let us say that the self is a multifaceted figuration that has within it assumptions of individuality extricated from others (call this, let us say, individuation) and, with this, the disallowance of other ways to move, think, emote, and enact – that is, a disallowance of escape from its delimited confines (call this carcerality). To quote a passage, hopefully an illuminative one: 'The institutions that we are fighting are not just the school, the police, the clinic, and the jail. It is also the self – the subject.'[1] The self curtails and presumes, which is to say that the self circumscribes and has criteria for entry – criteria that shuttle from the racialised and the gendered – which, if rebuked, dredge up a violent response. In short, the self is a regime.

And another idea: when speaking precisely, which I cannot do all the time, either because I am not at my best or because the context in which I find myself has not allowed for that to happen,

I say that I understand myself through nonbinariness rather than I *am* nonbinary. The nonbinary is the way I inflect the trans, and the trans, as theorised by a raucous group of brilliant thinkers – with whom I align and move and thus dissolve the discrete implications that inhere in my 'self' – is no mere medico-juridical alteration of corporeality. It is so much more. First, we must note that the self is predicated on certain logics that grant the self's validity as self. One of its chief logics, not to other logics' exclusion or lesser importance, is gender – to 'be' a 'self' and to be granted access to sociality one is required to be a properly gendered subject. We can then, secondly, offer trans and nonbinary as precisely an *improper* gender, perhaps even the declining of gender as such. Trans and nonbinary cannot hold, and do not want to hold, the self. Insofar as it might be said, in the wake of someone like Lacanian trans studies scholar Shanna T. Carlson, that a proper self and subject is predicated on the assumption of there *being* an unconscious sexuation from which gender is divorced, I, in my task of autotheorising the unself, aim to divorce gender from the province of the subject, the self, querying what 'I' even am when trying to move through a non(binary)-gender – perhaps the very unself autotheorised here. If I move through the nonbinary, my transness, I cannot properly be said to be a self, and that is perfectly fine with me. Indeed, quite desirable.

And yet, I can be said to write autotheory. A mere treatment of its constitutive terms – auto, or self, and theory – might lead one to think that autotheory is *quite* concerned with the self, with gaining an understanding of it, defining it, fleshing it out. It has thus been posed to me, as a scholar and thinker and writer given towards the radical project of undermining ontology and tenets of self, how it is that I come to autotheory as a mode of writing. My intellectual and sociopolitical penchants skew in the vein of desiring an outside to the identarian, the hubris of a coherent and transparent self, the presumption of an uncritiquable lived experience. How, then, is autotheory a genre for you, Marquis? It is a sincere question, and a perplexing one, to which I respond in a way not quite expected: I move through autotheory not as a reflection of the self's event; rather, autotheory provides the discursive occasion for excavating the conditions of the supposed self in service of its interrogation – and, too, the interrogation of other selves, other conditions. Through a refusal of individuation, and through an engendering of the trans and nonbinary, as my work is so often characterised, the very notion of 'self' loses and loses purchase, and loses it again. That is my autotheory. Put differently, it provides the opportunity to excavate the *encounter* and what it might permit us to learn that would bring about the dissolution of so many rigid, impenetrable requisites for how it is possible to encounter, to know, to live, to be. Autotheory, as I wield it, is to theorise the undermining of the 'self' such that other things become possible to know and become. Not 'self-theory' but 'un-self-theory', as it were.

What I shall do in this brief treatise is give an account of the account that is my own work, namely my first book, *Them Goon Rules: Fugitive Essays on Radical Black Feminism* and my latest book to date, *Cistem Failure: Essays on Blackness and Cisgender.*[2] This is a practice, indeed a languaging practice, I humbly and hopefully generously adopt from the inimitable Toni Morrison. As she writes in her germinal essay, 'Unspeakable Things Unspoken': 'Please forgive the use of my own work in these observations. I use it not because it provides the best example, but because I know it best, know what I did and why, and know how central these queries are to me.' 'Writing is,' she concludes, '*after* all, an act of language, its practice. But *first* of all it is an effort of the will to discover.'[3] And I feel and believe this, so deeply. What I try to discover is something else that is not the self, something that is more and less than the self. In the opening essays of each of these books, what I discover in writing is how the self is not needed for my purposes, because the writing is in service of something so much more.

Lastly, it bears being said explicitly, in line with the spirit of this chapter, that *Them Goon Rules* and *Cistem Failure*, and all my autotheoretical work, are not autobiography. This is not self-writing a *bios*. There is a documented lineage of the autobiography, the self-writing, one that goes back to Augustine's *Confessions* and its decidedly religious mastery of the self, which then moves into priority given to the modern individuated self. Robyn Wiegman, in the context of the autobiographical, writes: 'its claims to truthfulness and facticity have been sullied by the imprecision that accompanies human memory and by the psychoanalytically inflected suspicion that its devotees are willing to engage fabrication for their own narcissistic fulfilment, delivered under the cover of personal experience and subjective knowledge'.[4] The aim is not precision, nor narcissism, nor even personal or lived experience. Rather, the bounteous possibilities in *de*emphasising the purported 'self' and asking, through a deconstruction of a singular site of the personally experiential, how I am always and already given over to others is much more the aim.

Unruly goons

What opens 'Whence We Are Sent', the first essay in *Them Goon Rules*, are two epigraphs. The first is by Toni Morrison, who lives with me constantly. The second is by Lorna Goodison. It is brief, only seven words. 'I was sent, tell that to history', Goodison writes in her poem 'Nanny'.[5] I first discovered that passage in a piece of writing by Fred Moten. I do not remember which piece of Moten's prolific intellectual corpus the quote stems from, nor am I entirely sure it was written. Perhaps it was spoken in one of his beautiful riffs. But this does not matter. What matters is that Goodison was sent, and Goodison sent Fred (if I may), and Fred sent me. And, so many others – people and non-people – sent Fred and sent me, which also means that those who sent me may have also sent Fred, and those who sent Fred may have also sent me. In sending and being sent, not even the most systematic postal service in the world could track the lines that are not lines but worried and worrisome tremblings, vibrations even. Who sent whom does not matter. It is impossible to know, to track. So, it is impossible to know, to track, the 'I' that I supposedly am precisely because I was sent and am sending so much that even if tracks were being kept, which they are not and cannot be, 'I' would be more parts 'you' than anything else.

This multiplicity pervades 'Whence We Are Sent'. I recall, during the early stages of production, being asked by the publisher if I wanted the title essay to be first. And I was quite adamant about it not being first. The reason for this was not so much about 'Them Goon Rules' but 'Whence We Are Sent': in some ways, that essay *had* to go first, to set the stage for how the 'I' of the proceeding essays perhaps ought to be read. Indeed, readers needed to know that the subject of the essays – the 'auto' that was, in some ways, the scene of the theorising done throughout the essays – was fundamentally fractured, which, hopefully, fractured the reading experience as well. In short, that essay and the book as a whole seek to undermine the self in the service of another way to understand how to come to an encounter with who one is; indeed, to *encounter* who one is, not as an already-formed entity with clear boundaries but as a thing that is entangled with all things, which is also to say a thing that is uncertain, undergoing tremulous de-sedimentations. And this is alluded to in the Preface, where I write: 'That is the language I have been bred in, the language that has produced the struggle that troubles me and will hopefully, if I am marginally successful, trouble you.'[6]

The language spoken of is doing a very fundamental troubling, a troubling at the level, we might say, of ontology. There is a colloquial way such a word resounds, with a meaning that reflects a kind of being put off or made uncomfortable. But here, there is a seriousness with which the 'troubles me' is meant: the 'me' throughout these pages is troubled such that 'me' is rattled in ways that disallow the discretion and individuation indexed, popularly, to Me's and I's. Through the language of the text, I trouble the very definition, the very singularity, of 'me' – and, consequently, of 'you'. (And, even further, of 'us'.)

There is difficulty here too, I must confess. Few of us would unquestioningly welcome the kind of troubling of ourselves I am suggesting. Indeed, when one is met with the kind of encounter to which I allude – one that troubles you to your 'core' – one is much more likely to baulk at the troubling, assuming one is all good, as it were. And this is OK; I, too, have baulked at invitations to trouble myself and be troubled. But I was not, and am not now, so naïve as to think that asking someone to be troubled will be met with excitement. I knew that; I must have known that. So, what was I doing? Why was I insisting? My best guess is that I cared less about cogently coaxing others to do such troubling then and there, and more about letting readers know that you might be troubled and that is OK – it is OK to be troubled *and* to realise that this is a question you can ask yourself (and, too, ask of yourself). You do not need to let trouble into your home; you need only to know that troubling is there, and might one day be the only guest you ever wish to invite in.

The cast of characters in 'Whence We Are Sent' are close to my upbringing. They are those who, 'in Dickensian parlance, raised me by hand', and that includes my cousin Marcus, my brother Gordon, my mother, and my grandmother.[7] I could not write about 'me' without writing about 'them', as any Black feminist knows well. To speak to the ways my cousin and I played together, or the flipside of the behavioural coin that my brother posed in contrast to me, or my grandmother's philosophising, or my mother's authority, is to speak polysemously, polyvocally. I was sent by them, I write; I am here because of them, I write; what I can say is sayable precisely because so many others cultivated the conditions for me to say 'I write' – and then I write: 'This intimacy fissures boundaries imposed.'[8] To be so close to all these others and their voices, their histories, their various 'sents' is to narrate myself in ways that make it difficult to even say 'myself'. They are always and already bound up in the ability to say anything about me. And this is the precondition for the fissuring of imposed boundaries. I write this in this way because of Fred Moten, whose refusal of 'given ontologies' circulates throughout all that I write. 'Boundaries imposed' is to say 'given ontologies', but more particularly in this instance: the boundary that is the body, the individual. To fissure the body's individuality, its stand-aloneness, is to open it up to everything else that constitutes it, which is, maybe, everything. So, what even is a self in this context? What is a self that has neither its own body nor its own discrete narrative? What is a self that through and through comprises so many other selves, which comprise so many other selves, which comprise so many other selves, which are . . .?

This refusal of the singularity imbued into the self is given towards escaping. Insofar as selfhood is to be ontologically still and self-same across a range of vectors, that 'Whence We Are Sent' 'continue[s] to escape confinement' reckons with the urge to not be a self – to move and move, to not sit still, to respond to circumscription, which might be to say the ontological predicate for being a self, primordially cut off from other things, presumptively.[9] But there are so many others that are always here, with/in us, making us, allowing us to be us, but refusing to let the assumed 'me' and 'you' within the 'us' remain distinct. That is what, then, my mother's authority inflected, this sense of the more-than-oneness, always, of the presumed one:

> A polyphonic authority, my mother's verbal authorship of commands . . . her *'Cause I said so* exceeds her and exists before her. She said so, just 'cause, because Grandma said so, her mother said so, Auntie and cousin said so. ''Cause I said so' exists in excessive multiplicity in my mother, given weight by a lineage that has seen some things. Her 'I' is more than her. Her 'I' does not agree to the rules of singular subjectivity contained by presumptions of individualist authority. This polyphonic life my mother fashioned in our home is a refusal, a refusal of the ways in which the world imposes singular sovereignty on our lives. We can only mean one thing, the world tells us, so my mother's latching of an entire world to her utterances is an ardent rebuff of the gestures of individuality. When she speaks, she does so with a legion of others who come back, though they never left, showing us that we live together.[10]

Her ''Cause I said so' is more accurately a ''Cause *we* said so'. There are no I's here. There is no oneself here. This I learned.

Unhoused and unhomed

Of course, autotheory, like any genre of writing, is gendered. As one who writes autotheory *and* theory, it is very clear how the theory employed inhabits the space of seriousness, criticality, cerebrality, and thus, in the incessantly gendered landscape we occupy, masculinity. Lauren Fournier makes this clear and further notes that if such a masculine gendered coding is present with respect to theory, it is a coding 'that is compounded when compared in oppositional ways to the "feminized" genres of lifewriting and memoir', of which autotheory is a sibling.[11] I do not want to say that autotheory is 'feminized' in such a binaristic way, and do not think Fournier is implying a gendered binary either. But I also do not wish to say, in a manner of one-upspersonship, that autotheory 'is' trans. It is not, especially not simply by virtue of it being designated as autotheory. (And indeed, we can hear the gender-laden resonances here: designated or 'assigned' a *genre*, etymologically linked to *gender*. This is not lost on me.) Autotheory is not so much gendered or not gendered, at least for my purposes, as it is a terrain in which the very fundament of that which gender latches on to and moves through is interrogated such that it is, perhaps, vitiated.

The opening essay in *Cistem Failure*, 'Back in the Day', is a kind of taking stock of the moments that proved to be brief apertures into a burgeoning departure from gender. Tongue-in-cheekily, it is an accounting of the moments that made me nonbinary. With trans as my analytic guide, the essay moved through those early moments of nonnormative gender that might have not quite made it onto the radar of legible nonnormative genders. The trans, too, however, offered access into why the self was insufficient; the self was not what would save or even hold us in the end, this essay discovered, and it discovered this through gender's perpetual failing. Gender was and is too wedded to a self. Gender needs a self. And my nonbinariness, my transness, does not need gender. So, do the maths.

The essay opens with an articulation of trans that is 'an itch that things are not enough, a project of undoing, be it gender, institutions, the fabric of the social world'.[12] Most obviously we can link trans to gender and understand trans as a departure from and undoing of gender. But this brief sentence expands this. Because it is never simply about gender for me; it is about so much more, and about the things gender deputises to actualise itself. Namely, the body, the subject, the self. And that self is, at base, an enclosure, something that delimits an inside and an outside with clear boundaries. Erecting walls and roofs and foundations implies an architecture that stands out and away from the surrounding. Indeed, this is what architecture does – erect a thing that is then individuated, made discrete and standing out from the miasma of the undifferentiated. Architecture makes things that create a self, in the midst of all that is non-self.

So, in come the anarchitect and anarchitecture. They are terms I borrow from my friend Jack Halberstam (itself derived from the artist Gordon Matta-Clark and the Anarchitecture Group of the mid-1970s, whose art 'offers a fantastic legacy to young trans* artists who, as we will see, are less interested in making work within existing parameters for painting, sculpture, and/or performance than in tearing those parameters apart'). Jack is thinking about 'unbuilding' and (trans)genders, and to do that he offers the idea of anarchitecture.[13] As I write, moving with Jack:

> Yet the anarchitect tinkers with the building and its logics of buildingness. That anarchitect – who I'm sure uses *they/them* pronouns (for now), I hereby tentatively decree – ain't building nothing, really, just tearing things down and messing with stuff so that what the building is to be is, precisely, that tearing and messing. Because what a building is can only be so much, is only permitted to be so much. So the anarchitect, well, they give glimpses of the things buildings can't be, insisting on what isn't and maybe can't be 'there' – what has been necessarily voided in order for what is sanctioned to appear natural. And I like that. A lot. Because there is no fetishization of being at home or having a house to provide one with shelter. The desire for housedness is tweaked. There are other ways to feel sheltered and loved that do not rely on enclosing oneself in an impenetrable fortress. And maybe that desire that I had, inchoate as it may have been, is responsible for my infatuation with the trans, since transness, anarchitecturally, *offers an extensive vocabulary for expressing unbecoming*; anarchitecture, transly, is deployed *as a kind of wrecking ball that can knock and batter at the fortress of binary gender.* Unstitching the enclosure of the house's structural architecture is in fact more livable for some ways of becoming and unbecoming than the presumed house. I could not be loved, at least not all the way, in the house. It stanched too much. I needed more room than the architecture of the house could provide.[14]

Anarchitecture is an unbecoming. To *be* is to stand out, to have a defined architecture that is decidedly not other things. The walls are its own; there are juridical documents attesting to its proprietary standing. It is indeed property, unable to legally be trespassed on – because it is a self-contained entity, indeed a self, not-others. But the anarchitect *un*becomes, does not build to erect edifices but tears down, refutes, and vitiates various other selves. Those glimpses the anarchitect provides are the things that are not selves and cannot and do not want to be selves. It, we might say, makes things *un*exist since existence is predicated on possessing a selfhood that can be made discrete from other selves. Love and shelter need not be things bestowed only by closing off and extricating from others. This impulse is deeply trans, and my transness, the transness 'I' move through, does not want binary gender, does not want *gender*, does not want to erect a clearly delimited thing that is unlike others – a self.

So, what does it want? That is still up in the air. And maybe because it is not here and cannot be here. That 'subjectivity found and unfound elsewhere' I write about, pages later, is a subjectivity which is *not* the same as a self; subjectivity for me is much more robust, can hold and unhold so much more. That subjectivity does not abide the extant parameters of life because it lives imaginatively 'in the social world that will emerge after the abolition of this one, a terrain that is still consequential and attendant upon our sense of *(un)self even though it is not (yet) here*'.[15] That is what trans can offer: something not this, not self, not the confines of corporeality and identity. Just something else. Because the trans and how 'I' move through it via the nonbinary does not need or want a self. It is too busy trying to live in other unworlds that have long let go of all the lacklustre, unimaginative terrains that characterise and foundation this world. Why else would Dean Spade, in a reappropriative move, call trans people 'impossible people' if the trans did not yearn deeply, viciously for that which was not real, not possible?[16] The possible is here, and we wish for all that is not here.

Notes

1 From 'FUC 012 | Fred Moten & Stefano Harney – the university: last words', www.youtube.com/watch?v=zqWMejD_XU8&t=5353s (accessed 11 April 2023). See also '"Escape"-Bound on Twitter: "The Institutions That We're Fighting Is Not Just the School, the Police, the Clinic, the Jail, but It's Also the Self, the Subject." – Fred Moten / Twitter', Twitter, https://twitter.com/escapebound/status/1281329092495904775 (accessed 20 July 2020).

2 Marquis Bey, *Them Goon Rules: Fugitive Essays on Radical Black Feminism* (Tucson, AZ: University of Arizona Press, 2019); *Cistem Failure: Essays on Blackness and Cisgender* (Durham, NC and London: Duke University Press, 2022).
3 Toni Morrison, 'Unspeakable Things Unspoken: The Afro-American Presence in American Literature', *Michigan Quarterly Review,* 28 (1989), 19–20, original emphasis.
4 Robyn Wiegman, 'Introduction: Autotheory Theory', *Arizona Quarterly: A Journal of American Literature, Culture, and Theory,* 76:1 (2020), 2.
5 Goodison, 'Nanny', in *I Am Becoming my Mother* (London: New Beacon Books, 1995), p. 45.
6 Bey, *Them Goon Rules,* p. xii.
7 Bey, *Them Goon Rules,* p. 13.
8 Bey, *Them Goon Rules,* p. 5.
9 Bey, *Them Goon Rules,* p. 10.
10 Bey, *Them Goon Rules,* p. 13.
11 Lauren Fournier, *Autotheory as Feminist Practice in Art, Writing, and Criticism* (Cambridge, MA: MIT Press, 2021), p. 13.
12 Bey, *Cistem Failure,* p. 3.
13 See Jack Halberstam, 'Unbuilding Gender: Trans* Anarchitectures In and Beyond the Work of Gordon Matta-Clark', *Places Journal* (October 2018), https://doi.org/10.22269/181003 (accessed 20 July 2020).
14 Bey, *Cistem Failure,* p. 4, original emphasis.
15 Bey, *Cistem Failure,* p. 8, emphasis added.
16 Spade made this statement in a lecture, 'Trans Politics on a Neoliberal Landscape', delivered on 9 February 2009 at Barnard College, Columbia University, New York.

Part IV
Conceptualising the self

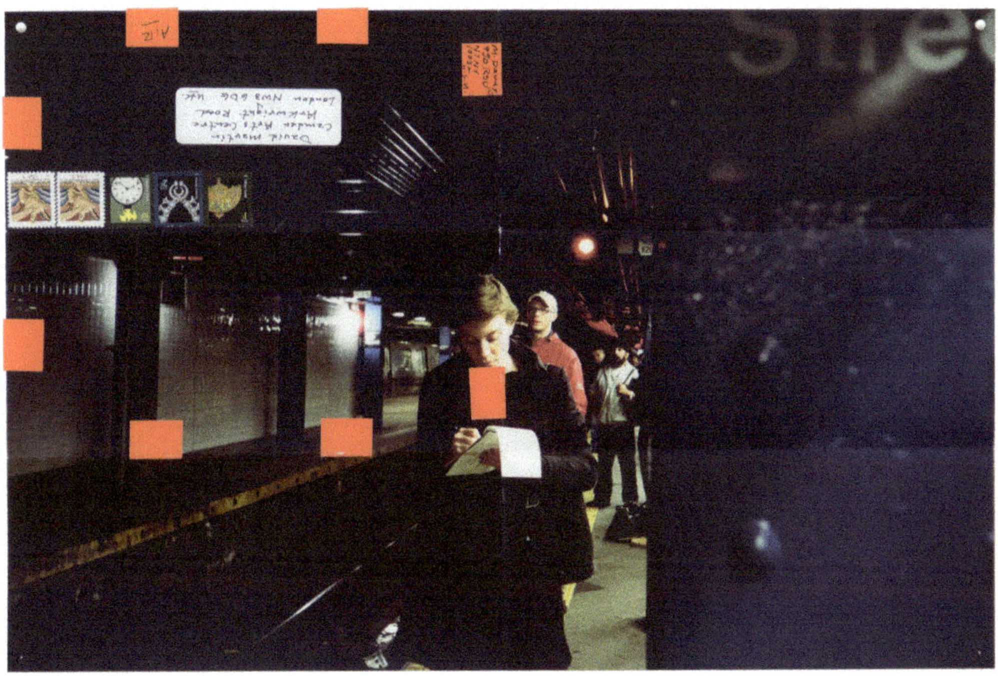

Moyra Davey, detail from *Subway Writers* series, 2011, C-print, tape, postage ink, 30 × 45 cm

8

'Sources questionable at best': Ree Morton's notebooks and sketchbooks

Abi Shapiro

In 1988, Franklin Furnace – an organisation dedicated to the collection and preservation of artists' books – displayed the notebooks and sketchbooks of the American artist Ree Morton to mark the acquisition of the books for their collection.[1] The exhibition took place just over a decade after the artist died, aged 41, in 1977 and it helped revive interest in her short nine-year career that spanned a remarkable gamut of genres from post-minimalism, to feminist art, conceptual art, land art, installation art, performance art, and the Pattern and Decoration movement.

The exhibition at Franklin Furnace, however, did not display any of Morton's artworks, showing only her notebooks and sketchbooks. Reviewing the exhibition for *The New York Times*, critic Roberta Smith wrote:

> these notebooks – which include everything from sketches and written plans for pieces to quotes from favorite writers to a rough draft of an application to the National Endowment for the Arts – narrate the ups and downs of life in the studio with particular vividness. And they may give a fuller feeling of Morton herself – her sense of humor, of poetry, and of intellectual curiosity – than her art quite had time to.[2]

Smith's review situates Morton's notebooks within the purview of autobiographical archive material rather than as artists' books. For Smith, the books offer a more authentic or 'fuller' link between the artist 'herself' and her artwork, even though – as I will discuss later – Morton chose to display parts of her notebooks as artworks in 1976. Smith's reading of Morton's notebooks as archival ephemera aligns with long-standing trends both in art history and exhibition displays where artists' autobiographical writings are often used in the interpretation of their artwork, yet frequently with reductive effects. This is particularly evident in cases where an artist's practice is understood to have autobiographical reference points and archival materials, such as notebooks and diaries, are presumed to provide causal links between an artist's work and their life.

I raise this as a concern not to challenge whether artists' notebooks should be put into interpretive service, but rather to propose that we need to consider more carefully *how* autobiographical sources are being deployed and what kind of knowledge this produces about the artwork and the artist. In terms of autobiography, the explicit use of the 'I' and the evocation of the self is particularly important in the study of art made by women because it is a charged act intended to give agency and legitimacy to the creative expression of one's lived experience. Yet, despite the increasing proliferation of artists' writing and archival materials being used hermeneutically in publications and exhibitions, these materials to a large extent remain critically and theoretically unexamined as sources.

Morton is a fascinating example of an artist who regularly drew inspiration from her personal relationships with her children, friends, colleagues, and lovers, as well as the places, objects, and landscapes she encountered. While Morton's extensive notebooks and diaries have been widely used by critics, curators, and historians to provide explanations for her work and its presumed autobiographical content, I would argue this has happened without much reflection on the complex and conceptual role of her notebooks in her practice with regard to writing and documentation. With the advent of several international major retrospective exhibitions in the last decade and Morton's work increasingly being collected by major museums, it is timely to explore the use of the notebooks in the emergence of her legacy as well as how we approach and use artists' diaries, notebooks, and sketchbooks in general.

The first part of this chapter surveys a range of new methodological approaches to women artists' writings in relation to autobiographical strategies and explores broadly how feminist critiques of established art-historical models have challenged problematic causal links between art and artist. I consider the value in looking at notebooks through a lens of gendered labour, particularly assessing how artists' writings each offer unique material and theoretical propositions from which to explore their working process as it relates to their lived experiences. The second section looks closely at different forms of work and labour expressed in Morton's practice across both her art objects and her notebooks. I discuss the projects she developed on holiday with her children and the circumstances of her domestic studios, in order to theorise the convergent forms of labour that expand our understanding of the artist's 'work' across her studio practice and in her writing.

Ree Morton

Although during her life Morton exhibited alongside notable artists – such as Eva Hesse, Bruce Nauman, Robert Morris, Richard Serra, Lynda Benglis, Sol LeWitt, Louise Bourgeois, Robert Rauschenberg, Joan Jonas, and Hannah Wilke – she has remained relatively obscure. A handful of major solo exhibitions have substantially improved the visibility of her legacy, but rarely is she mentioned in historical surveys of 1970s American art.[3] Given the limited exposure to her work, there is merit in rehearsing the basic story of her career as it bears on the discussion of her autobiographical artwork that follows.

Born in 1936, Helen Marie ('Ree') Reilly began making art relatively late in life, around the age of 29. In 1965, when she was already married to Ted Morton, with three young children under the age of 10, Morton enrolled in university evening classes, later graduating with a bachelor's degree in Fine Art from Rhode Island School of Art and Design. In 1968, after separating from her husband, Morton moved with her children to Pennsylvania to complete a postgraduate degree at Tyler School of Art in Philadelphia.

At Tyler, Morton became interested in the relationship between two- and three-dimensionality, engaging with contemporaneous minimalist and post-minimalist debates about medium specificity to produce a series of works in the late 1960s that challenged definitions of painting and sculpture. After graduating in 1970, Morton remained in Philadelphia, and between 1971 and 1972 she made over twenty-five large-scale installations using found objects and large painted wooden planks and beams arranged around the walls and corners of rooms. This marked the start of Morton's interest in immersive spatial installations, prompting her to seek out a larger studio space and further career opportunities in New York City. However, in order to do so, in 1972 Morton took the difficult decision to legally turn over full-time custody of her children to their father, who lived out of state.

In New York City, Morton immersed herself in the art scene of Greenwich Village and Soho, taking part in feminist art networks associated with Marcia Tucker and Lucy Lippard and working on projects with groups such as Anarchitecture – a collective of avant-garde performance artists, sculptors, dancers, and architects including Gordon Matta-Clark and Laurie Anderson. These networks honed Morton's approach to space, materials, and the body, and it was at this time that she began to integrate political ideas about gendered aesthetics, the built environment, and motherhood into her abstract minimalist sculptural pieces.

After 1973, Morton's points of reference in her work became increasingly autobiographical, likely due to her association with feminist activism, consciousness-raising groups, and self-help therapy methods, all of which encouraged auto-analysis. She began to deliberately use materials and forms deemed 'feminine', decorative, and kitsch to create large spatial installations that referred to her family, friends, and colleagues. For example, Morton created several installations adorned with items such as sculpted ribbons, pink bows, butterflies, and decorated cakes in order to mock and question feminine stereotypes in both serious and humorous ways. Steadily, her use of kitsch tropes gave way to more pointed explorations of feelings in the mid-1970s, and Morton engaged with gendered debates about 'bad taste' and the use of 'feminine' clichés, increasingly using language and text with regard to the challenge of expressing ideas such as sentimentality and love. In the spring of 1977, as she was in the midst of preparing for an exhibition at the School of the Art Institute of Chicago, Morton died from injuries she sustained in a car accident.

Ree Morton's notebooks

Anecdotal sources tell us that Morton's notebooks and sketchbooks were 'always at hand' and that 'they meant a great deal to her'.[4] Although Morton's use of notebooks started as early as 1968, when she was a student, their use became regular and sustained between 1973 and 1977, and Morton often worked across multiple books at the same time. During these four years, she interspersed documentation of her artistic processes amid diaristic passages ruminating on her experience as a woman and a single working mother.

The thirty-nine books are a fascinating and complex resource. The content, style, and forms of writing within them are vast, ranging from nonsensical poems, to detailed drawings of installations (since destroyed), recipes for soup, annotated philosophical tracts about aesthetics, grocery lists, as well as emotional passages about her concerns of being a competent mother. Shortly before Morton died in 1977, she wrote about her notebooks, stating:

> Data in these notebooks – accumulated over the years on a hit and miss basis using principles of selection mysterious to me which, furthermore, changes from year to year and which I could not recover if I wanted to. Sources questionable at best. My excuse for brazenly dipping into this preempted domain is that I have a special interest, one that does not recognize a difference in value between a good novel and a bad one, a comic strip or an opera. All are equally useful in explicating the character of styles of experienced activity.[5]

Morton's statement that the 'data' and 'sources' in her writing are 'questionable at best' was my starting point for understanding her notebooks as sites of creative work and not as repositories of factual information about her life. Here, Morton presents herself, in effect, as an unreliable narrator in her writing. This is a proposition more readily understood if we agree that the 'auto' in autobiographical art should not be taken as a stable or truthful expression of artistic identity. Rather, in the production of women's autobiographical art, the concept of 'self' and expression of agency unfolds in multiple and intersecting ways across art objects and writing.

My approach is indebted to the rise of 'autotheory' over the last two decades specifically – a term that Lauren Fournier describes as

> works of literature, writing and criticism that integrate autobiography with theory and philosophy . . . a term that describes a self-conscious way of engaging with theory – as a discourse, frame, or mode of thinking and practice – alongside lived experience and subjective embodiment, something very much in the *Zeitgeist* of cultural production today – especially in feminist, queer and BIPOC–Black, Indigenous, and people of color – spaces that live on the edge of art and academia.[6]

Charting the development of autotheory, Fournier ascribes the term to interdisciplinary practices that adopt self-reflexive, diaristic, and 'personal' strategies of expression that challenge the illegitimacy of making public the so-called 'private' lived experiences of individuals, particularly those whose lives are marginalised. Drawing on an autotheoretical approach not only embraces the impulse of evoking the self and embodied positionality as a social and political act in art-making, but it further expands the sites of creativity – such as notebooks, diaries, or sketchbooks – where we might look to find self-styled forms of agency within an artistic practice. This helps to consider the idiosyncratic connections between these 'private' forms of writing and the more public-facing objects (produced in the studio and later exhibited) that offer specific theoretical propositions about autobiographical strategies. In light of this, it bears thinking more generally first about what is at stake when we talk about the 'autobiographical' and 'biographical' relationship between art and artist, and looking at what existing methods and formats sustain such models, such as the monograph.

Feminist approaches to autobiographical material

Since the eighteenth century, the monograph has established a number of methodologies that have governed the way notions of art and artist are mutually codetermined.[7] Monograph conventions were largely unchallenged until feminist art historians in the 1970s, such as Linda Nochlin, addressed the way models of artistic 'genius' had been created by, and for, the legacies of white male artists.[8] These critiques exposed the marginalisation of artists according to exclusions based in or around bodily 'difference' and they began to explore new ways to historicise these subjects. This not only put the efficacy of the monographic tradition into question, but it raised concerns about the gendered instrumentalisation of biographical narratives.[9] Griselda Pollock's critiques of canons and their predefined relationships between artist and art object are particularly important:

> The preoccupation with the individual artist is symptomatic of the work accomplished in art history – the production of an *artistic subject for works of art.* The subject constructed from the art work is then posited as the exclusive source of meaning – i.e. of 'art' and the effect of this is to remove 'art' from historical or textual analysis by representing it solely as the 'expression' of the creative personality of the artist. Art is therefore neither public, social, nor a product of work. Art and artist become reflexive, mystically bound into an unbreakable circuit which produces the artist as the subject of the artwork and the artwork as a means of contemplative access to that subject's 'transcendent' and creative subjectivity. The construction of an artist subject for art is accomplished through current discursive structures – the *biographic*, which focuses exclusively on the

> individual, and the *narrative* which produces coherent, linear, causal sequences through which an artist subject is realised.[10]

Pollock explains how certain tropes and formats of biographical narratives in the monograph seek 'coherent' and stable identities in relation to artworks. The monograph therefore bolsters the myth of the 'singular, solitary genius' which maintains this model of artistic identity gendered as male, and thus unavailable to women.[11]

Gabriele Guercio, in his study of the monograph, similarly suggests that the chronological format of the monograph encouraged a preference towards the linear teleological and parallel progression of art and artist, securing a mutually coherent evolution of artistic style and personal identity culminating in the 'genius' model. He argues that the explicit focus on the interdependency of these narratives has resulted in the erasure of social and cultural contexts of art and artist, which is particularly problematic in the case of women reflecting on the personal and political circumstances of their experiences.[12]

The conventional model of writing in monographs is broadly known as 'biographism' – a literary term used for the explanation of a text relying on information known about the author's life.[13] Artist monographs have relied heavily on archival materials – such as diaries and notebooks – to legitimise biographism, which has in turn sustained assumptions that 'truths' about artists are evident in autobiographical material. Therefore, the interconnected legacies of the monograph and the methodologies of biographism have sustained the framing of primary (auto)biographical sources as factual, that is, containing answers and truths to facilitate interpretive frameworks. By extension, then, is it presumed that artists' diaries and notebooks also hold such truths?

One salient example can be seen in the legacy of the artist Eva Hesse, whose complex biographical events were recorded in the artist's extensive diaries.[14] Hesse's diaries have been used in Freudian-led psychobiographical interpretations of her oeuvre that have used the artist's traumas (her escape from Nazi Germany, her mother's suicide, and her experience of a brain tumour which later killed her) as interpretive frameworks.[15] Psychobiographical models are still very common today in art history and in gallery exhibitions where artist's notebooks, diaries, and letters are presumed to deliver 'insights into the mind' of the 'real' artist.[16] This supposed transparency of Hesse's self in her autobiographical writing was particularly apparent in 2016, upon the complete publication of Hesse's notebooks and diaries, when one critic remarked that the artist is now 'an open book'.[17]

The contested use of psychobiography in Hesse's legacy can be seen in a debate between two art historians during the mid-1990s. In an article published in the journal *October*, Anne M. Wagner detailed her critique of Hesse scholarship that made her 'mistrustful of the assumptions and reductions at the heart of Hesse's reputation'.[18] Wagner accused several writers by name – including Anna C. Chave – of 'martyrology' and 'collapsing the artist into her art'. Wagner bemoaned that, because Hesse spoke in her notebooks of the 'interconnectedness' of her art and life, scholars seemed permitted to use the artist's trauma to interpret her work. This, Wagner said, made Hesse a symbolic 'wound', where her femininity and trauma were doubly pathologised, instead of being celebrated as a successful post-minimalist artist.[19]

A year later, *October* published a letter by Chave responding to these criticisms in which she suggested that Wagner herself had proposed an unethical interpretative framework, wherein art historians may claim to know exactly how to separate a woman artist's lived experience from her artwork. She warned against policing the legitimacy of biographical narratives and further cautioned against the negative impact this could have on the legacy of women artists more generally if we *did not* consider the circumstances of the artist's life and her expression of agency in relation to how her work was produced.[20] This clash in views characterises a wider anxiety in feminist scholarship regarding the use of women artists' autobiographical art and writing.[21] Yet is it notable that both historians' positions still indicate a belief that an authentic or coherent identity is to be found in Hesse's diaries and in her work.

Feminist life-writing scholar Marlene Kadar offers instructive ways to reconceptualise this relationship between artists' autobiographical writing and their agency. She suggests that autobiographical materials like diaries and notebooks in literary studies are too often configured around binary models, such as truth versus fiction, masculine versus feminine, and public versus private. This tendency, she argues, has constructed false parameters in women's life writing, particularly where gendered bias has historically determined women's writing as private and domestic and therefore non-literary. Seeking an alternative approach, Kadar posits that 'life writing is best examined on an "uneven continuum" of objectivity and subjectivity, and fiction and non-fiction'. She goes on to suggest that '[t]here is no search for truth or the "real" but a mutual construction of knowledge between what the writer gives and what the reader understands'.[22] This is important, as it resists a presumed mastery over a subject and allows life writing to be understood more as an *encounter* that 'implicates self and other(s) in a context in which a dialectic of relationality is both acknowledged and problematized'.[23]

Adopting a similar idea for autobiographical art and writing, Sidonie Smith and Julia Watson consider 'autobiographical acts' as an 'interface.' This, they explain:

> foreground[s] us as viewers, who are addressed in and by the works, to participate actively, and oftentimes uncomfortably, in negotiating the politics of subjectivity. They invite us to confront our own participation in 'othering' the text, the image, and the 'woman' embodied before us. They invite us to re-vision the spectacle of femininity and to remake women as cultural agents of the autobiographical interface.[24]

Kadar's, and Smith and Watson's, propositions underscore the extent to which agency and authorship are mutually constructed and enacted through embodied encounters with autobiographical material, whether they are texts or works of art. Seen in this way, the dynamics between artists' autobiographical acts need not be viewed as disclosing truth or fiction, or as confirming authentic identity. Instead, autobiographical material is a site of encounter – an 'interface' – that permits more open-ended interpretations that do not pathologise the subject by making a causal link between her art and life.

Kristen Frederickson and Sarah E. Webb, in their feminist rethinking of the artist's monograph, propose a 'matrix' where the relationship between art historian and the artist-subject is configured as dialogic and collaborative – what Webb calls 'the convergence of authors' and artists' voices'.[25] Frederickson and Webb claim there will be gaps, misunderstandings, and contradictions which occur in the encounter with autobiographical material but that these anomalies and fantasies create more ethical accounts that act not as a '[retrieval of] the artist who is also a woman, but [as] a rethinking of the site of her inscription' in the format of the monograph. We must ask, they conclude, 'How are her notations [and] her works recorded, valued, made visible, qualified or erased?'[26]

In effect, these scholars propose that each artist's notebooks and diaries are material and theoretical propositions from which to develop unique models about how to explore their practice and its contexts. In this regard, I find Briony Fer's approach to Gabriel Orozco's notebooks particularly instructive: she describes them as 'disobedient objects' because they refuse to provide the answers she asks of them about the artist and his work.[27] Notebooks, she suggests, productively resist truths about their maker precisely because they invite us instead to 'reflect on the conditions of art's production'. This foregrounds artistic processes and labour rather than their identity, which is ultimately unstable and unknowable.[28]

This approach to autobiographical material in art-historical writing is key because it suggests that artists' notebooks are not material repositories of answers or truths, but that they open up theoretical questions about what is at stake in the power dynamics when we write about art and artists in art history.

The 'work of art' and 'artwork' as methodologies

In her book *Women Making Art: History, Subjectivity, Aesthetics,* Marsha Meskimmon argues that 'the *work* of art' can be understood to have multiple meanings: it is both a material object made from artistic labour *and* a process of interpretation performed by the viewer. Meskimmon suggests that looking at art made specifically by (the unstable gender category of) 'women' constellates the work of a female artist with the interpretive work of the viewer, through what she calls a 'double play of materiality and agency'. This locates the viewer as 'a partner in a dialogue with women making art rather than one in a position of a privileged interlocutor, explicating the inherent truths of women, art and cultural history'.[29]

Meskimmon proposes that shifting the locus of analysis towards the way in which meaning is produced through encounters, rather than searching for what an object means, results in expanding the definition of the *work* of art as a dialogue between artist and interpreter. This, she notes, requires us to think about the new kinds of knowledge produced in each encounter in order not to 'define in advance what women's art can mean', but to look at the ways in which we may work '*with* women making art . . . to create specific configurations of ideas, objects, images and texts'.[30] Meskimmon concludes by arguing that this dynamic 'forges the critical link between [artists'] thinking and making, between the materiality of the objects and the agency of artists and participant observers'.[31] This focus on agency and materiality links closely to Kadar's, Smith and Watson's, and Frederickson and Webb's ideas about the 'interface' between viewer and autobiographical material and the way in which these encounters ('working *with* women making art') allow us to resist mastery over a subject. While Meskimmon's theory is not specifically about autobiographical art or artists' writing per se, her approach to the mutual configurations of *work* extends to the way we might approach the processes of labour evident in Ree Morton's notebooks and art objects as they mutually bring about what she calls the 'critical link between thinking and making'.

Labour is a central theme in Angela Dimitrakaki's book, *Gender, ArtWork and the Global Imperative: A Materialist Feminist Critique.* Here, the author reconsiders artistic labour through the term 'artWork'. Where Meskimmon focuses primarily on the dialogic relationship produced between artist and viewer, Dimitrakaki locates the art object between the artist and their labour according to art-market economies and gendered conditions of production. Dimitrakaki examines how female artists at different points in history have become 'economic subjects', mitigated specifically through their gendered circumstances of work. She explains:

> The term 'artWork' is intended to take further feminist art history's partial displacement of the delivered artwork as the exclusive origin of meaning and rethink what 'process-based work' can possibly describe . . . artWorks engage with social phenomena associated, in many different and not always transparent ways, with globalisation as well with the processes and contexts of art making, including if, and how, a 'global imperative' has transformed the social role of the artist as a gendered individual.[32]

Dimitrakaki foregrounds how reading labour in art genders processes of making and equally how assumptions about gender influence interpretations of labour and art. Thus, to remove the art object as 'exclusive origin of meaning' is to look beyond the one-way, causal relationship between the artist and her art, and instead to view labour as a process that, as Dimitrakaki explains, can 'locate women artists within a broader framework of artistic production'. Dimitrakaki notes that this broader framework must take into account the various material *and* immaterial labours of women artists more broadly, opening out artistic labour to, for example, include and overlap with domestic labour. This, Dimitrakaki suggests, helps 'in tracing *how* the articulation of art as a gendered field of production is connected with gendered labor beyond art'.[33]

Both Meskimmon's and Dimitrakaki's theories of art, work, and labour have meaningful implications for Ree Morton's practice. Meskimmon's model of the *work of art* provides a way to analyse Morton's 'double play of materiality and agency' in her art objects and notebooks as a means to explore her labour and processes between both media as dialogic sites of encounter. Bringing in Dimitrakaki's expanded concept of artwork opens up Ree Morton's practice and her various kinds of 'work' to contexts of gendered labour in the 1970s. For example, it proposes that childcare was not a corollary to Morton's 'studio' art-making but that it was a part of her practice. This situates Morton as a subject produced by her gendered and economic context and implores us to explore how the circumstances of her work – in the studio and at home – affected and informed her autobiographical strategies.

'Vacation work': *Souvenir Piece* and *Weeds of the Northeast*

In 1973, Morton spent a summer holiday with her three children on the rural coast of Newfoundland, Canada – a trip she later described as 'the happiest summer of my life'.[34] Not only was the holiday time for Morton to spend with her children (who at this time were living with their father), but it also inspired a new body of work. Shortly after her return from Canada, Morton made the multi-part installation *Souvenir Piece* (figure 8.1), which consisted of four clusters of sculptural objects arranged in and around the edges of a room.[35] When the work was first exhibited at Artists Space in New York that October, Morton used the full scope of the room by placing objects both on the walls and around the floor, set at different heights to create dynamic material and spatial relationships between the installation's components. One of the clusters of objects in *Souvenir Piece* is a low green table, around fifty centimetres high, held up by precariously unsteady legs. Upon the table are items salvaged from the Canadian shore by Morton and her children.[36] The pebbles and stones, most of which are no bigger than a child's clenched fist, rest on small wooden battens of various heights like a series of miniature abstract sculptures on plinths. The low table and the display aesthetic bring to mind a child's abandoned game – as if the artist has turned the eponymous 'souvenirs' from the summer into a museological memorial. Another piece inspired by the same holiday is a series of works on paper called *Newfoundland Drawings* (also 1973). Each work presents abstract circular forms rendered in

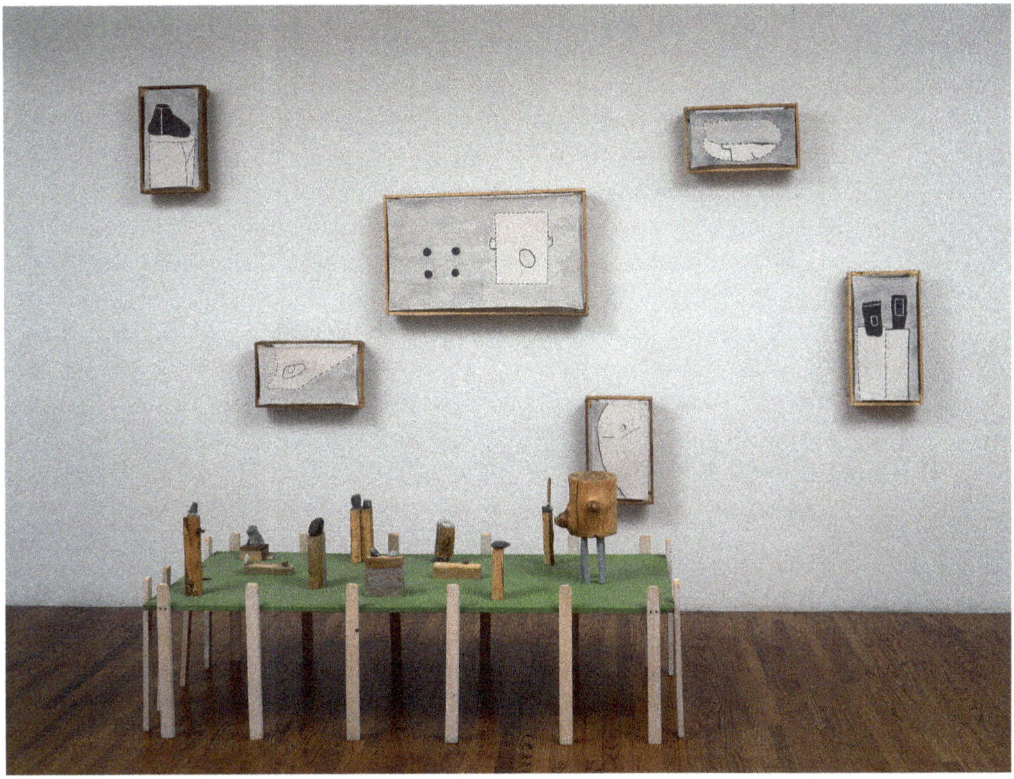

8.1 Ree Morton, *Souvenir Piece*, 1973, 6 acrylic on canvas and wood paintings; wooden table with 11 'souvenirs': acrylic, wood, and stones, paintings overall: 240 × 391 cm, table: 84 × 188 × 90 cm

pencil, abstractly referring, perhaps, to a cartographer's illustration of the rocky Newfoundland coastline as seen from above.

Although a holiday is meant to be a period away from work, Morton used the time with her three children to develop ideas for her practice. The notebook from the holiday contains documentary sketches and semi-abstract drawings of coastlines, plants, people, and found objects that would later appear in both *Souvenir Piece* and the *Newfoundland Drawings*.[37] Morton later said: 'a recent trip to NFLD [Newfoundland] has had a profound influence on my work, and keeping in mind topographical surroundings greatly affect my thinking'.[38] Not only was Morton responding to the Canadian coastal geography, but in her notebooks she was developing techniques, styles, and strategies *because*, not in spite of the fact, that she was working whilst caring for her children.

The following summer, in 1974, Morton took her children on holiday to the small, rural town of Tannersville in the east of New York State. She soon developed two series of works based on botanical textbooks she had bought for her children in Tannersville. The first series was *Weeds of the Northeast* (1974), comprising ten works on paper each representing leaves native to New York State based on scientific illustrations from a 1956 educational book of the same name.[39] However, unlike the detailed scientific illustrations, Morton's drawings are bright, colourful, and simply drawn, in a combination of pencil, crayon, and watercolour. Each is captioned with the leaves' colloquial names, such as 'corn cockle', 'sticktight', and 'teasel' (figure 8.2). Each leaf is set against a bright pink-and-red-patterned background and contained in a frame decorated with glitter. The gaudy and celebratory ornamentation of an everyday object implies a deliberate amateur aesthetic, suggestive of a childlike awe of nature.

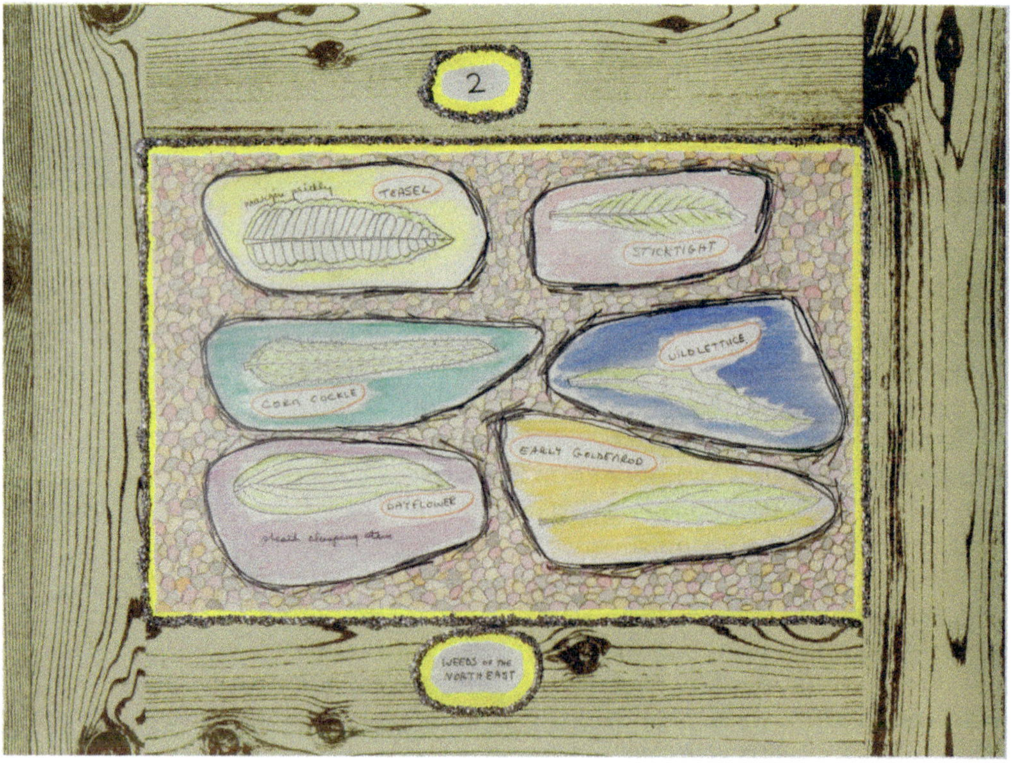

8.2 Ree Morton, *Weeds of the Northeast* 2, 1974, pencil, coloured pencil, glitter, silkscreen on paper, 48 × 63 cm

The second series of works on paper made after the Tannersville trip were inspired by a second book, *Wild Flowers Worth Knowing*, by the amateur botanist Neltje Blanchan, originally published in 1917.[40] Blanchan's book features simple illustrations of flowers with poetic descriptions of their features, origins, and medicinal uses, along with associated folk myths. In her notebooks, Morton made an entry for the 'The Borage Family' and its common names such as 'forget-me-nots', 'mouse ear [sic]', 'scorpion grass', 'snake grass', and 'love me', which she experimentally illustrated in banners as well as contained within a sculptural tombstone shape adorned with light bulbs. Adjacent on the page, in text that curls around the illustration, Morton copied Blanchan's poetic description: 'another dismal myth sends its hero forth seeking hidden treasure caves in a mountain under the guidance of a fairy. He fills his pockets with gold but not heeding the fairy's warning to "forget not the best" – i.e., the myosotis – he is crushed by the closing together of the mountain.'[41]

Morton made fourteen artworks inspired by Blanchan's book between 1974 and 1975, including seven works on paper and seven sculptures made of Celastic, a plastic-based material, each taking their titles from a plant's name or a phrase from the book.[42] Yet, unlike *Weeds of the Northeast,* where Morton represented the leaves or flowers as images, in the Celastic works she only represented the flowers by their names.

This use of language was a new direction for Morton's work. In a work on paper called *Trumpet Weed* (1974), three banners proclaim the phrases 'the ranks of floral missionaries need recruits', 'conspicuous advertisements', and 'trumpet weed'. Behind the banners, Morton drew and painted a woodland landscape in pale muted watercolours that contrast with the bold text floating in the foreground. Morton's notebooks show that she cut and matched passages from different parts of Blanchan's book in this work; instead of fidelity to the author's observations or indeed to the natural world itself, Morton reconfigured the plants' attributes to fictionalise nature by her own design.[43]

In the seven Celastic pieces inspired by *Wild Flowers Worth Knowing*, Morton selected shorter words or phrases which she then embossed onto three-dimensional banners.[44] Celastic is pliable, with a finished appearance similar to papier-mâché. It was originally created for cheaply fabricating theatrical props. When wetted with acetate, Celastic has to be quickly contorted freehand or moulded around objects before it sets, forming a rigid and robust cast that can then be painted or embellished. Morton used the material to emboss words into the surface of the banners, making clay letter-moulds around which to sculpt the Celastic. The banners were hung across walls or splayed across horseshoe-shaped sculptures which were then propped upright on the floor. Morton painted the banners in bright colours and sometimes decorated them with glowing light bulbs – as in the piece *Solitary or Rarely 2* (1974), which took its title from Blanchan's description of the rock-rose flower.

In an interview in 1975, Morton explained: 'I got involved with the language because it's very moralistic about the flowers' attributes. The reference to flowers also seems to pertain to people.'[45] In her notebooks, Morton twice called these her 'Autobiographical Wallflower Series', insinuating these works were not just about 'people' but also, ultimately, about herself.[46] Although it might be tempting to interpret the works through their titles, such as *Solitary or Rarely 2*, which could be references to Morton's loneliness or status as a single mother, this would result in the problematic causal and psychobiographical connections between art and artist that Griselda Pollock cautioned against when she spoke of the 'unbreakable circuit which produces the artist as the subject of the artwork and the artwork as a means of contemplative access to that subject's "transcendent" and creative subjectivity'.[47]

In this case, we cannot presume Morton's 'autobiographical flowers' tell us something authentic or definitive about the artist's psyche, simply because she frames them in reference to herself. By this I mean that Morton's evocation of the 'autobiographical' is not an invitation to pinpoint precisely *how* her artworks relate to her identity – how could we ever know this anyway? Rather, in the political act of referring to the self – which legitimises her agency as a woman and a mother who can draw on her own experience in her art practice – this opens up an autotheoretical interface where Morton's material outcomes invite us to contemplate the interrelated personal and political conditions of its process-based production. For example, we, as viewers of her 'holiday works', are aware that Morton's maternal responsibilities informed her material and aesthetic choices. Yet, her decision to represent flowers in such a playful, childlike, and 'feminine' way, as she does in *Weeds of the Northeast,* does not have to only be about her, her children, or her maternal experience. Instead, we can look at the way the evocation of these subjects infers her holiday, childcare, and the act of note-taking and sketch-making as all interrelated forms of labour, which together make up Morton's *work* of art. How might this more expansive definition of Morton's labour inform our reading of these works, when we think about the paradox of making art (i.e., working) while being on holiday (typically a time spent *not working*)? Reframing Morton's autobiographical work in this way helps us to complicate and redefine what is perceived as productive and unproductive artistic labour, not just at the stage of fabrication, but in the conceptual development of the work, as is evident in Morton's notebooks and sketchbooks. To do so locates, more precisely and more politically, how motherhood and parental care was (and is) implicated across and between different aspects of creative production, and perhaps – even more importantly – how it permeates daily life.

'Home work': domestic studios

In a notebook entry from 1975, Morton reflected on balancing work and home life: 'women are not any more part time than anyone else – very few artists of any sex do not work at something other than their art to earn a living, though its [sic] true that women often have three jobs instead of two'.[48] Morton may have been paraphrasing her friend, the critic and feminist activist Lucy Lippard, who, just a few years earlier, wrote that 'women often have three jobs instead of two: their art, work for pay and the traditional unpaid "work that's never done"'.[49]

By the mid-1970s, Morton was working 'three jobs' by balancing a studio practice, teaching, and caring for her children, often as a single parent (having regained custody by this time). Back in 1964, when Morton was taking evening art classes prior to starting her degree (while caring for her children aged 2, 4, and 7), her neighbour and friend Janis Porter described Morton's domestic studio space in Norfolk, Virginia: 'The small house had no ideal spot for her to paint, and with three small children around, privacy was at a premium. However, Ree found refuge in the large unfinished bath just off the ground floor playroom . . . she took refuge in her bathroom studio.'[50] A few years later in 1968, following the separation from her husband, Morton moved with her children to Pennsylvania to begin a master's degree. During her first year of graduate school, Morton moved into a small house with a basement for her studio. Curator Marcia Tucker, who at the time was Morton's art-history teacher and friend, remembered Morton 'literally working behind the washer/dryer in the basement of this suburban home'.[51]

Morton's circumstances were not unusual for women at the time. As Lippard remarked in 1976: 'I went to a great many women's studios and my preconceptions were jolted daily. I thought serious artists had to have big, professional looking spaces. I found women in corners of men's studios, in bedrooms and children's rooms, even in kitchens, working away. I thought important American art was large. I found women working small both out of inclination and necessity.'[52] Indeed, much of Morton's artwork made during these periods of using domestic studios were paintings and small sculptures. Unsurprisingly, when Morton was able to rent a studio away from her home, her practice transformed. Not only did Morton increase her capacity to work uninterrupted, but her sculptures and installations from this period were made using power tools, like chainsaws, that were obviously unsuitable around young children. I have argued elsewhere that Morton's acquiring of a non-domestic studio was a pivotal moment in the artist's career, as she began making installation art in 1972 – a period that also heralded a number of other women making installation art in the 1970s who have been widely overlooked.[53] By the time Morton arrived in New York City in 1972 to a much larger loft-studio, her immersive installations were taking up the entire room.

For Morton, her loft-studio in Greenwich Village marked a shift in her professional status. In a grant application made the year she moved to New York City, Morton wrote of how she had started out with 'three children, a naval husband and a home in a boring middle class development in Norfolk, Virginia', describing her story as 'a feminist classic: out of the kitchen, into the studio'.[54] Speaking in an interview in 1974, Morton said she had not seen herself as a professional artist in the early stages of her career:

> I was still not able to call myself an artist. I mean, I was a housewife, right? I was a mother, I had children, I had a family to take care of. And [being an artist] was something I did in my extra time. It was taking up a lot of time by then . . . The teachers would talk a lot about commitment, being committed to your work and somehow that word had a lot of implications that I couldn't accept . . . I would never say that I am an artist.[55]

Morton's difficulty in recognising her status as a professional artist illustrates what Alexandra Kokoli has called the 'misrecognised labor' in women's art practices. Underscoring the importance of recognising the different kinds of work that are involved in making art, Kokoli posits that labour is not only visible in the actions an artist takes towards an object, but that it is also enacted in corollary forms of work that facilitate artistic practice, such as non-artistic work that pays the bills as well as the unpaid domestic work of childcare. This, Kokoli suggests, means that notions of artistic labour prioritise paid productive labour over unpaid unproductive labour, resulting in problematic distinctions between the professional and the amateur, or what Kokoli calls 'real' work versus art-making as a 'labor of love'.[56]

Speaking to the same distinctions, Angela Dimitrakaki argues that, in the case of women making art, these binary distinctions of productive and unproductive work have been historically cleaved along spatial and gendered lines. She further outlines how qualities associated with the 'professional' male artist and his paid labour are sustained in opposition to women's 'private', amateur, unpaid art or 'hobbies' taking place in the home. These distinctions, Dimitrakaki writes, relate to 'women's association with the private rather than the public ... women [artists] were very much associated with the first term "the private", as in "the garden", "the kitchen", "the bedroom"'.[57] Virginia Woolf famously articulated as early as 1929 that 'a woman must have money and a room of her own if she is to write fiction'; the same could just as easily be said wherein an artist who is a parent must have childcare as well as a studio if she is to make art.[58]

Therefore, in not perceiving herself as a professional because of her domestic responsibilities, Morton self-deprecated herself as an amateur because art was something she did in her 'spare time', in bathroom and kitchen studios. In actual fact, by this point, Morton was exhibiting her work and earning money as a teacher. When Morton described her story as 'out of the kitchen, into the studio', she spatially tracked her own professional transition across these sites of labour. Moreover, she highlighted how entrenched the gendered spheres of private and domestic life are to perceptions of amateur creative work.

The artist's studio has long been a contested site of intersectional identity and labour, and while I cannot rehearse its extended scholarship here, it is important to remember that discourses of artists' studios have configured a particular relationship between gendered labour and space. We should therefore consider with more seriousness artwork made in spaces beyond the studio. What kind of non-traditional workspaces might exist – temporary or otherwise – that activate a different space of encounter with the *work* of art? Given that Morton's holiday notebooks were integral tools for developing ideas and documenting her surroundings, could her notebooks be conceived of as spaces of work? That is, as conceptual extensions of the studio? In what follows, I suggest that Morton's increasing use of text in 1974 was due to the way she was using notebooks as studios and studios as notebooks, which culminated in the artist's decision to exhibit and publish excerpts of her notebooks in 1976.

Exhibiting notebooks

Teaching – what Lippard called a woman artist's third job after childcare and art-making – was not only a way for Morton to support herself. It also allowed her to use her employers' studios. Shortly before Morton went on vacation to Tannersville in the summer of 1974, she took up a six-week teaching post at Montana State University. While there, Morton made only one artwork, *Bozeman, Montana*, named after the small town where she lived at the foot of the Rocky Mountains. The work consists of eleven sculpted Celastic words scattered across a wall, bracketed by two sculpted parentheses adorned with colourful light bulbs (figure 8.3). The enclosed words refer to people Morton taught or colleagues at the school ('Lowell', 'Scott', 'Curt', 'Mike', 'Sylvie', 'Manuel', and 'Richard'), activities she did in her spare time ('Pool', 'Beer', 'Fish'), and geographical features of Bozeman ('MTS' [mountains] and 'Sky'). These references to people, actions, and places fix this period of her teaching work in text. In her notebooks, Morton describes the piece as a 'tone poem' – a term referring to a narrative device in a musical score. An adjacent notebook page cites the poem's categories ('homages', 'souvenirs', 'commemorative', and 'memorial'), with the note 'cheap sentimentality . . . sayings as a way to remember friends'.[59]

If *Bozeman, Montana* is a memorialisation of friendship, then it offers a variation on Morton's commemoration to maternal love in *Souvenir Piece* made a year earlier. Instead of using beach pebbles and driftwood as found objects, Morton uses single nouns in a motif reminiscent of the lists and shorthand notes in her notebooks. *Bozeman, Montana* is a celebratory, enunciative work which seems to speak through its artificially coloured, shiny Celastic surfaces embellished with glitter and reminiscent of candy bar wrappers. Did Morton transcribe her private notations into sculpted words in order to make

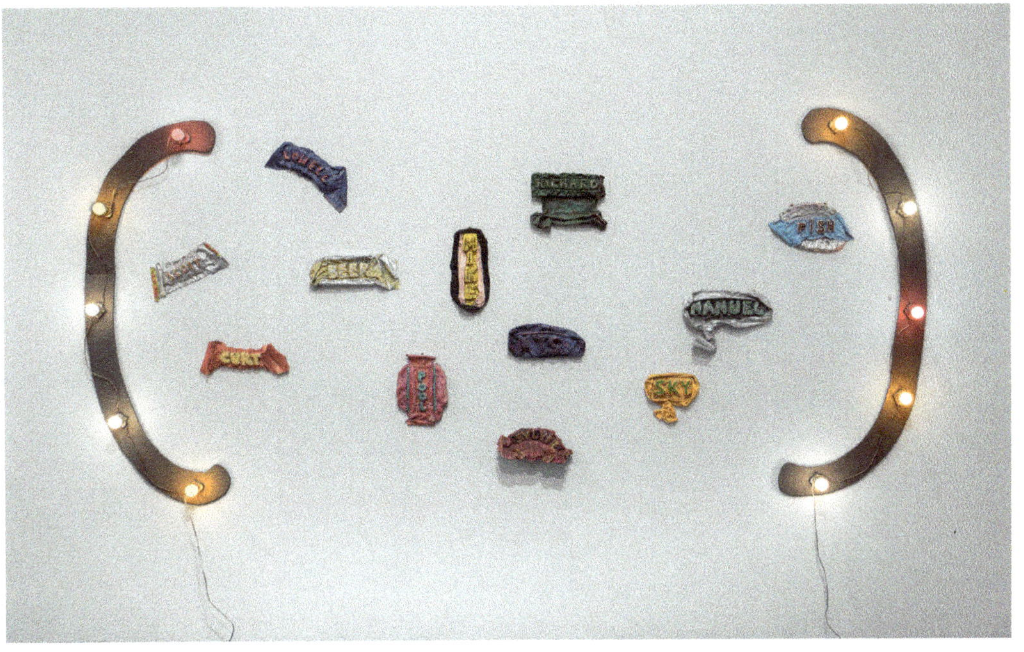

8.3 Ree Morton, *Bozeman, Montana*, 1974, enamel, flocking and glitter on wood and Celastic, coloured light bulbs, approximately: 213.5 × 335.5 × 8 cm

their 'cheap sentimentality' affective? *Bozeman, Montana* was made directly in response to Morton's labour as a teacher, work that supported her studio practice. She later recalled: 'I took some Celastic to Montana to demonstrate the potential to the students. I made my name out of clay and pushed the Celastic around it. As soon as I saw the words embossed on a hard surface, well, that was it.'[60] *Bozeman, Montana* was the first time Morton sculpted text in Celastic, which prompted her series of banner works based on Blanchan's book *Wild Flowers Worth Knowing* in 1974. For the rest of her career, Morton continued to use Celastic as a material through which feeling could take form in a way that signified the ambiguous aesthetics of kitsch, sentimentality, and femininity.[61]

Later in 1974, Morton wrote in her notebooks that she had 'a need to confess – in a public place'.[62] This passage was part of her development of the 1974 work *Something in the Wind* (figures 8.4 and 8.5), an outdoor installation for which Morton made over a hundred hand-sewn and colourfully painted flags for 'each person in my life that I have good feelings for . . . [as] a celebration for them and a means of identifying and locating myself in the world'.[63]

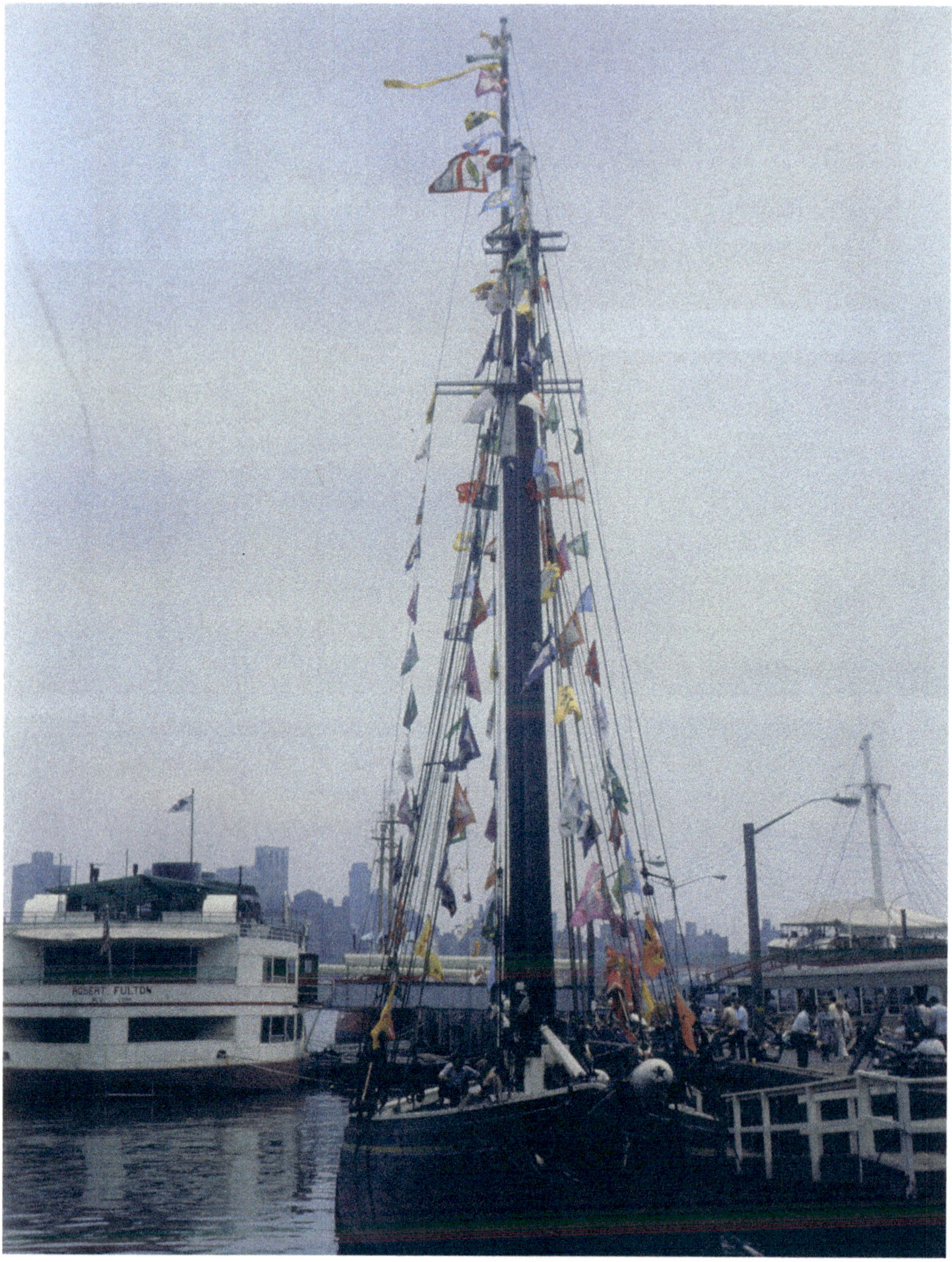

8.4 Ree Morton, *Something in the Wind*, installation view, 1975, acrylic and felt-tip pen on nylon, dimensions variable

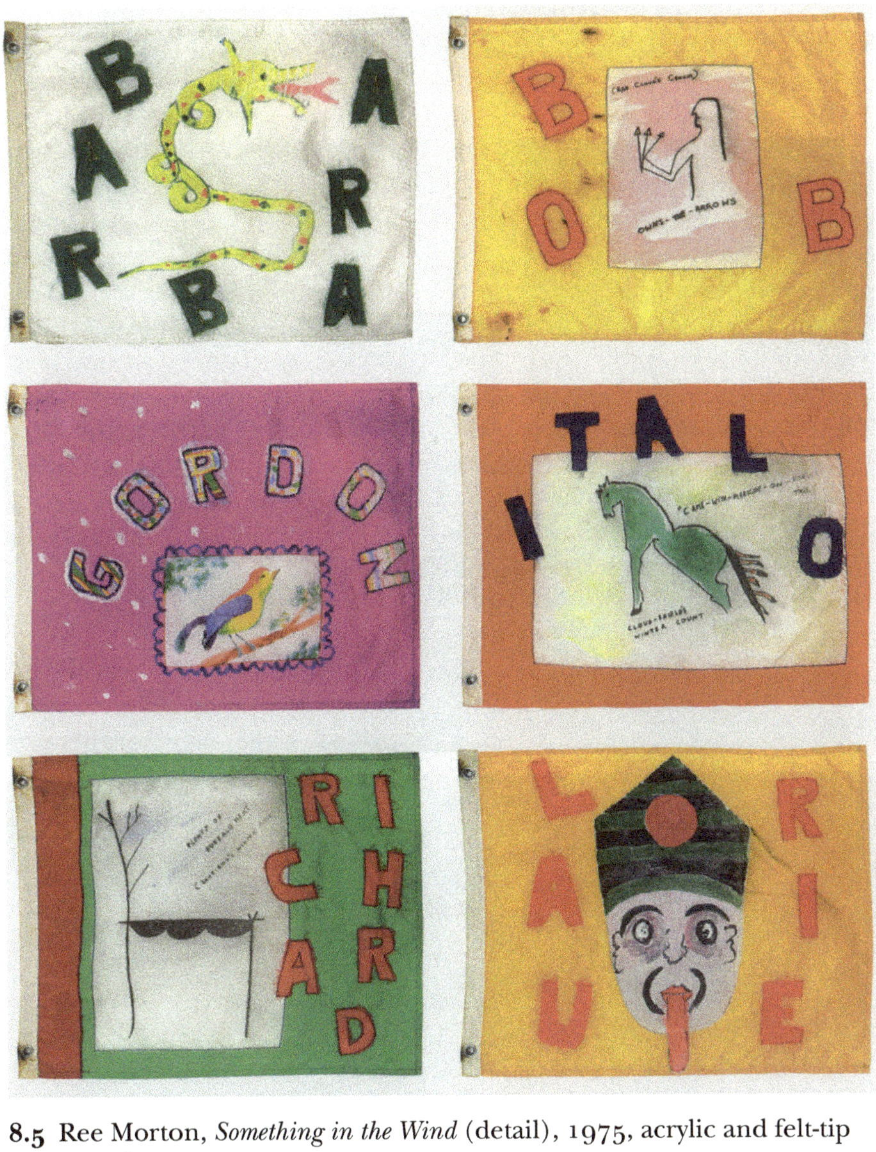

8.5 Ree Morton, *Something in the Wind* (detail), 1975, acrylic and felt-tip pen on nylon

Each flag included the name of the person it was made for and an accompanying illustration. For example, the flag made for Gordon Matta-Clark, her lover for a brief time in 1973, bears the emblem of a colourful bird perched on a branch surrounded by a decorative frame. The flags were shown in various outdoor configurations: first rigged onto an old schooner moored in the South Street seaport in

New York City in the summer of 1975, before being strung up at a friend's garden party, and later exhibited at the Woman's Building in Los Angeles.

The profound sentimentality of *Something in the Wind* marks Morton's deepening interest in the capacity of combining images and language to represent feelings. This arguably culminated in Morton's epic installation made only a year before her death, *Signs of Love* (1976, figure 8.6). This work showcased a range of signs, symbols, and words related to the representation of romantic heteronormative, platonic, and maternal affection.[64] The work includes handwritten words painted onto the wall, such as 'Poses', 'Symbols', 'Settings', 'Gestures', 'Atmospheres', 'Pleasures', 'Objects', 'Moments', and 'Signs of Love', as well as paintings of a Renaissance couple and sculpted Celastic objects such as roses, ladders, and laundry baskets. Here, word and image are interspersed in a tableau configuration, along two long intersecting walls and the floor, with Celastic again deployed for kitsch effect.

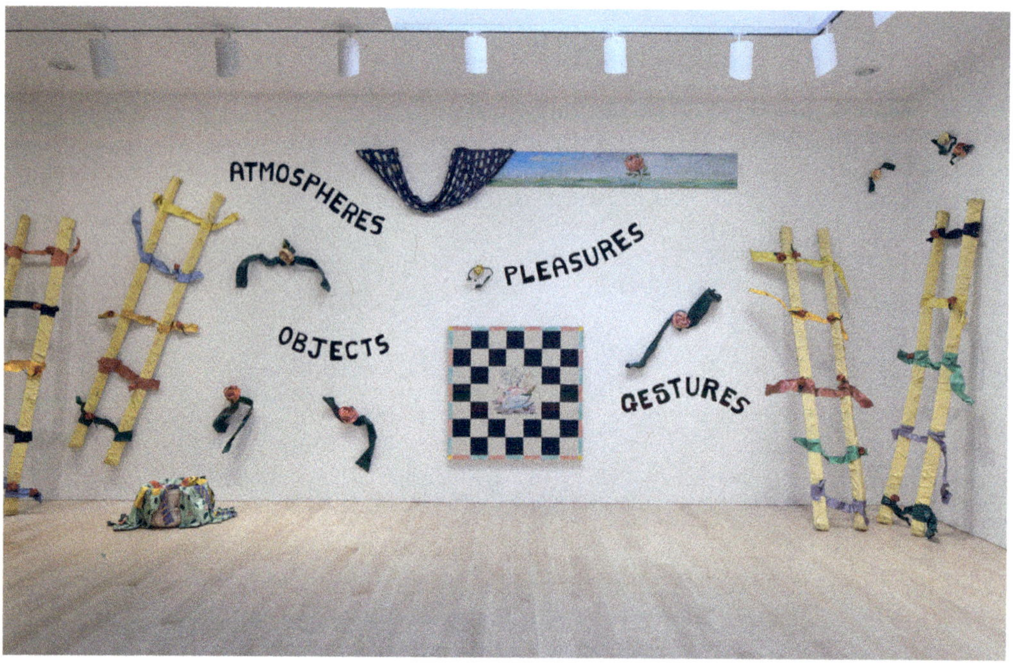

8.6 Ree Morton, *Signs of Love,* 1976, acrylic, oil, coloured pencil, watercolour, and pastel on nitrocellulose-impregnated canvas, wood, and canvas with felt, dimensions variable

In as much as *Signs of Love* explores how text and image exist within the scope of possible expressions of 'love', the artifice of Morton's materials and its theatrical display are arguably symbolic of the ultimate inadequacy of language to communicate the most ineffable feelings. If Morton was therefore aware of the representational limitations of language, it is interesting to consider that *Signs of Love* was in production around the same time she chose to publicly display her notebooks.

The first exhibition of Morton's notebooks was for the show *Preparatory Notes – Thinking Drawings* curated by Micaela Amateau Amato and Amy Snider. The show featured work predominantly by women, including Morton's best friend Cynthia Carlson, as well as Barbara Kruger, Joyce Kozloff, and Louise Bourgeois.[65] The exhibition featured artworks as well as artists' notebooks and sketchbooks, the pages of which were turned every few days by gallery staff.[66] Morton sent approximately six works on paper to the exhibition, along with three or four of her notebooks.[67] Curator Micaela Amateau Amato recalled:

> Ree and I went over her journals together in her studio and we discussed them with much excitement/pleasure/humor. I think we chose together which pages would be open, and which ones would be opened the following days . . . She loved the idea of the show and I believe she found it perfect for her own creative impulses . . . the layered process from the recesses of her imagination quickly jotted onto paper and then to real space (that included everything) was a blueprint of this comprehensive creative process for her.[68]

Two of the four works included were *Bozeman, Montana* and *Weeds of the Northeast.* Although it is not known which of Morton's notebook pages were shown during the exhibition, in juxtaposing artwork that explicitly made use of text drawn from documentation made in her notebooks, Morton made explicit the link between the object as the 'work of art' and her art's *work,* in which notebooks are as much art objects as indices of process.

The second exhibition of Morton's notebooks came a few months later in October 1976, in *Private Notations: Artists' Sketchbooks* at the Philadelphia College of Art. The show featured the notebooks, sketchbooks, and diaries of approximately sixty artists.[69] In her introduction to the exhibition, curator Janet Kardon said:

> For this exhibition books were collected from painters, sculptors, dancers, performance and video artists, representing a range of

> diverse sensibilities . . . For some artists their sketchbooks are portable easels or studios in which they work constantly; while for others, keeping a notebook is a discrete activity which may include working drawings for a specific project or commemorate an isolated experience. A turn of the page may juxtapose mundane jottings, recipes, shopping lists, addresses with serious visual or verbal observations. These informal 'autobiographies' often contain found objects: photographs, postcards, memorabilia – souvenirs of a specific time or location . . . There is no beginning, middle or end, but rather an aleatory storage arrangement of segments of time.[70]

Many of the artists included in Kardon's exhibition, including Sol LeWitt, Joseph Kosuth, Vito Acconci, and Michelle Stuart, were known for their use of language to record, observe, and represent ideas and systems in notebook or journal form. This conceptual use of language in the 1960s and 1970s is described by Liz Kotz as a tendency towards seeing text as a kind of material, where 'words were treated [by artists] in some sense like objects – to be looked at, and also to be accumulated, built up, moved around and broken apart'.[71] As such, many artists embraced the format of diaries, notebooks, journals, and sketchbooks as devices to represent temporal constructs.[72] The inclusion of Morton's notebooks in *Private Notations: Artists' Sketchbooks* not only aligns her work with this diaristic impulse in 1970s conceptual art but, coupled with the aptly titled exhibition, *Thinking Drawings*, shows a trajectory of exhibitions about the material traces of immaterial labour that clearly appealed to the artist.

In 1977, Morton once again made her notebooks public, this time in a book. Morton was one of fifteen artists included in *Individuals: Post-Movement Art in America* edited by Alan Sondheim, who described those included as artists with 'an emphasis on procedure, on "going through the work" as opposed to a perfected final product'.[73] Morton was invited to include material she felt best represented her practice. She gave Sondheim a mixture of photos and drawings of her artwork, an annotated postcard from California, and the title page of a book from 1872, as well as three pages that resemble her notebooks.[74]

Morton titled the book chapter 'Analects', a term which refers to a collection of philosophical treatises. The chapter is divided into nine parts: 'Locations', 'Recitations', 'Narrations', 'Observations', 'Definitions', 'Notations', 'Illustrations', 'Commemorations', and 'Prescriptions'. Each subtitle relates to the sections found in

Blanchan's *Wild Flowers Worth Knowing.* These subtitles refer to the same categories Blanchan applied to the methods of studying flowers and plants: the geographical origins of the species ('location'); the plant's Latin and colloquial name ('recitations'); the plant's folklore 'story' ('narration'); the plant's visible characteristics ('observations'); its 'meaning' ('definitions'); and its medicinal properties ('prescriptions').

The 'Notations' section features pages *resembling* Morton's notebooks (figures 8.7 and 8.8), but they are not – to my knowledge – copies from her original books. They appear to be composites of text and drawings of different artworks Morton made in 1974 inspired by Blanchan's book, as well as phrases taken from her notebooks. For example, in one section of 'Notations', Morton writes:

> memory and fantasy
> affection for the work
> sweet and sour color
> found words
> fragments not coalesced into sentences or sentenced
> sources outside of oneself, in order to get at oneself
> love the romance
> memorials to lost intentions
> sentimentality
> incorporate your existence
> find the meaning, change the meaning, contradict the original meaning
> advertising things painful and private
> invest with meaning, signs or tokens of a thought, a sentiment, or an event
> art from the heart[75]

These textual fragments, given little context, are simply presented in a list in the same way that Morton wrote out 'tone poems' in her notebooks. Some of the phrases are taken from Morton's older notebooks and integrated with other texts from various sources, many of which remain unknown to me. In this, 'Notations' might be understood as a partial and intentional 'autobiographical' performance of the artist's own 'thinking' and intellectual past labours, spliced with words borrowed from other books and temporal locations resulting in a language both dislocated and reconfigured as a meta-performance of the work of writing and drawing.

Morton chose to present collaged excerpts of her own notebooks and other anonymous fragments of writing from unknown

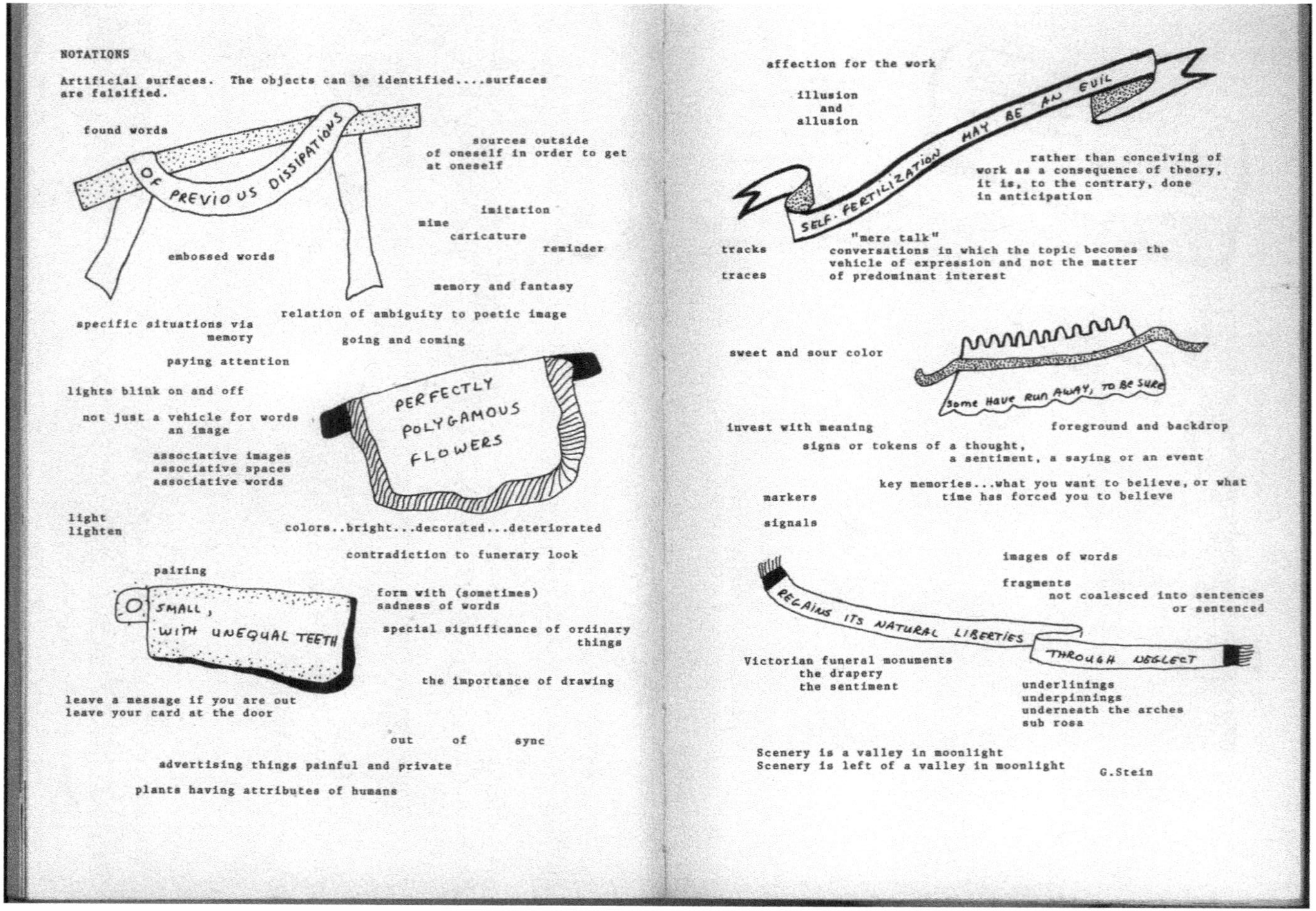

8.7 Ree Morton, 'Analects', 1976, published in Alan Sondheim (ed.), *Individuals: Post-Movement Art in America*, 1977, pp. 240–241

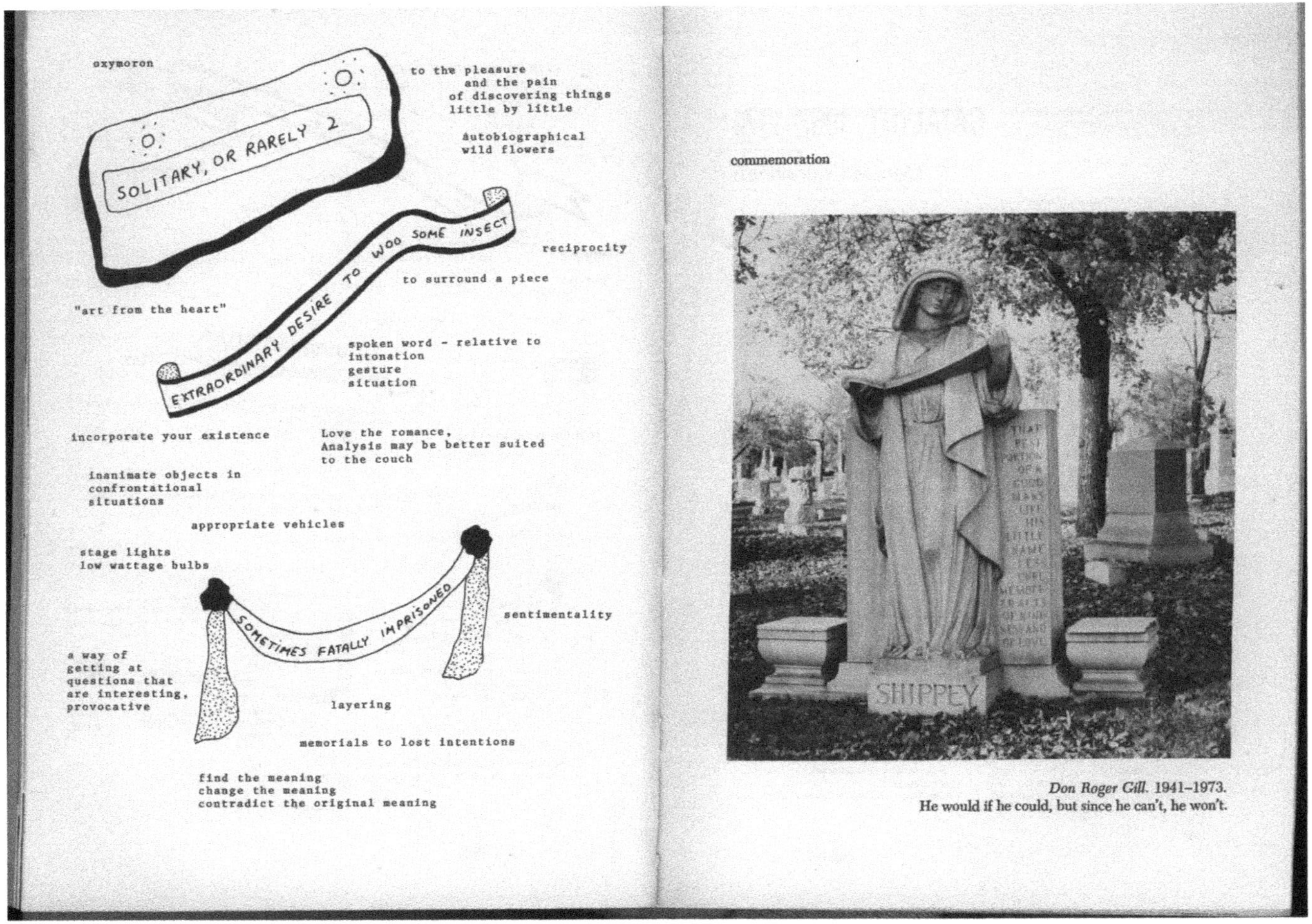

8.8 Ree Morton, 'Analects', 1976, published in Alan Sondheim (ed.), *Individuals: Post-Movement Art in America*, 1977, pp. 242–243

sources, effectively enacting what Kadar wrote about life writing being 'best examined on an "uneven continuum" of objectivity and subjectivity, and fiction and non-fiction'. Morton disrupts the authenticity of the autobiographical frame she poses within her own work. 'Notations' even appears to disclose its partial autobiographical strategies as a manifesto of statements – 'advertising things painful and private', 'sources outside of oneself, in order to get at oneself', 'art from the heart', and 'love the romance' – which seem to perform affectively next to what she called her 'autobiographical' flower drawings. This is part of the compelling autobiographical encounter with Morton's work: her juxtaposition of obscure personal references in the form of text and images rendered through symbolic materials conflate as much as they confound references to the artist herself. In this, the autobiographical status of both notebooks and artworks is evoked but also problematised as a theoretical proposition.

Giving an equivalence to Morton's art objects and her notebooks in her practice foregrounds the transmissions of language between the forms her practice adopts. Notational devices – scraps of words, statements, and decontextualised sentences – feature throughout her installations, suggesting that her notebooks were not merely spaces for developing objects she would later make in the studio. On the contrary, it posits that the installations were platforms from which to represent the processes in and of her notebooks. The books, in this sense, embody what Meskimmon calls 'the critical link between thinking and making, between the materiality of the objects and the agency of artists and participant observers'.

Critically reassessing the terms through which we understand autobiography when it comes to the labour of art-making, gendered agency, and the use of archival materials highlights the need for careful attention to the questions we ask of artists and how they inform the way we write about their subjectivities in relation to their work. The importance of materialist feminist critiques such as Meskimmon's and Dimitrakaki's shows the extent to which we need to rethink how we define and contextualise the labour of art-making, especially for women, and in turn how integral the concept of 'work' is in configuring relational and ethical autobiographical links between artists and their practices. For Morton, as for many other artists, this means reappraising archival ephemera such as notebooks, sketchbooks, letters, diaries, and in the case of later artists, electronic correspondence (such as emails, text messages, and social media posts) as sources from which to locate different iterations and nuances of art's 'work' and subjectivity as it materialises in our encounters with the autobiographical.

Notes

1 *The Sketchbooks of Ree Morton*, 7 July–27 August 1988, Franklin Furnace, New York City. The books are now held at the Museum of Modern Art (acquired in 2011) but are digitally available on Franklin Furnace's website, franklinfurnace.org/ree_morton_sketchbooks/index.php (accessed 16 May 2021).

2 Roberta Smith, 'Notebooks of An Artist Without Enough Time', *The New York Times*, 20 August 1988, Section C, p. 25. See www.nytimes.com/1988/08/12/arts/review-art-notebooks-of-an-artist-without-enough-time.html (accessed 14 November 2022).

3 Notable solo exhibitions include: *Ree Morton: Retrospective*, a touring exhibition that began in 1980 at the New Museum, New York; *Ree Morton, The Deities Must be Made to Laugh: Works 1971– 1977*, Generali Foundation, Vienna, 12 December 2008–1 March 2009; *Ree Morton: At the Still Point of the Turning World*, Drawing Centre, New York, 18 September–18 December 2009; *Ree Morton: Be a Place, Place an Image, Imagine a Poem*, Museo Reina Sofía, Madrid, 20 May–28 September 2015; *Ree Morton: The Plant That Heals May Also Poison*, Institute of Contemporary Art, University of Pennsylvania, Philadelphia, 14 September–23 December 2018.

4 Cynthia Carlson and Bill Beckley, interview with the author, 11 December 2013. For the full interview with Cynthia Carlson see Abi Shapiro, 'Ree Morton and Feminist Installation Art: 1968–1977' (PhD dissertation, McGill University, 2017), pp. 347–370.

5 Ree Morton, *76–77 Artist Sketchbook* (RM-15), p. 8.

6 Lauren Fournier, *Autotheory as Feminist Practice in Art, Writing, and Criticism* (Cambridge, MA: MIT Press, 2021), p. 7.

7 For more on the emergence of the monograph in the discipline of art history, see Gabriele Guercio, *Art as Existence: The Artist's Monograph and its Project* (Cambridge, MA: MIT Press, 2006).

8 Linda Nochlin 'Why Have There Been No Great Women Artists?' [1971], reprinted in *Women, Art and Power and Other Essays* (London: Thames & Hudson, 1989), pp. 145–178.

9 For a good overview of the key feminist critiques of the monograph, see Kristen Frederickson, 'Introduction: Histories, Silences, and Stories', in Frederickson and Sarah E. Webb (eds), *Singular Women: Writing the Artist* (Berkeley and Los Angeles, CA and London: University of California Press, 2003), pp. 1–20.

10 Griselda Pollock, 'Artists Mythologies and Media Genius, Madness and Art History' [1980], in Philip Hayward (ed.), *Picture This: Media Representations of Visual Art and Artists* (London: John Libbey, 1988), pp. 76–77, emphasis added.
11 For more on the unavailability of artistic identity for women, see Nochlin, 'Why Have There Been No Great Women Artists?', pp. 145–178.
12 Guercio, *Art as Existence*, p. 7.
13 For more on biographism in art history, see Mieke Bal, 'Narrative and its Discontents', in *Louise Bourgeois' Spider: The Architecture of Art Writing* (Chicago, IL and London: University of Chicago Press, 2001), pp. 35–37.
14 Eva Hesse's diaries were published in 2016. See Barry Rosen (ed.), *Eva Hesse Diaries* (New Haven, CT: Yale University Press, 2016).
15 Psychobiography is a subset method of biographism developed by Sigmund Freud which broadly presumes that a work of art (or any creative output) is a manifestation of the artist's psychic interiority. Freud developed this idea using the notebooks of Leonardo da Vinci. See Freud, 'Leonardo da Vinci and a Memory of His Childhood' [1910], in *Art & Literature*, Penguin Freud Library 14 (London: Harmondsworth Books, 1985).
16 For example, see the 2010 exhibition, *The Real Van Gogh: The Artist and his Letters*, at the Royal Academy in London, the title and institutional rhetoric of which revolved around the authenticity and truth of Van Gogh's artistic identity available in the letters.
17 Benjamin Sutton, 'A Psychological Portrait of Eva Hesse', *Hyperallergic*, 4 May 2016, http://hyperallergic.com/294315/a-psychological-portrait-of-eva-hesse (accessed 14 November 2022).
18 Anne M. Wagner, 'Another Hesse', *October*, 69 (Summer 1994), 59.
19 Wagner, 'Another Hesse', 55–67.
20 Anna C. Chave, 'Letter to the Editors', *October* 71 (Summer 1995), 146–148.
21 For a further analysis of the biographical interpretation of female artists, see Kristen Patterson, *Framed Receptions: The Biographical Discourses of Eva Hesse and Ana Mendieta* (PhD dissertation, Courtauld Institute of Art, University of London, 2008). For a discussion of ways to counter psychobiographic readings of women's art, see Griselda Pollock, *After-affects | after-images: Trauma and Aesthetic Transformation in the Virtual Feminist Museum* (Manchester: Manchester University Press, 2013).
22 Marlene Kadar, 'Introduction', in Kadar (ed.), *Essays on Life Writing: From Genre to Critical Practice* (Toronto: University of Toronto Press, 1992). p. 6.
23 Kadar, 'Introduction', p. 3.

24 Sidonie Smith and Julia Watson, 'Introduction', in *Interfaces: Women, Autobiography, Image, Performance* (Ann Arbor: University of Michigan Press, 2005), pp. 36–37.
25 Sarah E. Webb, 'Epilogue: Mark Making, Writing, and Erasure', in Frederickson and Webb (eds), *Singular Women: Writing the Artist*, p. 238.
26 Webb, 'Epilogue: Mark Making, Writing, and Erasure', p. 239.
27 Briony Fer, 'Constellations in Dust: Notes on the Notebooks', in Ann Temkin (ed.), *Gabriel Orozco* (New York: Museum of Modern Art, 2009), p. 24.
28 Fer, 'Constellations in Dust', p. 24.
29 Marsha Meskimmon, *Women Making Art: History, Subjectivity, Aesthetics* (London and New York: Routledge, 2003), p. 4.
30 Meskimmon, *Women Making Art*, p. 6.
31 Meskimmon, *Women Making Art*, pp. 4–5.
32 Angela Dimitrakaki, *Gender, ArtWork and the Global Imperative: A Materialist Feminist Critique* (Manchester: Manchester University Press, 2013), p. 11.
33 Dimitrakaki, *Gender, ArtWork and the Global Imperative*, p. 57.
34 Ree Morton, as quoted by Marcia Tucker in an interview with Allan Schwartzmann and Kathleen Thomas in November 1979; see *Ree Morton Retrospective: 1971–1977*, p. 32.
35 The entire installation is no longer extant; some of the components are missing or destroyed.
36 Morton's daughter Linda recalled: 'new foundland [sic], thank you wyn, collecting rocks on the shore'. See 'Morton's Recollections and Reflections', in *Ree Morton: Works 1971–1977*, p. 79.
37 See Ree Morton, *Notebook* (RM07: 1973–1974).
38 Morton, *Notebook* (RM30: 1973), p. 79.
39 The original name of the book, *Weeds of the Northeast*, has been credited by the authors of *Ree Morton: Works 1971–1977* as *Weeds of the Northeast: Aids to their Identification by Basal-leaf Characteristics* by Claude Ellis Phillips and V. J. Fisher, published by the University of Delaware, Agricultural Experiment Station, 1970 [first published 1956].
40 Neltje Blanchan, *Wild Flowers Worth Knowing* (New York: Doubleday, Page, 1917), p. 16.
41 Ree Morton, *May 74–June 45 Large Black Hard Bound Sketchbook* (RM-01), p. 51.
42 There are fourteen works with titles taken from *Wild Flowers Worth Knowing*. Those on paper are: *Jack in the Pulpit* (1974); *Yellow Clintonia* (1974); *Trumpet Weed* (1974); *Broom-Rape Family* (1974); *Bitter-Buttons* (1974); *The Stems, Too, Are Restless* (1974); and *Love Me* (1974). The Celastic works are: *Solitary or Rarely 2* (1974); *The Plant That Heals May Also Poison* (1974); *Terminal Clusters* (1974); *Fading Flowers* (1974);

Antidotes for Madness (1974); *Many Have Run Away To Be Sure* (1974); and *Devil Chaser* (1976).

43 See Morton, *Notebook* (RM01: 1974), pp. 49–54.

44 For more on Morton's use of Celastic, see Roksana Filipowska, 'Ree Morton's Celastic Turn', in *Ree Morton: The Plant That Heals Must Also Poison* (Philadelphia: Institute of Contemporary Art, University of Pennsylvania, 2019), pp. 248–251.

45 Ree Morton quoted in interview with Barbara Schwarz, Hannah Wilke, Jim Cobb, Alan Saret, and Eddie Shostak, 'Methods and Materials: New and Old', *Craft Horizons*, 35:6 (December 1975), 48.

46 Ree Morton, *Notebook* (RM29: 1975), p. 50; and *Notebook* (RM18: 1975), p. 8.

47 Pollock, 'Artists' Mythologies', pp. 76–77.

48 Ree Morton, *Notebook* (RM04: 1975), p. 11.

49 Lucy Lippard, 'Twenty Six Contemporary Women Artists', in *Twenty Six Contemporary Women Artists* (Ridgefield, CT: Aldrich Museum, 1971), reprinted in Lippard, 'Prefaces to Catalogues', in *From the Center: Feminist Essays on Women's Art* (New York: Dutton, 1976), p. 41.

50 Janis Porter, 'Marionette', in *Ree Morton: Retrospective 1971–1977*, p. 81. Porter met Morton in Norfolk, Virginia, in 1964, when Morton was taking evening classes before starting her degree. Both of their husbands worked away from home (in the US navy), and both had young children.

51 Marcia Tucker, quoted in interview with Ree Morton, *Ree Morton: Retrospective 1971–1977*, p. 10.

52 Lucy Lippard, 'Changing Since *Changing* (1976)', in *From the Center*, p. 4.

53 My doctoral thesis proposed that women have been widely omitted from histories of installation art. I take Morton's practice as a case study to investigate the significance of women's installation art to explore some of the reasons their work has been overlooked in art history. See Shapiro, 'Ree Morton and Feminist Installation Art', pp. 347–370.

54 Ree Morton, *Notebook* (RM05: 1974), p. 66.

55 Ree Morton in interview with Kate Horsfield and Lyn Blumental, *Ree Morton: An Interview* (1974), Video Data Bank, School of the Art Institute Chicago, Chicago, IL.

56 Alexandra Kokoli, 'The Work of Art as Labour', 22 June 2011, http://discussionsart.wordpress.com/2011/06/22/the-work-of-art-as-labour/ (accessed 22 May 2021).

57 Dimitrakaki, *Gender, ArtWork and the Global Imperative*, pp. 115–116.

58 Virginia Woolf, 'A Room of One's Own' [1929], in Michèle Barrett (ed.), *A Room of One's Own/Three Guineas* (Penguin: London, 2000), p. 3.

59 Morton, *Notebook* (RM01: 1974–1975), pp. 20–32.

60 Morton, cited in Schwartz, 'Methods and Materials: New and Old', 46–49.
61 For more on Morton's use of Celastic and feminine aesthetics, see Shapiro, 'Ree Morton and Feminist Installation Art', pp. 209–278.
62 Morton, *Notebook* (RM01: 1975), p. 31.
63 Morton cited in *Attitudes Towards Space: Environmental Art* (Los Angeles, CA: Mount Saint Mary's College of Art Gallery, 1977) unpaginated, reprinted in *Ree Morton: Retrospective 1971–1977*, p. 51.
64 For a rich discussion of this work, see Susan Richmond, 'The Sentimentality of Ree Morton's *Signs of Love*', *American Art*, 30:3 (Fall 2016), 92–111.
65 The show began at Woman-Centre in Boulder, Colorado, in May 1976 and later travelled to 80 Washington Square East Galleries, New York University, in February 1977. For more information on this exhibition, see *Ree Morton: Works 1971–1977*, p. 197.
66 Micaela Amateau Amato, email to the author, 25 March 2014.
67 Amateau stated: 'The drawings of Ree's were about 24 × 36' on heavy paper with pencil-washes and coloured pencils for "Let us Celebrate While Youth Lingers and Ideas Flow" and "Of Previous Dissipations" and "weeds . . ." and "Bozeman, Montana" installation. There were at least five or six pieces . . . text on all of them. They were hung vertically I think, as a piece in itself.' Email to the author, 25 March 2014.
68 Amateau, email to the author, 9 April 2014.
69 For a full list of contributing artists see Janet Kardon, *Private Notations: Artists Sketchbooks* (Philadelphia, PA: Philadelphia College of Art Press, 1976).
70 Kardon, *Private Notations*, p. 3.
71 Liz Kotz, 'Introduction', in *Words to be Looked at: Language in 1960s Art* (Cambridge, MA: MIT Press, 2007), p. 2.
72 Just a few examples of artists using diary or notebook formats at this time are Dieter Roth's dairy series (1964–1988); On Kawara's *Date Paintings* (1966–2014); Lee Lozano's *Write-Ups* and *Pieces* (1968–1971); Hanne Darboven's *One Month, One Year, One Century* (1971); Annette Messager's *Collection Albums* (1972–1974); Eleanor Antin's *Carving: A Traditional Sculpture* (1972), which is discussed in Chapter 9 of this book by Lucy Bradnock; and Andy Warhol's *Time Capsules* (1974–1987).
73 Alan Sondheim, 'Introduction', in *Individuals: Post-Movement Art in America* (New York: E. P. Dutton, 1977), p. xv.
74 Morton, 'Analects', in Sondheim, *Individuals*, pp. 226–243.
75 Morton, 'Analects', pp. 240–242.

9

'Hey Mom, I made it and I'm OK': self-help and 1970s conceptual art

Lucy Bradnock

Unnamed people casually speculate as to the whereabouts of an absent friend. A woman at a restaurant table gesticulates theatrically to resist offers of food from an unseen lunch companion. A mother advises her daughter about the best place to buy steak and shoes, suggests activities for relieving boredom, and ponders whether her suburban home is too large. In all three scenarios, which form the central exchanges in Allen Ruppersberg's *Where's Al?* (1972), Eleanor Antin's *The Eight Temptations* (1972), and Ilene Segalove's *The Mom Tapes* (1974), respectively, people try and to some extent fail to come together, their mildly unsuccessful encounters captured in photographs, text, and video.

These works epitomise the playful embrace of vernacular narrative forms that characterised Los Angeles conceptual art, which deployed anecdote and humour to attend critically to the linguistic, relational, and technological apparatuses of quotidian communication.[1] They also belong to a wider tendency towards autobiography and life narrative in 1970s video and performance art, in particular as enacted through the format of the pseudo-documentary. Across the United States, that period saw the apparatus of conceptual art brought increasingly to bear on discourses of the self, through the sort of 'subject-centred inquiry' that Jayne Wark identified as a specifically feminist conceptual mode.[2] What she charts is closely related to the procedure that Lauren Fournier has more recently described as 'performative life-thinking'.[3] Both practices are rooted in a sort of performative autoethnography, thus privileging the re-entry of subjectivity and first-person experience into what had previously appeared to many as the hermetic realm of conceptual art. Conceptual life narrative permitted a delineation of the subject-in-process even as it articulated a work of art in progress. This shift, which represented a rejection of the perceived death of the author, was concurrent with post-studio practices that developed in early 1970s Los Angeles, particularly at the California Institute of the Arts (CalArts), and that often explored conceptual ideas via popular media and its technologies.[4] Meanwhile, artistic projects that documented or made visible overlooked lives found a parallel in the feminist strategies of consciousness raising and collective action.

The conceptual approach to life narrative, as enacted in the works I describe above, related to another form of self-discourse that emerged in the early years of the 1970s: the increasingly popular emphasis on instrumentalised self-metrics and self-improvement embodied in the rise of popular psychology and self-help, the latter understood as both a practice and as an epistemology, that is at once a set of instructions that govern behaviour and a means of knowledge production. I propose that works like Ruppersberg's, Antin's, and Segalove's can be read in relation to the increased marketisation of the self and self-schemas delineated by the structural, ethical, and economic logic of self-help that came in the wake of the countercultural project of the previous decade. This is not to say that their work cited self-help sources directly, nor that they produced artwork as therapy (though Segalove has claimed as much on occasion, and her work and Antin's has been described in these terms by some critics). Rather, reading their work in relation to an epistemology of self-help, I suggest that Ruppersberg, Antin, and Segalove show how an increased attention to the process and procedures of subject formation is inevitably implicated in the logic of consumerism and capital.

Conceptual art and self-help share common structures, formats, and approaches, including list-making, record-keeping, task-setting, and iterative documentation; a resistance to formal academic learning in favour of self-guided tasks; an emphasis on process and a foregrounding of labour; a performative character; a quasi-scientific framework that deploys the language of objectivity even as it might pertain to subjective or creative practice; and the application of an organised system or framework to multiple sites or subjects. Self-help frames living as labour, epitomised in the idiomatic notion of 'working on yourself'. As they echo those of conceptual art, the strategies of self-help apparently reorient what Benjamin Buchloh famously described as 'the aesthetic of administration' towards the goal of self-actualisation.[5] That self-help situated life work in the public sphere, inhabiting media spaces as much as scientific or countercultural ones, only served to emphasise the public self as embedded in and performed via that communications network. Just as their contemporaries engaged critically with the economy of pictures in an era of mass communication, so Segalove and others used conceptual practices to critique these schematic economies of self-improvement.

Where am I?

In the 1972 work *Where's Al?* (figure 9.1) viewers are presented with a conceptual portrait of the artist figured through his perennial absence. Instamatic photographs of unidentified people are affixed to the wall with pushpins, interspersed with typed index cards that relate conversations about Ruppersberg in which friends or acquaintances (scripted merely as 'she' or 'he') engage in speculative chat about his absence and the reasons for it. Via the familiar strategies of conceptual art – the deadpan presentation of documentation, the bureaucratic display format, the focus on information above craft – *Where's Al?* delineates the social networks and quotidian interactions by which the self is constructed. Ruppersberg has described *Where's Al?* as ironic, on account of the contradictory nature of its central narrative, 'because I ain't there. But of course, I am there'.[6] Indeed, it plays on the implied but invisible body behind the camera in a manoeuvre that prods good naturedly at assumptions about documentary photography, conceptual art, and the impossibility of the Cartesian subject.

In some ways, *Where's Al?* relates to earlier works, such as the photobooks *23 Pieces* and *24 Pieces* (both 1970), which presented black-and-white photographs of city locations and empty hotel rooms, respectively, each deploying a conceptual, task-oriented approach to create narrative-laden collections of images. The latter would find three-dimensional form in 1971 as the installation *Al's Grand Hotel*, a fully functional, if surreal, hotel on Sunset Boulevard. Among its variously bedecked bedrooms, the Al Room contained seven life-sized, free-standing photographic cut-outs of the artist in various guises, each related in some way to his life or person (the cowboy, the hippie, and so on). If the undertaking of *Al's Grand Hotel* was to orient the conceptual project of *24 Pieces* towards the person of the artist (from the anonymous and generic hotel to one that is named after Ruppersberg himself), the Al Room presented that

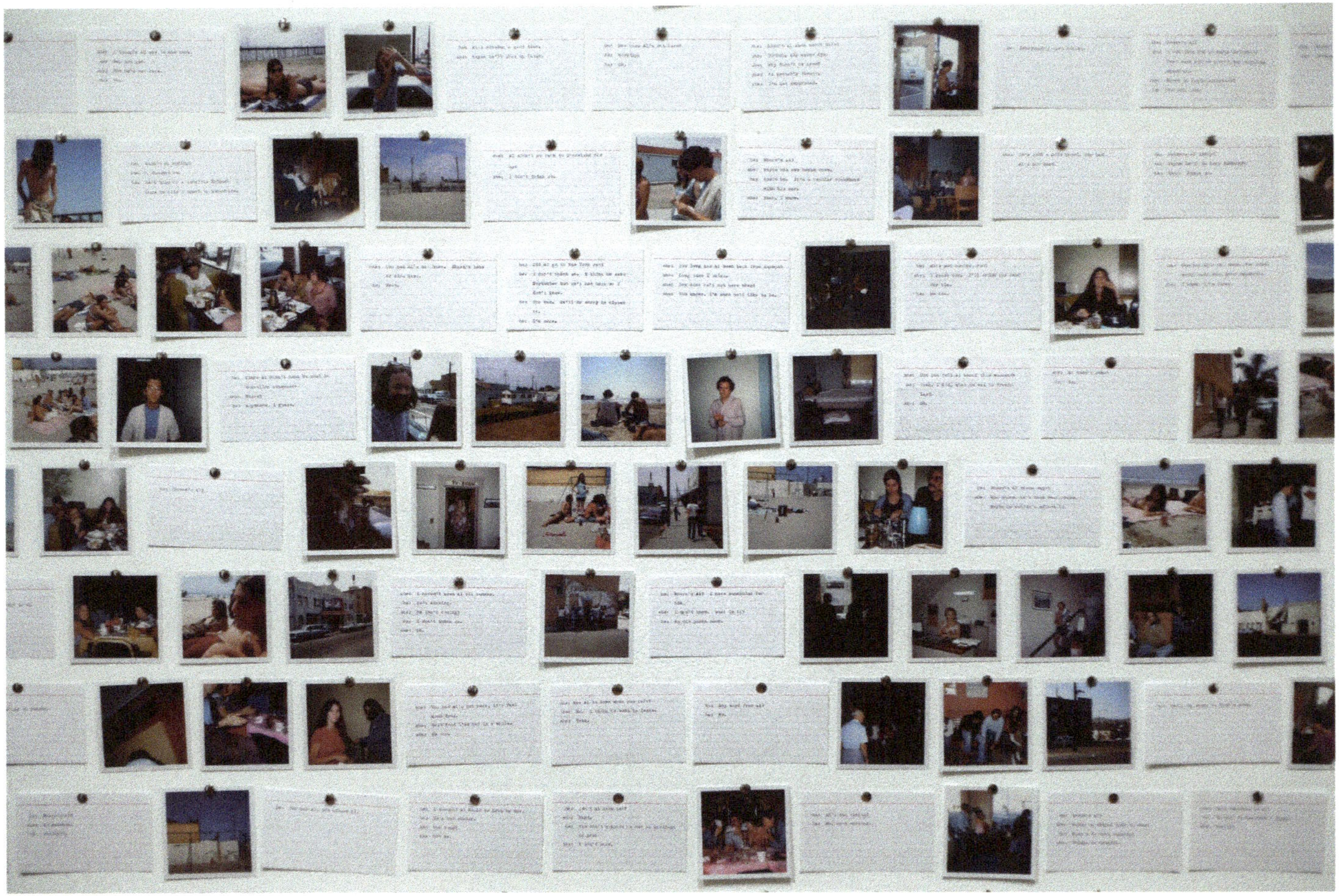

9.1 Allen Ruppersberg, *Where's Al?* (detail), 1972/2006, typewritten index cards and colour photographs, 139.7 × 215.9 cm overall installed

person as comprising multiple, easily identifiable personas, albeit those roles were quickly revealed as two-dimensional props. The Al Room and *Where's Al?* have much in common, in their theatricality, their playful approach to identity and identification, and their repeated iteration of the person of the artist, the former through a surfeit of Als, the latter an absence.

The photographs included in *Where's Al?* were shot over a long group weekend in Pismo Beach, California, a celebration of the tenth wedding anniversary of fellow artists Terry and Jo Harvey Allen. Although its location is not made explicit to the viewer, the atmosphere of relaxed conviviality and references to the festivities contained in the conversations that the work records cement its relevance to themes of locale and community identity; as Siri Engberg has noted, the images carry with them a sense of generic social ease, 'all in the context of hanging out. Al seems to be missing a good party.'[7] As Ruppersberg himself has explained, his pervasive absence points to an increasingly international profile for the young LA-based artist at the start of the 1970s, emphasising a shift from the local to the international in his movement between Los Angeles, New York, Amsterdam, and other art-world cities.[8] The 'trick' at the heart of the work might relate, too, to Ruppersberg's stated fascination with the magician and escape artist Harry Houdini.[9] For Thomas Crow, the work embodies a thematic elusiveness that is discernible in the work of Los Angeles conceptual and performance artists in the early years of the decade, who, he writes, 'tended to function under the sign of their own disappearance'.[10] For Crow, the dialectic of revelation and concealment of artists' bodies is a gesture of object-refusal and a negotiation of the tensions between the display of the self as a medium and the conditions of invisibility in the Los Angeles art world. If the title of *Where's Al?* emphasises geographical and corporeal absence, however, the conversational vignettes that the work presents link this status to personal attributes and behaviours, a reconstitution of sorts: on one card 'she: I thought Al was coming. / she: He was. / she: Maybe he's not up yet. He likes to stay up late sometimes'.

Across the surface of *Where's Al?*, the artist's perpetual failure to appear is cast in contradiction to the apparent reliability of the work's evidentiary format, embodied in the candid snapshots and unselfconscious chit-chat, as well as the index cards and pushpins. For Jacob Stewart-Halevy, Ruppersberg's approach to conceptual documentation is characterised by affected carelessness, in that it represents a deliberate failure to adhere to the rigorous commitment to indexicality practised by his conceptual predecessors: thus *Where's Al?* 'transposes the deskilling strategies of earlier Conceptual artists from the territory of the office to the sphere of leisure–from the perpetual performance of monotonous work to the shirking of responsibility, from the submission to predetermined protocols to the failure to adhere to them'.[11] According to Stewart-Halevy, this manoeuvre served at once to demonstrate a facility with the intellectual and artistic procedures of conceptualism and to signal distance from them. Information in *Where's Al?* is weighted with a personal narrative of tardiness and unreliability. A viewer is invited to join in the game, speculating as to the identity of the speakers, their relation to the artist, and the reliability of their assessments. Ultimately, however, the failure enacted in the work is not the artist's for not showing up, but rather the viewer's for taking documentation at face value, for assuming actual absence where really there is only the pretence of it (just as a visitor to The Al Room of *Al's Grand Hotel* might briefly assume actual presence instead of the fiction of it).

In the context of identity culture during the first years of the 1970s, *Where's Al?* also points to another important context for this approach to conceptual practice: in capturing and documenting the self via reiterative question-and-answer activity and its anonymous protagonists' repeated speculation about behavioural patterns and motivations, *Where's Al?* appears less like an investigative evidence board and more like a do-it-yourself psychological map, mimicking the structural logic of pop psychology, and populist self-discovery and self-help literature that was gaining traction in the aftermath of 1960s utopianism. *Where's Al?* functions as a self-audit of kinds, where the network that the work describes is in some senses a support system, albeit one that is lackadaisical and not always entirely supportive.

As Crow also notes, the snippets of dialogue in *Where's Al?* are presented in the format of the script or screenplay, which relates the work to that of other artists within Ruppersberg's milieu. These include John Baldessari, whose 1974 work *Scripts* drew on excerpts of couples' dialogue from found Hollywood screenplays, and Ilene Segalove's video cycle *The Mom Tapes* (1974–1978), in which droll and somewhat wooden exchanges unfold between the artist and her charismatic mother Elaine. The Los Angeles location of both invites comparisons with the movies, but we might also relate these works to the structured, question-and-answer dialogue that comprised one tool in an arsenal of self-help strategies aimed at self-improvement and self-fulfilment. As Stewart Justman has described it, the self-help genre as it emerged in the early-1970s United States was characterised by its apparently systematic and reliable approach, in which a regime of 'formulas, exercises, and charts representing so many instructions for the re-programming of the self' were designed to appeal to a mass audience previously inexperienced in therapeutic procedures.[12] Self-help offered guidelines, tools, and specific strategies for self-evaluation, self-knowledge, and self-actualisation that are echoed in the work of Ruppersberg, Baldessari, Segalove, and others, even as the structural logic of self-help mirrored conceptual art's orientation towards process and tautological documentation.

Inevitably the genre of self-help intersects with an interest in the politics of domestic and creative labour, play, and pedagogy, particularly as these pertain to the practice and purpose of art-making. Artistic improvement and self-improvement are similarly invested in structured manuals that reduce actualisation to a series of achievable steps or tasks and are often aimed at amateurs. Their ironic take-up by conceptual practitioners reflected a strategic rejection at CalArts and other institutions of the conventions of academic art education, including life drawing.[13] The forms and structures of self-guided amateur art learning in particular were explored by Baldessari and those artists associated with his post-studio classes, with their emphasis on pedagogy, technology, and deadpan humour. These include, for example, works of Baldessari's such as *Wrong* and *The Spectator is Compelled* (in which photographic rules from an amateur photography book are presented in a deadpan tone along with demonstrative photographs that transgress them); Jack Goldstein's *The Portrait of Père Tanguy* (1974, in which a hand traces the outline of the eponymous Van Gogh painting from a colour reproduction);[14] Bas Jan Ader's *Self-Portrait Making a Face Like Barney Bear* (in which the artist draws a cartoon bear in the pictorial style derived from an instructional manual);[15] and the segment titled 'Oh, If Only I Could Draw' from Segalove's *The Mom Tapes* (1974–1978). Such projects rework the tautological emphasis of earlier conceptual art practice via the semiotics of art pedagogy, thus reimbuing conceptualism with humour and narrative (or perhaps revealing the narrative subject that was always present even in apparently analytic conceptual practice). They might also be understood in relation to the kind of deskilling that Stewart-Halevy had in mind.

Developing out of the utopian project of the late 1960s, with its multitude of alternative lifestyle manuals, the self-help movement reoriented responsibility for better living from the collective to the individual, and eschewed intergenerational teaching in favour of task-based self-actualisation. Just as the works that I am discussing both originated in and responded to conceptual art, so, according to Justman, was self-help 'at one a parody and an offshoot of the idealism of the 1960s revolt'.[16] Self-help made visible and legible to the lay person the schematic structure of the self that all therapeutic methods proposed, emphasising the performed and performative nature of its own processes.[17] While therapy was undertaken increasingly in the spaces of the support group or the television show, self-help also facilitated individual task-oriented self-improvement via other formats. Eva S. Moskowitz has described, for example, a variety of therapeutic products and associated mail-order catalogues launched during the 1970s, that often focused on ludic strategies of self-improvement, including feelings-based board games, publications, and greetings cards.[18] Products such as the The Ungame, a non-competitive communication board game developed by the Californian author and mother Rhea Zakich in 1972, were released onto the home therapy market.[19] The Ungame was typical of the marketisation of do-it-yourself home therapy tools that co-opted American leisure time for the labour of self-improvement, via a series of prompts intended to facilitate dialogue and open discussion. Katherine Doniak has persuasively linked the structured dialogic methods of such products to the process-oriented nature of conceptual art, particularly as it developed in the context of Baldessari's post-studio, finding in both an interest in the nature and structure of play.[20]

Self-help also represented a temporal shift from conventional child-rearing and collective utopian projects, both of which relied on reviving the traditions and the past wisdom of previous generations in a contemporary context. In comparison, and distinct from psychoanalytically inflected practices, self-help insisted on 'living in the moment', paying attention to the present self in the service of future actualisation. A similar emphasis on the present was discerned by critics viewing the work of Segalove and her contemporaries in the exhibition *Autobiographical Fantasies* in 1976: when critic Sandy Ballatore described the work of Segalove in terms of 'the "right now" introspection mania characteristic of this culture and this decade', it was not merely the work's apparent timeliness that she emphasised, but also its insistent occupation of the present tense.[21] Thus an emphasis on method inherited from conceptual and process art practices is oriented towards the self as it is experienced in the present moment, a self-in-progress articulated via the marketised systems of self-help. In this regard, the dialogue in *The Mom Tapes* is constitutive rather than merely narrative: Segalove's self comes into being in relation with her mother, with the generational, societal, and economic implications of that process.

I'm OK – you're OK

The rise of self-help – in which we are invited to audit ourselves according to an established schema and commit to a structured improvement plan – coincided with the advent of the hand-held video camera, which documented and shaped the experience of domestic life via the logic of the home movie. In Segalove's work, both also coincide with the economy of television, with its potential for confessional reality formats and commercial advertising alike. It is no coincidence that 1973 saw the airing of what is considered the first reality television programme, *An American Family*, which chronicled across twelve episodes a seven-month period in the lives of the Loud family, in their home in Santa Barbara, California.[22] In that programme and Segalove's video, the work of subject formation and apprehension played out via familial interactions captured by the camera for the small screen.

Segalove's video cycle *The Mom Tapes*, shot on Portapak between 1974 and 1978, comprises eight segments, each featuring Segalove's mother Elaine wandering through and around the Segalove family home in Beverly Hills, or addressing Ilene via voiceover. The result is something that mixes the tone of a surreal anthropological interview with a televised celebrity home tour. Life advice goes hand in hand with consumer recommendations, as Ilene's mother responds to her litany of queries about how to alleviate boredom (in a segment titled 'Mom, I'm bored') or where to buy clothing, food, and other products (in 'Mom, where can I get . . .', figure 9.2), and gives her advice on how to stay safe when out alone (in 'Underground Walkway', figure 9.3). In other segments, Elaine reflects on whether the family home is too big now that her children have moved out (in 'Professional Retirement Home'), how to protect herself from damaging sun rays while enjoying the pool in her back yard (in 'Skin Cancer'), and discusses Ilene's tendency towards art, in

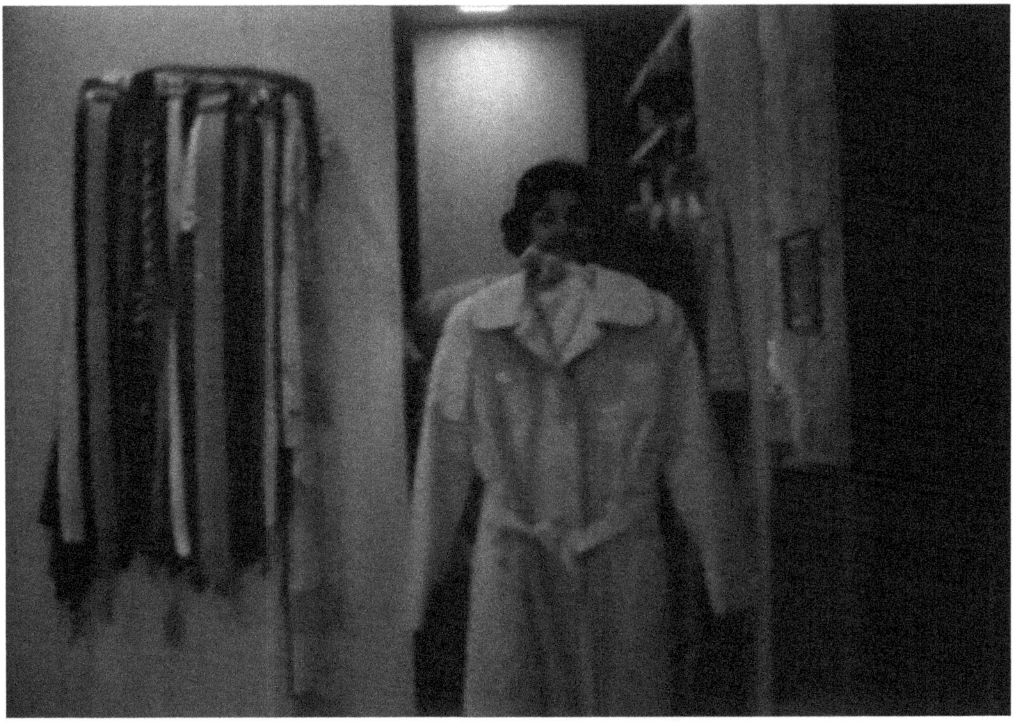

9.2 Ilene Segalove, 'Mom, where can I get . . .' from *The Mom Tapes* (still), 1974–1978, single-channel digital video, transferred from U-Matic videotape, black-and-white and colour, sound, 26 min. 52 sec.

implicit comparison with her own amateur desire to learn to draw (in 'The Red Shoes' and 'Oh, if only I could draw'). In a postscript titled 'Cold Coffee', she leans out of a window to relate an anecdote about a family dinner, before promising her daughter 'when I think of another story, I'll call you. Remember, I know your telephone number.' In a manner similar to *Where's Al?*, the quasi-documentary format belies the casual, anecdotal, and sometimes intimate nature of the vignettes presented. The tension between the two impulses – objective and deeply subjective – is maintained in the occasionally stilted dialogue and the insistently invisible presence of Ilene behind the camera, her voice posing questions but her face not seen until towards the very end, when she gently encourages her mother to take speed reading instead of art class.

With its focus on quotidian domesticity, with the attendant boredom, loneliness, and frustration experienced by the middle-class housewife, *The Mom Tapes* has been read persuasively from a

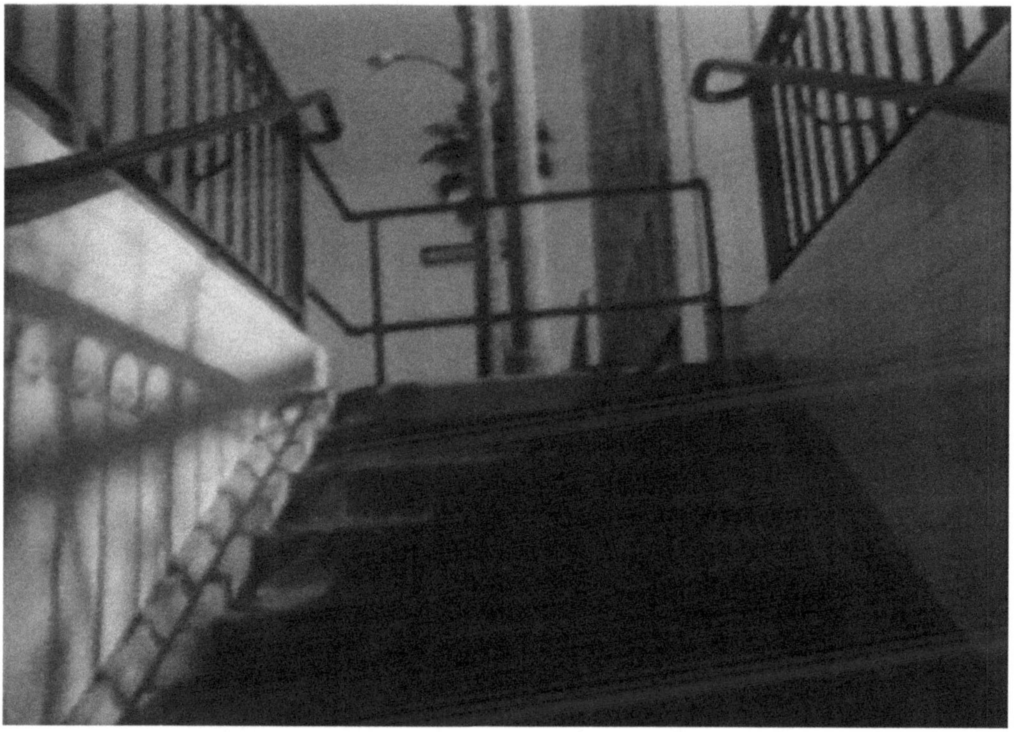

9.3 Ilene Segalove, 'Underground Walkway' from *The Mom Tapes* (still), 1974–1978, single-channel digital video, transferred from U-Matic videotape, black-and-white and colour, sound, 26 min. 52 sec.

feminist perspective. The work is not so much a straightforward portrait of her mother, of course, as it is an exploration of the relationship between the two women. Indeed, a comparison with *Where's Al?* permits a reading of *The Mom Tapes* that focuses on Ilene herself, as inevitably constituted from her mother's advice and experiences. The work's affectionately didactic logic is coded as explicitly intergenerational and feminine, according to which Ilene's mother inducts her into middle-class adulthood and womanhood via a set of rules intended to delineate personal behaviours, interpersonal relationships, and commercial imperatives as all equally important. The back-and-forth structure, never quite a dialogue, feels at times akin to a game, one oriented around the transactional, push-and-pull nature of familial relationships, in particular those between mother and daughter. Structured as a call and response in the initial segment with its repetition of the phrase 'Mom, where can I get . . .', these interactions perform the process of transitioning to adulthood, as articulated via those roles and concerns conventionally gendered feminine. In collaborating with her mother, even as the older of the two women serves as a kind of foil for Segalove's deadpan humour, *The Mom Tapes* proposes intergenerational cooperation that can serve both women (it feels appropriate that Segalove first showed the work at the Los Angeles Woman's Building). In equal parts instructional and reflective, Ilene's mother is at once a voice of reasoned advice and one of constraint: her reaction to her daughter venturing through an underpass is simultaneous curiosity, wariness, and dismissal, even when her daughter makes it to the other side unscathed: 'Mom, I made it and I'm OK', Ilene declares, to which her mother responds with a warning: 'Next time, you might not be so lucky.'

The 1970s turn towards life narrative and autobiography in art has often been linked to the politics of consciousness raising, in which the personal became the political, empowering both speaker and listener through the process of shared narrative. The dynamic that is enacted in *The Mom Tapes*, however, also calls into question inter-generational wisdom sharing and suggests that the game being played is not as productive as at first it seems. Segalove's questions leave little space for acknowledging her mother's answers: what unfolds is emphatically not a conversation. And although her mother's direction to look in the department store Loehmann's for a suitable raincoat seems plausible, her advice not to venture into an underpass is met with resistance by the young Ilene, whose shaky camerawork charts the subterranean journey regardless of her mother's warnings. The underpass incident assumes mildly epic proportions in *The Mom Tapes*, serving as the denouement of the series' first interaction between Ilene and her mother. Its culminating phrase, 'I made it and I'm OK', echoes, albeit not explicitly or deliberately, the titular rhetoric and methodology of the famous self-help publication *I'm OK – You're OK*, a 'practical guide to Transactional Analysis' written by psychologist and psychiatrist Thomas Anthony Harris. Reading both *Where's Al?* and *The Mom Tapes* in terms of the transactions that they map emphasises their conceptual focus on the relations between process and product, here oriented towards the construction and maintenance of the self.

First published in 1969, *I'm OK – You're OK* had an extended run on *The New York Times* best sellers list in 1972 and was at the heart of the early 1970s self-help boom. The book popularised the theories of interpersonal interactions that had been developed by California-based psychiatrist and psychotherapist Eric Berne and described in his 1964 book *Games People Play*, which proposed the transaction as the foundational unit of social intercourse.[23] In glossing these ideas for a wider audience, Harris's book presented a systematic model for practical emotional training, 'rather than a confessional or an archaeological exploration of the psychic cellars'.[24] The book included strategies for decoding the physical and verbal clues that comprised social transactions according to 'I' and 'you' positions, each designating a positive or negative 'OK' status, with four possible permutations. It offered advice on how to replace 'crossed' transactions (those that hinder communication, such that one or both people are 'Not OK') with 'complementary' ones (those that encourage it and therefore result in the ideal permutation indicated in the book's title). Harris drew on Berne's proposed three states, that of Parent, Child, and Adult, which Harris summarised as being characterised by taught concepts, felt concepts, and learned concepts, respectively, and that are proposed to coexist in all people.[25] As opposed to the model of Ego, Superego, and Id, Berne's (and by extension Harris's) Parent–Child–Adult states are defined by real-world experiences, which Harris describes according to the analogy of the tape recorder: 'the state is produced by the playback of recorded data of events in the past, involving real people, real times, real places, real decisions, and real feelings'.[26] As Harris outlines in *I'm OK – You're OK*, the Child state is characterised by pronouncements received passively ('without editing') from the Parent, which Harris describes via the analogy of a tape recorder that plays without interruption a litany of statements, warnings, and rules that are received unquestioningly by the Child.[27] The Child state is therefore focused on internal felt experience of the world, while the Adult state is defined by an exploration of the world and the formation of opinions independently of the Parent's ideas or regulations. Notably, Harris's use of the tape recorder and data analogies reflects the arrival of home-cassette technologies during the latter 1960s as well as the broader cultural influence of technology discourses and systems theory.

By the end of the decade, the book's influence was widely felt in educational settings as well as American homes, with schools running 'OK Week' activities that encouraged kindness, self-understanding, and relationship-building. One such initiative resulted in the publication of an accompanying *I'm OK, You're OK Field Guide* (produced with Harris's permission), which included a set of suggested activities for parents, faculty and staff, students, and the wider community: 'Conduct a faculty meeting in which no problems are presented'; 'Conduct a smile contest'; 'Conduct a class meeting on the topic "What is OK about our school?"', the last including the instruction to 'Show the meeting on videotape to students or hold the meeting over the school intercom.' Juxtaposed with those 1970s experiments in participation, spatial practice, and communication technologies being undertaken at CalArts, it is tempting to read these 'OK Week' activities in the same tone as the typed list of suggested class assignments produced by Baldessari for his post-studio class in 1970.[28] The latter's opening gambit – 'Imitate Baldessari in actions and speech. Video' – sets the tone for a list that is equally invested in recording technologies and the rules that tacitly shape social and creative interactions.

My intention is not to draw a direct causality between Harris's book and the conceptual projects being undertaken in Baldessari's class, whose students included Segalove. Nor is it to say that *The Mom Tapes* is a direct illustration of the ideas set out in *I'm OK – You're OK*. But the popularity of Harris's book during the first half of the 1970s offers a useful backdrop to understand the video, in which the artist, mostly invisible to the viewer, is delineated via a set of transactional encounters with her mother in the spaces that she inhabits. Indeed, in the sense that they implicitly map or document relations between people, both *Where's Al?* and *The Mom Tapes* might be described as concerned with social transactions, according to which the self is made present through the description of its interactions with others (the friends gathered for a weekend party or the mother wandering around an empty nest). Though not explicitly framed as such (and though the familial terms adopted by Berne and Harris are symbolic rather than literal),[29] the transition in the first episode of *The Mom Tapes* from the apparently passive reception of advice and admonition to an independent exploration of the world, articulates the move from Parent to Adult ego state: Ilene's venturing into the underpass thus operates as a moment of breaking free and independent self-formation, even as the maternal voice of warning continues unaffected. As she emerges, the declaration 'I made it and I'm OK' marks that transition. In the typically bathetic style of Segalove's deadpan humour, the scene of this transformation is one of suburban mundanity that feels anything but transcendent.

Where's Al? also includes what Harris might have termed 'crossed transactions' – among the conversations that it details, several indicate a lack of interest or refusal to assign motivation, appearing as conversational and intersubjective dead ends that frustrate communication and communion – 'he: Where's Al? / she: Who knows?' or 'she: Where's Al? / he: Indisposed'. On one card the question, 'he: Where's Al?', dangles with no answer at all. These unsatisfying exchanges are characterised by the absence of knowledge and curiosity alike, representing a scenario in which Al alone bears responsibility for his failure to appear. This shift of emphasis – from the group to the individual – echoes a broader social shift in psychological responsibility and labour during this period, a reorientation from the expert voice of the therapist to an emphasis on the individual via the accessibility of popular self-actualisation strategies. In the burgeoning culture of self-help, the individual takes ownership of their own journey, reliant only on their own determination or ability to follow the instructions set out in easily available literature and associated products. Others are unimportant or indifferent. In this context, we might read the performance of motherly advice (sometimes sought, sometimes unsolicited) in *The Mom Tapes* as echoing the tone and structure of popular advice columns, self-help literature, and pop psychology, which aimed to replace the familial guidance of mother–daughter relations with structured (and marketised) advice.[30] Products and advertising go hand in hand with subject formation as it plays out in white middle-class America, with the setting of Segalove's video typical of the suburban audience targeted by pop psychology and self-help marketing.

Pictures and self-help

In the slender catalogue of the 1977 exhibition *Pictures*, held at Artists Space in New York, Douglas Crimp described the works of a group of contemporary American artists as critically engaging with pictures as a signifying structure that usurps reality.[31] Jack Goldstein and others included in Crimp's exhibition no longer looked to uncover the truth beneath or behind representation but focused their attention on the opacity of the picture in and of itself and the pictorial economy within which it is embedded. In the context of Los Angeles, Goldstein, William Leavitt, Billy Adler, and others focused this investigation on the film and television industry, taking as their subject the industry's visual cues, codes, and conventions, in order to draw attention to their generic absurdity.

In line with this impulse that is oriented towards the apparatus of communication, we might read works such as *Where's Al?* and *The Mom Tapes* as invested not in revealing any sort of true self (thus not confessional per se), but in mapping or performing the representational mechanisms by which the subject is delineated in the era of marketised self-help. The field that they describe is one in which the commercial logic of the self (its life work, as in the business of living) is articulated as much in the realm of pop psychology as in the television advertisement, the movie leader, or the department store display. In line with the Pictures generation (and other Los Angeles artists who took media representation as their subject), their attention falls on the mediation enacted via pop psychology, cheap claims for art as therapy or autobiography, and the structures of self-help, which is framed as the new society of the spectacle. We are reminded that even as these constitutive schemas are revealed, we become tangled in another schematic logic produced to determine and guide procedures of self-actualisation. Such explorations are closely related to feminist artistic practices that sought to reveal, often through performance, the schematic and systematic construction of the normative (gendered) subject. They also relate to the fraught debates around conceptual art, which, like self-help, demanded attentive and systematic processes oriented towards self-reflection that often manifested as tautology; both conceptual art and self-help thus trod the precarious line between eschewing hegemonic value systems and susceptibility to marketisation.

The sense in which self-actualisation is tangled up in the technological and cultural logic of picturing is at the heart of Eleanor Antin's *Carving: A Traditional Sculpture* (figure 9.4), in which a grid of black-and-white photographs document the artist's body over a period of five weeks between 15 July and 21 August 1972, during which she reduced her food intake. The work mobilises the act of dieting as the paradigmatic action of self-improvement performed in public and links both its action and its outcome to the mode of photography as proof of change. As viewers, we are invited to peer at Antin's body in order to discern barely perceptible differences (Antin lost around ten pounds over the course of the project), deploying a scrutinising gaze that precludes any notion of self-improvement as liberation or empowerment, even as it also undermines the supposed objectivity of photography and conceptual art alike.[32] Although the photographs are visually reminiscent of mugshots, Antin's positioning against a door serves as a reminder

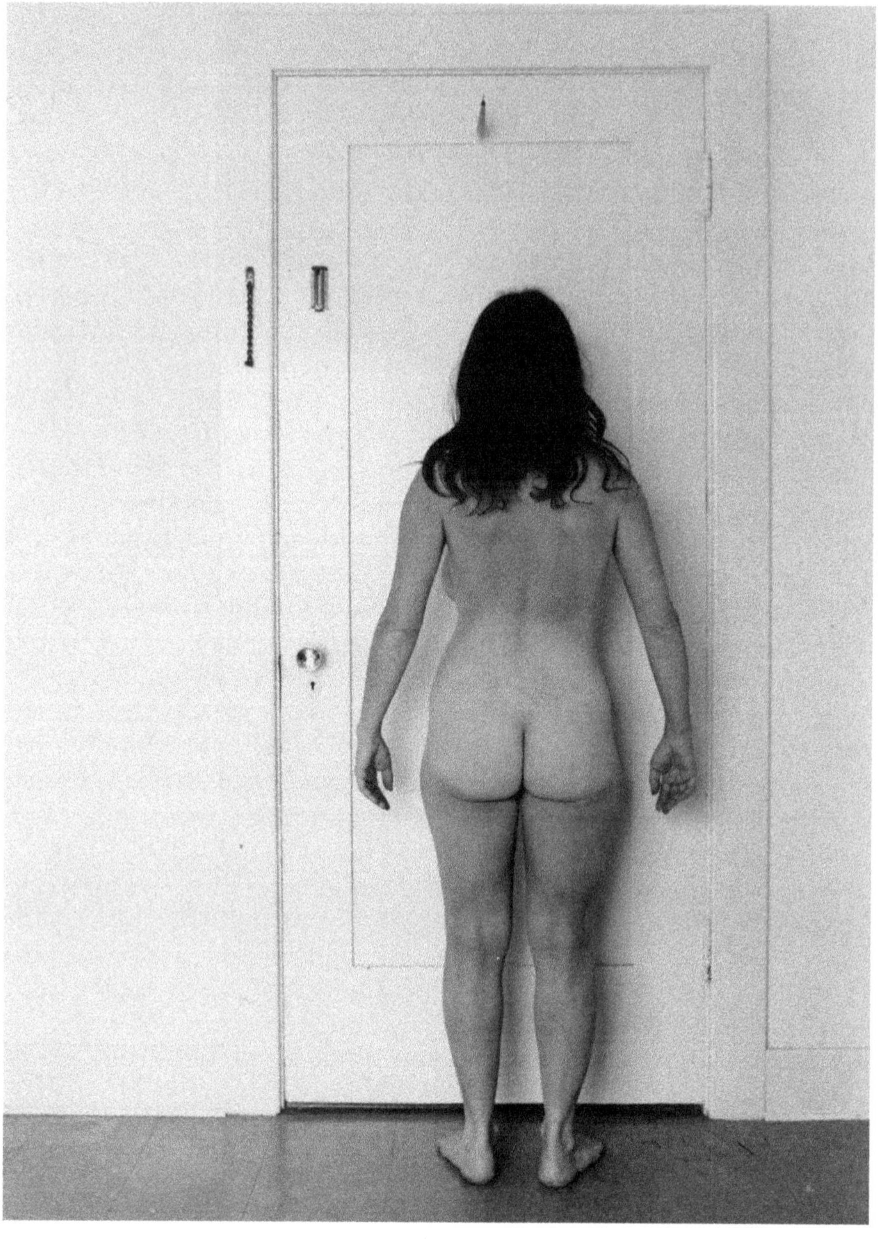

9.4 Eleanor Antin, *Carving: A Traditional Sculpture* (single photograph detail), 1972, 148 gelatin silver prints and text panel, each photograph: 17.7 × 12.7 cm; text panel: 39.4 × 26 cm; installed: 79.4 × 518.2 cm

of the intimate scale of her undertaking and the way in which self-improvement necessitates a negotiation between private and public, a process that is inevitably gendered. A related work called *The Eight Temptations* (1972, figure 9.5) makes explicit the transactional implications of *Carving*. The work comprises eight colour photographs depicting Antin seated at a restaurant table, her hands raised in ever more melodramatic gestures as if rejecting increasingly insistent offers of food, a camply ironic performance of self-denial.

Taken together, *The Eight Temptations* and *Carving* underscore that dieting is a private action that is performed in public, often announced via a declaration to others and assessed by their scrutinising gaze, the body held to account. The early 1970s saw a proliferation in popular diet-advice books, which sat alongside other self-help titles on bestseller lists. Regimes that advocated the consumption of single foodstuffs in place of full meals – the 7-Day Milk Diet, the Grapefruit Diet – were often sponsored by corporate entities or produce associations, while the 1970 Sexy Pineapple Diet was conceived by the husband-and-wife team Inge and Sten Hegeler, who had made their names dishing out relationship advice in their book *The X.Y.Z. of Love*. In this context of the marketised crossover of relationship and so-called health advice (save your marriage by getting thin), and in light of what I am reading as the feminist projects of Ruppersberg and Segalove, it is not coincidental that the field of self-help, even in the 1970s and even in the field of diet and nutrition, was one dominated by male authors even as it was aimed predominantly at women readers, as Nicos Kefalas has observed.[33] Antin makes clear that self-improvement here involves the negotiation of interpersonal interactions that can put pressure on the ability to achieve self-actualisation, in a manoeuvre reminiscent of Harris's positions (here, surely, 'You're OK – I'm Not OK'). In *The Eight Temptations* it is not the artist who is the invisible participant in these transactions, but the viewer, cast in the role of tempter, or derailer of good intentions.

To read the works I have described in terms of the subject transactions that they delineate or imply is to recognise that the play of absences that Crow identifies in Los Angeles art of the early 1970s is not always, or not entirely, symptomatic of an anxiety about artistic professionalism. If we locate the work of Ruppersberg, Segalove, and Antin within an epistemology of self-help, we see the ways in which they exist at the confluence of identity-formation, market logic, and ideal self-picturing. Set against the early 1970s backdrop

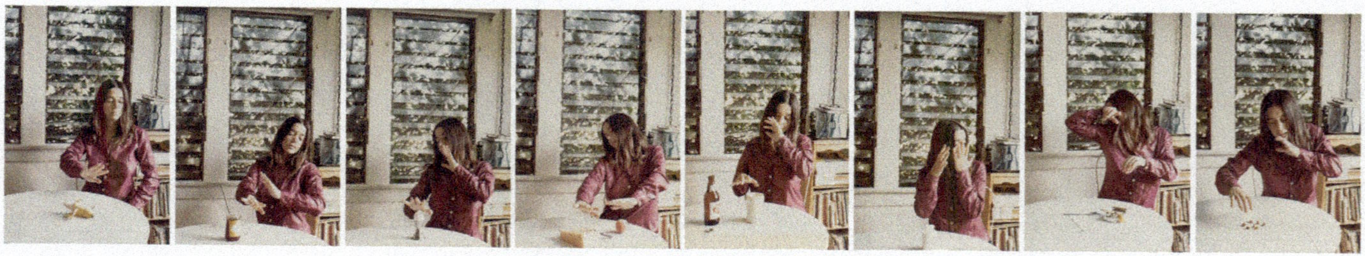

9.5 Eleanor Antin, *The Eight Temptations* (detail), 1972, eight chromogenic prints, each 17.8 × 12.7 cm

of self-help, *Where's Al?*, *The Mom Tapes*, and *The Eight Temptations* emerge accordingly as humorous critiques of the idea that art should be therapeutic, and the widespread demand that it should be revelatory or confessional. That is, they negotiate the demands for emotional labour made by contemporary art audiences, political movements, and therapeutic groups alike. They also ask how and where we might locate the boundaries of life (improvement) work? Whom does the labour of self-help implicate, and what are its logics? While straightforwardly biographical art history was long viewed as a reductive manoeuvre that dislocated the work of art from its historical, political, and economic context, when understood according to the epistemology of self-help, it was, on the contrary, inevitably and irrevocably implicated in, and shaped by, those economies. As much as they play with the role of life narrative as (and in) art and its histories, the works that I have examined also have something to say about the stakes of conceptual art in the era of self-help. Rather than using conceptual art strategies to tautologically document the process of artistic labour, Ruppersberg, Segalove, and Antin deploy diagrams, documentation, structured conversational formats, and other devices to document the process of 'working on' themselves. In doing so, they highlight the parallel imperatives that governed self-help and conceptual art alike, revealing both to be embedded in the logic of capitalism.

In 1979, Segalove added to the binary positions articulated in the 'I'm OK – You're OK' formula, a third, implied presence that made explicit the commercial and visual entertainment imperatives that underpinned the self-help movement: the phrase 'TV Is OK', inscribed on a car licence plate. Segalove used the phrase as the name of her putative production company, complete with business cards that bore the declaration, and the licence plate appears in a 30-second video work of the same name.[34] In a photographic self-portrait from around 1984, a frame from the video appears on a television set behind the artist, its upper-right background position akin to a comic strip thought bubble hovering above the pensive Ilene's head, such that medium and message are presented at once as external tools of the trade and internal monologue (figure 9.6). While the short declaration 'TV is OK' could be read as a defence of television viewing as an activity increasingly occupying American homes, we might also read it as staging TV as a subject, in line with Segalove's broader impetus to frame it as both emotional facilitator and family member alike. Indeed, television was a crucial protagonist

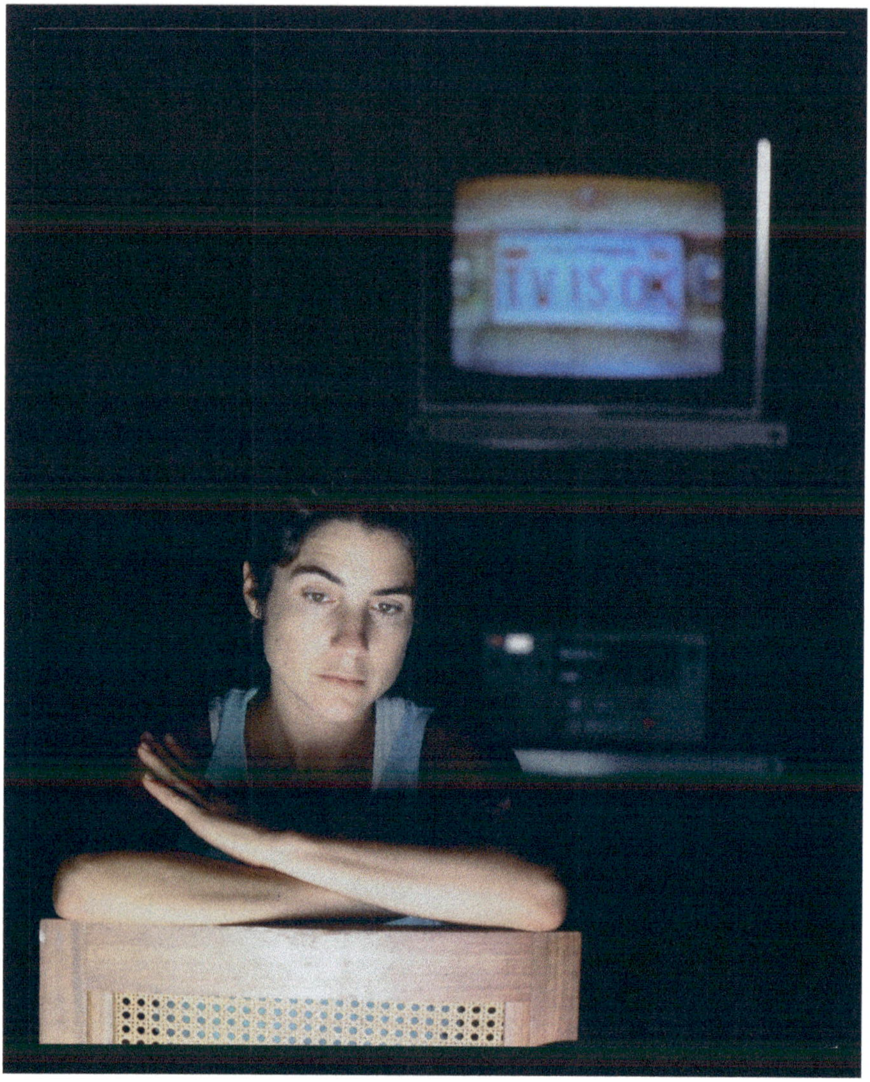

9.6 Photograph of Ilene Segalove, *c.*1984

in the kinds of discussions, games, and relationship-building that had been occupying American middle-class households across the decade. Lifework here is reoriented as cultural product and tool of mass communication via the ultimate vanity plate as symbol of success, in a gesture that makes explicit the commercial logic that governs the self-schema as it is performed in public, but apparently concludes that all is well: 'I made it and I'm OK.'

Notes

I offer my thanks to Ilene Segalove and Eleanor Antin. An early version of this research was presented at the University of Sussex, for which opportunity and the discussion it engendered I thank Francesco Ventrella.

1 See, for example, Constance Lewellan (ed.), *State of Mind: New California Art circa 1970* (Berkeley and Los Angeles, CA and London: University of California Press, 2011); Damon Willick (ed.), *Valley Vista: Art in the San Fernando Valley, CA, 1970–1990* (Los Angeles, CA: Angel City Press, 2014); and Jacob Stewart-Halevy, 'California Conceptualism's About-Face', *October*, 163 (2018), 71–101.

2 Jayne Wark, 'Conceptual Art and Feminism: Martha Rosler, Adrian Piper, Eleanor Antin, and Martha Wilson', *Women's Art Journal*, 22:1 (2001), 42.

3 Lauren Fournier, *Autotheory and Feminist Practice in Art, Writing, and Criticism* (Cambridge, MA: MIT Press, 2021), p. 14.

4 See Glenn Phillips, *California Video: Artists and Histories* (Los Angeles, CA: Getty, 2008), pp. 4–8.

5 Benjamin H. D. Buchloh, 'Conceptual Art 1962–1969: From the Aesthetic of Administration to the Critique of Institutions', *October*, 55 (Winter 1990), 105–143.

6 Ruppersberg in Leah Ollman, 'In the Studio: Allen Ruppersberg', *Art News*, 1 March 2018, www.artnews.com/art-in-america/features/studio-allen-ruppersberg-63475 (accessed 14 November 2022).

7 Siri Engberg, 'As the Crow Flies: Following the Path of Allen Ruppersberg', in Engberg (ed.), *Allen Ruppersberg: Intellectual Property, 1968–2018* (Minneapolis, MN: Walker Art Center, 2018), p. 32.

8 Oral history interview with Allen Ruppersberg, 27 October 2017–15 January 2018, Archives of American Art, Smithsonian Institution, Washington, DC.

9 Allen Ruppersberg interviewed by Marie B. Shukus, in Rebecca McGrew and Glenn Phillips (eds), *It Happened at Pomona: Art at the Edge of Los Angeles, 1969–1973* (Los Angeles, CA: Pomona College Museum of Art, 2011), p. 227.

10 Thomas Crow, 'The Art of the Fugitive in 1970s Los Angeles: Runaway Self-Consciousness', in *Under the Big Black Sun: California Art 1974–1981* (Los Angeles, CA: MOCA, 2011), p. 44. See also Crow, 'The Picture of Allen Ruppersberg as a Young Man', in *Allen Ruppersberg: Intellectual Property, 1968–2018* (Minneapolis, MN: Walker Art Center, 2018), p. 242.

11 Stewart-Halevy, 'California Conceptualism's About-Face', 78. By his own admission, Stewart-Halevy considers Ruppersberg, but not Antin and Segalove, in his account of California Conceptualists.

12 Stewart Justman, 'The Uncaged Bird: Pop Psychology and Its Sources', *Salmagundi*, 157 (2008), 133. See also Mercè Mur Effing, 'The Origin and Development of Self-help Literature in the United States: The Concept of Success and Happiness, an Overview / El Origen y Desarrollo de la Literatura de Auto-Ayuda en los Estados Unidos: El Concepto de Éxito y Felicidad. Vision General', *Atlantis*, 31:2 (December 2009), 125–141.
13 See Gary Alan Fine, *Talking Art: The Culture of Practice and the Practice of Culture in MFA Education* (Chicago, IL: University of Chicago Press, 2018), p. 56.
14 See Michael Lobel, 'Postmodernism between Art and Film: Jack Goldstein's *Portrait of Père Tanguy*', in Rebecca Peabody et al. (eds), *Pacific Standard Time: Los Angeles Art 1945–1980* (Los Angeles, CA: Getty, 2011), pp. 246–247.
15 See Crow, 'The Picture of Allen Ruppersberg as a Young Man', p. 242.
16 Justman, 'The Uncaged Bird', 131.
17 See Eva Illouz, *Saving the Modern Soul: Therapy, Emotions, and the Culture of Self-Help* (Berkeley and Los Angeles, CA and London: University of California Press, 2008), pp. 178–179.
18 Eva Moskowitz, *In Therapy We Trust: America's Obsession with Self-Fulfilment* (Baltimore, MD: Johns Hopkins University Press, 2001), pp. 219–224.
19 The Ungame is distinct from earlier examples, in that it was aimed at home use by non-specialists, as opposed to products such as the Talking, Feeling, and Doing Board Game, which was launched in 1968 but aimed at use by specialist child therapists in a professional therapeutic context.
20 Katherine Doniak, 'Feed Your Head: Conceptual Art and the American Counterculture' (PhD dissertation, University of Nottingham, 2019).
21 Sandy Ballatore, 'Autobiographical Fantasies', *Art Week*, 7 (14 February 1976), p. 1, 16. For a discussion of the exhibition see Lucy Bradnock, 'Autobiographical Fantasy and the Feminist Archive', *Archives of American Art Journal*, 60:1 (Spring 2021), 44–61.
22 Jeffrey Ruoff, *An American Family: A Televised Life* (Minneapolis, MN: University of Minnesota Press, 2002).
23 Thomas A. Harris, *I'm OK – You're OK* (London: Pan, 1973), p. 12. Berne's model was first published as 'Transactional Analysis: A New and Effective Method of Group Therapy', *American Journal of Psychotherapy*, 12:4 (October 1958), 735–743.
24 Harris, *I'm OK – You're OK*, p. xvii.
25 Harris, *I'm OK – You're OK*, pp. 16–35.
26 Harris, *I'm OK – You're OK*, p. 18.
27 Harris, *I'm OK – You're OK*, p. 19.
28 Michael L. Bundy, 'Field Guide to a Human Relations Week', *School Counselor*, 26:3 (1979), 172–177.

29 Harris explains that 'Parent is not the same as mother or father, Adult means something quite different from a grown-up, and Child is not the same as a little person.' Harris, *I'm OK – You're OK,* p. 15.

30 It is important also to acknowledge the significant links between self-help and feminism, particularly in the form of the feminist self-help health movement started by Carol Downer in 1971. See Debra Brody, Sara Grusky, and Patricia Logan, 'Self-help Health', *Off Our Backs,* 12:7 (1982), 14. See also Hannah Grace Dudley Shotwell, 'Empowering the Body: The Evolution of Self-Help in the Women's Health Movement' (PhD dissertation, University of North Carolina at Greensboro, 2016).

31 Douglas Crimp, 'Pictures', in *Pictures* (New York: Committee for the Visual Arts, 1977), p. 3.

32 Eleanor Antin cited in Howard N. Fox (ed.), *Eleanor Antin* (Los Angeles, CA: Los Angeles County Museum of Art, 1999), p. 44.

33 Nicos Kefalas, 'Self-help and Self-promotion: Dietary Advice and Agency in North America and Britain', in Mark Jackson and Martin D. Moore (eds), *Balancing the Self: Medicine, Politics and the Regulation of Health in the Twentieth Century* (Manchester: Manchester University Press, 2020), pp. 131–132.

34 Ilene Segalove papers, 1960–2021, Box 1, folder 1, Archives of American Art, Smithsonian Institution, Washington, DC.

Part V

I remember . . . remember me

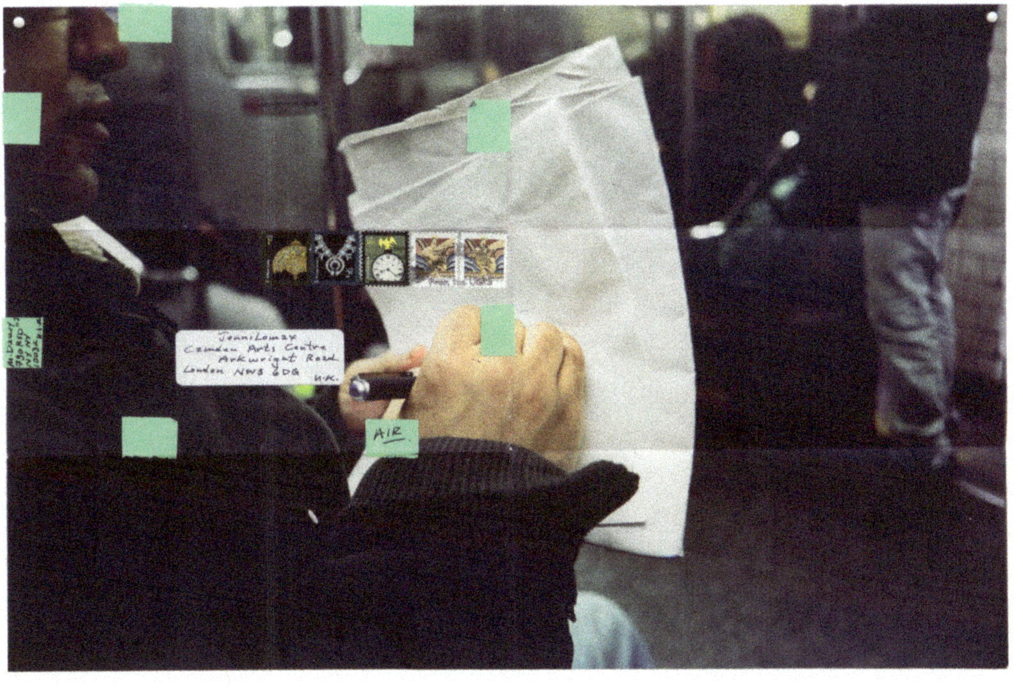

Moyra Davey, detail from *Subway Writers* series, 2011, C-print, tape, postage ink, 30 × 45 cm

10

A wall for apricots: dedication and loss in Anne Truitt's minimalism

Miguel de Baca

This chapter concerns two sculptures, made by the American artist Anne Truitt in the 1960s, that share a single, idiosyncratic title: *A Wall for Apricots.* Truitt fabricated the first in 1966, of welded slab aluminium painted with flat zones of industrial marine coating (figure 10.1). Already it was an exception. Up to that point, Truitt was known mainly for elegantly painted wooden planks and volumes, a style she innovated starting in 1961, making her one of the first artists to be associated with what would come to be known as minimalism. But, owing to a shift in her studio practice upon moving to Tokyo from Washington, DC, between the years of 1964 and 1967, Truitt began creating sculptures with metal. These sculptures were not critically successful, confirming the artist's own doubts. When considering works for inclusion in a career retrospective at the Corcoran Gallery of Art in 1971, Truitt sensed that her aluminium, Japanese-made sculptures did not fit within her overall aesthetic, and she destroyed most of them. The second *A Wall for Apricots* (figure 10.2) was made in 1968, after Truitt had arrived back in the United States and returned to working with wood painted with thinned washes of Liquitex acrylic, her preferred medium. Truitt sanded back between layers of paint to achieve the ambiguous, multifaceted, colourful surfaces that are now a hallmark of her practice. This sculpture takes the form of a rectangular column, Truitt's favoured shape after 1967, and one that she deployed almost exclusively for the next forty years.[1]

The sharing of a title between two artworks in the same artist's oeuvre is not seemingly that extraordinary, and one should not assume that the title of an artwork will reveal its 'content', particularly for non-objective artworks in which content is deliberately

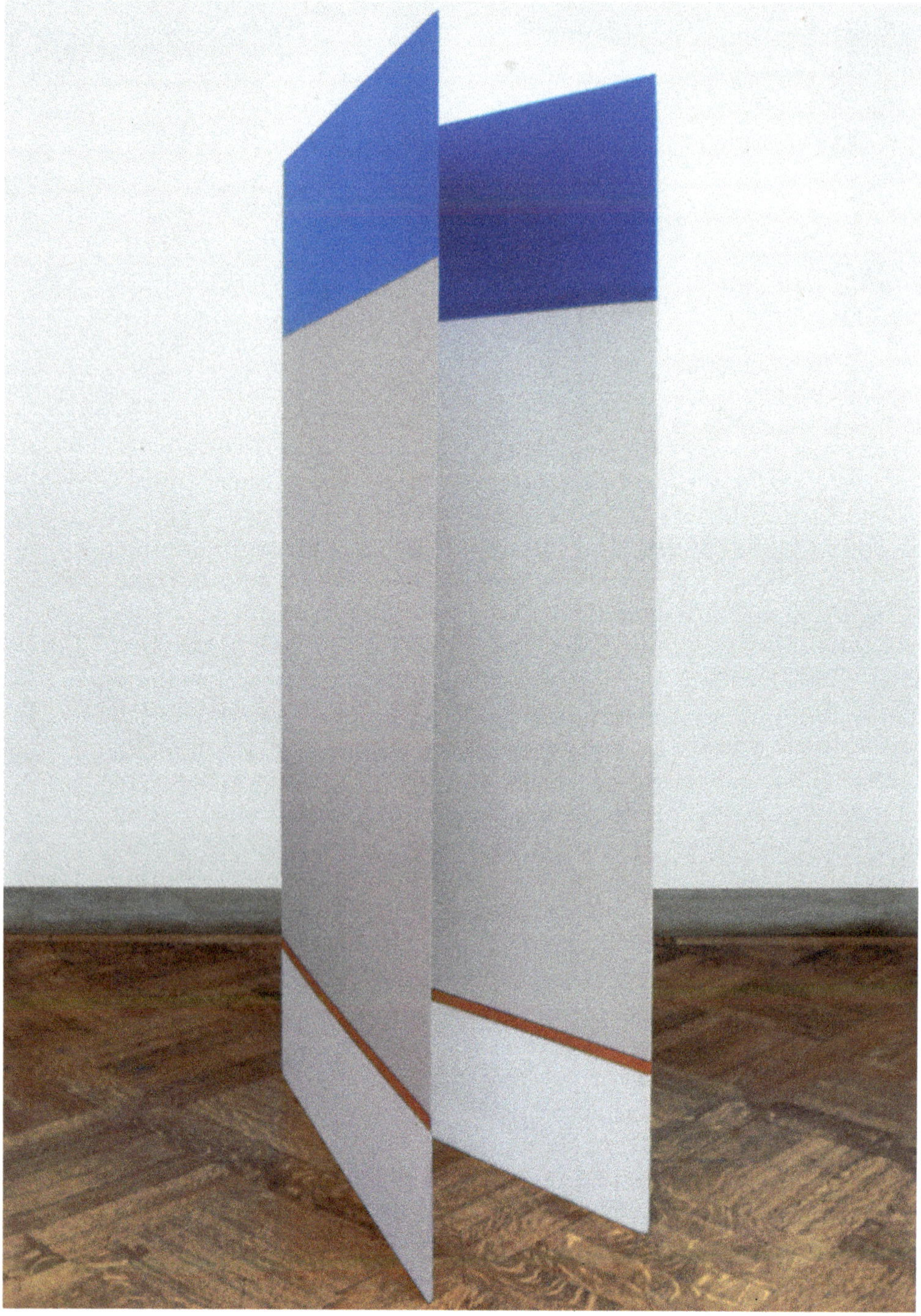

10.1 Anne Truitt, *A Wall for Apricots*, 1966, acrylic on aluminium, 199 × 100 × 43 cm

fugitive. Many artists at mid-century decided to withhold titles for this very reason, and leaving a work untitled is a trope in abstract art going back at least to the early twentieth century. It was not necessarily uncommon to select a title that establishes a mood or sensibility, even for high-modernist abstraction. Take, as a ready example, the infamously downbeat titles of Frank Stella's *Black Paintings* (1958–1959): totally abstract, monochrome paintings evocative of relentless gloom.[2]

Although a title is an unstable signifier, one that may undoubtedly be kept aloof from the artist's intentions, for the beholder the title may imply meaning and provide a suggestive context – even if that context is at first obscure.

The destruction of the first *A Wall for Apricots*, and the title's resurfacing in a later mode in which the artist was perfecting a durable mature style, suggests that these words do not merely constitute an arbitrary signifier, but instead one deeply involved in the artist's process and its desired aesthetic effect. Truitt's titles often insinuate a relationship between the viewer and the sculptural object, a subject that many early minimalists had also addressed in their radical appraisals of the phenomenon of sculpture itself, to find its meaning in contemporary terms. The Truitt title frequently advances what the literary historian Gérard Genette has called a 'zone of transaction, a space that is essentially pragmatic and strategic' in his consideration of what is known as the 'paratext', that is, written matter that is adjunct to the main story or narrative: notes, dedications, prefaces, and – importantly for our purposes – titles and subtitles.[3] Genette studies this paratextual phenomenon in the writings of Marcel Proust, the French author, whose influence on Truitt happened to be profound. The objective of this Proustian strategy, which is to structure and mediate the reader's encounter of the main text, can also be applied to the relationship between the title, sculpture, and beholder of Truitt's work. I believe this is especially poignant in Truitt's case because we happen to know that *A Wall for Apricots* was dedicatory, having been made in memory of the artist's dear friend Mary Pinchot Meyer, who was murdered in the autumn of 1964.

Truitt's devotion to Proust was lifelong. In 1953, she undertook a published translation of the French scholar Germaine Brée's *Marcel Proust and Deliverance from Time* (1955), a critical assessment of Proust's masterwork, *la Recherche*, a novel in seven volumes published between 1913 and 1927. To translate it, Truitt familiarised herself with Proust's work, which she described as a 'turning point'.[4] She was

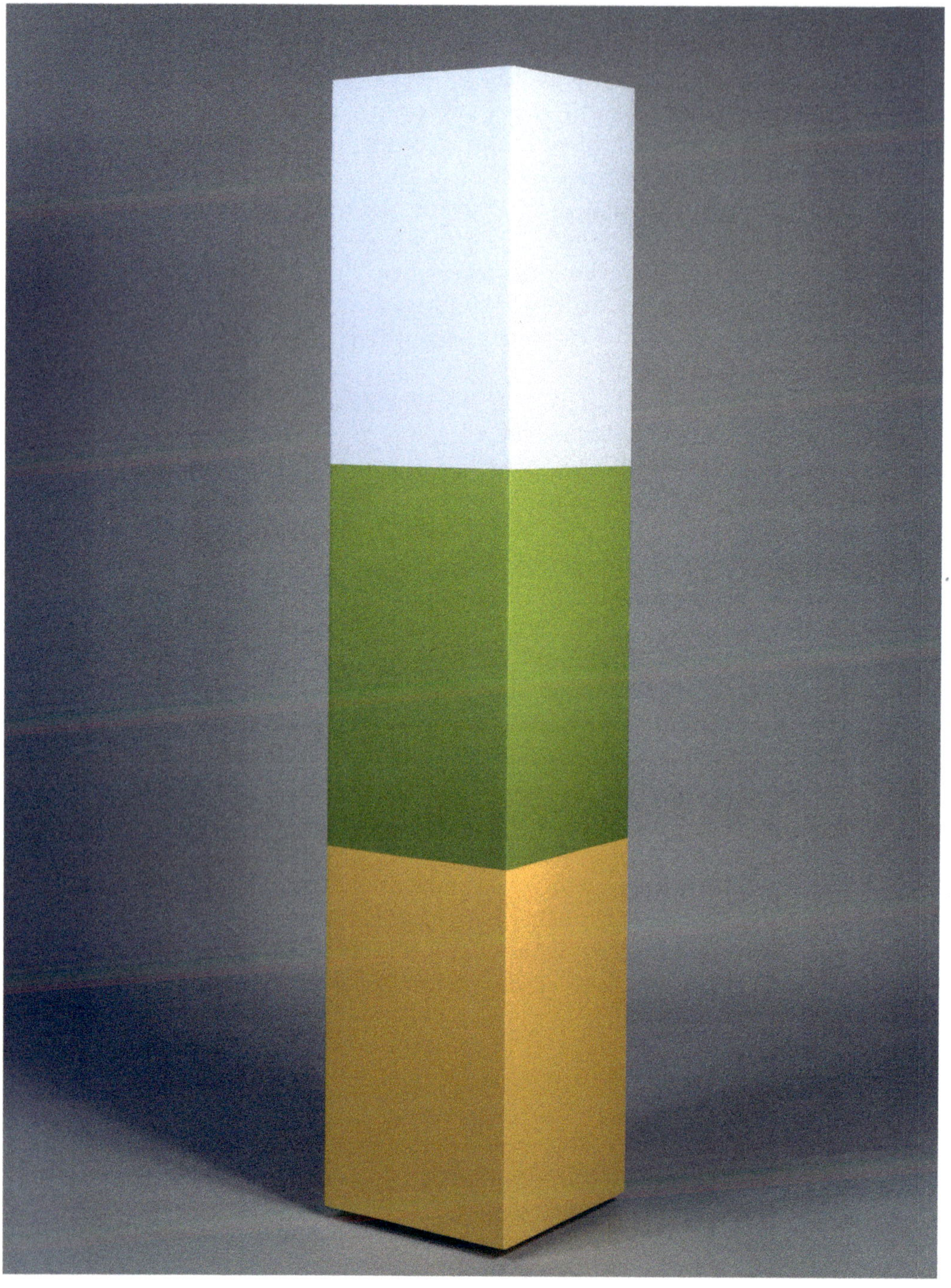

10.2 Anne Truitt, *A Wall for Apricots*, 1968, acrylic on wood, 185 × 36 × 36 cm

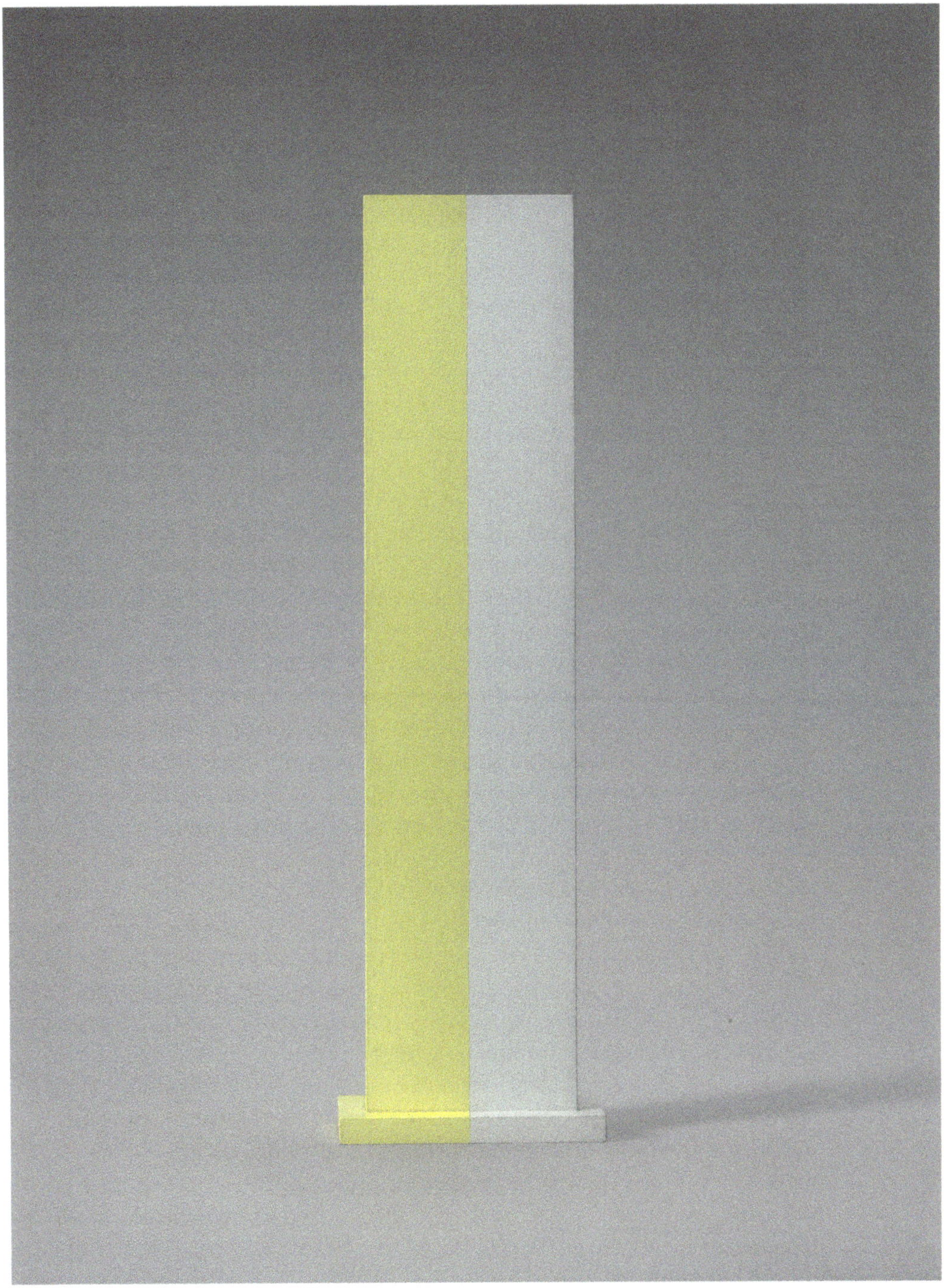

10.3 Anne Truitt, *Mary's Light*, 1962, acrylic on wood, 136 × 38 × 18 cm

drawn to the fundamentally Proustian concept that sensory stimuli in the regular environment could produce powerful and spontaneous memory effects. Such a return, however potent, does not reproduce the past, but rather creates intensity in the present experience: one that is not only excited by a single memory, but also potentially by the intervening time and other memories that give that memory a special meaning. One of the focuses of Brée's book was Proust's extensive narration of how memories are deeply interconnected and recur across one's lifetime, which unites the volumes as a coherent autobiographical artwork. Brée's scholarship opened Truitt's horizons to Proustian concepts of memory and sensation just as she was beginning to think of herself seriously as a sculptor and was in the larger sense thinking of what an artist's life would be like. It would also structure a significant encounter with a Barnett Newman painting in 1961 that launched her into minimalism, which I discuss further below.

Although it is not directly mentioned in Truitt's reflections on Proust, it stands to reason that Proust's unique style of narration, with its incorporation of elaborate paratextual matter, would have been noticeably evident to her. According to Genette's interpretation of *la Recherche*, the paratext is where the reader observes porousness between the text of the novel and Proust's relationship to the whole novel as a work of art. Genette also identifies the paratextual elements as a 'threshold' between the reader and the author. The belaboured section titles and intertitles, dedications, and even the unusual lack of certain customary publishing practices such as a preface amount to guidelines to the reader, all given in the author's own voice. Naturally, how one reads a novel will necessarily be guided by individual insights. But as literary critic Jane Lavery writes, 'peritextual devices establish a sense of purpose and prompt the reader to step into the text itself and to read on', and can serve as much to anchor meaning as to disrupt it, or to stir ambiguity.[5] Despite the scholarly debate on whether Proust's novel was intended to be read as a work of fiction (a book about a character named Marcel) versus autobiography (the story of Proust), the author's extensive paratext places his authorial voice forcefully in the story anyway. And the fact that Proust changed paratextual matter from edition to edition indicates the evolution in his own thinking about the novel and how it could be made better or more aesthetically whole through these textual signposts, either for himself as the artist or on behalf of his ideal reader. Truitt learned a great deal from the relationship that Proust had to his novel and his coming-into-being as a mature author.

Truitt's artworks are abstract and non-textual, so the only evident paratext is found in their titles. These titles rarely, if ever, illuminate meaning, but like Proust's paratext, they invite an entrance into perception given in the artist's own voice. It was not uncommon for Truitt to employ dedicatory titles evoking both personal and public significance. The sculpture *Mary's Light* (1962, figure 10.3) was one of Truitt's first sculptures in the pared-down aesthetic of minimalism after having worked through an expressionistic phase in her early career, and it is also titled after the same Mary that would later be tragically killed. Although *A Wall for Apricots* does not name her outright, a recorded interview with Truitt in 1998 reveals its origin: the artist remembered that she and Meyer were together at a dinner party at which, during a conversation game, the host asked each of the guests to write down three things they loved and three that they abhorred. Truitt remembered that two of Meyer's loves were 'white walls' and 'apricots'.[6] The shape of *Mary's Light* even suggests the fragment of a wall, although in this period, Truitt was primarily designing her work after the memory of various architectural details, most prominently the fences, tombstones, and white wainscotings characteristic of the colonial landscape of her childhood home on the Maryland coast. In any case, it is certain that *A Wall for Apricots* held a significance that was totally and privately elegiac to the artist herself, which its later iconoclasm renders unrecoverable. The second *A Wall for Apricots,* however, reveals the turn in Truitt's practice. Here, the sculpture confidently instantiates a sense of the private within the public domain – a sculpture that reveals as much as it conceals. This fugitive condition validates the viewer's uncertainty as a mode of perception and meaningfully resists transparency and resolution.

Truitt and Meyer became close friends within a devoted network of artists and intellectuals working in Washington in the 1950s and 1960s. Although New York held sway over the production of contemporary art in the United States in the middle of the twentieth century, the American federal capital enjoyed a vibrant art scene enabled by a highly educated class of governmental bureau chiefs and the substantial presence of a liberal free press. For example, Anne Truitt's husband, James, was a leading journalist for *Newsweek.* These men, and their equally educated and erudite wives, formed a salon culture connected by small, yet robust, galleries and museums such as the Jefferson Place Gallery, the Institute of Contemporary Arts, and the Washington Gallery of Modern Art. President John F. Kennedy and his wife, Jacqueline, who came into the White House in 1961, were symbolic of the cosmopolitanism enjoyed in Washington during this optimistic era. Those in the political and artistic scenes were connected by mere degrees of separation because the elite in Washington were socially compact: the Truitts were invited guests to Kennedy's inauguration, and Meyer was the subject of scrutiny as the president's alleged mistress.[7]

In those heady days, the leading artistic figures in Washington were Morris Louis and Kenneth Noland, colour-field painters who earned a national reputation through representation at the André Emmerich Gallery in New York. Noland, who taught studio classes at the Catholic University of America before devoting himself to painting full-time, was especially influential on both Meyer and Truitt. Meyer's signature particoloured discs evoke especially Noland's early bullseye style. As Truitt wrote to the critic Clement Greenberg in 1963, Meyer's work was 'imitative of Ken's . . . soaked in flat areas of spiral color, close in value, varied in hue'.[8] Truitt was also influenced by Noland, from whom she rented a small studio in the Dupont Circle neighbourhood of Washington. As she wrote in a highly personal, unsent letter to Greenberg in 1965: '[I]t was not Ken's work that influenced me . . .. It was his self, his experience as an artist, generously shared.'[9]

Truitt and Meyer were not only friends, but also professional interlocutors for one another. Meyer was Truitt's companion on a crucial trip to New York in 1961, where they visited the 'American Abstract Expressionists and Imagists' exhibition at the Guggenheim Museum. Together they viewed and discussed artworks by Ad Reinhardt and Barnett Newman. Truitt was felled by one Newman painting that, years later, the artist wrote about as a Proustian reaction in her published artist's journal *Daybook* (1982): 'What did I *know*, I asked myself. What did I *love*? . . . The fields and trees and fences and boards and lattices of my childhood rushed across my inner eye as if borne by a great, strong wind. I saw them all, detail and panorama, and my feeling for them welled up to sweep me into the knowledge that I could make them.'[10] Upon returning to her studio in Washington, she constructed *First* (1961, figure 10.4), which, as its title suggests, was the artist's first sculpture in a newly adopted style of geometric simplicity. *First* consists of three vertical, white-painted pales cut to resemble a picket fence, the kind of fence Truitt remembered from

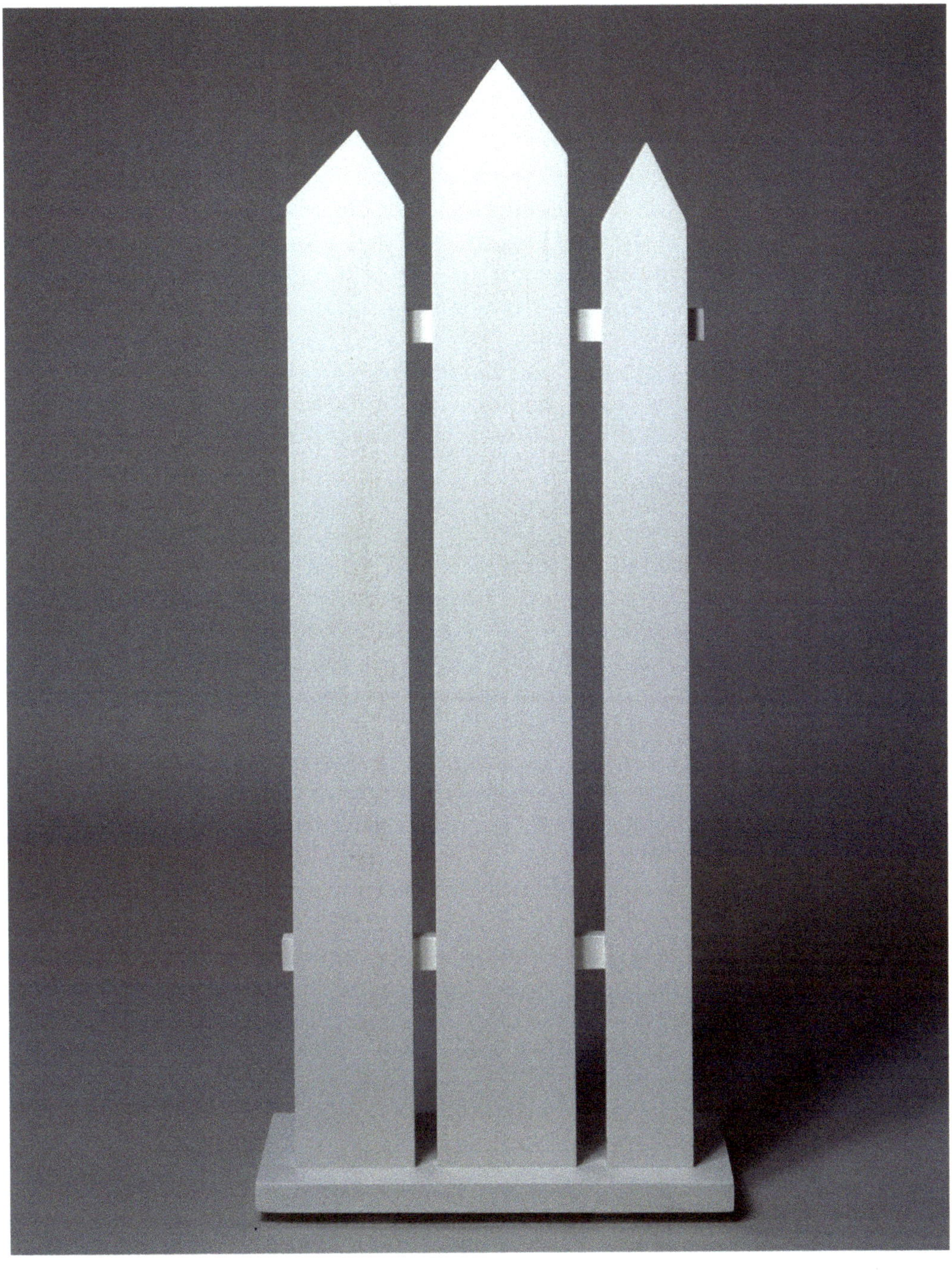

10.4 Anne Truitt, *First*, 1961, latex semi-gloss enamel on poplar wood, 112 × 45 × 18 cm

her childhood, and the kind of fence enshrined as an image and a metaphor in American cultural memory.[11]

First reveals both Truitt's sited, sculptural response to Newman's painting specifically and to the practice of painting more generally. Compellingly in *Daybook*, Truitt wrote of her desire to set a painting free into three dimensions: here, a painting's flatness refers to a limitation that the artist was interested in challenging. Like a painting, a fence is a surface with a front and back. However, *First* is a structure unlike a painting, allowing the viewer to occupy one or both sides. The viewer becomes acutely aware of the spatial dynamics that solicit their body into a relationship of inside and outside, strongly connoting inclusion and exclusion. However, Truitt's art is not purely denotative, but is instead a process of mediation between the object and the viewer: the space of its beholding provides a sensory context in which visual and embodied perception spark associations with images and memories in the viewer's mind. Truitt's ensuing practice was about subtleties that break through ordinary perception when presented with these objects in the space of a room. Ultimately, Truitt's art demonstrates clearly that a moment of perception cannot be abstracted either from its immediate context or from its references to the past. The intuitively remembered meanings of a shape, a colour, or an armature are, in fact, the underlying matter of perception itself.[12]

As she continued working in 1962 and 1963, Truitt became ever more attentive to how her sculptures opened up such horizons of spatial experience. After experimenting for some time with conventional bases for her planks and plinths, she eventually exhibited works directly on the floor – one of the first artists at the time to do so – as a way of announcing the sculpture's consistency with the viewer's zone of encounter. As the scale of these sculptures grew larger, Truitt identified colour as the formal property that her work singularly magnified in the viewer's visual plane. In fact, regarding *Valley Forge* (1963), a large, wall-shaped volume, Truitt spoke of colours that were 'cantilevered', at once grounded on the vertical axis and suspended on the horizontal one. Her deployment of an architectural vocabulary to describe colour was consistent with her resistance to the localising impulse of the canvas. As colour was set free from its relationship to a flat surface, it was also liberated from codes of traditional painterly meaning – set adrift in space, quickening in the viewer's perceptual apparatus.[13]

In 1964, Truitt's husband, James, accepted a position as the Asian bureau chief of *Newsweek*, headquartered in Tokyo, and the Truitts moved from Washington to Japan. During this period, Truitt's main concern remained the analysis of boundaries between shapes and spaces. As she noted on a scrap of paper in January 1964: 'A space enclosed by a heavy, fat line will have more psychological bulk than when enclosed by a thin line.'[14] As a practical matter, Truitt was unable to work with wood in Tokyo because it was too cumbersome and expensive. Instead, she turned to sheets of lightweight aluminium. Unlike joined wood, the sculptural edge is a soldered line, a neatly drawn seam that brings the metal plates together into an enclosed volume. As a result, there is a lightness to the work that betrays not only the materiality, but the solemn effect that Truitt wished the sculptures to provoke. When these works were shown at the André Emmerich Gallery in 1965, Greenberg thought the sculptures were made of cardboard: in other words, decorative and elementary rather than rigorous.[15] Although she would later rebuff some of the critic's coolness, at the time, Truitt agreed.

While James was immersed in the Japanese cultural scene as a result of his journalistic work, Truitt remained at an arm's length in her studio. The preferred style in Tokyo at the time was neo-Dada sculpture, painting, and assemblage. American artists Robert Rauschenberg and Jasper Johns were received enthusiastically into the Japanese avant-garde, but their work was formally remote from Truitt's austere geometries.[16] Notwithstanding, there was a buzz surrounding Truitt, resulting partly from her novelty as a 'woman artist'. A feature interview in the *Asahi Shimbun* from 22 March 1964 introduced her as 'not just an ordinary housewife, but also a *mama-san* sculptor', using the term for the woman in charge of a geisha house.[17] Truitt's presence in the Japanese art world was eccentric and most likely understood mainly in the context of her husband's connections. Through an eventual friendship struck with the sympathetic dealer Kasuo Shimizu, Truitt was able to secure a solo show at his Minami Gallery, a pre-eminent contemporary art space in Tokyo, known especially for exhibiting trendsetting art from abroad.

One week before her important opening at Minami in October 1964, the unthinkable happened. Truitt received the upsetting news that Meyer had been shot at point-blank range while on a morning walk in the fashionable Washington neighbourhood where they both had lived. In an urgency to find the killer, charges were brought against Raymond Crump, Jr, a Black man whose presence was conspicuous in that wealthy, white area, but eventually dropped due to a lack of evidence. The murder remains unsolved to this day.[18]

Although stricken with grief, Truitt remained in Japan after Meyer's death, knowing that she was soon to make the arduous air journey to the United States for her sophomore show at Emmerich early in 1965. Much has been made outside art history of the furtive phone calls within the Truitts' network of *cognoscenti* in Washington in an effort to hide Meyer's diaries from those who might sensationalise her friendship with President Kennedy.[19] Such personal stress exacerbated Truitt's instincts that her studio work was off course, and she went into a medical depression. As she wrote to her friend, the California mosaicist Louisa Jenkins, in 1965: 'What I appear to be suffering from is a reactive depression, the result of countless strains . . . I'm afraid that my sin has been that ancient one of hubris: I thought I was strong enough to bear anything. But the way life is, is much harder than I had imagined.'[20]

When Truitt returned to Japan after her 1965 show at Emmerich, she ceased making soldered sculptural boxes and began to think more progressively about the formal property of scale. Confronted by the harsh criticism of these earlier works, Truitt wrote to Emmerich that she wished to do away with her previous aesthetic altogether, instead to pursue sculptural work so gigantic that it would declare an entire environment, possibly intended to be sited out of doors. At this scale, the viewer would have no choice but to encounter these works spatially. We are today accustomed to such sculptural environments by way of the land art movement in the late 1960s and early 1970s, but in 1965, Truitt's conceptualisation was unique.[21]

Alongside an awakening interest in scale (the massive sculptures she saw in her mind's eye were untenable in Japan), Truitt began to place her work for the first time in an art-historical trajectory. She wrote in her studio notes on 23 October 1965 that 'when the form and the color are one – CUBISM. Color can be/is independent of form. Colors will lock together and dominate the real shape of the piece. The form will be determined by the color NOT by the height, depth, width of the physical sculpture itself.'[22] This line of thinking reveals that, up to that point, Truitt might have accepted shape as a limiting condition of sculpture, just as analytic cubists in the early twentieth century accepted flatness as the limiting condition of painting. Their efforts resulted in the rejection of verisimilitude as the highest goal of depiction and the realisation that painted visual representations stand in somewhat of an arbitrary relationship to that which they represent. By going beyond the aims of cubism, Truitt wished to experiment with colour as the formal quality that mediates a sculptural relationship to its surrounding space. In such a paradigm, colour would take a leading role in the aesthetic language of sculpture, one less dependent upon local, predictable relationships to shape and composition, and thus freed to dictate form.

By citing cubism, Truitt was thinking of herself within a modernist legacy – even one that she was free to pick apart. Hand in hand with this new self-conception was a more highly self-conscious criticism of an art world that she shared with other artists who were women. For instance, Truitt's correspondence with the painter Helen Frankenthaler was particularly active in the period that she lived in Tokyo. Frankenthaler contacted Truitt to express great sympathy after Meyer's shocking death in 1964, and wrote apace in 1965 and 1966, sharing news about their mutual showings at Emmerich. In a letter from 10 October 1966, Frankenthaler complained of her sheer exhaustion leading up to an opening, which seemed to have been provoked by the whims of the men around her: 'playing nurse' to her husband, the painter Robert Motherwell, after an injury, and 'dealing with the pros and cons of André [Emmerich], Clem [Greenberg], Ken [Noland], *ad infinitum.* You know the score . . . we've discussed it, I think.'[23] In the closing of a letter to Truitt in 1967, Frankenthaler signed the postscript, 'Love, Woman Artist'.[24]

There were so few women working as artists who enjoyed the same high level of success as Truitt and Frankenthaler in the early 1960s, but it came at a great personal cost. Truitt no doubt felt this acutely while she was in Japan, a move that she made specifically as a wife and mother, and directly because of her husband's acceptance of a job abroad. Truitt's professional life was disadvantaged by being away from the United States. Living abroad also withheld the closure she might have felt if she had been living in Washington at the time of Meyer's death. Meyer's own artistic career was hindered by the perception that her work too closely followed Noland's example, and dealers might have shied from her because of assumptions about her relationship to Kennedy. And so, within Truitt's attempt to think of her practice beyond cubism, the classic paradigm of twentieth-century modernism, there resides also a willingness to strike at the authority of modernism in general: its logic, critique, the whispering art world that supported it, and its predominating masculinity. It makes sense that she would choose colour to achieve her goals, as it is the most elusive formal property and was the least codified in high-modernist art criticism. It is also, and possibly for those very reasons, the quality that Greenberg liked the least about Truitt's sculptures – more on which below.

But first, a refocusing question: What is within our grasp for understanding *A Wall for Apricots* as motivated by Truitt's new resolve, in which the memory of Meyer's death is implied? The 1966 version exemplifies where Truitt arrived in her practice – it is a flat sheet of aluminium bent on a brake, declaring a narrow, interior semi-enclosure, standing flush on the ground without a supportive base. The small fold is not merely self-reflexive, but rather opens to the outside, declaring an interior space. Truitt made twelve of these folded works, exhibiting but a single one of them only once in Tokyo in 1967. On the evidence, it appears that these works gave the artist no lasting satisfaction in working her way out of the problems of quality or decoration that Greenberg identified after the second show at Emmerich. But out of these folded sculptures, it became clear that Truitt wanted to preserve an expansive sense of space – a reference to the floor as the site of experience – but without the literal enclosing gesture of the fold.[25]

As she was making these folded works, Truitt also explored interior versus exterior positioning through the familiar motif of fences in several works on paper, and therefore a conceptual return to the origin of her practice in 1961 and the ideas that underpinned her critical success.[26] The fragmented fence was the key architectural object that sprung to mind at her first beholding of Newman's influential work at the Guggenheim, a memory now haunted by that of her companion and interlocutor, Mary Meyer, on that original journey to New York in 1961 (figure 10.5). Therefore, the title 'A Wall for Apricots' can be seen as a mnemonic cue that permitted Truitt at last to associate Meyer with a foundational change in her life as an artist and ensuing critical success, and to push further the relationship between the work of her private mourning and the public space of its deployment.

To return to Genette's theory of the paratext, the phrase 'a wall for apricots' is not merely autobiographical (although it must seem so), but also makes the sculpture present for the viewer, whose body is already strongly insinuated by being able to encounter the work on the floor and to imagine their enclosure by the central crease. Considered as an intermediate text attached symbolically to the sculpture, the title wards off intent by imparting ambiguity: the

10.5 Anne Truitt, *Truitt '66 [19]*, 1966, acrylic and graphite on paper, 26 × 35 cm

'wall for apricots' known by one beholder's imagination will diverge from another's, and ultimately point away from the artist, preserving her privacy even within a sculptural situation oriented formally to the viewer's space and habit of seeing. Truitt herself acknowledged this in 1975, saying that the subject of her titles is 'an area of great privacy and great intimacy. . . . The only thing that concerns me with the spectator is . . . the fact that he doesn't see what I see. That worried me for a long time. And then I came to terms with the fact.'[27] Truitt's esoteric titling practice was not new in 1966, but *A Wall for Apricots* provides an especially generous example for examining its functionality: preserving a sense of elusive privacy in a space where the viewer is deeply involved.

As I have elsewhere argued, the folded aluminium sculptures freshly addressed Truitt's interest in activating space and motivated the more urgent interest in colour to emerge. The artist spent the remaining short time in Tokyo focusing on the spatial effects of colour achieved in works on paper, such as in the small sheets of *washi* rice paper soaked in various pigments which she produced in 1966. The curved lines in these 'glazed papers' realise tentative boundaries between soaked colours that seem to delimit their own space, by receding, hovering, and pulling away. Truitt began to see how she could apply this effect of colour to geometric forms through *sumi* ink drawings, of which fifteen are extant, all similar in composition: two perfectly straight, side-by-side stripes of different values of brownish grey, painted from edge to opposite edge (figure 10.6). When they were made, Truitt signed the drawings horizontally. After she returned to the United States in 1967, the artist re-signed the works vertically. The reorientation reveals that Truitt was beginning to comprehend chromatic subtlety in the context of precise, vertically rectangular shapes.[28]

Return (1967), as its title suggests, is the first sculpture Truitt made after returning to the United States from Japan: a slender wooden column, painted on each of its faces with vertical stripes in barely offset shades of fuchsia. Its relationship to space is held in tension with the perception of its brilliant colour that solicits the beholder's attention. The effects of value on the sculpture's surface confuse the eye: are they a factor of the ambient light, or of the colours' internal luminosity? Truitt's work awakens in the knowledge that our eyes are connected to our bodies; from some vantage points, it is unclear whether the beholder is looking at the sculpture face-on or obliquely. At last, Truitt found a way of evoking such space through colour rather than literalising space as in the interior angles of her folded work.[29]

The second *A Wall for Apricots* (1968) follows *Return*. It is a sparse but muscular rectangular column, which exemplifies the formal vocabulary she perfected after she returned to Washington. Instead of red, white, blue, and beige, the latter sculpture is painted with anomalous colours: bluish white, chartreuse, and bright orange-yellow strain against the crisp boundaries between them and against the sculptural edge. As a column, it necessarily involves a relationship to the viewer's natural body. As James Meyer astutely observed in 2009, its segments pertain to the head, the torso, and the legs – thus, encountering this sculpture is not unlike seeing parts of ourselves in a radical reorientation.[30] Significantly, this sculpture's effulgent surfaces also challenge the beholder's ability to hold each glance in the memory of the preceding one as they move around it to see the whole, telescoping between form and surface from side to side.

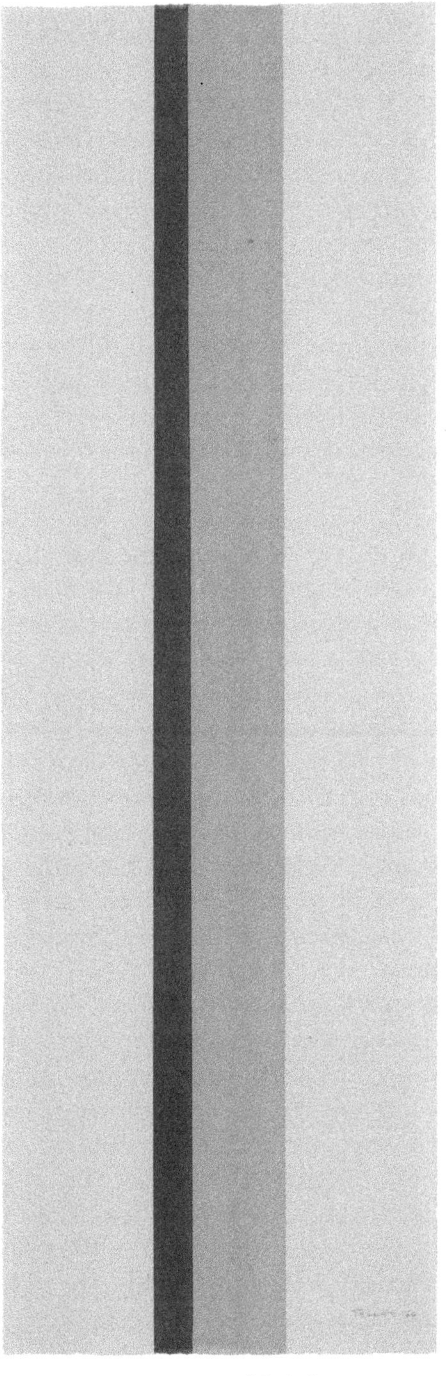

10.6 Anne Truitt, *Sumi Drawing [5]*, 1966, ink on paper, 69 × 22 cm

Most importantly with respect to the trajectory of her career, after her return to Washington, Truitt was emboldened to pursue colour as a subject in itself and to claim for it a special importance in her practice. Although the viewer may feel an initial attachment to what a given colour represents, upon further reflection Truitt's hard-to-name hues are fundamentally unfixed, enlisting a range of transmutable meanings held in active tension. Using *A Wall for Apricots* as an example, the orange band may refer to the apricot in the title, but upon reflection, it is too bright and yellow – therefore, the relationship is arbitrary. Taken in concert with the impossibility of comprehending the entire physical form of these new, monumental sculptures in a single glance, there is something deliberately fugitive in Truitt's new work that seduces us into the storehouse of our own memories but purposefully resists assimilation therein.

The unwieldiness of Truitt's sense of colour also redoubles the complexity of her relationship to both the colour-field painters Louis and Noland and the largely monochromatic minimalists with whom she would later be grouped. The valences of meaning Truitt associated with both colour and memory were not translatable to either modernist painting or minimalist sculpture, and her use of colour was singled out as a quality of difference. As aforementioned, Greenberg's 1968 discussion of Truitt in the fashion magazine *Vogue* portrayed her use of colour as a 'feminine sensibility'. According to the critic, if she had embraced a monochromatic palette, she would have achieved a more masculine look and would have been recognised as a pioneer.[31] Masculinity was Greenberg's shorthand for quality, and he found most sculptural minimalist art unconvincing and connotatively feminine regardless of the gender of the artist. But in Truitt's case, the use of colour was conspicuous because she was a woman, and it was understood to be merely biographical. Truitt was not ignorant of the ways in which she was feminised because of the colours of her sculptures yet proceeded to identify colour as the most important feature of her practice moving forward.

The first, Japanese-made *A Wall for Apricots* lends an example in which the artist's biography provides the general context for an artwork – the shocking death of a dear friend, feeling at odds in the studio, a growing awareness of suffocating masculinity in the modernist art world – but one where the title repels exact attribution. And this is perhaps its greatest success, given that its formal qualities did not capture Truitt's ambitions after 1965. The second, Washington-made *A Wall for Apricots*, however, is ebullient.

Through colour and space, it signifies a process of recognising colour that is open-ended and incomplete. It also finds its footing in the column, a neutral form subordinated by colour; a column does not resemble anything except itself, and when considered in light of Truitt's complex palette, is both monumental and subtle. Rather than the apotropaic function of 1966, the 1968 titular paratext clarifies the viewer's awareness of multiple uncodified meanings – the artist's, the public's, the individual viewer's – to be present at once; it is generously unfixed.

At last, I return to the parlour game from which the title originated. The hosts of the dinner party had asked each guest to write down three things they loved, but thus far we have only discussed two: walls and apricots. On the matter of Mary Meyer's third love, Truitt said, 'I have forgotten.' The inconclusiveness of Truitt's recollection teaches us something about the fundamental nature of how memory can be at once vivid, partial, and inconclusive. The poignancy of what we remember about our lost ones derives not from abundance but from a profound and subconscious discrimination – from our mind's obdurate refusal to reveal. For Truitt, it is this quality of memory that motivated her expression.

Notes

1 The fullest recounting to date of Anne Truitt's early career is found in my book, *Memory Work: Anne Truitt and Sculpture* (Oakland, CA: University of California Press, 2015).

2 Brenda Richardson, *Frank Stella: The Black Paintings* (Baltimore, MD: Baltimore Museum of Art, 1976). Richardson's essay has inspired plenty of further debate; see especially Benjamin H. D. Buchloh, 'Painting as Diagram: Five Notes on Frank Stella's Early Paintings, 1958–1959', *October*, 143, Abstraction: A Special Issue (Winter 2013), 127–44.

3 Gérard Genette, 'The Proustian Paratexte', trans. A. G. McIntosh, *SubStance*, 17:2 (1988), 63–77.

4 De Baca, *Memory Work*, pp. 5–6.

5 Jane Lavery, 'Ana Clavel's *Las Violetas son flores del deseo* and Peritexuality', *Hispanic Research Journal*, 14:2 (2013), 161.

6 James Meyer, 'The Bicycle', in *Anne Truitt: Perception and Reflection* (Washington, DC: Smithsonian, 2009), p. 52n.22.

7 De Baca, *Memory Work*, pp. 28–30. See also Nina Burleigh, *A Very Private Woman: The Life and Unsolved Murder of Presidential Mistress Mary Meyer* (New York: Bantam Books, 1998), p. 282.

8 Clement Greenberg papers, 1937–1983, Archives of American Art, Smithsonian Institution, Washington, DC.
9 Anne Truitt, 'Letter to Clement Greenberg, 1965' (10 December), in Alexandra Truitt (ed.), *Always Reaching: The Selected Writings of Anne Truitt* (New Haven, CT: Yale University Press, 2023), p. 61.
10 Truitt, *Daybook: The Journal of an Artist* (New York: Penguin, 1982), pp. 151–2.
11 De Baca, *Memory Work*, pp. 13–38.
12 De Baca, *Memory Work*, pp. 13–38.
13 De Baca, *Memory Work*, pp. 61–80.
14 Truitt, miscellaneous notes, box 1, folder 19, Anne Truitt Papers, Special Collections Department, Bryn Mawr College Library, Bryn Mawr, PA (hereafter ATP).
15 Clement Greenberg, letter to Anne Truitt, 18 June 1966, box 12, folder 21, ATP.
16 De Baca, *Memory Work*, pp. 86–87.
17 Truitt, 'Japan Interview, 1964', in *Always Reaching*, p. 42.
18 In addition to Burleigh, the circumstances are summarised more recently in Lance Morrow, '44 Years Later, a Washington, D.C. Death Unresolved', *Smithsonian Magazine*, December 2008, www.smithsonianmag.com/history/44-years-later-a-washington-dc-death-unresolved-93263961 (accessed 1 January 2021).
19 Burleigh, *A Very Private Woman*, p. 246.
20 Truitt, letter to Louisa Jenkins, 14 December 1965, box 15, folder 2, ATP.
21 De Baca, *Memory Work*, pp. 97–98.
22 Truitt, studio note dated 23 October 1965, box 1, folder 19, ATP.
23 Helen Frankenthaler, letter to Anne Truitt, 10 October 1966, box 14, folder 8, ATP.
24 Frankenthaler, letter to Anne Truitt, 3 January 1967, box 14, folder 8, ATP.
25 De Baca, *Memory Work*, pp. 100–102.
26 De Baca, *Memory Work*, pp. 103–105.
27 'Anne Truitt interviewed by Howard Fox', in *Sun and Moon: A Quarterly of Literature and Art*, 1 (1976), reprinted in *Always Reaching*, pp. 151–152.
28 De Baca, *Memory Work*, pp. 103–105.
29 De Baca, *Memory Work*, pp. 108–109.
30 Meyer, 'The Bicycle', p. 50.
31 Greenberg, 'Changer: Anne Truitt', in James O'Brian (ed.), *Clement Greenberg: The Collected Essays and Criticism, Volume 4: Modernism with a Vengeance, 1957–1969* (Chicago, IL: University of Chicago Press, 1993), pp. 288–91.

11

Ode to forgetting

Moran Sheleg

> For the important thing for the remembering author is not what he experienced, but the weaving of his memory, the Penelope work of recollection. Or should one call it, rather, a Penelope work of forgetting?
>
> Walter Benjamin, 'The Image of Proust'[1]

Forgetting Penelope

It begins with a red square. A red square with its centre seemingly cut out, overlaid with a giant graphic stitch. Or a crosshatch, depending on your perspective. Diamonds travel up and down along the insides of this intersecting form, suggesting movement and an indelible sense of drama animating its geometries (figure 11.1). Turn over this scene and the drama continues within the next, where three rows of red squares are piled up on top of each other in descending order of size, resembling precarious columns (figure 11.2). Attached to an orange linen ground, their edges recall the large stitch-like shape seen before, itself a printed pattern that has been quartered and threaded back together again. As one thumbs through the textile pages of *Ode à l'Oubli* (*Ode to Forgetting*), these kinds of visual doublings occur everywhere, both visually and textually. Colours, shapes, and configurations come together, fall apart, and reassemble, in a way reminiscent of a memory game. Or a game made of the second-hand, stitched-together bits and pieces retained from the past that form memory itself.

Completed by Louise Bourgeois in 2002, eight years before her death at the age of 98, this would be the first of the artist's so-called fabric books and the first compilation of fabric collages to take this format; made using scraps of old clothes and other fabric household

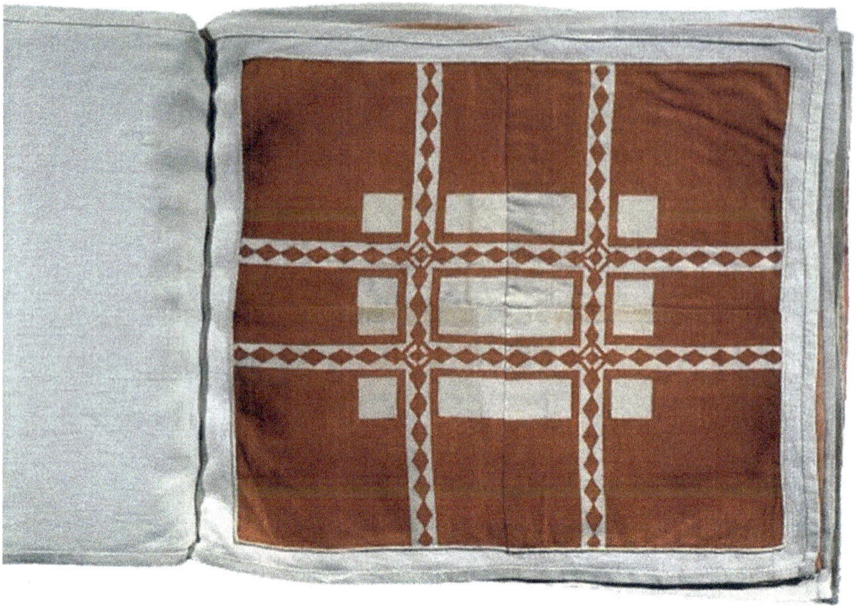

11.1 Louise Bourgeois, *Untitled*, no. 1 of 34, from the illustrated book, *Ode à l'Oubli*, 2002, fabric collage, 27.3 × 30.7 cm

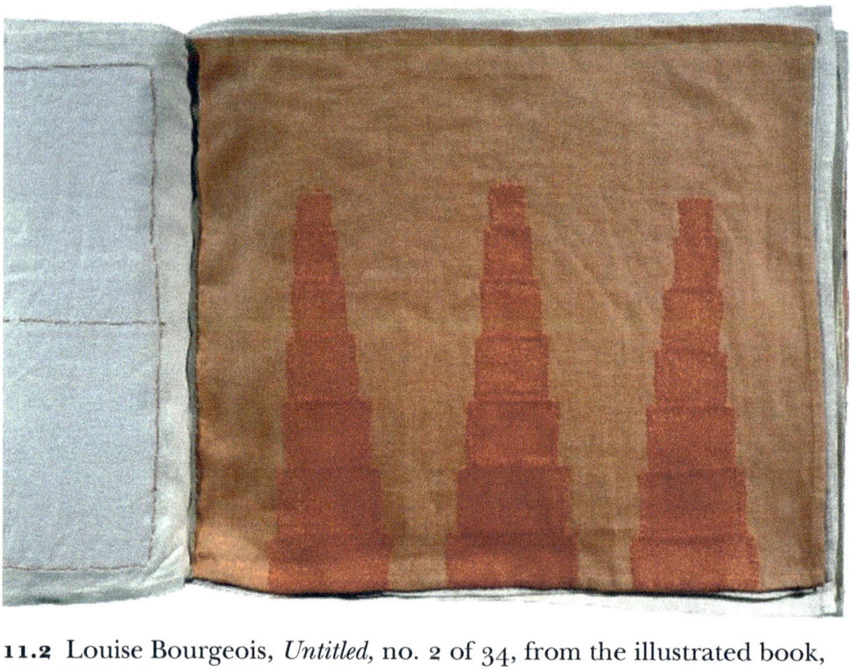

11.2 Louise Bourgeois, *Untitled*, no. 2 of 34, from the illustrated book, *Ode à l'Oubli*, 2002, fabric collage, 27.3 × 30.7 cm

items (sometimes soiled and bearing marks of use) sewn onto linen hand towels that act as the ground for each of its pages, themselves preserved in the artist's wedding trousseau. Bourgeois married the art historian Robert Goldwater in Paris in 1938 and moved to New York the same year. Like much of Bourgeois's work, *Ode à l'Oubli* contains imagery and words echoed in other works spanning the many decades of her career, including the diaries and notebooks she kept, many of which detail her extensive experience with and knowledge of psychoanalysis (which the artist kept a secret for decades).

In a later fabric book and portfolio of prints, *Hours of the Day* (2006), Bourgeois turned to the image of the clock as a temporal measure, accompanying each of the 24 hours depicted with an epithet. For number eighteen in the portfolio, Bourgeois has assigned in French*: J'aimais les jours de Penelope / Oublie la* (*I love the days of Penelope / Forget her*) (figure 11.3). Referring to the character from Homer's epic poem *The Odyssey*, Penelope is, of course, the ultimate weaver and, consequently, the archetypal mother of memory. Her daily attempt to stave off the advances of unwanted suitors by weaving a memorial shroud for her absent husband, Odysseus, which she unpicks every night, has become a nebulous metaphor for the processes of self-creation and destruction held in the communal psyche. For Sigmund Freud, she (and other women weavers from antiquity, including Arachne, Ariadne, Philomela, and the three Moirae, whose task it is to tell stories through their labour of cloth-making) symbolised the unconscious web that constitutes a subject's inner world.[2] For his daughter Anna, herself a child psychoanalyst, Penelope's practice of patience mapped onto the work of weaving together an image of the patient's young mind during sessions, while she in turn threaded her own clothes.[3]

When Walter Benjamin reversed the terms of Penelope's production in his analysis of Proust's *la Recherche* (a line from which opens this chapter), he also highlighted the destructive impulse underlying the creative act of remembering and, indeed, writing.[4] As Jerry Flieger points out, Proust's narrator is plagued with forgetfulness as well as debilitatingly poor health at the very moment that he decides to write what would become his epic novel. Having found his '*vocation*' while on '*vacation* from ordinary daily commerce', Marcel, described as 'the anti-social artist', 'has become "ex-centric", disorientated, given over to a kind of amnesiac wandering among a jumble of resurrected images and experience'.[5] This sense of mental dislocation also extends to temporal drift – night and

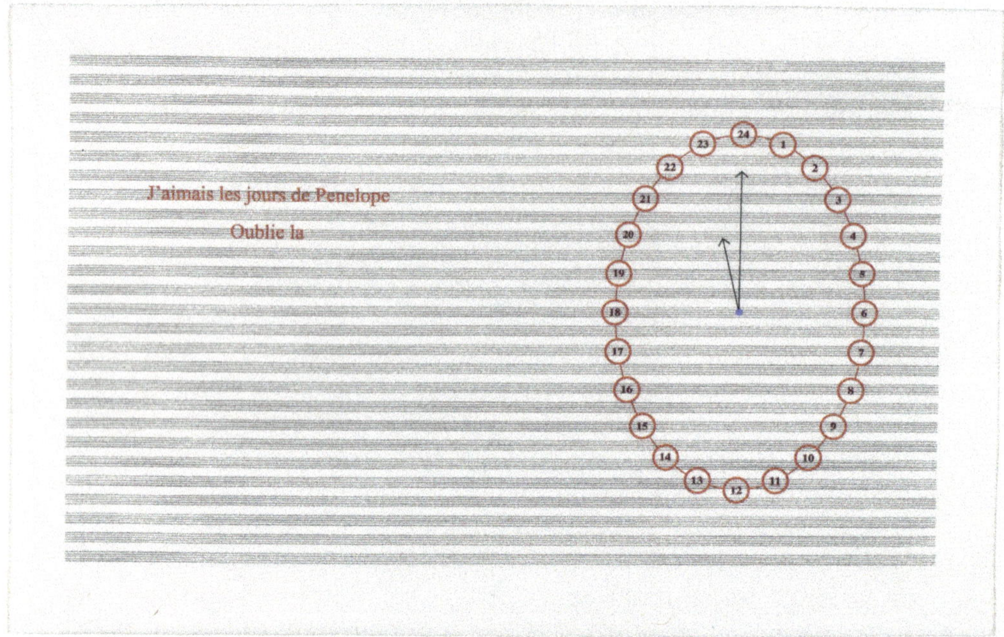

11.3 Louise Bourgeois, *Untitled*, no. 18 of 24, from the portfolio *Hours of the Day*, 2006, digital print, composition: 35.3 × 60.8 cm; sheet: 44.5 × 68.5 cm

day become one indistinguishable stretch for the writer struck with chronic asthma, suffering from insomnia, and prone to daydreams. Like Penelope, who weaves and unravels continuously to delay time, his labour is also timeless, not bound by the limits of daily work yet always defined by the prospect of death. A convalescent by the end of the book, Proust's body becomes a site of undoing just as his memory enables the process of recollection and recording to begin.

One imagines the aged Bourgeois in a similar state: sitting up in bed unable to sleep, in her dilapidated brick rowhouse in Chelsea, Manhattan, surrounded by half-completed artworks and hordes of objects collected over the years, snipping and sewing, sewing and snipping. She may be a nonagenarian but inside she feels like a little girl. In the corner of her room, crouching in a glittering web, she sees a small spider and smiles. The creature has long stood as a symbol for her mother, a tapestry restorer, who has become like one of the mythical women of antiquity with whom Bourgeois herself occasionally identifies.[6] Yet the spider also stands for an incarnation of the artist who makes, the artist who is herself a mother. Lying on her lap, the most recently completed page of her fabric book into which she has stitched a rectangular panel of white cotton, that announces in large, red, printed letters: 'I had a flashback of something that never existed' (figure 11.4).

This vignette too never existed, at least not as described here. Rather than a solitary endeavour – and rather questioning the image of the isolated weaving woman in favour of the collaboration of the workshop floor, like that of the women workers in her mother's restoration business where Bourgeois also worked as a girl – Bourgeois employed a seamstress, Mercedes Katz, to help compile her fabric books. There is, however, an image that exists of a very elderly Bourgeois in bed (figure 11.5). Quite unlike the other photographs taken between 2008 and 2010 by her friend the Dutch photographer Alex Van Gelder, which show her famous playfulness and ease in front of the camera, here we see her in repose,

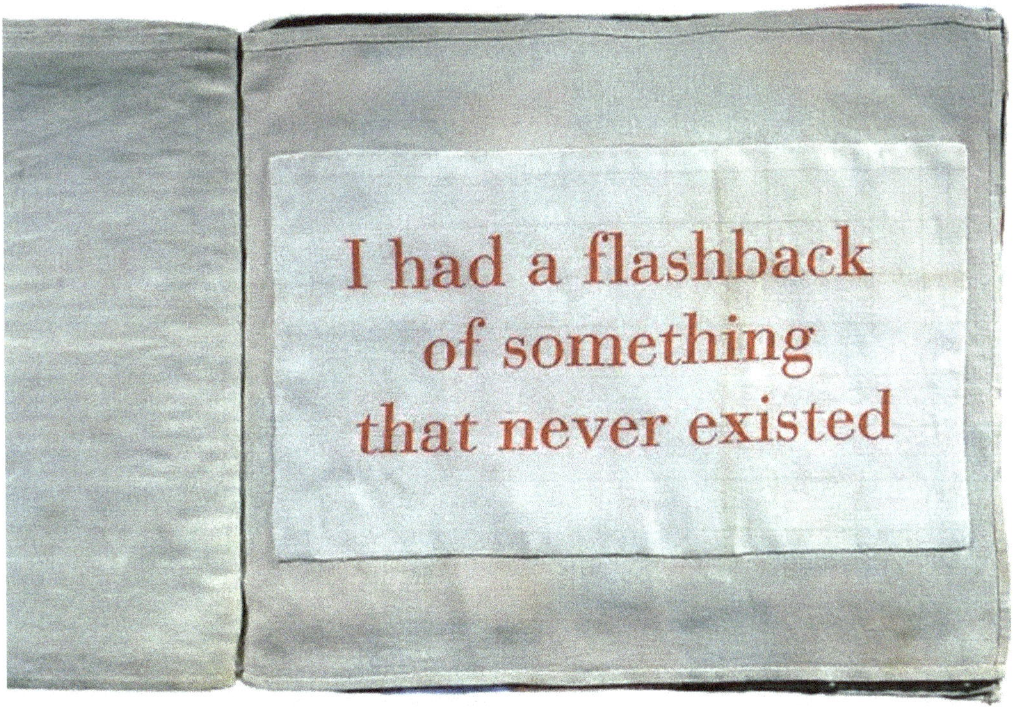

11.4 Louise Bourgeois, *I Had a Flashback of Something that Never Existed,* no. 18 of 34, from the illustrated book, *Ode à l'Oubli,* 2002, lithograph on fabric, 27.3 × 30.7 cm

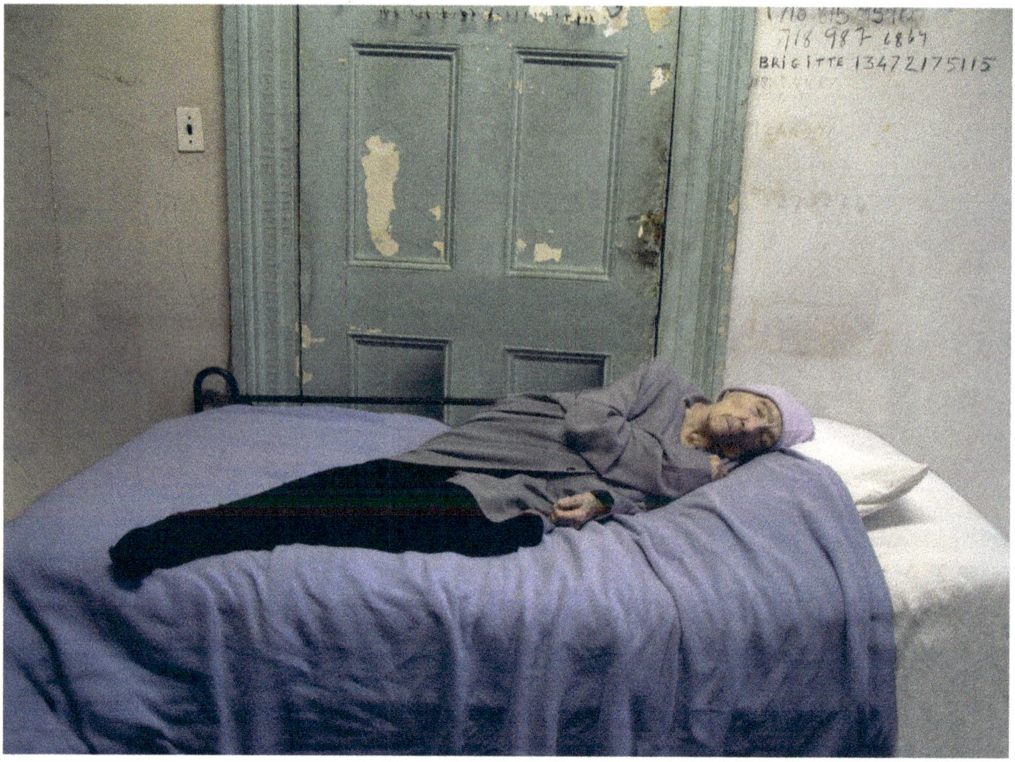

11.5 Alex Van Gelder, Louise Bourgeois in bed, 2009

inactive, eyes closed.[7] Swaddled in a grey cardigan, her head covered with a soft lilac hat, the artist lies over the blanket of her made bed, itself propped against a door with peeling mint-green paint. Is this a performance of infirmity, a counter-image to that of her robust creativity? Or a quiet moment of rest and reverie caught by the ever-wakeful eye of the camera? Although also a self-confessed insomniac (see her *Insomnia Drawings* from the 1990s), Bourgeois recorded her dreams, which sometimes appear in her diaries as loose-sheet writings, seeing within their forms the outlines of otherwise inaccessible memories, approximating what she called 'the return of the repressed'. This phrase, taken from Freud's thesis on how the conscious mind attempts to suppress traumatic experiences only for them to suddenly reappear later in time (either through dreams, phobias, or 'neurotic behaviours'),[8] is the second of the two textual phrases nestled among the abstract patterns that make up *Ode à l'Oubli* (figure 11.6). It would also be the title of a collected volume

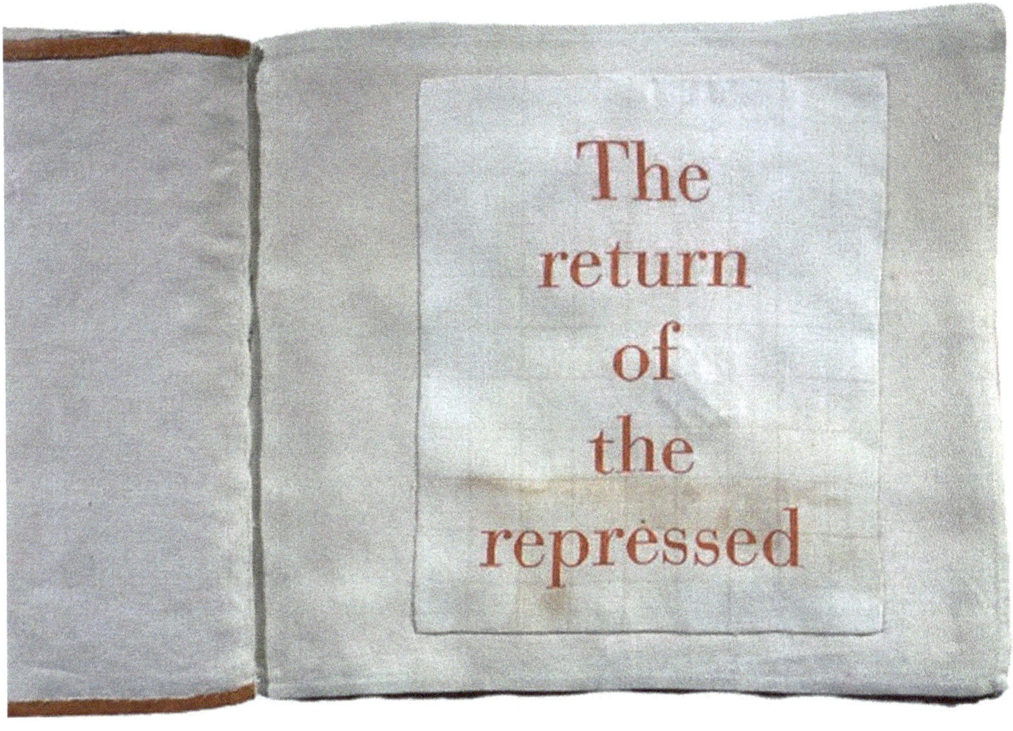

11.6 Louise Bourgeois, *The Return of the Repressed,* no. 18 of 34, from the illustrated book, *Ode à l'Oubli,* 2002, lithograph on fabric, 27.3 × 30.7 cm

of Bourgeois's psychoanalytical notes published in 2012, coinciding with a related exhibition at the Freud Museum in London, where Bourgeois's sculptural work *Janis Fleuri,* a double-headed phallus, hung above the analyst's tapestry-covered couch.[9]

While a key figure for Bourgeois, Freud would also come to stand for all that had to be overcome through her art: namely, the monopoly of the paternal on childhood experience and the idea that one's work was a faithful product of the internal feelings that gave rise to it. The reparative aspect palpable in Bourgeois's mode of recalling the past (both her own and that of art history more generally) in order to work through it has been discussed at length by others, particularly with recourse to alternative models of psychoanalysis, such as that offered in the writings of Melanie Klein.[10] In what follows, I attempt to bolster the established literature on Bourgeois by suggesting a literary (or Proustian) counterpart to the psychoanalytic (Freudian/Kleinian) frame of reference for

Bourgeois's work, particularly the fabric books. One in which the undoing of narrative, and indeed of subjectivity itself as the ground upon which life stories take shape, is just as vital as – and increasingly essential to – its making. This is not to discount Bourgeois's obvious and deep engagement with psychoanalysis, but to complicate the apparent seamlessness between it and her work, to pull at the threads of another story embellished within its holes.

My own use of metaphor here leads me to the question of method (for the writer), or process (for the artist), as a mitigator between the metaphorical and the literal. Psychoanalysis, in its attempt to align the past with the present and thus understand them as one and the same, works on a metaphoric basis.[11] While used extensively in *la Recherche* and even identified by the author as an artistic process akin to 'metamorphosis' (or the remaking of one thing into something else),[12] Proust's own metaphors, as Gérard Genette has noted, usually amount to metonymy, by which things are not so much taken as other things but aligned on the basis of their shared proximity to an environment, location, or person, with which the writer sets up a resemblance (or a whole catalogue of resemblances).[13] Although comparable to association, a technique of huge importance to both Freud and Proust, metonymy involves an act of renaming (for example, mother as spider) that cements this proximity as the grounds for a substitution of form.[14] In Bourgeois's work, we can see both the psychoanalytic and literary forms of metaphor and metonymy at play, sometimes simultaneously. Yet in her own process of recollection through making – the manual labour of work as a working through of the past in the present – we also see them broken down into their constituent parts, sometimes to be rebuilt into something else, sometimes to be committed to meaninglessness.

For example, the model of metaphor provided by psychoanalysis is literally cut apart in the way the fabric books themselves are made. While containing several examples of woven textiles, the stitching together of offcuts from personal, historied bits of old clothes and other pieces of fabric onto monogrammed napkins to make something like a pattern book of abstractions suggests a closer affinity with *découpage* than weaving, making Bourgeois a *découpeur* (or 'cutter'), as well as a stitcher.[15] As Lynne Cooke has pointed out, scissors appear time and again as a visual motif in Bourgeois's work, as do, of course, the suture and the spool of thread.[16] Yet, the stitching of these 'pages' read more as bindings, as in the assembling of a codex, than bound-up wounds. Their passages of decorative embellishments and flourishes of embroidery, that bear little resemblance to mending and no immediate restorative function, set among abstract patterns and printed text disconnected from any larger context beyond the bound page, work to further question the narrative thread of the fabric books as a metaphorical body of work. As does the design of the editioned book's pages, which can be easily detached to hang on the wall (when exhibited, they are often displayed in a grid format) or be considered individually and put back together again.[17] The tension between the handmade (or the manual) and the machine-fabricated, evident in much of her work, here also reaches a climax in the juxtaposition of image and text, which would be solidified in the print version of the volume made in 2004. A distinction should therefore be made between the psychic reparative charge of the figure of the spider, with all its mythological and literary overtones; its relation to what I want to call the re-membered maternal body; and the imagined products of its labour. I use the term 're-membered' in the sense of being opposite to 'dismembered', a word derived from the old French *desmembrer*, meaning to pull apart at the limbs. Sarah Bernthal has proposed such a dynamic in her reading of the medieval poet Marie de France's *Laüstic,* in which the acts of sewing and writing become 'metaphors for regenerating the mutilated female body'.[18] This mutilation, Bernthal relates, often involves the mouth, rendering women mute and unable to tell their stories (the reparation that takes place here, then, while metaphorical, is primarily narrative).[19] My claim is that in making such metaphors materially literal, by holding the symbolic at arm's length but always keeping it within reach, Bourgeois's fabric books reinstate the maternal body as a narrative object (central to both psychoanalysis and literature but often made mute and passive by them) that is both re-membered (put together) and forgotten (pulled apart) in the process of giving and living life, and of making art. But they also work to undo its mythical, sphinx-like status, offering an image of the mother – whether good or bad – capable of both recalling and forgetting its own past.

That's my madeleine

The continuing significance of the maternal is, of course, central to both Bourgeois and Proust. Mothers dominate the world unfolding across the volumes of *la Recherche,* not least the narrator's own, who famously provides him with the most potent vehicle for remembrance in the form of a small, unassuming cake, which brings about a moment of sheer, explosive rapture. In 1994, Bourgeois made a group of drypoint etchings which she published as a portfolio entitled *Autobiographical Series,* a compilation of motifs primarily lifted from source images dating back to the 1940s. One composition dates from 1986 and originated with the tracing of an actual pair of scissors. Across its fourteen plates we see familiar scenes, such as the artist working on a sculpture; washing her hair in a sink while naked as an anonymous man looks on, his face reflected in the mirror; two pairs of shears connected by a thin line (often described by Bourgeois as an 'umbilical cord' tethering these cutting implements); and a naked woman giving birth to a baby whose head protrudes from her. Moments recalled from childhood, scenes of childbirth, voyeurism, and physical as well as psychic separation sit alongside references to artistic creation and family dynamics. Through the scraping away of matter on the printing plate to the accumulation of rolled ink and transfer of the image onto another surface, the process by which these images are rendered echoes the life processes recorded within them, setting up an intrinsic yet delicate relationship between the literal, the metaphorical, and the mnemonic. Another series of prints, from 1999, features *Madeleine* (figure 11.7), a Proustian motif in which the bust of a figure – apparently topless but wearing a necklace, their head covered with either a bandage or a hat reminiscent of the cloth cap worn by the artist in the Van Gelder image mentioned above – devours the shell-shaped sponge, teeth bared and eyes and tongue protruding with cartoonish fervour. Bourgeois spoke several times about Proust's famous scene, on one significant occasion relating that:

> Time is a tributary of light, of twilight, of the night and dawn. And full daylight. That's my madeleine. That's what I say to myself when time has passed. It's mostly a function of the eyes, of light. It could be a function of the heat that rises into the radiator. It could be the smell of a good meal. Or it could be the music of Mozart that filters throughout the house. That is, it's a function of the five senses.[20]

Inverting Proust's passage, in which the author states that 'the sight of the little madeleine had recalled nothing to my mind before I tasted it',[21] Bourgeois highlights the primarily visual basis of her understanding of the passing of time. Taste, along with touch, is not

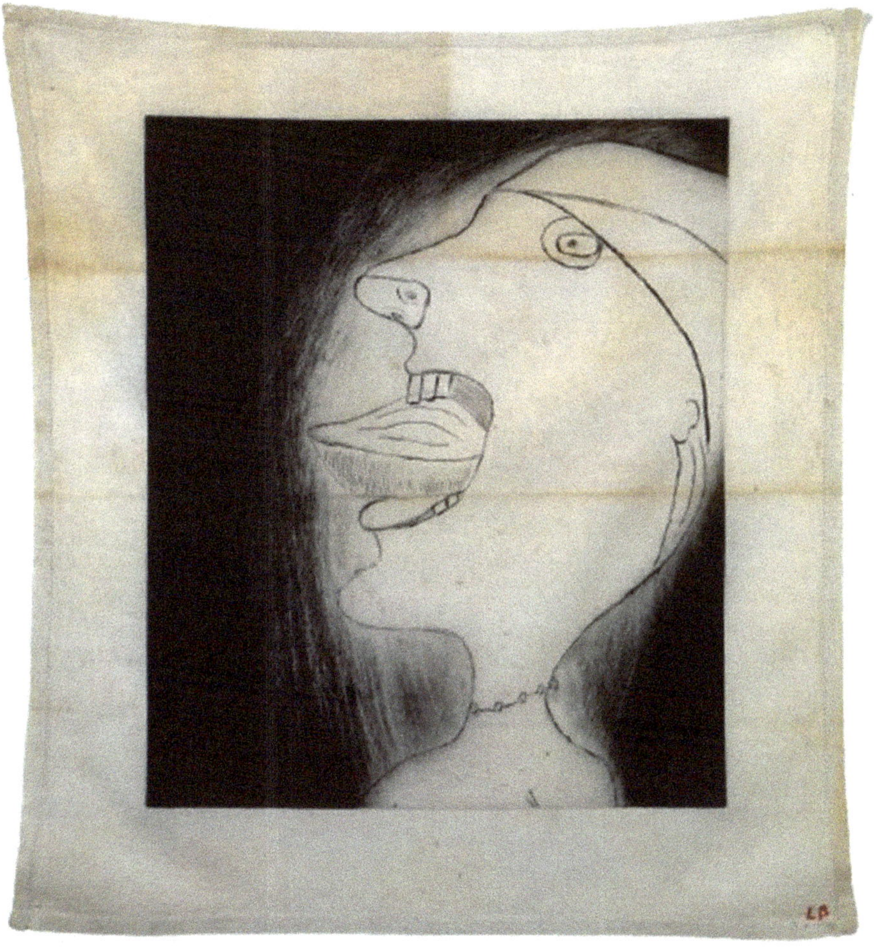

11.7 Louise Bourgeois, *Madeleine*, 1999, drypoint on fabric, plate: 30.2 × 25.1 cm; sheet: 40.6 × 37.1 cm

actually mentioned by name. Yet, in her work the image of the open mouth appears again and again, as in the large fabric head, *Untitled*, itself a prop in another portrait of the artist taken by Van Gelder (figure 11.8), as well as in Bourgeois's own expression. While being opened to receive, or caught mid-speech, these doubled mouths also suggest defiance, as when the weaning infant refuses food by pushing it out with their tongue or offers a show of playful impertinence by sticking their tongue out. They could be seen as a pair of mouths that poke fun and wound before they can be wounded, to return to Marie de France, but that also offer a point of contact. For while the protruding tongue renders one verbally mute, albeit by self-volition, it still communicates a message, even if that message is a denial. This triumvirate between consuming, expressing, and denying reaches a head in *Ode à l'Oubli*, where abstraction mediates the narrative impulse of the visual and textual phrases collated and fixed together within its pages.

In the summer of 2011, the author Rachel Cusk visited *Suites on Fabric*, a small exhibition featuring several works by Bourgeois held at the Marlborough Gallery in London, the catalogue for which opens with Van Gelder's image of the artist holding *Untitled*. Writing eight years later, Cusk recalled her impressions of the intimate display in which cloth is employed as a ground upon which to draw but also with which to build. Referring to the 2007 series of digital prints, *The Fragile*, Cusk sees within its variously bulging and arachnid female forms at once a toughness and a delicacy reflective of pregnancy and, consequently, of motherhood as conveyed through a dual point of view:

> Here the child speaks, tracing the maternal form again and again – drawing Mummy, the dextrous spider who spins and weaves. These are a child's perception of the primary image of its parent, yet their knowledge is her knowledge too, her knowledge of her own body as an unstable form. Resolution is sought in these fused perceptions: perhaps the artist herself can, through her child, return to the child-like state of freedom and creativity. And she remains, after all, a daughter: the spider, Mummy, belongs to her too.[22]

Through these remembered images, Cusk continues to consider the resonance of the spider for Bourgeois beyond the autobiographical frame of reference to which it is often ascribed. For Cusk, it appears as a foil to the 'countercurrent of memory' that animates Bourgeois's artistic project – a point I will return to shortly.[23]

Cusk's own project as a writer has itself involved intense reflection on the mother–child relationship as experienced first-hand, in real time. In *A Life's Work* (2001), she explores the daily tedium, uncertainty, and extremity of pregnancy and life with a young infant with a level of honesty that garnered much criticism as well as praise upon its publication. Putting its reception aside, the book's attempt to inhabit the maternal condition also reimagines the form of the memoir. Elsewhere, Cusk has referred to what she calls 'the feminist principle of autobiographical writing' as an old but 'inherently radical' form, 'because women haven't finished evolving. They're still a work in progress, and there is always an inherent radicalism,

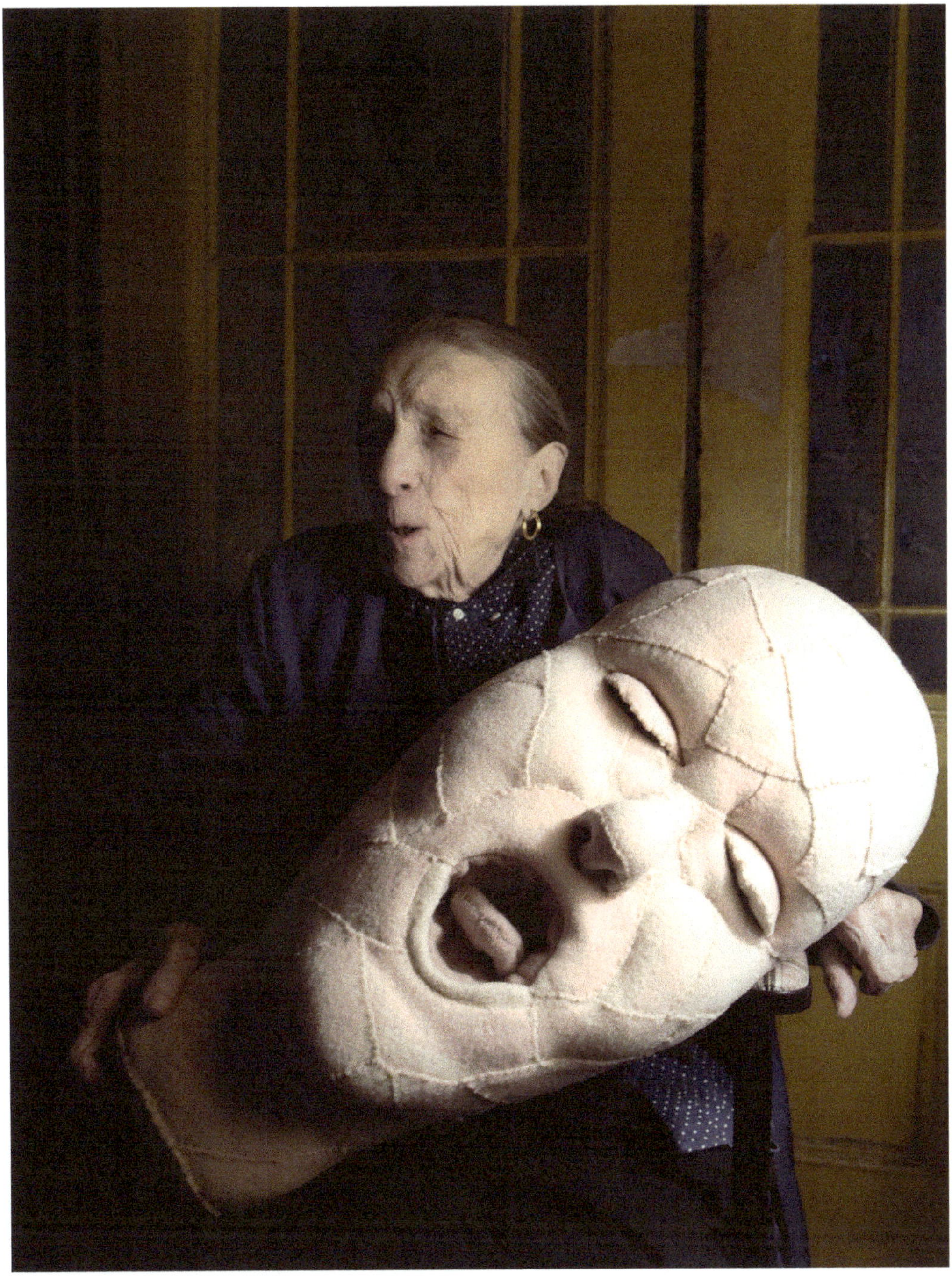

11.8 Alex Van Gelder, Louise Bourgeois with a fabric sculpture in progress in 2009

a principle to a woman writing about her own life.'[24] This radicality, however old, has always animated life-writing by women and the thin line it toes between autobiography and fiction. As Virginia Woolf famously stated in 1928: 'Fiction is like a spider's web, attached ever so lightly perhaps, but still attached to life at all four corners. But these webs are not spun in midair, by incorporeal creatures. They are the bodies of suffering human beings, and are attached to grossly material things, like health and money and the houses we live in.'[25] Woolf's acknowledgement of the corporeality of women's experience as the basis of fiction reintroduces the material, the bodily, and the political into the psychoanalytically informed view of Proust's world as one of profound disorientation, at least as imagined by Freud, Benjamin, and even Gilles Deleuze, who famously likened the narrator of *la Recherche* to a spider who 'sees nothing, perceives nothing, remembers nothing', but instead acts as a receptacle for sensations to which she (for Deleuze's spider is gendered female) automatically reacts.[26]

In her essay on Bourgeois, Cusk writes: 'Through the process of memory the artist recovers balance. She is released from her tortured body, becomes unbodied, returns to objectivity.'[27] In another text, Cusk evokes a passage from *Swann's Way* to again posit the objectivity essential to literature, or art, that draws on autobiography: 'The reattachment of the subjective self to the material object is where much of the labour of writing lies – labour because, in this one sense, writing feels like the opposite of being alive. The intangible has to be reversed back into tangibility; every fibre of the subjective perception has to be returned to the objective fact from whence it came.'[28] If Bourgeois's spider is such an object, or abstraction, or 'theoretical object' that poses questions about art and its making, as Mieke Bal has furthermore proposed, then Cusk seems to suggest it can also offer a creative imperative, and a place from which to speak, for the artist who invests it with such weighty subjective charge.[29] To see the spider as mother, and as me, is to provide oneself with a 'feeling of reality' that allows one to write, or create, fiction. Or perhaps it is the result of the spider's labour, the web (which, as Benjamin pointed out, is the meaning of the Latin *textum*, from which 'text' derives),[30] which offers the objectivity needed to write, after having lived through, one's own stories. Spinning a web here appears akin to spinning a yarn. And in the process, a transformative line is drawn between the subjective and the objective; a once severed connection not mended so much as re-membered.

Webs, in the form of triangular strips of lined or otherwise segmented cloth, stitched together in the round, proliferate across Bourgeois's fabric works, where they are sometimes doubled or tripled, their centres often resembling eyes or mouths. A single, irregular web appears in *Ode à l'Oubli,* its rudimentary form stitched out of small pieces of light pink and cornflower blue, all converging into a tiny centre point, a cluster of stitches, in the middle of the page (figure 11.9). Having become solid, its gaps filled in with fabric, the web no longer resembles a trap but a vortex. Proust uses the image of a swirling vortex to describe the effect love has on our view of the people we care for, which he describes as 'an animated system' through which their appearance is (almost violently) made to 'adhere to . . . coincide with' our memory of them so that we do not recognise them as they are.[31] Objectivity seems nigh on impossible amid such a maelstrom. And yet, in Bourgeois's work, it perseveres, turning those ravaged features back into

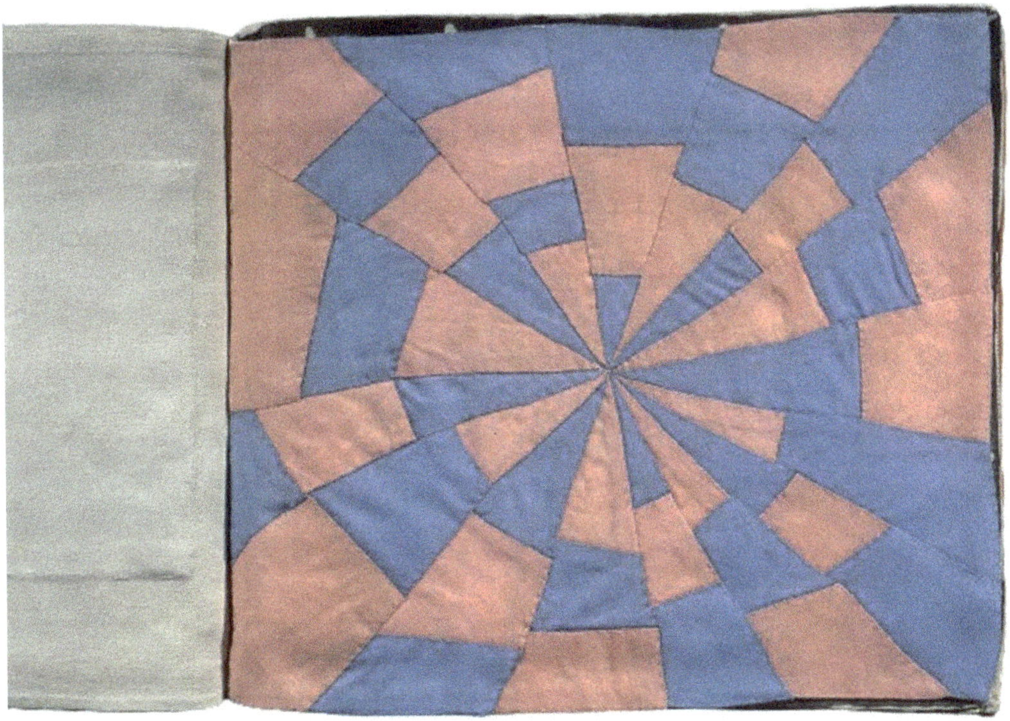

11.9 Louise Bourgeois, *Untitled,* no. 19 of 34, from the illustrated book, *Ode à l'Oubli,* 2002, fabric collage, 27.3 × 30.7 cm

something resembling reality but clearly augmented by the passing of time.

Another vortex, composed of concentric rings in the same colours as the web-vortex described above, appears on the penultimate page of *Ode à la Bièvre*, a further fabric book made later the same year (2002). Having recalled in her writings the many rivers near which she lived during her life – from the Creuse and Bièvre in France where she grew up, to the Seine in Paris and the Hudson in New York – Bourgeois would pay further homage to their significance in a series of works on paper produced in 2007, *La Rivière Gentille.* The fluidity of water, here emphasised in that of watercolour and gouache paint, also reappears as a figure of memory. The river seems to appear as another member of the Bourgeois family, while also providing them with the raw materials needed to make a living – their choice to live by the Bièvre dictated by its rich tannin stores that proved essential to their tapestry restoration business.

In the opening chapter of her 2009 book, *The Last Supper,* Cusk similarly recalls her time living on the banks of the River Avon in Bristol with her young family and how the noise from the traffic running along the gorge that crosses the river would rise 'like a vortex', keeping her up at night (another insomniac).[32] As well as facilitating life, like Bourgeois's Bièvre, the Avon holds within it a passage of time stretching from the dinosaurs to 'the stub of humanity', where it abruptly ends, rendering the future 'blank'. Walking her children to school every morning, Cusk imagines their little uniformed bodies, which mark them as 'modern schoolchildren', being swept up in 'the great impersonal wave' that is their 'moment of history'.[33] Water, the original wellspring of life and harbinger of its catastrophic end, also harbours within it a countercurrent to memory: the unknowable void of the future.

I string together these shared images (or metonymic metaphors, to echo Genette on Proust) of web, vortex, and river to build a fragmentary picture of what we might call a form of anti-memoir: a work that flits between autobiography and fiction, operating through the mutually dependent acts of retrieving and obliviating involved in the artwork that doubles as a 'lifework'. Benjamin suggested Proust himself as one such image, formed out of his own text, as 'the highest physiognomic expression which the irresistibly growing discrepancy between literature and life was able to assume'.[34] The attempt to glean something about the artist from their work, while perhaps ultimately doomed to fail, may itself reveal more than any single image (or collection of images) could about the life codified within it.

Anti-memoir

In 1967, André Malraux published *Anti-Memoirs*, a largely autobiographical book that also reads as a quasi-historical document, its chronology 'scrambled' and conveyed as if through a stream-of-consciousness narrative. Writing on the structure of Malraux's many-volumed 'unconventional memoirs', of which *Anti-Memoirs* would be the first, Peter Tame notes how it resembles 'the way we often perceive [memories] in their raw state in the unconscious. They emerge, fade, and re-emerge in a mysterious, seemingly random rhythm, like the horses on a moving merry-go-round, as Malraux himself describes them.'[35] Key to Malraux's entwining of personal and cultural history, Tame claims, is mythopoesis, or the making of myths. Here historical figures from Charles de Gaulle (who elected Malraux as France's first Minister of Cultural Affairs in 1958) to Mahatma Gandhi take on mythic status, as does the writer himself through his accounts of them. The writing of history – quite literally as *his story* – becomes a form of metamorphosis through which extracts from fiction are repurposed to create something that exceeds personal memoir, or the limits of one's own experience, and comes to embody something like 'a cultural product', passed down through generations and augmented by each retelling.[36] As Mignon Nixon, Griselda Pollock, and Rosemary Betterton have variously emphasised, Bourgeois similarly crafted her life story as a 'palimpsest' through its repeated retelling and restaging through her art and writing, which has come to exceed and even 'dispense' with the limits of her own 'self'.[37]

Writing on the work of Proust and Bourgeois (as well as Samuel Beckett), Catherine Crimp claims that within both 'childhood becomes a myth for imagining the process of creation'.[38] Analysing how the child figure is recast as a double for the work of art, Crimp attributes the separation that characterises the artist's relationship with their own past – one we all experience through the inaccessibility and lack of control we have over our memories, as well as the increasing distance from infancy we experience as we age – as a driving force of this myth. The child we faintly remember being but are now estranged from comes to symbolise the irrepresentability of all origins, including that of the artwork. Or, to reverse this, the artwork becomes a cipher for the separation the artist experiences from their own origins and that of all their works, which together operate to cast doubt on the myth of beginnings.[39] Keen to distance biography from her reading, borrowing heavily from Maurice Blanchot's theories on literature, Crimp is also quick to glide over the differences of gender as well as the place of the maternal in this account of the artwork's relationship to childhood as an idea rather than an experience. Yet, her thesis raises an interesting question if made to address those very oversights: could this literary myth of the creative child, which doubles as a metaphor for the artwork and for that of the *memory* of the maternal, function to counter 'the cultural myth of the mother as the object, never the subject, of aggression or desire', the adherence to which many have recognised as a limitation of psychoanalysis (whether Kleinian or Freudian)?[40] Put more simply, could the memory of the maternal counter its mythical muteness?

While not directly dedicated to her mother (unlike *Ode à Ma Mère,* a portfolio of nine prints made in 1995), *Ode à l'Oubli* suggests itself as one such undoing of the memory of the mother as a mute, passive object. Having described her own mother as soft-spoken and stoic, the mother that is memorialised within them seems to be not Bourgeois's own mother but herself as a mother, albeit in the purely artistic sense. Standing as an anti-memoir of (the image of) her mother – i.e. the spider who sustains, protects, and contains the child at great cost to her own agency – it also acts as a lifework of the artist-mother who, in making this artwork-child, casts into oblivion, or forgets, the traditional role of the mother-object.

It seems pertinent that *Ode à l'Oubli* ends, like it begins, with a red square. In place of the giant stitch sits a navy centre square, intersected with horizontal red lines. A void at the heart of the vortex. Back in 1987, Donald Kuspit suggested that 'Bourgeois's entanglement with her mother, not her father, is becoming clear as the inner content of her work. She has filled the void of mother/artist in spirit as well as substance, an Oedipus replacing the mother instead of the father, a Sphinx whose Secret is that a story about a relationship to a father is really a story about a relationship to a mother.'[41] Finding the literary resonances within this psychobiographical frame of reference, *Ode à l'Oubli,* as a paradigm of the fabric books, suggests the place where fiction and autobiography meet and collapse into each other to the point of oblivion. Glorifying in this oblivion, it doubles as a memorial to it.

Notes

1 Walter Benjamin, 'The Image of Proust' [1929], in Hannah Arendt (ed.), *Illuminations: Essays and Reflections*, trans. Harry Zohn (New York: Schocken Books, 2007), p. 198.
2 Liliane Weissberg, 'Ariadne's Thread', *MLN*, 125:3 (2010), 665–666.
3 Weissberg, 'Ariadne's Thread', 661.
4 Bourgeois owned a 1986 edition of Benjamin's collected writings, *Illuminations: Essays and Reflections*, and referred to his 'study of Proust' in an entry of her audio diary from September 1973 [01:29:45; AV_00986_01 © The Easton Foundation/VAGA at ARS, NY]. Author's correspondence with the Easton Foundation, 28 February 2024.
5 Jerry Aline Flieger, 'Proust, Freud, and the Art of Forgetting', *SubStance*, 9:4:29 (1980), 66, original emphasis.
6 'The most important person in my life was my mother. My "Spiders" [often entitled *Maman*] are an ode to her'. Bourgeois cited in Ulf Küster, *Louise Bourgeois: Art to Read* (Ostfildern: Hatje Cantz, 2011), p. 23. In this short book, Küster identifies Arachne and Medea, alongside Penelope, as figures who held particular significance for Bourgeois, who directly mentioned Penelope and Medea in her notes.
7 These would be published, prefaced with an essay by Hans Ulrich Obrsit, in Van Gelder, *Louise Bourgeois: Mumbling Beauty* (London: Thames & Hudson, 2015).
8 Sigmund Freud, 'Repression', *The Standard Edition of the Complete Psychological Works of Sigmund Freud*, trans James Strachey and Anna Freud (London: Hogarth Press, 1957), vol. 14, p. 146.
9 Philip Larratt-Smith (ed.), *Louise Bourgeois: The Return of the Repressed Vol. II: Psychoanalytical Writings* (London: Violette Editions, 2012). This would be followed by an exhibition catalogue: Philip Larratt-Smith and Juliet Mitchell, *Louise Bourgeois: Freud's Daughter* (New York: The Jewish Museum and New Haven, CT: Yale University Press, 2021).
10 Not only, but perhaps most compellingly and thoroughly, by Mignon Nixon in *Fantastic Reality: Louise Bourgeois and a Story of Modern Art* (Cambridge, MA: MIT Press, 2005). See also Jerry Gorovoy, *Louise Bourgeois: The Spider and the Tapestries* (Ostfildern: Hatje Cantz, 2015).
11 For an introduction to the much-discussed relationship between psychoanalysis and metaphor, see Antal F. Borbely, 'Chapter 23: Metaphor and Psychoanalysis', in Raymon W. Gibbs, Jr (ed.), *The Cambridge Handbook of Metaphor and Thought* (Cambridge: Cambridge University Press, 2012), pp. 412–424.
12 'Naturally enough, what he had in the studio were almost all seascapes done here at Balbec. But I was able to discern from these that the charm of each of them lay in a sort of metamorphosis of the objects represented, analogous to what in poetry we call *metaphor*, and that, if

God the Father had created things by naming them, it was by taking away their names or giving them other names that Elstir created them anew.' Proust, *In Search of Lost Time, Volume 2: Within a Budding Grove*, trans C. K. Scott Moncrieff and Terence Kilmartin, revised by D. J. Enright (London: Random House, 2010), p. 479, emphasis added.

13 See Gérard Genette, 'Proust and Metonymy', reprinted in Susanna Lee (ed.), *Marcel Proust, Swann's Way: The Moncrieff Translation, Contexts, Criticism* (New York and London: W. W. Norton, 2014), pp. 433–452.

14 For more on association and its mutual use by Freud and Proust, see Christie McDonald, *The Proustian Fabric: Associations of Memory* (Lincoln, NE: University of Nebraska Press, 1991).

15 Bourgeois would directly employ weaving in another fabric book from this time, *The Woven Child* (2003). As Lynne Cooke has shown, Bourgeois employed weaving in various forms within her work since the 1960s but held ambivalent feelings about its efficacy as an artform, particularly in the hands of others. See Cooke, 'Weaving, Materials and Metaphor', in *Louise Bourgeois: The Woven Child* (London: Hayward Gallery, 2022), pp. 20–25.

16 Cooke, 'Weaving, Materials and Metaphor', p. 22.

17 There is a video of Bourgeois's hands leafing through the pages of the book.

18 See Sarah Bernthal, 'Dismemberment and Remembrance in the *Lais* of Marie de France', *Pacific Coast Philology*, 54:1 (2019), 20–37.

19 Bernthal, 'Dismemberment and Remembrance', 20.

20 Bourgeois cited in Paulo Herkenhoff, 'Louise Bourgeois: Femme-temps', in Jerry Gorovoy and Pandora Tabatabai Asbaghi (eds), *Louise Bourgeois: Pink Days and Blue Days* (Milan: Fondazione Prada, 1997), p. 269.

21 Proust, *In Search of Lost Time, Volume 1: Swann's Way*, trans C. K. Scott Moncrieff and Terence Kilmartin, revised by D. J. Enright (London: Random House, 2010), pp. 54–55.

22 Rachel Cusk, 'Louise Bourgeois: *Suites on Fabric*', in *Coventry* (London: Faber & Faber, 2019), p. 143.

23 Cusk, 'Louise Bourgeois', p. 144.

24 Cusk cited in 'Interview with Rachel Cusk', *White Review*, No. 14 (July 2015), p. 127.

25 Virginia Woolf, *A Room of One's Own* [1929] (London: Renard Press, 2020), p. 51.

26 'The spider too sees nothing, perceives nothing, remembers nothing. She receives only the slightest vibration at the edge of her web, which propagates itself in her body as an intensive wave and sends her leaping to the necessary place.' Gilles Deleuze, *Proust and Signs* [1964], trans. Richard Howard (London and New York: Continuum, 2000), p. 117.

27 Cusk, 'Louise Bourgeois', p. 144. Cusk reiterates the theme of 'artistic objectivity in the face of the most fiercely subjective materials' – this time, in reference to the fabric works – in her text published as part of the catalogue for the artist's large 2022 exhibition at the Hayward Gallery in London. Cusk, 'The Fabricated Woman', in *Louise Bourgeois: The Woven Child*, p. 30.
28 Cusk, 'How to Get There', in *Coventry*, p. 185.
29 Bal qualifies this term to mean 'works of art that deploy their own artistic, and, here, visual, medium to offer and articulate thought about art'. Mieke Bal, 'Narrative Inside Out: Louise Bourgeois' Spider as Theoretical Object', *Oxford Art Journal*, 22:2 (1999), 104.
30 Benjamin, 'The Image of Proust', p. 198.
31 Proust, *In Search of Lost Time, Volume 3: The Guermantes Way*, trans C. K. Scott Moncrieff and Terence Kilmartin, revised by D. J. Enright (London: Random House, 2010), p. 156.
32 Cusk, *The Last Supper: A Summer in Italy* (London: Faber & Faber, 2009), p. 3.
33 Cusk, *The Last Supper*, p. 4.
34 Benjamin, 'The Image of Proust', p. 197. Just before this passage, Benjamin also uses the image of a river to describe the singularity of *la Recherche*: 'From its structure, which is fiction, autobiography, and commentary in one, to the syntax of endless sentences (the Nile of language, which here overflows and fructifies the regions of truth), everything transcends the norm.'
35 Peter Tame, 'From Mars to Mnemosyne: The Idea of Culture in André Malraux's *Antimémoires*', in Tame, Dominique Jeannerod, and Manuel Bragança (eds), *Mnemosyne and Mars: Artistic and Cultural Representations of Twentieth-century Europe at War* (Newcastle upon Tyne: Cambridge Scholars Publishing, 2013), p. 258.
36 Tame, 'From Mars to Mnemosyne', p. 263.
37 See Rosemary Betterton, 'Louise Bourgeois, Ageing, and Maternal Bodies', *Feminist Review*, 93 (2009), Birth, 30.
38 Catherine Crimp, *Childhood as Memory, Myth, and Metaphor: Proust, Beckett, and Bourgeois* (Oxford and New York: Legenda, 2013), p. 29.
39 Crimp, *Childhood as Memory, Myth, and Metaphor*, p. 29.
40 As highlighted by Nixon in *Fantastic Reality*, p. 12.
41 Donald Kuspit, 'Louise Bourgeois: Where Angels Fear to Tread', *Artforum*, 25 (March 1987), 120–121.

12

A life's work

Jo Applin

To speak of 'a life's work' is to conjure the single-minded pursuit or principal undertaking of a committed individual. To describe a 'life's work' is to emphasise the *longue durée* of that commitment. A 'lifework', on the other hand, is a relatively recent neologism that is as likely to take the form of an orchestrated one-off activity as it is the kind of drawn-out endeavour that best describes a 'life's work'. It finds an analogue in literary studies, whether in the form of life-writing or its more recent casting as 'autofiction', a mode of writing typically framed as a self-consciously creative merging of art and life; the one proving difficult to disentangle from the other.

Of course, the question of biography – its uses and misuses as a critical tool for interpretation – is a vexed and familiar one within the history of art, largely debunked as a means of getting to the heart of what a work ultimately 'means' or represents. And yet, creative bodies of work still tend to be bracketed into individual epochs and developmental stages and periods by curators, critics, and historians, and even when such taxonomies are couched in various forms of apology or caution, they still hold sway. These categories might include 'juvenilia' and 'early work'; 'ephemera'; 'mid-career', and finally 'late style', whether understood as a late-life blooming or as a sign of senescence and decrepitude, although in fact 'late works' are notable largely for their tendency for being overlooked, as awkward or embarrassing.[1] When 'late work' is addressed, writers tend towards the elegiac or blandly celebratory, focusing on the work of already successful, often male artists, where late style is framed as another form of codified 'genius'. We can count the exceptions on one hand. Surprisingly, the question of age rarely features in such debates, and certainly not at the level of methodology. When ageing is raised as a line of enquiry, it is often in the service of biography. However, to speak of 'a life's work', or even a 'lifework', is in part to speak about the life course, a concept defined in the 1960s by gerontologists as a means of analysing the complicated psychosocial process of ageing, from youth to old age, although this process is not limited solely to linear progression or chronology.[2] As well as important questions relating to time, ageing speaks – loudly – to issues of inequality and gender: about who gets to age, and how. 'Is age a class?' queried Viola Klein, one of the first British sociologists to focus on women, and whose own late work was an unfinished project on women and ageing.[3]

Ageing is also a material and conceptual condition of the work of art which, like the body, undergoes its own deterioration over time. Many artists have worked with precarious materials with this in mind. The American sculptor Eva Hesse wryly accepted that the latex sculptures she made in the 1960s would perish, noting that 'life doesn't last, art doesn't last'.[4] Hesse was, in part, reflecting on her own situation: in 1970 she died from the brain cancer that was already at an advanced stage when she made this comment. Such a statement was both deeply personal and absolutely of a piece with the times, something reiterated in Hesse's insistence that 'art and work and art and life are very connected'.[5] And yet – perhaps understandably, given most people's discomfort with the topic of ageing (and, relatedly, death) – art is rarely written about at length in relation to the life course and ageing, despite ageing permeating all aspects of the individual's lived experiences. To that end I propose that ageing is uniquely placed as a frame through which to think about a life's work, and about the lifework, in a manner that both encompasses and extends beyond consideration of figurative representations of ageing bodies or withered materials.

The life course as a life's work

When in 1945 the Finnish painter Helene Schjerfbeck made her final self-portrait at the age of 82, it marked the end point of a life's work dedicated to charting her own image (figure 12.1).[6] Each of her self-portraits was based on a similar format: her face fills the middle of the canvas or sheet of paper, her defiantly jutting chin and piercing, hooded eyes levelled back at her own brush. The portraits are freighted as much with psychological as physical differences and intensities. Much has been made of Schjerfbeck's self-portraits

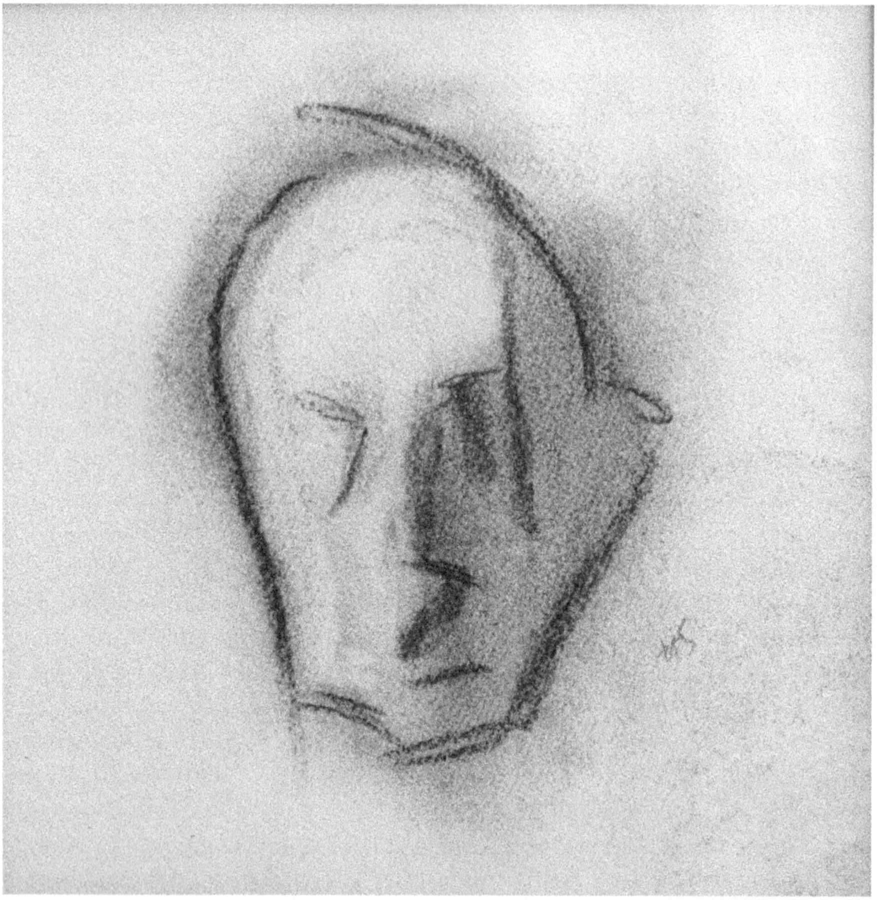

12.1 Helene Schjerfbeck, *Last Self-Portrait*, 1945, charcoal on paper, 17.5 × 17 cm

as documents of the artist's reckoning with her own life, from a difficult childhood that included a prolonged period of convalescence, to her later isolation and ill health. However, in the last two years of her life Schjerfbeck upped the intensity and frequency of her self-portraits as she turned her attention to her body's ageing, making approximately twenty self-portraits. Viewed collectively, the self-portraits do not narrate a life moving inexorably in the direction of old age from youth. Nor do they add up to anything like a decisive statement about the life course. Rather, the self-portraits are punctuated by repeated refrains and motifs, as well as abrupt formal changes of direction. They resist a chronologically ordered self-imaging that could amount to a comprehensive or summary statement either about the artist's life, or the ageing process in general. We might say Schjerfbeck's self-portraits add up to a statement about the impossibility of imaging a cogent representation of the ageing self, whether in psychological or physiognomic terms.

Over time, Schjerfbeck's drawn and painted line increased in intensity as her forms reduced in detail. In her final self-portrait, barely more than a small sketch, an angular skull-like visage floats against a blank background. These formal shifts tend to be described in biographical terms, as underscoring the sense of isolation, vulnerability, and encroaching old age the artist was experiencing as she painted them, although this is to assume, first, that we know what that process looks like and, second, that it is somehow readily recognisable in such abstracted forms.[7] In gerontological terms, this process of self-analysis is called a 'life review', an expression first coined by Robert Butler in 1963.[8] The 'life review' holds therapeutic value in its encouragement of the elderly subject to reflect on their life course. The aim is to retrospectively impose a narrative flow to the series of disjointed events that collectively constitute a life lived. It is intended as an end-of-life treatment for the individual, a therapeutic rerouting of the familiar process of 'reminiscence' so often associated with older people, and its rather less focused yet, as Butler wrote, therapeutically recognised correlate, 'rambling'.[9] The task of the gerontologist is to listen to the patient, some of whom may struggle to articulate or remember much at all, others of whose narratives tend towards 'garrulity, repetitiveness, and reminiscence'; to seek significance in the seemingly 'insignificant' detail to those 'forces shaping life'.[10] It is, Butler wrote, 'a looking-back process that has been set in motion by looking forward to death'.[11] What better example of the 'lifework' is there than the production of a 'life review', albeit one aimed not exclusively at those end-of-life encounters but applicable to any process of self-conscious 'looking back'? Divorced from its therapeutic remit and repurposed as a creative act, the life review can aim not so much at making good, or making sense, or even making 'better' or narrating one's lived experiences, but instead at helping others articulate those moments when such attempts at making sense fail or break down. In her important work on psychoanalysis and ageing, Kathleen Woodward has described such a state as closer to that of reminiscence in that it tends towards the 'fragmentary and partial'.[12] How might we think of the lifework focused not on linear narrative, or order and sense, but on those moments of caesura and pause, on an incipient collapse of sense and meaning that may just as readily mark an individual's life (or even, as Butler cautions, lead to the most 'extreme form of total catastrophe': the decision to bring one's life course to an abrupt end by suicide)?[13]

Ageing as abstraction

Schjerfbeck's *Self Portrait with Red Spot* (1944, figure 12.2) was painted a year before her last self-portrait. The body has been fleshed out, with rounded shoulders and chest supporting the wraithlike bald head that has been rendered in contrasting sharp angles to the shrouded form. This painting is unusual in other ways. Schjerfbeck has added a small, vivid red patch of paint to the lower lip of the face, just below the dark chasm that sits where the mouth should be, open as though mid-yawn, or yell. It is a charged, horrifying even, image. The small red mark jars against the otherwise monochrome palette as an anomaly. It reads as an accidental as much as intentional mark and appears to have no place in the formal structure of the work. It is extraneous, a disturbance in the visual field. This red-blotted irruption exemplifies the kind of radical abstraction that lies at the heart of Schjerfbeck's process of self-imaging. It speaks to questions about the ageing body, the life course and that process of retrospection, and its disavowal, more explicitly than any number of painted wrinkles and frail limbs could hope to convey. What is it that Schjerfbeck wants, here, to bring into visibility, and why do so in such an intractable manner? For this is a portrait not easily described in terms of age, gender, period, or style. The red mark represents the fundamental unknowability of old age via abstract, not figurative, representative means. It captures instead a sense of estrangement and surprise experienced at the precise moment the artist recognises herself in old age, a form of lifework irreducible to figurative or narrative account.[14]

In her writing on Doris Lessing's novels about old age, which Lessing wrote under the pseudonym Jane Somers, Nonia Williams argues that Lessing 'identifies a failure of representation' of the elderly within literary narratives. Their absence stands as an abstraction at the heart of otherwise narrative forms.[15] Williams suggests that Lessing's writing 'registers the need for different language and forms within which to communicate the "delightful surprises" of ageing – a term that is both serious and playful' for

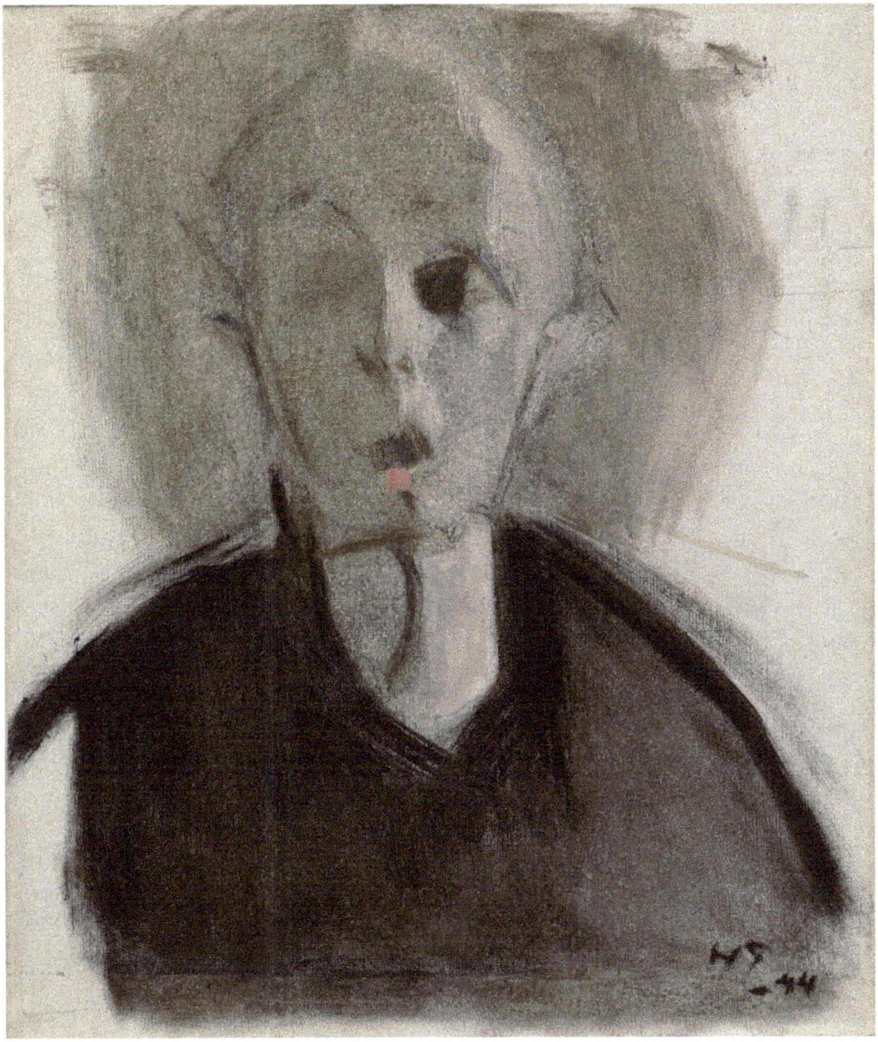

12.2 Helene Schjerfbeck, *Self-Portrait with Red Spot*, 1944, oil on canvas, 45 × 37 cm

Lessing and, I would argue, Schjerfbeck, who similarly at no point relinquishes formal innovation or 'surprise' in her fictionalised interrogation of self.[16]

Aged 85, Lessing returned to the theme of ageing in her essay 'Old', describing the different shape time takes as we age. It becomes, she wrote, more 'fluid'.[17] And while it may be 'entertaining to look at an old face, on a bus perhaps, and imagine how it

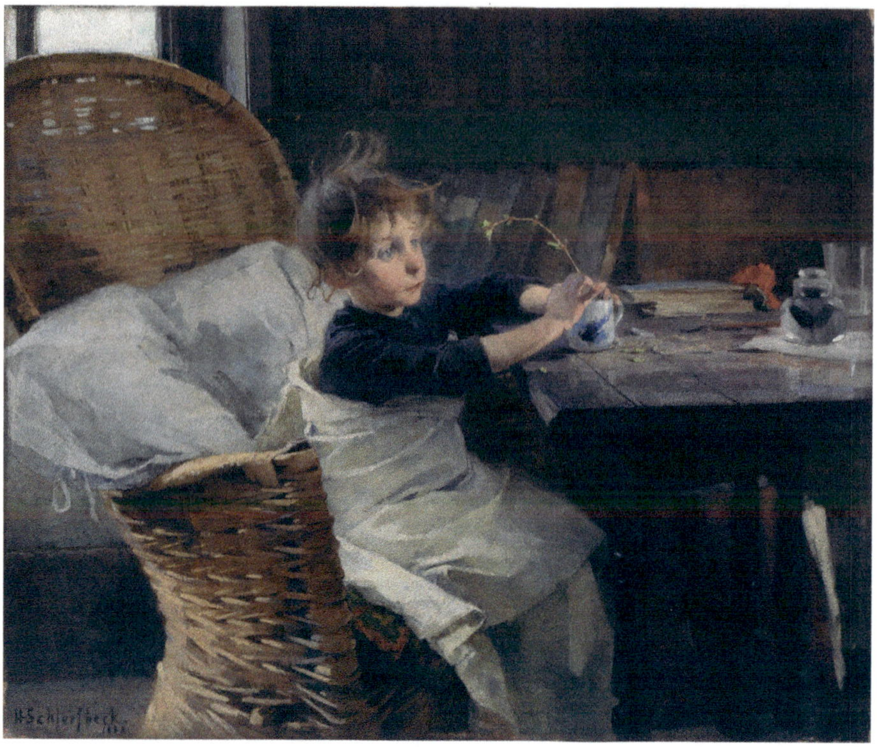

12.3 Helene Schjerfbeck, *The Convalescent*, 1888, oil on canvas, 92 × 107 cm

must have been young', within 'this fluidity' there is 'a permanence, for the person who looks at the old face in the mirror is the same as the one who shares your earliest memories'.[18] We can rethink the temporal 'flow' of Schjerfbeck's painting *The Convalescent* (1888, figure 12.3) in such fluid terms. Schjerfbeck painted *The Convalescent* in her twenties, an 'autofictional' portrait of the artist's early years. Rather than demarcate her 'late' work such as *Self-Portrait with Red Spot* as utterly distinct to this earlier painting, the two address each other across time in a form of what age-studies scholar Margaret Morgonroth-Gullette has dubbed 'age-autobiography', and Lessing more simply as a 'mirror', from the delicately graded brushwork and details that underscore the child's young age, from the game being played, to the youthful feet dangling from the too-high chair. In a similar vein, the white bedsheet wrapped around the child may foreshadow the coming of age and death as imagined by the artist's younger, twenty-something self.[19]

Schjerfbeck's later self-portraits made in her advanced years resolutely refused the narrative structure and formal composition of *The Convalescent*. In that final self-portrait, age registers instead at the level of a refusal, a 'failure of representation', as Williams put it.[20] Schjerfbeck's formal innovations in her final portraits operated via abstraction and dissonance, suggestive of an impending breakdown of form and subjectivity, reduced to a bare minimum, what in another context Elizabeth Barry has described as 'the contingency of old age' in the writing of Roland Barthes and Proust.[21]

When in 1971 Simone de Beauvoir published her groundbreaking book on ageing, just over twenty years after *The Second Sex* (1949), she also addressed the failure of representation that is so often the fate of the older woman.[22] Then in her early sixties, Beauvoir turned her attention to the invisibility of the older woman in Western society, citing Proust's description of ageing as a form of abstraction in *la Recherche*: 'And now I understood what old age was – old age, which, of all realities, is perhaps the one of which we retain a purely abstract notion for the longest time and the one we have the hardest of times giving shape to as a concept and reality.'[23] The fact of ageing's intractability found blunter expression forty years later when the critic Joan Didion, then in her seventies, responded to her doctor's complaint that she had made an 'inadequate adjustment' to ageing by pointing out that in fact she considered herself to have 'made no adjustment whatsoever to aging'.[24]

In Theodor Adorno's well-known essay on 'late style', he argued that the best kind of 'late work' is defined by a productive form of failure or dissonance at the level of form, not biography.[25] 'The only way to arrive at a revision of the [dominant] view of late style would be by means of the technical analysis of the works under consideration', as opposed to the usual reliance on biography.[26] Although he was not writing about old age per se, Adorno was discussing the late point in an artist's career which often coincides with their own advanced years, when the life and the work seem to merge one into the other. Adorno famously concludes his essay, which takes Beethoven as its case study, with the claim: 'In the history of art late works are the catastrophes.'[27] For Adorno, Beethoven's late works were a riposte to the contemporary bourgeois order, epitomising 'the idea of surviving beyond what is acceptable and normal'. The catastrophe was, for Adorno, in fact productive, signalling a new means of engaging with the material that was not and should not be reducible to the 'life' of the artist. On the contrary: 'The maturity of the late works of significant artists does not resemble the kind one finds in fruit. They are, for the most part, not round, but furrowed, even ravaged. Devoid of sweetness, bitter and spiny, they do not surrender themselves to mere delectation.' Rather, late works 'lack all the harmony that the classicist aesthetic is in the habit of demanding from works of art'.[28]

Life into art

Some time in the middle of the twentieth century the concept of an artist's 'lifework' took on a new and highly specific, self-conscious cadence at the hands of a younger generation of avant-garde artists. This generation was keen to rid itself of the trappings of an advanced art that privileged the atemporality of high modernist abstraction, what in another register Adorno described as a 'classicist aesthetic'. These artists began to incorporate into their work elements of their own lives, as well as that of the contemporary milieu in which they lived, in opposition to the abstract paintings of their predecessors. Happenings and environmental installations replaced wall-bound abstract-expressionist paintings, expanding the logic of an all-encompassing visual field into a fully three-dimensional and temporally bound experience. While not 'late works' in terms of the artists' ages at the time of making, this turn towards making lifeworks did mark a late and decisive moment in the life course of advanced art in the United States at mid-century. Famously, Robert Rauschenberg called his works 'Combines', a combination of painting and sculpture, as well as art and life. He described them as deliberately straddling the life–work divide with the oft-repeated statement: 'Painting relates to both art and life. . . . (I try to work in that gap between the two).'[29] Rauschenberg's contemporary Allan Kaprow was similarly an advocate of mining that gap, proposing that 'the line between art and life should be kept as fluid, and perhaps indistinct, as possible', a statement echoed in Hesse's later acknowledgement of the productive muddling of art and life and life and art.[30]

Kaprow developed his definition of the artist as one who blurs the line between art and life over the following years, although his insistence that value was to be placed not on art that fit discrete categories but which sought connection and 'ties to the "real" world, rather than the art world' was less appealing to those for whom such a 'blurring' was a luxury they could ill afford and for whom staving off the world and its threats to infiltrate the time carved out to make art was a daily reality.[31] In those instances, the importance of making time to work was less a liberation than a struggle, notably for women and people of colour, for whom entry into the art world was already an uphill struggle. Reflecting on her own working practice, in her fifties Schjerfbeck reflected how it was precisely those 'ties' to the 'real world' that were to be avoided to maintain the specificity and space for her painting practice apart from her daily life. Clear delineation rather than a blurring of the line between art and life governed her approach, as the only way to avoid turning her life into a spectacle and to keep it firmly in the realm of abstraction, not 'reality'. In stark contrast to Kaprow's claims some forty or so years later, Schjerfbeck wrote: 'I try to hold a sharp boundary *around* art. I do not let it go over into reality, as in an old panorama.'[32]

Life as work

It is necessary to recognise how the blurring of art and life for many women is simply a description of a situation where they have neither the time nor the emotional, psychological, or economic capacity to attend fully to either. In most cases, life (whether caring responsibilities, other kinds of paid work, and so on) frequently trumps, rather than complements, the making of art. Blurring in such instances is not so much welcome as to be avoided at all costs. The American artist and feminist Ida Applebroog experienced that sense of invasion in the late 1960s as a young mother of four children, struggling to find the time to focus on her art. The blurring of art and life was less in her case a creative motor than a daily burden in need of constant policing. Describing the feeling of arriving at her studio ready to work, Applebroog noted how hard it was to shake off her domestic duties in a way distinct to that of her male contemporaries. 'All this stuff on my back,' Applebroog later remarked, 'how the postman looked at me that morning, what happened in my personal life, what did my dealer say to me, what did my friend say on the telephone – all the different things that go on in your mind. What do I have to do? What appointments do I have?'[33] For Applebroog, a young family was an impediment to the kind of time necessary to make her work, and for a period she maintained her own separate apartment in which to work unimpaired. The African American artist Faith Ringgold similarly recounted how in the early years of her success she kept a separate apartment to her husband ring-fenced specifically for her art, not domestic life as wife and mother, stating: 'my apartment is not for the comfort of others but for my art work'.[34] It was in this space – this 'room of her own' apart from the other pressures on her – that Ringgold was able to work on her quilts, her soft doll sculptures, and other projects divorced from the day-to-day demands placed on her time.

Tasked with all that remembering and recording (birthdays, opening hours, whether there is enough milk in the fridge), it is no wonder the very act of charting one's life finds specific, limpid expression in the work of many women, whether through force of circumstance or choice as a form of 'lifework'. The point is, of course, that the avant-garde celebration of work that blurred the line between art and life is a privilege not available to everyone, however much one may fight for the space and capacity to do so. Most notably this was a struggle played out in the lives of many women artists who, like Applebroog, acknowledged the problems they experienced in securing the time to work. When life rears in their work it is often through an overtly political lens in the form of feminist critique, not celebration, of that blurring. Examples include Applebroog's *Living* series of paintings from the 1990s, in which domestic life muddles with unsettling scenarios with unclear narrative form as though haunting the daily to-dos and activities of the calendar and dates for which each painting is named and numbered (see figure 12.4).[35]

We might substitute the term 'multitasking' for 'lifework' in this instance as getting closer to what Applebroog was gesturing towards: the familiar, highly gendered term describing what many women must simply do to live up to the expectations placed upon them as wives, mothers, colleagues, and caregivers. The difficulties in managing the gulf between art and life falls unevenly not just to women, but specifically to women of colour and working-class women lacking a financial safety net provided others by family or marriage. Howardena Pindell subsequently recalled her experience as the only woman of colour affiliated with the cooperative AIR Gallery in the 1970s while working at the Museum of Modern Art, New York, and the stark difference between her life and that of her white married peers. Pindell could only get to her work after she had finished her day job, a situation that saw life and art less in tension than stark opposition to one another. In another instance of the uncomfortable bridging of art and life, Pindell's video work *Free, White and 21* from 1980 recounted a series of racist experiences she had encountered since childhood. As Pindell lists the many instances to the young

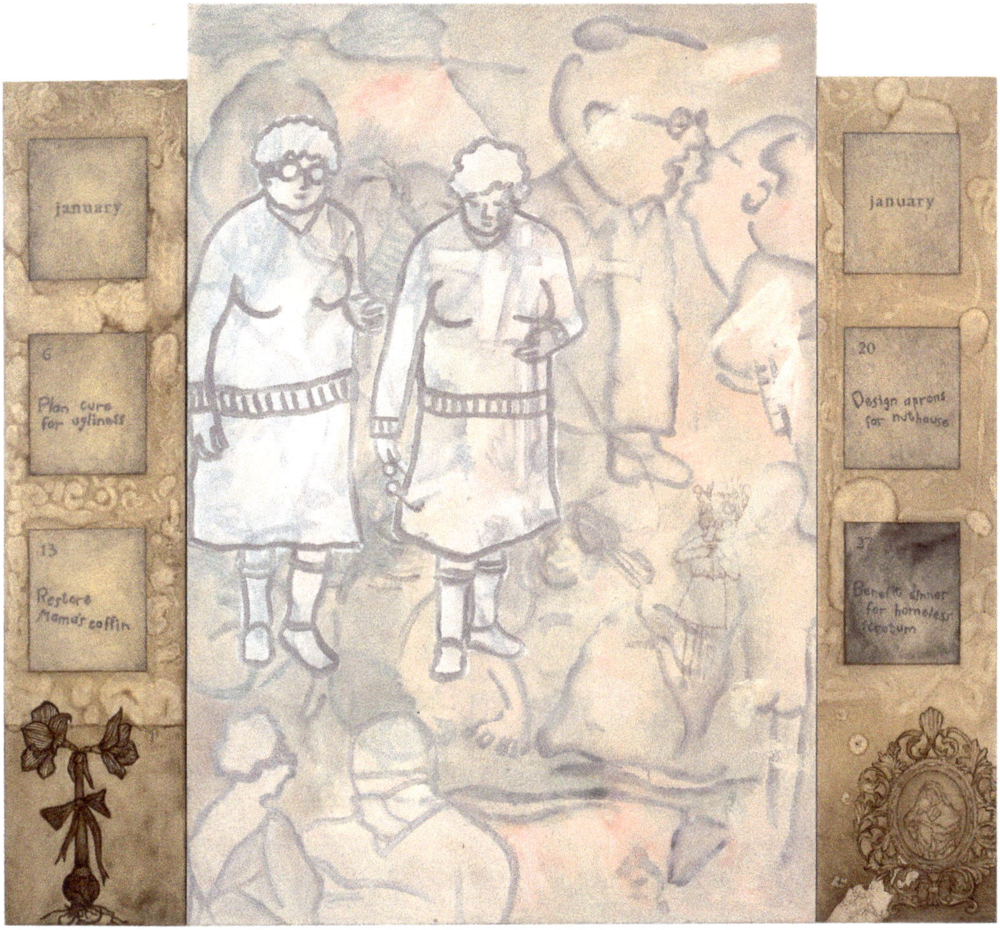

12.4 Ida Applebroog, *1956*, 1995–1996, oil and resin gel on canvas, 3 panels: 182.8 × 193 × 4.4 cm

female interviewer, played in the video by Pindell in whiteface, the interviewer refuses to accept that these were racist incidents at all.

We can describe Pindell's chronological charting of her lived experiences as what the psychoanalyst Danielle Quinodoz calls, in her work on ageing, an 'internal life-history', a version of Butler's 'life review', in which Pindell attempts to make sense of who she is by stringing together a series of incidences of who she once was (the work is also about memory, after a serious car accident during which Pindell sustained head injuries which meant she suffered from memory loss). As Butler argued, the therapeutic benefits of reshaping one's life in retrospect is to give it meaning, an internal coherence or history complete with narrative arc, explanation, and linking of discrete events into a continuous thread. In Pindell's case the white interviewer substitutes the role of the gerontologist, failing at the first hurdle as they refuse to listen, and so to give voice and agency to their subject as they tell their story, laying bare the potential pitfalls of a therapeutic process in which both parties are not working in concert but at odds.

Despite the struggles, women artists have frequently – as in the case of Pindell and Applebroog – worked to explore the fraught relationship between art and life in their work to powerful and critical ends. It is possible to see the anecdotes and experiences recounted by women artists keen to stake a claim in their life for their art from a different perspective, noting less the pressures of time than its passing, and the manifold ways they make this manifest in their work. Louise Bourgeois famously marked the end of her domestic responsibilities and multitasking efforts after her husband died and her children left home by ripping out the family kitchen and replacing it with a simple hotplate. It was a decisive gesture through which she reclaimed the house as her own working space. The point was less to reduce the house to her life's work, or to suggest her life was now an artwork – the line remained carefully maintained in even her most seemingly personal and autobiographical works. Bourgeois knew well the fault lines that ran between one's inner and outer sense or performance of self and was well-versed in psychoanalytic theory, including undergoing extensive periods of analysis as an adult.

In addition, Bourgeois began to carve out a language of ageing and autobiographical reflection that is determinedly not reducible to the body or life of the artist, most notably in her *Cell* installations that she began to make in 1989, when in her seventies. In these, Bourgeois combined personal items, salvaged architectural materials including doors, wire mesh, mirrors, and sculptural fragments, to the extraordinary series of stitched doll-like forms she began to make in fabric in her later years from materials hoarded and saved over the course of her life, alongside the oversized metal spiders, whose encroaching forms and telling title *Maman* speak as much of protection as fear and attack (figure 12.5). Far too well-versed in psychoanalytic theory for an interpretation that takes as its basis the artist's 'life', Bourgeois instead self-consciously obfuscated, deliberately planting clues as decoys and signs of a life lived from the perspective of the older woman who now looks back over the life course in a

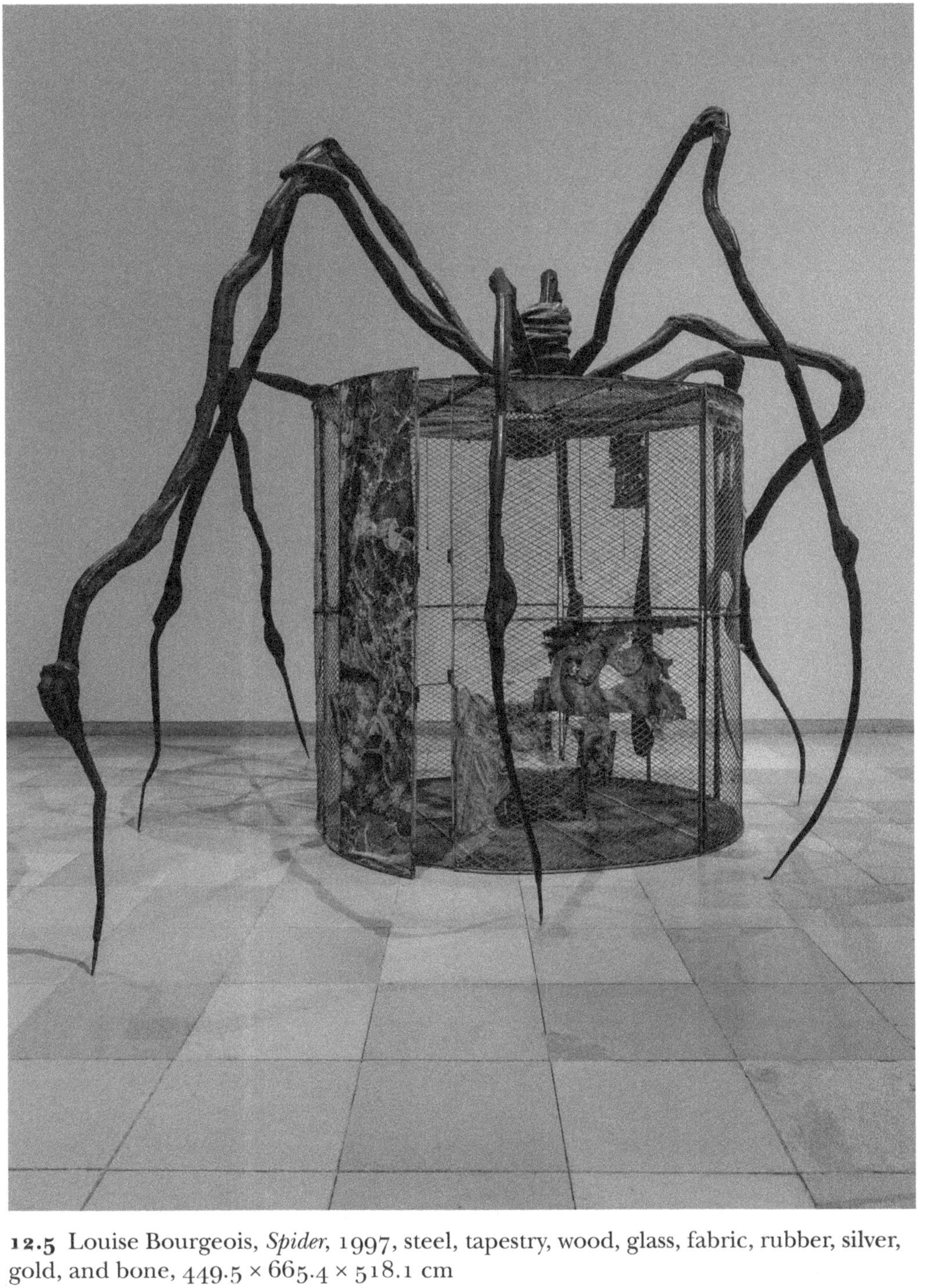

12.5 Louise Bourgeois, *Spider*, 1997, steel, tapestry, wood, glass, fabric, rubber, silver, gold, and bone, 449.5 × 665.4 × 518.1 cm

non-chronological manner, reflecting, rearranging, reordering, and reviewing her life.

Active ageing

In his posthumously published essay on 'late work', Edward Said, after Adorno, also challenged the often held assumption that we tend to think of the artist's life and work as one and the same.[36] When artists actively explore the gap between art and life as a condition or motif of their work, in all its various forms, breakdowns, and failures, the resulting lifework is a complex amalgam of self and not-self, of past and present folding one into the other. As Said argues, with the onset of old age, artists begin to adopt new 'idioms' that challenge the apparent 'timeliness' of their earlier works, upsetting any fixed ideas about chronology or biography.[37] In her book *Growing Old*, Quinodoz also places the idea of chronological time as an organising principle under pressure. She proposes we consider alternative, creative ways of charting a life, those 'small seconds of eternity' that can be experienced by the ageing subject during their retrospective reflection on their life, whether in the form of the 'lifework', or the therapeutic process of the life review, or 'internal life-history', in Quinodoz's terms. Quinodoz advocates for the therapeutic benefits of a creative blurring of past and present in our self-reckoning. This recalls in part Didion's wondering about the passage of time, which she also described as a non-linear experience, the radical abstraction that lies at the heart of the ageing experience and its visual representation. Quinodoz is interested in those who age 'actively' not 'passively', that is, those who have the capacity, or will, to stop and reflect on their life rather than merely experience it as 'a juxtaposition of repetitive snapshots' that repress any sense of 'intentionality'.[38] Quinodoz proposes we can 'either look at our life as a whole and in a synthetic manner, thereby giving it coherence', or instead see it as 'a series of juxtaposed events that have little or nothing in the way of internal links to draw them together'.[39] The distinction she draws could be described as one who experiences themselves, and the life course, as comprising a series of meaningless, repetitive daily activities and experiences, and those for whom the life is akin to and as malleable as art, and it is no surprise that Quinodoz furnishes her argument with examples of such active ageing by visual artists: we might call the 'internal life-history' the therapeutic lifework *par excellence.*

Schjerfbeck decided to age actively. This much is made clear in her radical repurposing of the self-portrait in those last two years of her life, a complicated meeting of retrospection and projection that is in no way reducible to a 'late', weakened, or elegiac style. We might propose in fact that the artist – ageing or otherwise (for we are all, always, ageing) – is ideally placed to actively interrupt and interrogate the ageing process, given how works of art so frequently beg the question of time's passing, historical narrative, and the representation of self. Quinodoz describes the capturing of that abstract moment where things, for a time, come together outside time – that 'second of eternity', as a 'reflection on a reflection'.[40] As Butler and Quinodoz in their own ways make clear, the 'life review' (or internal life-history) functions as a necessary period of retrospection, marking an active reckoning with the passing of time in all its abstract and figurative modalities, from radical, red, misplaced marks to the more familiar wrinkled brows and 'furrowed', spiny forms described by Adorno. To this end, it provides a model for thinking about the lifework, about a *life's work* through the lens of ageing at both the level of content but also, importantly, form.

Notes

1 For two classic texts on late style see Theodor W. Adorno, 'Late Style in Beethoven', in *Essays on Music* (Berkeley and Los Angeles, CA and London: University of California Press, 2002), pp. 564–568; and Edward Said, *On Late Style: Music and Literature Against the Grain* (London and New York: Bloomsbury, 2007). See also Thomas Crow and Karen Painter (eds), *Late Thoughts: Reflections on Artists and Composers at Work* (Los Angeles, CA: Getty, 2006).

2 Life course theory has its roots in the first half of the twentieth century, in the work of scholars such as Karl Mannheim's pioneering study on generations from a sociological perspective. For a recent analysis, see 'Chronological Age: A Useful Category of Historical Analysis', in *American Historical Review*, 125:2 (April 2020), 371–459.

3 Klein died in 1973, shortly after retiring from the University of Reading the previous year. See E. Stinea Lyon, 'Viola Klein: Forgotten Émigré Intellectual, Public Sociologist and Advocate of Women', *Sociology*, 41:5 (October 2007), 839–840. Many thanks to Griselda Pollock for drawing my attention to Davis's work, and her archive at the University of Reading.

4 'At this point I feel a little guilty when people want to buy [latex works]. I think they know but I want to write them a letter and say it is not going

to last . . . life doesn't last, art doesn't last, it doesn't matter.' Eva Hesse cited in Cindy Nemser, 'An Interview with Eva Hesse', *Artforum*, 8:9 (May 1970), 59.

5 Hesse cited in Nemser, 'An Interview with Eva Hesse', 59. Hesse died that year, aged 34.

6 Schjerfbeck died the following year. For a recent comprehensive overview, see the catalogue for the recent exhibition of her work at the Royal Academy in London: Rosie Hore (ed.), *Helene Schjerfbeck*, trans. Tomi Snellman (London: Royal Academy of Arts, 2019). The exhibition included a room dedicated to Schjerfbeck's extraordinary series of self-portraits which informed my own reading of her work here. At the symposium accompanying the exhibition, papers by Sophie Oliver and Griselda Pollock have been instrumental to my thinking about her work.

7 For more on her career, see Leena Ahtola-Moorhouse (ed.), *Helene Schjerfbeck: 150 Years* (Helsinki: Ateneum Art Gallery/Finnish National Gallery, 2012).

8 Robert Butler, 'The Life Review: Interpretation of Reminiscence in The Aged', *Psychiatry*, 26:1 (February 1963), 65–76.

9 Butler, 'The Life Review', 65.

10 Butler, 'The Life Review', 72.

11 Butler, 'The Life Review', 65.

12 Kathleen Woodward on ageing and literature, in particular her chapter 'Telling Stories: Aging, Reminiscence and the Life Review', *Doreen B. Townsend Center Occasional Papers*, 9 (1997), viii–17.

13 Butler, 'the Life Review', 68.

14 The literature on portraiture is by now extensive. See for instance Tamar Garb, *The Painted Face: Portraits of Women in France 1814–1914* (New Haven, CT and London: Yale University Press, 2007); Richard Brilliant, *Portraiture* (London: Reaktion Books, 2013), and Joanna Woodall (ed.), *Portraiture: Facing the Subject* (Manchester: Manchester University Press, 2014).

15 Nonia Williams, '"No Hip Muffs": Female Ageing in Doris Lessing's Fiction and Correspondence', *Critical Quarterly*, 63:1 (April 2021), 67.

16 Williams, '"No Hip Muffs"', 67.

17 Doris Lessing, 'Old', in *Time Bites: Views and Reviews* (London: Fourth Estate, 2004), pp. 215–216, p. 216.

18 Lessing, 'Old', p. 216. For a discussion of this, see Williams, '"No Hip Muffs"', 67–81.

19 Margaret Morganroth Gullette, *Aged by Culture* (Chicago, IL: University of Chicago Press, 2004), p. 153. See also Gullette, *Declining to Decline: Cultural Combat and the Politics of the Midlife* (Charlottesville, VA and London: University of Virginia Press, 1997).

20 Williams asks: 'what are the chronologies, forms, devices and narrative perspectives of Lessing's writing of age in her novels?' Williams, '"No Hip Muffs"', 67.
21 Elizabeth Barry, 'The Moment of Truth: Proust, Barthes, and the Contingency of Old Age', *Textual Practice*, 32:3 (2018), 489.
22 For a critical literature on mid-life see Carleen Brice, *Age Ain't Nothing but a Number: Black Women Explore Midlife* (Boston, MA: Beacon Press, 2005); and Gullette, *Declining to Decline*. For an excellent recent account of the mid-life crisis and male chauvinism see Susanne Schmidt, *Midlife Crisis: The Feminist Origins of a Chauvinist Cliché* (Chicago, IL: University of Chicago Press, 2020).
23 Simone de Beauvoir, *The Coming of Age* [1970], trans. Patrick O'Brian (New York: Warner Paperback Library, 1973), p. 11.
24 Joan Didion, *Blue Nights*, p. 137.
25 Adorno, 'Late Style in Beethoven', p. 565.
26 Adorno, 'Late Style in Beethoven', p. 565.
27 Adorno, 'Late Style in Beethoven', p. 567.
28 Adorno, 'Late Style in Beethoven', p. 564.
29 Robert Rauschenberg, 'Untitled Statement', in Dorothy C. Miller (ed.), *Sixteen Americans* (New York: Museum of Modern Art, 1959), p. 58.
30 Allan Kaprow, *Assemblages, Environments and Happenings* (New York: Harry N. Abrams, 1966), p. 188.
31 Kaprow, 'The Education of the Un-Artist Part III' [1971], reprinted in Jeff Kelly (ed.), *Allan Kaprow: The Blurring of Art and Life* (Berkeley and Los Angeles, CA and London: University of California Press 1993), p. 131.
32 As cited in Michelle Facos, 'Helene Schjerfbeck's Self-Portraits: Revelation and Dissimulation', *Woman's Art Journal*, 16:1 (Spring–Summer, 1995), 15.
33 Ida Applebroog, 'Power, Feminism, and Art', *PBS Art:21*, 2005, https://art21.org/read/ida-applebroog-power-feminism-and-art (accessed 4 July 2023). On Applebroog's feminism see my 'Generational Objects: Ida Applebroog's History of Feminism', *Oxford Art Journal*, 40:1 (Spring 2017), 133–151.
34 Faith Ringgold, 'Faith Ringgold Makes Dolls and Art', *Essence* (July 1979), 114.
35 On this, see my 'Generational Objects: Ida Applebroog's History of Feminism'.
36 Said, 'Thoughts on Late Style', *London Review of Books*, 5 August 2004, 3.
37 Said, 'Thoughts on Late Style', 3.
38 Danielle Quinodoz, *Growing Old: A Journey of Self-Discovery* (New York and London: Routledge, 2010), p. 2.
39 Quinodoz, *Growing Old*, p. 2.
40 Quinodoz, *Growing Old*, p. 196.

Index

Note: 'n.' after a page reference indicates the number of a note on that page. Literary works (indicated in *italics*) and illustrations (indicated by page reference in **bold**) can be found under authors' or artists' names.

EU authorised representative for GPSR:
Easy Access System Europe, Mustamäe tee 50,
10621 Tallinn, Estonia
gpsr.requests@easproject.com

www.ingramcontent.com/pod-product-compliance
Ingram Content Group UK Ltd.
Pitfield, Milton Keynes, MK11 3LW, UK
UKHW051310191025
3307IPUK00037B/34
* 9 7 8 1 5 2 6 1 7 2 4 7 1 *